European Spring

Why Our Economies and Politics are in

a Mess – and How to Put Them Right

PHILIPPE LEGRAIN

ISBN: 1782924809

ISBN 13: 9781782924807

5411703342

CONTENTS

ACKNOWLEDGEMENTS... vii

INTRODUCTION: Pain, fear and loathing xiii

PART I: A LONG, DARK WINTER 1

1. TWO CURRENCIES, ONE CRISIS 3
Why Britain and the eurozone have similar failings

2. A FIASCO MADE IN FRANKFURT, BRUSSELS
AND BERLIN.. 46
A tragedy in five acts

3. THE AUSTERITY DELUSION 97
All pain, no gain

4. PANIC! 126
How the euro came close to collapse

5. IT'S NOT OVER... 168
How to fix the crisis in the eurozone for good

6. GRAND DESIGNS..202
How to complete the half-built euro house

7. NORDIC LIGHTS, BRITISH GLOOM 227
Why Britain's long-delayed recovery is dysfunctional

PART II: SPRING?...255

8. THE EAGLE ALSO LANDS..................................... 257
Why Germany is not a role model for the rest of Europe

9. REFORMS THAT ADD UP 279
Why economies ought to be more adaptable, dynamic
and decent

10. ADAPT!.. 301
How to cope with and adjust to change
11. DYNAMIC 336
How to create new ideas and businesses
12. DECENT 392
A fairer society with opportunities for all
13. DEMOCRACY IN EUROPE............................... 407
Why the EU is still a good thing, but needs to change
14. THE POLITICS OF CHANGE.............................. 434
Why we need a European Spring

ABOUT THE AUTHOR... 449

ACKNOWLEDGEMENTS

Writing a book is an intensely individual effort, yet it also requires the stimulus and support of a great many people. My agent Jonny Geller and his assistant Kirsten Forster have been very helpful. A big thank you to everyone else at Curtis Brown who has assisted in some way. It has been good working with the dynamic team at Amazon's createspace who publish books much faster and more flexibly than traditional publishers tend to. I am extremely grateful to George Soros, whose analysis of the political economy of the eurozone crisis has been masterful, for very kindly providing an endorsement for *European Spring*. Thank you to Heather Grabbe and Kim Forepaugh for their help with that and much else.

Over the course of my career, some people have been particularly good to me. I owe Nick Barr, my tutor at the London School of Economics, a huge debt of gratitude. Edward Lucas gave me my first break in journalism, aged seventeen, followed closely by Anthony Robinson at the *Financial Times*. Bill Emmott hired me at *The Economist* back in 1997 and has continued to be very supportive. Simon Long kindly provided comments on the manuscripts of my three previous books; I spared him the ordeal this time: he is suffering enough from Spurs' misfortunes. Mike Moore and his wife Yvonne have been true friends ever since I worked for Mike at the WTO; I admire him immensely. Annie Maccoby and Erik Berglöf are wonderful friends, wise counsels and an inspiration.

Over the past three years working for President Barroso, I have met many interesting people whom I cannot all name here. I'd like to thank President Barroso for the opportunity to make a difference in tackling the crisis in the eurozone. His assistant Rita Castro Dias has always been very kind. I'd also like to thank Jean-Claude Thébault, the director-general of the Bureau of European Policy Advisers, for his support. I have made many friends among my colleagues in BEPA, not least Graeme Carter, Paola Colombo, Paola Rossi and Anne Glover. Antonio Missiroli, Joao Marques de Almeida and Matti Maasikas have since gone on to greater things. A special thanks to everyone in BEPA's Analysis Team, whom I led for three years, and to my wonderful assistants Carmen Tresguerres and Lynn Scavée in particular. Baudouin Regout, Eric Peters and the rest of the team have been great.

Elsewhere in the European Commission, I'd like to thank Vice-President Neelie Kroes and her team for asking me to contribute to efforts to abolish roaming and create a single market for mobile networks. Ryan Heath has become a good friend. Thank you too to Ed Bannerman and Chantal Hughes for their friendship. Cecilia Malmström and her team fight the good fight on immigration; Kristina Lindahl now does so in Sweden. I have also worked well with Marc Vanheukelen and Jonathan Faull. At the European Council, I have always been stimulated by Shahin Vallée, who has a fine mind and a good heart. Peter Praet is a force for good at the European Central Bank. I also built good relations with many other policymakers and diplomats; you know who you are.

After Dominique Strauss-Kahn resigned and Christine Lagarde replaced him, the International Monetary Fund became more of a voice of reason in the eurozone crisis. Thank you to David Lipton, Min Zhu, Nemat Shafik, Olivier Blanchard, José Viñals, Mahmood Pradhan, Stijn Claessens and many others for our stimulating exchanges. I also worked closely with the World Bank's Europe and Central Asia team, notably Philippe Le Houérou, Indermit Gill and Dirk Reinermann, together with Kaushik Basu and his predecessor as chief economist, Justin Lin. Dilip Ratha, the Bank's migration guru, has been particularly supportive.

I have learnt a lot from my friends and acquaintances in the think-tank world. Fredrik Erixon of the European Centre for International Political Economy (ECIPE) is an old friend; his co-director Hosuk Lee Makiyama a newer one. Razeen Sally was very helpful with *Aftershock*. Ann Mettler and Paul Hofheinz, the dynamic duo who drive the Lisbon Council, where I used to be a senior fellow, have always been a source of support and advice. Charles Grant, Simon Tilford and everyone at the Centre for European Reform are great; all the best to Hugo Brady in his new job. Many thanks to Mattias Goldmann, Andreas Bergström and everyone at FORES in Stockholm, who have invited me to speak many times and published an updated Swedish edition of *Immigrants: Your Country Needs Them*. Thank you too to Roger Liddle, Olaf Cramme, Michael McTernan, Renaud Thillaye and everyone at Policy Network, who have also involved me in many interesting events.

Good ideas are sparked by stimulating conversations with a wide variety of people. I'd also like to thank Rob Johnson and Eric Beinhocker at the Institute for New Economic Thinking (INET); Adam Posen, Fred Bergsten, Arvind Subramanian, Nicolas Véron, Jakob Funk Kirkegaard, John Williamson and others at the Peterson Institute; Pascal Lamy; Danny Sriskandarajah at Civicus; Clive Crook; Jean-Pierre Lehmann at the Fung Global Institute; Sebastian Mallaby and Robert Kahn at the Council on Foreign Relations; Rob Shapiro at Sonecon; Richard Reeves at Brookings; Susan Lund at the McKinsey Global Institute; Michael Leigh and Ian Lesser at the German Marshall Fund of the US; Jan Techau and Sinan Ulgen at Carnegie Europe; Tyson Barker (now at the State Department) and Andy Cohen at the Bertelsmann Foundation North America; Stijn Hoorens and Svitlana Kobzar at RAND Europe; Vivien Pertusot at Ifri; Mark Leonard and everyone at the European Council on Foreign Relations; Jean Pisani-Ferry (formerly at Bruegel); Nick Pearce, Eileen McGowan and Will Straw at IPPR; Loukas Tsoukalis at ELIAMEP; Michael Clemens and

Owen Barder at the Centre for Global Development; Geoff Mulgan and Stian Westlake at NESTA; Jonathan Portes at NIESR; Shannon Pfohman and Michael Privot at ENAR; Carl Dolan at Transparency International; Catherine Fieschi at Counterpoint; Michiel van Hulten of Vote Watch Europe; Rainer Münz at Erste Group; Claire Fox at the Institute for Ideas; and Austin Williams of Bookshop Barnies.

Internet entrepreneurs such as Gi Fernando, Rajeeb Day and Michael Breidenbrücker are a huge inspiration. Thank you to Frédéric Michel for his kindness and support over the years and for introducing me to so many interesting people. Thank you to Peter Mandelson, Ben Wegg Prosser (a very old friend), Stephen Adams and everyone at Global Counsel. David Bowers and Dominic White at Absolute Strategy Research are always insightful and David has been particularly kind; thank you to Beth McCann for introducing us. Diane Coyle at Enlightenment Economics is lovely. Varun Chandra has been very kind. I have had many stimulating conversations with Gene Frieda at Moore Capital Management. Among bank economists, Stephen King at HSBC, Willem Buiter at Citi, Erik Nielsen at Unicredit and George Magnus, formerly of UBS, stand out. Julian Callow at Barclays is consistently positive about Europe. Thanks too to Paul Adamson and Hendrik Bourgeois. Jason Collins is a great guy. Bernard Snoy has been very kind and helpful. Susan Hitch is a lovely woman.

In the academic world, I have enjoyed setting the world to rights over a beer with Kevin O'Rourke; his work with Barry Eichengreen and others is superb. It was great to host Anat Admati and Martin Hellwig to present their cracking book, *The Bankers' New Clothes*. Paul de Grauwe, now of LSE, has been incredibly insightful about the crisis. Simon Hix is a guru on European politics; Henrik Enderlein on eurozone institutions. It was a privilege to attend a gathering of Nobel-winning economists in Lindau in August 2011, where I met many exceptional people.

Among the press, it was great to catch up with my old friend Luke Baker, who has done an excellent job as Reuters' bureau chief in Brussels and has a fine team across Europe. The Breakingviews team founded by Hugo Dixon are also excellent. At *The Economist*, thank you to John Micklethwait for his support for my previous books. I look forward to reading *Unhappy Union*, John Peet and Anton La Guardia's book about the crisis; Zanny Minton Beddoes and I have often had converging opinions about it. Saugato Datta, who has since moved on, is a great guy. At the *Financial Times*, I have enjoyed many stimulating conversations with Martin Wolf, my former colleague Gideon Rachman, Gillian Tett, Peter Spiegel, Alex Barker and many others. I recently had the pleasure of meeting Martin Sandbu who is writing a book about the euro which will doubtless be excellent. Wolfgang Münchau's Eurointelligence is required reading for anyone interested in the crisis. At the *Wall Street Journal*, Stephen Fidler, who covered the Latin American debt crisis in the 1980s, is particularly perceptive; Simon Nixon understands the role of finance better than most economic commentators; and Matina Stevis can see things from both a Greek perspective and an external one. Thanks too to Philippe Ricard at *Le Monde*; Olaf Storbeck at *Handelsblatt* (now at Reuters); Pablo Rodriguez Suanzes at *El Mundo*; Nikos Chrysorolas and Yannis Palaiologos at *Kathimerini*; Caroline de Gruyter at *NRC Handelsblad*; Rebecca Christie at Bloomberg; and David Charter at *The Times*. Also at *The Times*, Oliver Kamm is an old friend and Danny Finkelstein a new one. A big thank you to Kenneth Murphy at Project Syndicate for publishing my pieces about the crisis, as well as to Richard Baldwin at Vox. My friend Tove Lifvendahl at *Svenska Dagbladet* and Peter Wolodarski at *Dagens Nyheter* have also been kind enough to commission pieces by me.

In the conference world, the Wilton Park team have invited me to speak at many interesting conferences, not least in China. Thank you too to everyone at M3 Global and KPMG. Many thanks to the

Warwick Economic Summit for inviting me to speak several times. Howard Duncan of Metropolis is a star. Thanks to Alexander Crawford and the team at the Tällberg Forum, the Ax:son Johnson Foundation, and Stefan Kumarage Schou at DI. Thank you to everyone else around the world who has invited me to speak.

My friend Edie Lush introduced me to the British American Project (BAP), through which I have met many special people – not least Michael Hayman, who is kindly throwing his formidable energies and those of his excellent team at Seven Hills into helping to publicise this book.

A huge thank you to my father for tirelessly ploughing through and providing comments on initial drafts of this manuscript and for much else. My brother Pierre provides advice and help in all sorts of ways. Lots of love to them and to Mum, Milli, Elizabeth and Morag; to Patrick, Natasha and all the Fairweathers; and to Ivar, Christina and Joanna Tombach.

This book is dedicated to my many good friends, some of whom I have already mentioned. Among others, I would also like to thank Allison Gallienne, Asma Bashir, Ayisha Piotti, Cathleen Farrell, Chris and Emily Foges, Colin and Shirley Iles, Daniele Deiana, Dusch and Rebecca Atkinson, Farid Tabarki, Frank Paget, Gabe Adams, Gary Cox, Gideon Lichfield, Harry Rich, Hugo Macgregor, James Burgess, Jo Malvisi, Johan Nordin, John Cormack, Jonathan Rauch, Josh Caffe, Kelly McSherry, Kevin Goatcher, Linda Pearson, Mark Alefounder, Mark Westhenry, Martyn Fitzgerald, Mike Anderson, Nick Morton, Nick Tulk, Paul Bates, Priit, Katre and the Vanatoa family, Raffaele Orsini, Richard Garratt, Richard Scandrett, Rob Gunns, S-J Heany, Simon Sadler, Sophie Pittaway, Tashi Mannox, Tim Laxton and Viviana Staiano. Peter and Marion Doyle mean the world to me. Above all, thank you for everything to David Sanderquist.

INTRODUCTION:
PAIN, FEAR AND LOATHING

I haven't had a pay rise for over eight years, but everything else has gone up so I can't see how I am better off. I have tried getting another job with better pay but am too old so have to stick where I am. My husband lost his job a couple of years ago, did manage to get another one but it is thirty miles each way and costs a fortune in fuel – roll on retirement, or maybe not. We are surviving just!

Dyeb, responding to claims that living standards in Britain are rising, 2014[1]

I've enjoyed a better life than my parents and they had better lives than my grandparents. I've come here to protest because I fear the same may not be true for my children.

Protester in Portugal, 2012[2]

Like passengers on an up escalator, Britons and other Europeans for decades enjoyed seemingly effortless rises in living standards year after year. Expanding economies and swelling social spending lifted nearly everyone up. Each generation could look forward to much better lives than previous ones. Yet in recent years, this growth escalator has broken down. It has been creaky for a while: since the turn of the century, productivity growth has been sluggish across most of Europe – and

---

1   http://www.bbc.co.uk/news/uk-politics-25869001?postId=118503118#cosmment_118503118

2   http://www.ft.com/cms/s/0/132e4706-001a-11e2-831d-00144feabdc0.html

wage rises even slower. But piling on debt provided an artificial boost, while bubbly house prices and financial trickery blinded people to the risks. Then the financial crisis and the panic in the eurozone threw a spanner in the works and the escalator went into reverse. The long slump and governments' subsequent budget cuts have exposed the chasm between the fortunate – and sometimes undeserving – few who continue to thrive and the majority who are struggling. Many people have fallen far – not least the twenty-six million Europeans who are out of work, many of them for a long time.[3] In Britain, real wages have fallen by nearly a tenth.[4] A typical British household is no richer than a decade ago.[5] Even the much-vaunted German escalator has stalled. The average German earns fractionally less than fifteen years ago.[6]

Some parts of Europe have been in freefall. In Greece, where national income has shrunk by a quarter, children scavenge through rubbish bins for scraps for food, while hospitals run short of medicine.[7]

3   http://epp.eurostat.ec.europa.eu/statistics_explained/index.php/Unemployment_statistics. In January 2014, 26.2 million people in the EU were unemployed.

4   Between March 2008 and December 2013, average weekly wages rose from £439 to £478. Over the same period, consumer price inflation was 19.5 per cent. So real wages fell by 8.9 per cent. Office for National Statistics, average weekly earnings – total pay, seasonally adjusted; deflated by all-items consumer-price index.

5   According to the Office for National Statistics, median equivalised disposable household income in 2012 was no higher than in 2004. While more recent figures are not yet available, median incomes are likely to have continued falling. http://www.ons.gov.uk/ons/dcp171776_341133.pdf

6   Federal Statistical Office of Germany, index of real earnings, January 2010 = 100. Index for 1999 is 102.1; index for 2012 is 101.7. Provisional figures suggest real wages fell by a further 0.2 per cent in 2013. https://www.destatis.de/DE/ZahlenFakten/GesamtwirtschaftUmwelt/VerdiensteArbeitskosten/RealloehneNettoverdienste/RealloehneNettoverdienste.html https://www.destatis.de/DE/PresseService/Presse/Pressemitteilungen/2014/02/PD14_058_623.html

7   http://www.nytimes.com/2013/04/18/world/europe/more-children-in-greece-start-to-go-hungry.html

In Spain, where more than one in four people are unemployed, suicide is now the top cause of death after natural causes.[8] In Ireland, where house prices have halved, nearly one in five homeowners are in arrears on their mortgages on their depreciated homes, while the cost to Irish people of bailing out the banks that made all the bad mortgage loans comes to €14,000 each.[9] In Italy, more than two in five young people are out of work; in Greece and Spain, nearly three in five are.[10] Across Europe, fifteen million people below the age of thirty are neither in employment nor education.[11] A lost generation is in the making. Is it any surprise that young Europeans are having even fewer babies since the crisis and that someone emigrates from Portugal every four minutes?[12]

Fortunately, prospects look less bleak than in 2012, when panic stalked the markets and the euro seemed on the brink of collapse. Finally, most European economies are growing again, while markets are buoyed up by easy money. But after the longest and deepest recession since the Great Depression of the 1930s, and even with exceptional monetary support, the recovery is the flimsiest on record. Much of Europe remains lumbered with broken banks and crushing debts. Most of Europe suffers from record-low investment and

---

8   http://www.theguardian.com/world/2013/sep/05/spanish-helpline-rise-callers-considering-suicide

9   Figures for mortgage arrears are from http://www.centralbank.ie/press-area/press-releases/Pages/ResidentialMortgageArrearsandRepossessionsStatisticsQ42013.aspx The direct cost of Ireland's bank bailout was €64 billion. The population of Ireland in 2012 was 4.58 million.

10   Eurostat, harmonised unemployment rate for 15-24s, December 2014. Code: teilm021

11   http://www.ft.com/cms/s/0/34e7f42a-da88-11e2-8062-00144feab7de.html

12   http://www.demogr.mpg.de/en/news_press/press_releases_1916/economic_crisis_lowers_birth_rates_3250.htm Portuguese emigration figure is a personal calculation based on data in http://www.bbc.co.uk/news/world-21206165

feeble productivity growth. All of Europe is ageing fast – and without immigration most countries' workforces are set to shrink. Thus Europe seems destined for prolonged sluggishness and global decline. Depressingly, an overwhelming majority of Europeans – Britons as well as French, both Germans and Spaniards – think their children will have a worse life than they do.[13]

What has gone wrong with Europe's economies? Why has recovery from the financial crisis taken so long? Why did the euro nearly collapse – and might it yet do so? Are stagnation and decline inevitable? If a brighter future is possible, what needs to be done? Should the rest of Europe try to emulate Germany? Or are there better economic models?

The present economic pain and fear of the future are poisoning politics too. Many people have lost faith in seemingly self-serving politicians, technocrats and elites in general, all of whom have so far failed to solve the crisis, let alone to set out a compelling vision of a brighter future. Social tensions within countries are multiplying, as are political frictions between them. Understandable anger at the flagrant injustice of bailouts for rich bankers and budget cuts for poor schoolchildren overlaps with a despicable scapegoating of outsiders, in particular immigrants. Scots will vote on whether to split from Britain in September 2014, Catalans from Spain in November. Germans and Greeks are at each other's throats. The project that binds Europeans together – the European Union – has never been more unpopular; Britons may even vote to leave. The EU's crowning achievement, the euro, is increasingly perceived as a sadomasochistic straitjacket. This anti-establishment, anti-foreigner, anti-EU mood is fertile ground for extremists and snake-oil salesmen. In May 2014's European elections, xenophobic and reactionary parties

---

13   http://www.debatingeurope.eu/2013/05/17/new-poll-dramatic-rise-in-pessimism-in-the-eu/#.Uk_yuYbrzlY

such as Britain's UKIP and France's Front National look set to do exceptionally well. The far-left seems likely to top the poll in Greece. An anti-establishment movement headed by a clown may come first in Italy. Worst of all, many are losing faith in democracy itself.

Are you angry that the economy has been driven off a cliff, while many of those responsible have escaped scot-free? Are you depressed by policymakers' failure to improve things? Are you anxious that prospects for the future look grim and troubled that politics is taking a nasty turn? Are you eager for an alternative, positive prospectus for economic and social progress? Or perhaps you assume things are bound to get better? In any case, this book is for you. *European Spring* explains what's really wrong with Europe's economies and its politics – and how to put them right.

The Great Divergence

It often takes time for economies to recover from a big financial crisis – and they don't come much bigger than the recent one. Household spending remains depressed while people try to pay down their debts. Banks cut back their lending while they repair their balance sheets. Companies are reluctant to invest when future demand for their products is so uncertain. Capital and labour are not instantly redeployed to new businesses and sectors of the economy with the potential to grow. Even so, Europe ought to have made faster progress than this.

Cast your eyes across the Atlantic: while America is doing poorly by its own standards, it is doing much better than Europe. Even though the financial crisis originated in the United States, its economy has grown much more since then than Germany's, let alone Britain's.[14] Unemployment is much lower than in most of Europe and

---

14   By Q4 2013, the US economy was 7.3 per cent larger than in Q1 2008, Germany's was 2.9 per cent larger and Britain's was 1.3 per cent smaller.

has fallen to its lowest rate since late 2008.[15] Household debt has fallen significantly. Banks are lending again. Companies are starting to invest. New areas of growth are emerging: the next wave of the digital revolution, a manufacturing renaissance fuelled by cheap new sources of energy, booming exports to fast-growing emerging economies such as China and Mexico.

When the chaotic collapse of an American investment bank, Lehman Brothers, in September 2008 plunged the global economy into a tailspin, Britain and the eurozone initially tracked America's progression. They collapsed together in late 2008, hit rock bottom in mid-2009 and rebounded in 2010. But after that, their paths diverged. Investment and growth in America continued to recover, while they flatlined in Britain and plunged in parts of the eurozone. This divergence is in large part due to catastrophic mistakes by both British and eurozone policymakers, who killed off the recovery while failing to deal with the economy's real problems.

By late 2013, some European economies, notably Greece and Italy, were still shrinking. Many were flatlining. Most – including Britain's – were still smaller than before the crisis. Germany's was a mere 2.9 per cent larger than in 2008.[16] On the plus side, many countries' exports have picked up – Spain's are booming. Unfortunately, Britain's haven't, despite the much weaker pound. Countries that piled up huge debts to foreigners over the past decade – notably Ireland, Spain and Portugal –

Eurostat, gross domestic product at market prices, seasonally adjusted and adjusted for working days, index 2005=100. Code: namq_gdp_k

15   In December 2013, the US unemployment was 6.7 per cent, the lowest rate since October 2008. http://data.bls.gov/timeseries/LNS14000000 In the EU, the unemployment rate was 10.9 per cent in November 2013. http://epp.eurostat.ec.europa.eu/statistics_explained/index.php?title=File:Unemployment_rates,_seasonally_adjusted,_November_2013.png&filetimestamp=20140108092325

16   In Q4 2013, Germany's GDP was 2.9 per cent higher than in Q1 2008. Eurostat, gross domestic product at market prices, volume, seasonally adjusted and adjusted by working days. Code: namq_gdp_k

are no longer adding to them. Worryingly, Britain is again an outlier: its current-account deficit is larger than in 2007.[17]

Depressingly, after six years of slump and four of austerity, European households are nearly as lumbered with debt as before, while public debt is still rising. Many banks are zombies – neither infused with enough fresh capital to lend, nor killed off. Businesses either can't or won't invest. Promising sectors of the economy are often starved of the resources to grow or stunted by regulatory constraints, an aversion to taking risks and barriers to competition. Often, it seems as if Europe is not just taking ages to get back on its feet; it is actually digging a deeper hole for itself. Germany is exporting deflation to the rest of the eurozone. Much of southern Europe may be sinking into a debt trap. Meanwhile, the British government is trying to inflate yet another housing bubble ahead of the election due in 2015. The UK's recent burst of growth looks dangerously unsustainable: even though wages are still falling, debt-laden consumers are saving less and in some cases borrowing to spend more. It is not a pretty picture.

The Great Stagnation

Things aren't just bad now. The future seems bleak too. Prominent economists talk of a "new normal" of permanently low growth, a "great stagnation" of innovation and even of the "end of growth" in the West altogether. (Others, on the contrary, think innovation is speeding ahead, but fear that humans will lose the "race against the machine" and that robots will steal people's jobs.) There are certainly many worrying signs. The twin engines of higher living standards – productive investment and productivity growth – have long been faltering. Most of Europe has fallen further behind America's

---

17 Office for National Statistics, balance of payments statistics. The UK's current-account deficit was 2.2 per cent of GDP in 2007 and 3.8 per cent of GDP in 2012. In Q3 2013, it was 5.1 per cent of GDP. http://www.ons.gov.uk/ons/rel/bop/balance-of-payments/q3-2013/bop-time-series--q3-2013.html

productivity levels; only Ireland and much poorer ex-communist economies in central and eastern Europe have been catching up.[18] Britain's productivity record over the past decade is as poor as the eurozone's. Germany has performed worse than Greece. Italy did worst of all: a big fat zero.[19]

Europe's productivity pipeline is blocked. Not enough new businesses are launched. Start-ups have trouble lifting off. Growth in promising small companies often stalls. Established businesses don't innovate enough or invest enough in future growth. With a few notable exceptions such as Skype, Spotify and Shazam, the internet revolution has largely happened elsewhere. The new giants of our digital world – Google, Apple, Amazon, Facebook, Twitter, LinkedIn, PayPal, eBay – are all American. There is no European equivalent of Silicon Valley.

Europe isn't just falling further behind the US; it also faces evergreater competition from China, India, Brazil, Mexico, Turkey, Korea and other emerging economies – not just in lower-end manufacturing but also in higher-tech sectors. Apple's biggest rival in smartphones? Not Finland's Nokia, but Korea's Samsung. The world leader in solar panels? No longer Germany, but China. Britain's biggest manufacturer? India's Tata (which owns, among many things, luxury car maker Jaguar Land Rover).

Demography may not be destiny, but Europe's population trends look pretty dismal all the same. As the post-war baby boomers retire over the next fifteen or so years, the burden on smaller younger generations will be huge. In 2010, there were nearly four people of working age for every person aged sixty-five and over; without migration,

---

18   OECD, labour productivity growth in the total economy, change in GDP per hour worked, 2002–12

19   See Chapter 1 for more details.

there will be fewer than two-and-a-half by 2030.[20] The challenge isn't just financial, it's practical: who will care for the massed ranks of pensioners? As the labour force shrinks (as it already is doing in many European countries) and even more so as the population declines (as Germany's has been doing since 2004), economies will need to notch up faster productivity growth and investment merely to stand still. But if the economy is likely to stand still, why invest? To make matters worse, Europeans are much more risk-averse than Americans – less likely to start a business, less willing to embrace innovations such as genetically modified (GM) foods, nanotechnology or shale gas, less willing to accept any risks at all in their lives – and people tend to become even more conservative as they age. While the American Dream is one of restless self-improvement, the European Dream often seems to consist of a quiet life.

Increased immigration could be part of the solution to these challenges, but as experience shows in Britain, one of the few countries where the workforce is still rising thanks to new arrivals, this remains highly controversial.

Europeans can't even comfort themselves that their flaccid economy is getting greener. Despite all the costly policies that Europe has introduced, greenhouse-gas emissions from electricity generation are rising in Europe, whereas in the US, despite policymakers' inaction, they are falling. The EU's flagship emissions-trading scheme (ETS) has flopped. While the US is dashing for cheaper and cleaner shale gas, Europeans spurn shale while burning more filthy coal. Many countries, notably Germany, are also committed to phasing out nuclear energy, which will further increase emissions (and costs). As a result, energy prices are much higher in Europe than in the US, hitting consumers and

---

20 Personal calculations from Eurostat, Europop2010 (Eurostat Population Projections 2010-based). Code: proj_10c2150zmp. The ratio of 15–64s to over-64s is 3.86 in 2010 and 2.45 in 2030.

curbing growth. Without greater energy investment, the lights might even go out.

Let me be clear: I'm not saying that America is perfect, nor that Europe should try to become like America in every respect, simply that in many respects Europe is doing worse than the economy against which it tends to benchmark itself – which ought to be troubling. Pulling all this together, the danger is that Europe will get stuck in a semi-permanent winter, a prolonged period of poor growth and global decline akin to Japan's experience over the past two decades since its own bubble economy burst.

Political perils

It could be worse than that. Whereas the Japanese have displayed a remarkable stoicism and political stability during their long economic winter, Europeans are unlikely to be as accepting. The crisis has exacerbated existing political tensions and created new ones. The social fabric is fraying in many countries. People are increasingly turning on each other – and lashing out at foreigners too. Many no longer trust mainstream politicians, technocratic policymakers and elites in general, all of whom seem captured by vested interests and incapable of improving the lot of ordinary people. That leaves the door open to extremists and charlatans who scapegoat outsiders and peddle false solutions. Politics is turning nasty, fractious and inward-looking – with unpredictable consequences. Ultimately, our open societies could be at risk – and so too could democracy: witness how the neo-Nazi Golden Dawn has profited from the disintegration of Greek society or the authoritarian turn that Hungary is taking.

While belt-tightening is never easy, it helps if the pain seems fairly shared. But while politicians may proclaim that "we're all in this together", that's not how it feels to most people. During the boom years, people tolerated the widening chasm between rich and poor because it felt like everyone was benefiting from growth. But now that the pie is stagnant or shrinking, those who are doing well (or deemed not to be suffering enough) are increasingly resented, especially if others feel that they don't deserve their rewards. This rage is understandable and sometimes justified: bailed-out bankers do leech off the rest of society, as do Italy's grossly overpaid and often corrupt politicians. But unfortunately, it is often misdirected: most immigrants contribute to society and most unemployed people are unlucky, not lazy. Unless the real issues are addressed, this anger threatens to tear society apart and morph into a generalised anti-capitalist rage that would make us all worse off.

Trust in mainstream politicians has also been shredded. They failed to prevent the crisis, have been unable to resolve it and seem to prioritise their own interests over those of society as a whole. Since the crisis began, voters have turfed out incumbent governments of all stripes – left, right and technocratic – nearly every time they have had a chance.[21] The rare political survivors are all in countries that had come through the crisis pretty well – Sweden, the Netherlands, Poland and Austria – and even they are now in danger of being toppled.[22] Only Germany's Angela Merkel has sailed through the crisis

---

21 The incumbents thrown out include: Conservative New Democracy in Greece in October 2009 and then the Socialists in May 2012, the Socialists in Hungary in April 2010, Labour in Britain in May, Fianna Fail in Ireland in February 2011, the Centre-Party-led coalition in Finland in April, the Socialists in Portugal in May, the centre-right coalition in Denmark in September, the Socialists in Spain in November, the government in Slovenia in December , the centre-right in Slovakia in March 2012, President Nicolas Sarkozy in France in May, and both the Communists in Cyprus and Mario Monti, Italy's technocratic prime minister turned politician, in February 2013.

22 Sweden's centre-right coalition, which was re-elected in 2010, faces an uphill battle in 2014. The Dutch prime minister, Mark Rutte, only scraped through in 2012, albeit with a different coalition partner. Poland's centre-right coalition, which was

unscathed, winning re-election in 2009 and again four years later (although her coalition partners lost all their seats in parliament).

There is nothing wrong with throwing out unpopular governments; on the contrary, it is the essence of democracy. The problem is that their replacements have pursued broadly similar – and therefore largely unsuccessful – policies and have soon become deeply unpopular too. Only a year after he beat Nicolas Sarkozy in 2012, François Hollande had record-low approval ratings for a French president. Angry and disenchanted voters are increasingly turning away from establishment parties altogether. Again, this is not inherently bad: when an entire political class has failed, periodic democratic renewal can be positive. The problem is that voters aren't being offered sensible alternatives and are turning to extremists and charlatans instead. While Italians have only themselves to blame for repeatedly re-electing Silvio Berlusconi, it is understandable that they are angry at their often self-serving political class and feel let down by Mario Monti, the technocratic prime minister who plunged a largely unreformed economy into deep recession. Yet Beppe Grillo's anti-establishment Five Star Movement, which got more votes than any other single party in the 2013 elections, does not offer a coherent alternative.

Worse, most of these "populist" parties are xenophobic and reactionary. In Britain, the anti-immigrant and anti-EU United Kingdom Independence Party (UKIP) did surprisingly well in the 2013 local elections and may come first in the May 2014 European ones. In France, Marine Le Pen's fascist National Front (FN) polled nearly a fifth of the vote in 2012 and now tops the polls. In the Netherlands, Geert Wilders' anti-immigrant Freedom Party (PVV) is ahead in the polls again. Timo Soini's eurosceptic True Finns – now rebadged The Finns in case anyone doubted their Finnishness – are the largest

---

re-elected in 2011, is lagging in the polls. Austria's grand coalition also scraped back into power.

opposition party. Belgium's biggest party is hardline Flemish nationalist Bart de Wever's New Flemish Alliance (N-VA); a smaller nationalist party, Vlaams Belang, is even more extreme. In Sweden, the neo-Nazi Sweden Democrats entered parliament for the first time in 2010 and are now polling a tenth of the vote. In Denmark, the xenophobic Danish People's Party (DF) has also rebounded. Austria's far-right Freedom party gained over a fifth of the vote in the 2013 elections. Jobbik is a menace in Hungary. In Greece, the neo-Nazi Golden Dawn has rapidly gained support, not least from policemen, allowing its members to beat up and even murder immigrants with impunity until a government crackdown in late 2013. All these parties may do particularly well in the European elections. Even though the European Parliament's powers are greatly enhanced, voters tend to be unaware of this. In the absence of an open democratic debate about Europe's future, people often cast protest votes, if they bother to vote at all.

Fortunately, some countries are less affected by the far-right virus. Germany's Nazi past has largely inoculated it against extremism for now, as have Spain's and Portugal's more recent experience of fascist dictatorship. That said, Spain's ruling Partido Popular was founded by one of General Franco's former ministers. And *Deutschland schafftsichab* ("Germany Is Abolishing Itself"), an anti-immigrant tract by Thilo Sarrazin, a Social Democratic politician who used to be on the board of the Bundesbank, the country's highly respected central bank, was a huge bestseller.[23]

European Disunion

The crisis is not just tearing societies apart; it is pitting countries against each other. Old national stereotypes have been revived – and new grievances created. Whenever I speak in Germany, people assert

---

23   Thilo Sarrazin, *Deutschland schafft sich ab*, DVA: 2010

that Greeks are lazy; in fact, they tend to work much longer hours than Germans do.[24] According to a Pew Research Center survey, 18 per cent of Germans deem Greeks the least trustworthy people in the EU, and a further 18 per cent think the Italians are.[25] This mistrust is reciprocated: one in four Greeks deem Germans the least trustworthy Europeans.[26] So too is the scorn. Germans are deemed the most arrogant people in the EU by one in two Greeks, one in three Italians and one in four Spaniards.[27] They are also seen as the least compassionate Europeans by a majority of Greeks and nearly a third of Italians and Spaniards.[28] Worse, it has become increasingly common in southern Europe to label Germans as Nazis.

A crisis that could have been a unifying force – Europe acting together to tackle overmighty, dysfunctional cross-border banks – has instead become a divisive one, pitting creditors against debtors. Creditor-in-chief is Germany, which has used its clout to subvert EU institutions for its own selfish ends. As George Soros rightly observes, "The euro crisis has already transformed the European Union from a voluntary association of equal states into a creditor-debtor relationship from which there is no easy escape."[29] No wonder a massive 88

---

24   OECD, Average annual hours actually worked per worker, 2011. Greece is 2,032, Germany is 1,413 http://stats.oecd.org/Index.aspx?DatasetCode=ANHRS

25   To their credit, a third of Germans answered "don't know" or refused to give an answer.

26   Pew Research Center, Global Attitudes Survey, Spring 2013. Q44b: "In what European Union country, if any, are people the least trustworthy?"

27   *Ibid.* Q45a: "In what European Union country, if any, are people the most arrogant?" A plurality of Britons, French people and Germans think the French are the most arrogant.

28   *Ibid.* Q46b: "In what European Union country, if any, are people the least compassionate?" 57 per cent of Greeks say the Germans.

29   http://www.project-syndicate.org/commentary/a-simple-solution-to-the-euro-crisis-by-george-soros#ks2zqsVfBqj49ojP.99

per cent of Spaniards and 82 per cent of Italians think Germany's influence on the EU has become too strong.[30] More than half of French respondents agreed.[31] Three-quarters of Spaniards and Italians also think Germany is not showing enough solidarity with the rest of the eurozone. More than three-quarters of Spaniards believe that an increasingly German EU would be bad for Spain, while 70 per cent of Italian and British respondents voiced similar concerns.[32] A whopping 87 per cent of Greeks have a negative opinion of Germany's Chancellor Merkel.[33]

Unsurprisingly, support for the EU has also collapsed. As recently as spring 2010, 77 per cent of Spaniards had a favourable opinion of the EU; three years later, that had plunged to 46 per cent. In France, the EU's approval ratings fell from 63 per cent to 41 per cent over the same period – lower than in traditionally Eurosceptic Britain, where support dipped from 49 per cent to 43 per cent. Only one in three Greeks has a favourable view of the EU.[34] Polls suggest that Britons might even vote to leave the EU if given the chance – which they may get if the Conservatives win the general election in 2015 or if Labour and the Liberal Democrats match David Cameron's referendum pledge.

While the EU was once associated with prosperity, it is now linked with austerity and recession. Remarkably, Europeans now

---

30 That was up from 67 per cent of Spaniards and 53 per cent of Italians in late 2011. http://www.ft.com/cms/s/0/73f73f76-da75-11e2-a237-00144feab7de.html

31 56 per cent of French respondents agreed.

32 http://www.ft.com/cms/s/0/73f73f76-da75-11e2-a237-00144feab7de.html

33 Poll for Kathimerini and TV Skai, reported by Citi, Euro Area: Sovereign Debt Crisis Update, 16 July 2013

34 Pew Research Center, Global Attitudes Survey, Spring 2013 and previously, Q9f, Those having a very favourable or somewhat favourable opinion of the EU. Support for the EU has, however, held up in Poland (68 per cent), Germany (60 per cent) and Italy (58 per cent)

overwhelmingly feel that their national economy has been weakened by the economic integration of Europe.[35] Only in Germany, among the countries surveyed by the Pew Research Center, are a small majority more positive.[36] But despite the ongoing crisis in the eurozone, a majority of respondents in France, Germany, Italy, Spain and Greece want to keep their common currency rather than return to national ones.[37] All have strong political reasons for wanting to stay in the euro, not to mention a desire to keep their savings denominated in a strong currency and a fear of what euro exit might entail. Even so, support for the euro is falling.

European Spring?

How does Europe get out of this mess? Is ongoing sluggishness inevitable? Should politicians simply muddle through, massage down people's expectations and manage decline? Do people have to turn to extremists for alternative solutions?

Consensus opinion in Europe is overwhelmingly pessimistic. This book takes a more positive view. It unflinchingly explains how European countries face deep-seated economic and political problems that have been exacerbated by wrong-headed policies in recent years. But it argues that stagnation, decline and a lurch towards political extremism are not inevitable: the future can be much brighter if Europe changes course. We need to dispel bad ideas, confront

---

35   Pew Research Center, Global Attitudes Survey, Spring 2013. Q31: "In the long run, do you think that (survey country's) overall economy has been strengthened or weakened by the economic integration of Europe?" Three in five Spaniards think so, as do two in three Britons, three in four Italians and more than three in four French and Greeks.

36   Pew Research Center, Global Attitudes Survey, Spring 2013, Q31. 54 per cent of Germans think their country's economy has been strengthened by European integration.

37   *Ibid*, Q83.

vested interests and improve our institutions. To escape from this long, dark winter, we need a European Spring: both economic and political renewal.

European Spring is structured as follows. The first half of the book looks at the ongoing repercussions of the banking and debt crisis. Chapter 1 explains the common causes of the crisis in Britain and the eurozone, how they have made similar mistakes and how they face common longer-term challenges. Chapters 2 to 4 detail why the crisis took a particularly virulent turn in the eurozone. Chapter 5 explains why the crisis is not over and what needs to be done to resolve it, while Chapter 6 sets out how to make the euro succeed longer term. Since the chapters are largely self-standing, British readers who are not overly interested in the eurozone can skip Chapters 4 to 6 (or even Chapters 2 to 6) if they like. Chapter 7 looks at how economies outside the eurozone have fared, points out how poorly Britain has done and explains why its long-delayed recovery is dysfunctional.

The second half of the book looks at how to build a brighter future after the crisis. Chapter 8 considers whether Germany really is a model for the rest of Europe. Chapter 9 sets out my personal view of what makes a good economy, tracks the progress that has been achieved over the past century and suggests that our understanding of how economies work (and hence how to build better ones) is often flawed. Chapters 10 to 12 explain how European economies need to become more Adaptable, Dynamic and Decent in order to thrive: they need reforms that ADD UP. Chapter 13 looks at how to make the EU more democratic and therefore more effective (and why Britain would be crazy to leave in any case). Chapter 14 concludes with suggestions about how to save European politics from nasty extremists, create a more open democracy and bring about a European Spring.

Dissenting voices

European Spring is often very critical of European policymakers and institutions. Since the spinners in Brussels may try to discredit me, let me get my rebuttal in first. Line of attack one may be: he's British, so he's not really European. I am indeed a British citizen (not to mention a human being: a citizen of the world). I was born in London and have lived most of my life there (while travelling widely). But like it or not, Britain *is* part of Europe. Moreover, my father is French and my mother Estonian, so that makes me as European as someone who is wholly German or Portuguese – if not more so. I speak fluent French and good Spanish and have no problem understanding Italian newspapers or Portuguese films. I even speak a few words of Estonian.

More importantly, in my three years as independent economic adviser to the president of the European Commission and head of the team that provides him with strategic policy advice, I lived up to the institution's ideals as a guardian of the common European interest. I didn't hire my compatriots, let alone family friends, or primarily associate with them. I didn't take orders from the government back home. I always advised what I thought was best for Europeans in general, rather than what was good for the banks in my country or for my personal advancement.

Line of attack two may be: he's not really "pro-European". Again, bad luck. I spent two-and-a-half years as chief economist and then director of policy at Britain in Europe, the pro-European campaign. I think the EU is an amazing achievement, as Chapter 13 explains. I strongly believe in closer cooperation both within Europe and internationally. I recognise that nation-states still matter, but wouldn't shed a tear if they disappeared. I think it's wonderful that goods (though unfortunately not most services), investment and above all people can move freely across the twenty-eight member states of the European Union – and I wish those huge benefits were extended as widely as possible. Where the EU is advancing a positive agenda globally, we can achieve more together than we can alone – and where it isn't, we can try to change it. But unfortunately, the EU and the eurozone are often dysfunctional – and I believe they are heading in the wrong direction. It is precisely because I am pro-European and want the best for all Europeans that I passionately want the EU and the euro to succeed and am so critical of what has gone wrong.

Is it anti-European to want the costs of the crisis to be shared more fairly? Is it anti-European to want to hold to account the people who got us into this mess and are failing to get us out of it? Is it anti-European to want Europe to be better governed and more democratic? If I can criticise the British government without being anti-British, surely I can criticise EU institutions without being anti-European? Likewise, criticising Angela Merkel's policies does not imply being anti-German. Let us not fall prey to political manipulation by people in authority who think they are above criticism. Pointing out EU policymakers' mistakes is not treachery; it is expressing a well-meaning point of view. Lots of European citizens agree: Are they all "anti-European" too? If that makes the authorities unhappy, perhaps, to paraphrase Bertolt Brecht, they ought to dissolve the people and elect another.

Line of attack three may actually revolve around substance: he's wrong, the crisis strategy was the best that was politically possible at the time, it is now working, the EU is not perfect but it is heading in the right direction, and so on. Great: bring it on. We desperately need a genuine, open debate about the future of Europe (and Britain's place in it). Please read on to find out my analysis of what has gone wrong and how to put it right – then decide for yourself and make your voice heard.

PART I:
A LONG, DARK WINTER

1

TWO CURRENCIES, ONE CRISIS

Why Britain and the eurozone have similar failings

> *The UK government's economic policies are too European. Not too pro-European, clearly. Nor too oriented towards Europe. They are too European in that they are inflicting on the British economy the same misguided approaches whereby European leaders have perpetuated the euro crisis.*
>
> Adam Posen, former member of the Bank of England's monetary-policy committee, 2013[38]

Stepping off the Eurostar train in London, it feels a world apart from Brussels. Whereas the Gare du Midi is depressingly dark and dingy, St Pancras station is upliftingly bright and modern. Having shuttled back

---

38   Adam Posen, "The UK is very European – in its mistakes", *Financial Times*, 22 February 2013 http://www.ft.com/cms/s/0/cdcfe152-7b79-11e2-8eb3-00144feabdc0.html

and forth between Europe's financial capital and its administrative one each week for the past three years, I am particularly aware of their differences – and their similarities. Brussels isn't a patch on London. But contrary to the prevailing view that what ails the eurozone is very different to Britain's predicament, the similarities are striking. Many of their problems are alike. They have made similar policy mistakes. And in many respects, they need comparable economic prescriptions.

Policymakers in Britain like to flatter themselves that they are very different (read: "better") to those in Brussels and Berlin – and vice versa – but they often think alike. Listen to a speech by Britain's finance minister, George Osborne, his German counterpart, Wolfgang Schäuble, or his eurozone equivalent, Olli Rehn, and it is uncanny how they all mouth the same mantra: reducing public borrowing is the top priority and a precondition for sustained economic growth. Tragically, when Greece's debt problems came to a head in 2010, Britain, Brussels and Berlin all misdiagnosed the wider crisis as primarily fiscal, when it is in fact mainly financial. As a result, instead of fixing the banks and writing down excessive private-sector debts, all three pressed on with front-loaded austerity without doing enough to boost short-term growth in other ways – with similarly depressing results. That a recovery of sorts finally began in 2013 scarcely excuses those mistakes, while the scars from this period and many of the other problems endure. For instance, Royal Bank of Scotland made a further £8.2 billion in losses in 2013, while credit to businesses in the eurozone contracted at a record rate.[39] To cap it all, both Britain and the eurozone are failing to face up to their huge (and often similar) longer-term challenges.

---

39 RBS figures are from http://www.bbc.co.uk/news/uk-england-26364715. Credit to businesses in the eurozone contracted by 3 per cent in the year to December 2013 and by 2.9 per cent in the year to January 2014. http://www.ecb.europa.eu/press/pdf/md/md1401.pdf

The crisis in Britain, the eurozone and indeed across the Western financial system – from the mighty United States to tiny Iceland – is the result of massive bad lending in the years up to 2007 by a dysfunctional and dangerously fragile banking system, fuelled by excessively low interest rates and abetted by the complacency (and sometimes the complicity) of regulators and politicians. Investors underestimated risk and misallocated capital on a massive scale, inflating a property and financial bubble of unprecedented scale and scope, financed by reckless lending by both international banks and local ones. Europe's outsized banks – notably German, French and British ones – were at the heart of it.[40] They poured money into bonds backed by dodgy American subprime mortgages and made more complex bets on US house prices. They also made huge mistakes nearer to home. Together with local banks, they financed rampant property speculation in Britain, Ireland, Spain, the Netherlands and elsewhere. They gave huge loans to Portuguese consumers, even though the local economy wasn't growing. They lent to the Greek government as if its debt was as safe as Germany's. The result was a huge build-up of debt both within the financial sector and in the economy at large. In Europe, most of this bad lending to the real economy was to households; some was to companies; only in Greece was it primarily to the government.

Despite their differences, the similarities between what happened in Britain and various eurozone economies are glaring. In both Britain and Ireland, the financial sector came to dwarf the economy: bank assets grew to six times the size of the economy in the UK, eight times in Ireland.[41] The explosion of financial-sector debt

---

40   See, for example, Hyun Song Shin, "Global savings glut or global banking glut?", Vox. eu, 20 December 2011 http://www.voxeu.org/article/global-savings-glut-or-global-banking-glut

41   High-Level Expert Group on Reforming the Structure of the EU Banking Sector, chaired by Erkki Liikanen, 2 October 2012 http://ec.europa.eu/internal_market/bank/docs/highlevel_expert_group/report_en.pdf

in Britain between 2000 and 2007 exactly parallels the rise in the Netherlands[42] – and in both countries household debt rocketed as a share of disposable income by a similar proportion over the same period.[43] In Britain as well as Spain, house prices roughly trebled in the decade to 2007.[44] When the US housing bubble burst, both British banks (notably, Royal Bank of Scotland) and German ones (such as Commerzbank and many state-owned Ländesbanks) made such huge losses on American mortgage-backed securities that they were bailed out by their respective governments. Both the British government and eurozone ones subsequently extended a blanket taxpayer guarantee to all bank debts.

In *Aftershock: Reshaping the World Economy*, which I wrote in 2009, I explained the intricacies of what went wrong across the Western financial system.[45] The first half of this book focuses on the failures in Europe, particularly since 2010. For a broader and more detailed account of the pre-crisis years, notably of the excesses in the United States, please see *Aftershock* or one of the many other books about the crisis. Nouriel Roubini's *Crisis Economics* is particularly good.[46]

Table A1.2: total number and assets of monetary financial institutions by country (March 2012)

42 OECD, Debt of financial corporations, as a percentage of GDP, DBTS12GDP

43 OECD, Household debt as a share of gross disposable income, DBTS14_S15GDI In the UK it rose from 112.39 per cent in 2000 to 174.15 per cent in 2007, that is by a factor of 1.55; in the Netherlands it rose from 163.72 per cent in 2000 to 242.37 per cent, that is by a factor of 1.48.

44 See Nationwide House Price Index, http://www.nationwide.co.uk/hpi/historical.htm and http://www.cotizalia.com/cache/2008/07/03/46_europa_preocupa_mucho_ajuste_inmobiliario_espana.html

45 Philippe Legrain, *Aftershock: Reshaping the World Economy After the Crisis*, Little, Brown: 2010

46 Nouriel Roubini with Stephen Mihm, *Crisis Economics: A Crash Course in the Future of Finance*, Allen Lane: 2010

Manias, Panics and Crashes

Left to its own devices, the financial system has an inherent tendency to run away with itself and then blow up, as Charles Kindleberger's magisterial history of *Manias, Panics and Crashes* shows.[47] That was forgotten in the long period of stability after the Great Depression of the 1930s when the banking system was caged and predominantly national and financial crises seemed consigned to less-developed economies. When banking crises struck Norway, Sweden and Finland in the early 1990s, the lessons went unheeded (see Chapter 7). The crisis that began in Asia in 1997 and threatened to drag down the Western financial system a year later was an even louder wake-up call – as I explained in my first book, *Open World: the Truth about Globalisation*, written in 2001.[48] But seduced by the ahistorical, self-serving nonsense that the financial system was "efficient"[49] – which entailed that regulation should be minimised and economic models could ignore it entirely – policymakers complacently chose to do nothing. In fact, as thinkers as varied as Kindleberger, Friedrich Hayek, John Maynard Keynes, Hyman Minsky and George Soros have pointed out, the financial system is intrinsically unstable, because it involves bets about an unknowable future that can prove self-fulfilling for a (long) while. That the future is fundamentally uncertain is not a matter for academic debate; it is the essence of the human condition. Only a fool with a spreadsheet thinks it is a known (normal) probability distribution. Since nobody really knows what the future may hold, nobody knows what the prices of financial assets ought to be. So they take their cues from others – and since

---

47   Charles Kindleberger, *Manias, Panics and Crashes*, Wiley: 1978

48   Philippe Legrain, *Open World: the Truth about Globalisation*, Abacus: 2002

49   Financial markets were deemed efficient in the sense that prices set by the market were "right" since they were determined by rational investors acting on all available information and mistakes were rapidly corrected by other profit-seeking investors.

human beings are emotional and fallible social animals, they often get caught up in collective delusions, while sceptics are ignored or have an incentive to follow the crowd. If enough people bet the same way – and banks continue lending more to them so that they can go on raising their stakes – their mistakes can be self-validating for years before fundamentals finally intrude and prices correct.

In the bubble years, several false ideas seemed to justify investors' irrational exuberance: the mistaken belief that house prices in America and elsewhere couldn't fall; the absurd notion that supposedly God-like policymakers such as US Federal Reserve chairman Alan Greenspan, UK finance minister Gordon Brown and European Central Bank (ECB) President Jean-Claude Trichet had abolished the age-old cycle of boom and bust[50]; the delusion that financial crises didn't happen in advanced economies; and the misconception that all government debt was safe. All of that seemed to justify Western banks taking ever greater risks with ever more debt – and thus with ever less margin for error – while investors got caught up in the belief that speculation was the path to effortless riches.

When speeding cars collide on the motorway, causing a pile-up that hurts careful drivers too, the focus quickly turns to who might have prevented the carnage. Clearly, much of the blame lies with the reckless drivers themselves. Believing they had the driving skills of Lewis Hamilton on a Formula One racetrack, bankers abused regulatory laxity, put their foot down – and turned out to be losers tailgating on the motorway. Often, they crashed because of bad bets within the financial system. Where they came unstuck because of bad loans to households and companies, those borrowers are also responsible, albeit less so than bankers who were supposedly experts at pricing assets

---

50 As Bill White has observed, in the 1980s the fight against high inflation was justified on the grounds that it was 'necessary' for macroeconomic stability. Then, somehow, it morphed into the belief that price stability was 'sufficient' for such stability.

and assessing borrowers' creditworthiness – and paid handsomely for it – and had a better view of the overall picture. But responsibility also lies with those who failed to enforce a safer speed limit: central bankers, financial regulators, bank supervisors and politicians in both Europe and the United States.

By keeping interest rates too low for too long, central bankers fuelled this deadly race. Like the Fed, the Bank of England and the ECB focused too narrowly on consumer-price inflation and turned a blind eye to the dangers of soaring credit growth, both domestically and across borders, and the resulting asset-price inflation.[51] During that period, the West benefited from two big disinflationary shocks: the entry of China into global markets and the rapid diffusion of improvements in digital technology across the economy. This, in effect, expanded global supply and pushed down global prices. Instead of accommodating this price fall – which is "good deflation": the sort we experience with the collapse in the price of laptops or flat-screen TVs – central banks kept interest rates too low to offset this. Lax US monetary policy spilled over internationally, helping to fuel Europe's credit boom.[52] As UK house prices soared, the Bank of England sat on its hands. The ECB held real (that is, inflation-adjusted) interest rates below 1 per cent between mid-2001 and 2005.

When central bankers finally began to raise interest rates, it was too little, too late. Worse, they did nothing to sound the alarm about financial excesses. On the contrary, as late as 2006, ECB President Trichet welcomed the fact that investors were willing to lend to the

---

51 For example, gross capital flows both within the eurozone and into and out of it nearly tripled between 2002 and 2007. Source: Philip Lane, "Capital Flows in the Euro Area", *European Economy*, Economic Papers 497, April 2013. Capital flows in and out of Britain also soared.

52 See Hélène Rey's excellent "Dilemma not Trilemma: The Global Financial Cycle and Monetary Policy Independence", paper presented at Jackson Hole, August 2013. http://www.kansascityfed.org/publicat/sympos/2013/2103Rey.pdf

Greek government on almost as good terms as to Germany's as evidence of the euro's success.[53] This convergence of bond yields, in turn, was validated by the ECB's collateral lending rules, which treated all eurozone government bonds as if they were "risk-free". As for the Bank of England, when Northern Rock suffered the ignominy of a run in September 2007, the first on a British bank since the nineteenth century, it was asleep at the wheel.

While central bankers provided the rocket fuel, financial regulators allowed bankers to drive faster with souped-up engines, while skimping on safety measures. In both Britain and the eurozone, financial regulation was often inadequate and sometimes perverse. If you finance a house purchase by putting down only a 2 per cent deposit and borrowing the other 98 per cent, you are taking a huge risk. If the house goes up in value by 2 per cent, you have doubled your

---

53   For example, in the Mais Lecture at Cass Business School on 11 May 2006, Trichet said: "It is sometimes argued that the convergence in euro area government bond spreads which was seen in the run-up to Monetary Union is evidence that the process of financial integration may be detrimental to the functioning of market discipline, the latter being the influence exerted by markets on governments by pricing different risks of default. This reasoning, however, neglects the fact that the observed convergence in government bond yield spreads mainly reflected the closer coordination of monetary policies across euro area countries – an overall compression of risk premia also observable in other markets and outside the euro area – and the ensuing convergence of inflation expectations across countries, as well as the progressive elimination of uncertainty regarding exchange rate movements and, finally, the disappearance of intra-euro area exchange rate risk by the time the euro was introduced. Since 1999, government bond yield spreads have mainly reflected differences in liquidity and in perceived credit risks, which in turn reflect the sustainability of the countries' fiscal positions... There is little doubt that the progress in financial integration witnessed in euro area government bond markets over the last few years has helped to improve the efficiency of financial markets in general and of government bond markets in particular." http://www.ecb.europa.eu/press/key/date/2006/html/sp060511_1.en.html

equity – but if it falls by a mere 2 per cent, your capital is wiped out. If at that point you had to refinance your mortgage, you would probably not be able to. If banks finance their assets with mostly debt and only a little equity, they have even less margin for error, since they typically need to continually refinance their debt. Yet global rules agreed in the Swiss city of Basel not only set wafer-thin capital requirements, they also allowed banks to use their own flawed risk models to determine how big a capital buffer they needed to operate safely.[54] Given that bank bosses' bonuses depended on hitting targets for returns on equity, they had a huge incentive to borrow more to amplify their returns – and unsurprisingly, the banks' models deemed this to be safe. European banks ended up even more reliant on debt than American ones did. By 2007, UK banks were financing every £100 of lending with an average of £97 of debt and only £3 of shareholders' equity (and much less in some cases).[55] Eurozone banks were relying on as little as €2 of equity and €98 of debt. No wonder so many European banks were wiped out – or should have been, if governments hadn't stepped in with taxpayers' money.

Capital requirements weren't just too lenient and too easily gamed by bankers; they were also skewed to encourage banks to buy government debt. Shamelessly, governments connived in the fiction that public debt was risk-free, allowing banks to borrow as much as they wanted to buy as much government debt as they wanted. Unfortunately, some of the governments to which banks lent, notably Greece, are now insolvent. While eurozone banks were particularly big buyers of government bonds, British ones joined in too. In early

---

54 The risk models wrongly assumed that future returns were normally distributed, with the parameters of the distribution determined by market fluctuations in recent years.

55 http://www.bankofengland.co.uk/publications/Documents/fsr/2010/fsr27sec4.pdf

2010, British banks had a $13.5 billion exposure to Greek, Irish and Portuguese government debt – much less than French banks' $56.1 billion or German ones' $36.4 billion, but more than Spanish banks' $11.7 billion or Italian ones' $6.4 billion.[56]

It's not just central bankers and financial regulators who encouraged or ignored bankers' excesses, so too did the financial police, who failed to step in to stop bankers' recklessness. Britain's financial watchdogs prided themselves on their "light touch" – ie, soft-touch – approach. Instead of reining in the City of London's excesses, they became cheerleaders for it. Their Continental counterparts were more suspicious of the City's "casino capitalism", but just as corporatist in championing, rather than curbing, their country's banks. Financial self-interest and economic nationalism often overlap. Infamously, Jacques de Larosière chaired a high-level group tasked by the European Commission in 2008 with writing a report for EU leaders on EU financial regulation and supervision while on the payroll of France's biggest bank, BNP Paribas. Perhaps unsurprisingly, the report argues that banking oversight should involve "more reliance on judgement" by wise, impartial financial supervisors in his vein.[57] For the most part, international watchdogs such as the European Commission and the International Monetary Fund (IMF) failed to bark. Only Bill White at the Bank for International Settlements spoke out (and was first ignored then rubbished).

Last but not least, blame lies with politicians who are meant to take a wider view of financial safety yet failed to protect voters' interests. As Britain's finance minister from 1997 to 2007, Gordon Brown argued that what was good for the City of London was good for Britain,

---

56 Bank for International Settlements, *Quarterly Review*, September 2010. Foreign exposures to Greece, Ireland, Portugal and Spain, by bank nationality, end-Q1 2010

57 Report by the High-Level Group on Financial Supervision in the EU chaired by Jacques de Larosière, 25 February 2009, Recommendation 1

seeing the City's profits as a means of paying for a Scandinavian-style welfare system with American levels of tax.[58] As City minister, Ed Balls, now the opposition Labour party's finance spokesman, championed London's light-touch regulatory approach. The ties between the French government and BNP Paribas are so intimate that its traders boast that it is inconceivable that the government would let it fail. Spain's *cajas*, local savings banks which financed a big chunk of the country's property bubble, likewise had incestuous links with both local and national politicians. Germany's Ländesbanks, which are largely owned by its regional governments, serve as political piggy-banks for projects that cannot be financed out of taxes. Given such free rein, it is no wonder that Europe's financial system ran away with itself.

From bubble to bust

The party grew wilder as the decade went on, but in 2007 and 2008 the music finally stopped. When the US housing bubble burst, over-leveraged banks incurred huge losses on their poorly securitised exposure to subprime mortgages. The first European bank to collapse was a German one, IKB Deutsche Industriebank, which was bailed out by the government in Berlin in the summer of 2007. As the problems that began in the US subprime-mortgage market spread, wholesale financial markets froze. Banks stopped lending first to each other and then to the rest of the economy. Cross-border lending collapsed. Gross capital flows (movements of money) in and out of eurozone economies plunged from some $5 trillion in 2007 to around $1 trillion

---

58   On the eve of becoming prime minister in 2007, and only three months before Northern Rock collapsed, Gordon Brown spoke in glowing terms of "a new golden age for the City of London". http://www.hm-treasury.gov.uk/press_68_07. htm What was good for the City was good for Britain: "Let me say as I begin my new job, I want to continue to work with you in helping you do yours, listening to what you say, always recognising your international success is critical to that of Britain's overall."

in 2008 to less than $500 billion a year later.[59] Whereas foreigners had poured $1.5 trillion into Britain in 2007, they yanked out $1.2 trillion in 2008.[60] Credit to the real economy plunged. Again, the parallels between Britain and eurozone countries are uncanny. Having grown by 13 per cent in 2008, lending to households and non-financial businesses in Britain slumped by 5.3 per cent in 2009; in Spain 12.3 per cent growth was followed by a 3 per cent fall.[61]

As banks stopped lending, property bubbles burst and exalted expectations of future growth were revised down, people realised they were less wealthy than they had assumed. Their debts suddenly loomed larger, while creditors felt less confident that they would be repaid in full. So everyone tried to spend less (and save more) at the same time – and since one person's spending is another's income, this plunged the economy into recession. It's not just households' balance sheets that suddenly looked less healthy; so too did those of the banks that lent to them. Banks responded by cutting their outgoings still further, curbing credit even to sound borrowers, notably smaller businesses, and deepening the recession. Companies took fright too, cutting investment and firing workers. All this slashed tax revenues and swelled social spending, notably on unemployment benefits, resulting in larger government deficits. EU governments also joined in global efforts to arrest the world economy's collapse with a coordinated fiscal stimulus in 2008–9: tax cuts and spending increases, financed by increased

---

59   Personal calculations from Philip Lane, "Capital Flows in the Euro Area", *European Economy*, Economic Papers 497, April 2013, Figure 1

60   Charles Roxburgh et al., "Global Capital Markets: Entering a New Era", McKinsey Global Institute, September 2009

61   Eurostat, Private credit flow in per cent of GDP - non consolidated - annual data. Code: tipspc10

borrowing.[62] Without this stimulus, the recession would have been much deeper. For the most part, then, high government borrowing is a *consequence* of the crisis, not the cause of it. Greece is the exception, not the rule.

When the crisis struck in 2007, public deficits were below the limit of 3 per cent of gross domestic product (GDP) prescribed by EU fiscal rules in Britain and throughout the eurozone, except in Portugal, where it was 3.1 per cent. (It subsequently emerged that Greece had been cooking the books; its deficit in 2007 was not 2.8 per cent, but 6.5 per cent.) Britain had a deficit of 2.8 per cent of GDP; Spain a surplus of 1.9 per cent.[63] Nor did the level of public debt seem alarming. Spain's was low (36.3 per cent of GDP) and falling, Ireland's even lower (25.1 per cent) and stable. Britain's had risen from a low of 37.7 per cent of GDP in 2002 to 44.2 per cent in 2007, but was still comfortably below the EU limit of 60 per cent of GDP. A few countries had debts that were stable but a bit above the EU limit: France (64.2 per cent), Germany (65.2 per cent) and Portugal (68.4 per cent). Italy's debt was much higher (103.3 per cent) but also stable.[64] Greece's debt, it turns out, was even higher (107.4 per cent) and rising.

With hindsight, Osborne, Schäuble and Rehn argue that governments borrowed too much in the pre-crisis years. But if you showed the figures for government borrowing from 2000 to 2007 to independent experts who didn't know that tax revenues were unsustainably inflated by a huge bubble and the resulting consumer boom,

---

62   In December 2008, EU leaders agreed an initial €200 billion fiscal stimulus – equivalent to around 1.5 per cent of GDP – including a €30 billion boost for lending to smaller businesses through the European Investment Bank. European Council, Presidency Conclusions, 11/12 December 2008, 17271/1/08 REV 1. By June 2009, they were talking of a €500 billion stimulus – albeit spread over 2009 and 2010.

63   Eurostat, general government deficit/surplus, per cent of GDP. Code: tec00127

64   Eurostat, general government gross debt, per cent of GDP. Code: tsdde410

would they have sounded the alarm about fiscal profligacy and the risks of a debt crisis? Had they known Greece's true situation, they would certainly have been alarmed. They would have warned that Italy's situation was precarious. They would have recommended that France, Germany and Portugal keep an eye on their debt levels. They might have had a few concerns about Britain's deficits, but not about its debts. They would have been intensely relaxed about Spain and Ireland. That is not just my opinion. Were policymakers and politicians at the time – who didn't realise there was a bubble – warning about government borrowing running out of control? The European Commission wasn't.[65] The IMF wasn't. And nor was Osborne, then in opposition as the Conservatives' financial spokesman.

Had you noticed the financial bubble before it was too late, say 2005, would your policy advice have been to prioritise tax rises and spending cuts to try to strengthen public finances and slow the

---

65   The European Commission's directorate-general for economic and financial affairs, then headed by Klaus Regling, who has since been appointed to run the European Stability Mechanism, not only failed to raise the alarm, they actually deemed that Spain was running surpluses and set to continue doing so, even after stripping out the effect of the economic cycle. The figures can be found in the various editions of European Commission, Directorate General ECFIN, Economic and Financial Affairs, Cyclical Adjustment of Budget Balances. http://ec.europa.eu/economy_finance/db_indicators/gen_gov_data/adjustment/index_en.htm

In Spring 2007, they determined that Spain had a cyclically adjusted deficit of 0.1 per cent of GDP in 2003 and surpluses of 0.1 per cent of GDP in 2004, 1.6 per cent in 2005 and 2.3 per cent in 2006; by Spring 2013, they had revised down their view, judging that Spain had a cyclically adjusted deficit of 0.8 per cent of GDP in 2003, a deficit of 0.5 per cent in 2004, a surplus of 0.8 per cent in 2005 and a surplus of 1.5 per cent in 2006. In Spring 2008, when the crisis had already begun, they reckoned Spain had a cyclically adjusted surplus of 2.4 per cent of GDP in 2007 and would continue having surpluses of 1.1 per cent in 2008 and 0.9 per cent in 2009; by Spring 2013, their view was that Spain actually had a cyclically adjusted deficit of 0.9 per cent of GDP in 2007, 4.7 per cent of GDP in 2008 and 9.2 per cent of GDP in 2009.

consumer boom – remember that inflation was not out of control – or to get a grip on financial excesses? The former would have been a damage limitation policy that addressed the symptoms of the problem, while the latter would have tackled its root cause. Undeniably, policy-makers are guilty of many grievous errors. But the main reason why Europe is in such a mess is not that they overlooked *fiscal* profligacy in the pre-crisis years. It's they that failed to notice or do anything about the dangerous *financial* excesses. Often, indeed, they cheered them on. That is a calamitous error of judgment by both Osborne and Balls, the German government and the Spanish one, as well as by the European Commission, the ECB and the Bank of England.

Balance-sheet repair

Since the bubbles burst, the primary cause of the enduring weakness of Europe's economies has been the efforts by households and banks to repair their balance sheets. (Policymakers have also exacerbated and spread the misery, as we shall see.) Households in Britain, Ireland, Portugal, Spain, the Netherlands and Denmark have huge debts. In some countries, notably Portugal and Ireland, companies' total debts are dangerously high too; in many countries, including Britain and Italy, many business loans have gone sour.[66] Both local banks in those countries and the foreign banks that lent to them, notably French and German ones, are also often in trouble. Weak spending in post-bubble economies in turn has knock-on effects for countries that export a lot to them, not least Germany. So the way to promote a rapid recovery is to accelerate this balance-sheet repair.

One way is to try to make households feel wealthier by inflating the prices of their assets, such as shares, bonds and property. That is the purpose of quantitative easing (QE), whereby the US Federal

---

66   OECD, debt of non-financial corporations as a percentage of GDP. In 2012, the figure was 306 per cent in Ireland, 230 per cent in Portugal and 104 per cent in Britain.

Reserve and the Bank of England have "printed" money to buy assets, mostly government bonds. But while QE may have limited the downturn in Britain, it did not spark a recovery – and relying too much on overzealous monetary policy risks reviving the bubble economy rather than encouraging a shift to more sustainable and balanced growth. If investors think asset prices are only temporarily inflated and so don't feel any wealthier, QE isn't much of a stimulus to growth. But if they do feel wealthier and borrow more, QE can be dangerous, because their financial situation would then become even more precarious. Having spent £375 billion, the Bank of England stopped buying assets through QE in October 2012.

Another way to accelerate the balance-sheet repair is to reduce the debt burden – by keeping interest rates very low, through inflation or by writing them down. Insofar as banks pass them on to borrowers, very low official interest rates reduce households' and companies' interest payments – and may enable them to repay the principal faster. Inflation may be the eventual solution to the crisis, but it is hard to generate in a slump – although because of the pound's plunge Britain has had some. Debt write-downs are always possible but tend to be fiercely resisted by creditors.

A third way is to try to increase people's incomes so that they can pay down their debts more quickly, continue spending while they do so (or find higher debts more bearable). Governments can borrow to invest, boosting spending now and production later. Companies could all decide to invest more too – but are unlikely to do so if they expect future demand for their products to be weak. Businesses could try to boost their foreign sales, but that is hard if their major export markets are depressed too. At the very least, governments should support households' efforts to save by continuing to borrow themselves.

In the latter half of 2010, when I was first approached by the president of the European Commission, José Manuel Barroso, to provide him with independent economic advice, I advocated a three-point plan for resolving the immediate crisis. First, perform an honest assessment of the balance sheets of European banks and force them to write down bad loans, test how they would cope with severe economic and financial stress, compel viable banks to raise plenty of additional capital to provide a buffer against past losses and possible future ones – and wind down unviable banks. Second, conduct a candid appraisal of whether the government, households and companies in each country are likely to be able to repay their debts in full and write down those that are unsustainably high. Third, combine measures to boost investment – both nationally and at an EU level, notably through the European Investment Bank – with reforms to boost future growth, in order to support demand while households pay down debts and help economies adjust towards new and more sustainable sources of growth. My advice was designed for the eurozone but it could also have been applied to Britain.

Had my three-point plan been followed in full, Europe's economies would have recovered much faster and would now be in much better shape. Unfortunately, both Britain and the eurozone took a different course. They have tried to rescue every bank without forcing them to fix their problems, creating zombie banks that sap the economy's strength. They have failed to recognise that many debts are unpayable, still less deal with the problem. And they lurched into collective, front-loaded, slash-and-burn austerity without doing enough to promote the investment and reforms needed to boost growth. Predictably, the results were disastrous.

State-sponsored zombies

Ever since the crisis began, EU governments have tried to prop up nearly every failing bank at taxpayers' expense without forcing them to face up to their losses. Typically, governments first deny that difficulties exist. They then try to paper over problems with subsidised loans and guarantees. Finally, when a bank is on the brink of failure, they inject just enough taxpayers' money to keep it afloat, without repairing its balance sheet enough to make it a viable lender. This "pretend and prop up" approach reflects policymakers' capture by banking lobbies as well as their fears about whether voters – and in some cases, markets – will accept even bigger bailouts. The upshot is that Europe has ended up with the worst of both worlds: government-backed but undercapitalised zombie banks that fail to lend, hamper the economy from adjusting and growing again, and drag down governments' finances with them.

Bailing out the banks is monstrously unfair, because taxpayers are paying for the mistakes made by bankers and those who financed them. Failing to force them to restructure is perverse, because it has impeded the strong recovery that policymakers and everyone else are so desperate for, at huge human cost. Together, these two policies are dangerous. First, because they damage public finances, both directly through the cost of the bailouts (and potential future ones) and indirectly through the slump in tax revenues and rise in social spending in economies depressed by a zombie banking system. Second, because banks that do not suffer sufficiently for their past mistakes are more likely to make even bigger ones in future – in effect, government support is an invitation for banks to speculate at taxpayers' expense. Last but not least, placing banks' narrow interests ahead of the common good destroys trust in the honesty and competence of policymakers and institutions, opening the door to extremists and ultimately threatening support for democracy itself.

In Ireland, the cost of saving the banks and their creditors has threatened to sink the state. The direct cost to Irish taxpayers of paying off the creditors who financed banks' bad lending is so far €64 billion, around half of the value of everything Irish residents produced in 2011. On top of that, there is the indirect cost of the slump in living standards since 2008.[67] Given how huge and precariously financed British banks are, Britain was lucky to escape Ireland's fate. So far the losses have been huge, but not unbearable.

Some will argue that governments had no choice but to back-stop banks, since the alternative was a Lehman-style panic. But that is not true. The lesson from Lehman was not that governments must save all banks, but rather that failed banks should be restructured or killed off in an orderly way rather than a chaotic one. In the absence of legal mechanisms for winding down banks in an orderly fashion, insolvent banks should either have been nationalised, restructured and recapitalised before being sold off again (as Norway did during its banking crisis in the early 1990s) or new "good banks" created and the old "bad banks" wound down, as I argued in *Aftershock*.[68]

> *Either option — nationalisation or the creation of new good banks — would have been infinitely preferable to the current mess. It would have boosted the economy, because the freshly capitalised good banks, unburdened by the old bad loans and securities, could have quickly resumed their proper function of lending to sound companies. It would have deterred banks and their creditors from taking big, destabilising risks in future. It would have placed less of a strain on government finances. And it would have been much fairer, since banks and their creditors would have paid most of the price for their mistakes rather than*

---

67 http://ftalphaville.ft.com/2010/11/08/397221/the-likely-cost-of-irelands-bank-bailout/ GNP figure in 2012 is €127 billion: https://namawinelake.wordpress.com/2012/12/16/irelands-gnp-and-gdp-in-2012/

68 See in particular pages 72-75 of *Aftershock: Reshaping the World After the Crisis*, Little, Brown: 2010.

taxpayers. By clearing the decks, the new banks could have started afresh, chastened.[69]

Critics will say that such ideas are crazy, yet nationalisation is precisely how the IMF typically advises governments to deal with bank failures, while variants of the good-bank proposal were put forward at the time by luminaries such as George Soros, Willem Buiter (then a professor at London School of Economics, now chief economist of Citi, an American bank), and Nobel-winning economist Joseph Stiglitz.[70] I concluded:

> *The reason why these proposals were rejected is not because they were barmy. It is because bankers' huge lobbying power and policy-makers' capture by financiers' self-serving ideas persuaded them that banks had to be bailed out for the common good. But it was the banking system – not the bankers who got us into this mess – which needed to be saved. We will pay a huge price for this mistake in higher taxes, slower growth and greater instability for years to come. And unless sweeping reforms are enacted soon, this botched rescue paves the way for an even more devastating future crisis.[71]*

Bailing out the banks was bad enough. Failing to fix their balance sheets has compounded the mistake. While there is much to criticise about how the US handled its banking problems, its approach has been more vigorous than Europe's and palpably more successful. As

---

69   *Ibid*, page 74

70   See http://online.wsj.com/article/SB123371182830346215.html and http://blogs.ft.com/maverecon/2009/01/the-good-bank-solution/

71   Philippe Legrain, *Aftershock: Reshaping the World After the Crisis*, Little, Brown: 2010, page 75.

early as May 2009, the US government completed its "stress tests" of how American banks might cope with severe market conditions and then recapitalised them. Bad loans have been vigorously written down. The Federal Deposit Insurance Corporation – a government agency that insures bank deposits, supervises some banks and manages the restructuring and winding down of failed ones – has sold or closed down 475 banks since 2008, including Washington Mutual, then the US's largest savings bank.[72] By 2013, banks were lending again.

In Europe, much less has been done. Only in June 2012 did the European Commission finally publish its proposed common EU rules for tackling problems at distressed banks by "bailing in" the creditors of viable banks and winding down unviable ones – and the new rules would come into force only in 2018. A "bail-in" involves writing down the value of creditors' bonds or converting them into shares. Many countries – Britain, Germany, the Netherlands, even Greece – have moved faster to enact new procedures for dealing with failed banks safely without calling on public money. But only Denmark has used them voluntarily, in 2011 (and since rowed back). Cyprus was bullied into doing so in March 2013 by the EU and the IMF (when those who took losses were mostly Cypriot and Russian depositors, rather than French and German banks and investors). In neither case did this provoke a broader panic; Denmark has rowed back because local banks persuaded the government that this put them at a disadvantage to banks in other countries that were not bailing in creditors.

Now that legal mechanisms for restructuring and winding down banks in an orderly fashion do finally exist in many EU countries, there is even less excuse for regulatory forbearance and taxpayer bailouts. Yet as recently as February 2013, the Dutch government bailed out SNS Reaal, a bank sunk by bad property loans, while leaving

---

72 http://en.wikipedia.org/wiki/List_of_bank_failures_in_the_United_States_ (2008–present). Checked on 18 May 2013

senior bondholders untouched. The rescue is expected to increase public borrowing by at least 0.6 per cent of GDP.[73] Does anyone really doubt that German taxpayers are still on the hook for Deutsche Bank and the Ländesbanks – or French ones for BNP Paribas and Société Générale, both deemed "national champions"? Would Britain let Barclays fail?

EU bank supervisors have mostly connived in banks' efforts to sweep problems under the carpet. In many cases, the results of bank stress tests have not even made public: those of the UK's periodic ones since 2008 haven't been, nor were those of the first EU-wide ones in September 2009.[74] Even when the findings have been published, their Panglossian conclusions that all is well with most banks have quickly been discredited. Four months after the second round of EU-wide stress tests in July 2010 which gave the Irish banking system a clean bill of health, Ireland was forced to seek a €67.5 billion loan from the EU and IMF, €35 billion of which was directly for its banks. After that farce, the European Banking Authority (EBA), a body set up in January 2011 to coordinate the work of banking watchdogs across the EU, promised that the third round of EU-wide stress tests in July 2011 would be more rigorous. Yet only a week after the EBA's inaugural effort had identified a small capital shortfall at the Caja de Ahorros del Mediterráneo, a small Spanish savings bank, it collapsed and received a much bigger bailout from the Spanish authorities. Three months later, Dexia, a Franco-Belgian bank that passed the EBA stress test with flying colours, also folded. In June 2012, the Spanish government obtained a €100 billion credit line from the EU, again to support banks that the EBA had deemed in fine fettle. But repeating the old trick of denying and papering over problems, Madrid decided after

---

73   http://uk.reuters.com/article/2013/02/01/uk-dutch-finance-cbank-idUKBRE9100A420130201

74   http://www.ft.com/cms/s/0/645b24e6-adbc-11e2-82b8-00144feabdc0.html

further bogus stress tests that its banks needed only €40 billion (for now). The banks that have failed are only the tip of the iceberg: many more are zombies propped up by infusions of central-bank cash and government guarantees.

To be fair, the EBA is only partly to blame for all these mistakes. While its stress tests have been unduly lenient and deeply flawed, notably in their treatment of banks' holdings of government bonds, national regulators, egged on by governments, have also supplied incomplete and inaccurate information because they are captured by domestic banking lobbies and do not want to admit to failures on their watch.[75]

Financial watchdogs may finally be beginning to bark. In March 2013, after conducting a review of the quality of banks' assets, the Bank of England's Financial Policy Committee (FPC), which is now charged with overseeing the overall health of the UK financial system, determined that banks were overstating their capital by £52 billion at the end of 2012. The estimated shortfall was mostly due to banks not making big enough provisions for likely losses on bad loans and trades. But it was also because they were gaming the risk weightings on which capital requirements are based.[76] And they were also underestimating the likely costs of the many scandals in

---

75 http://www.eba.europa.eu/-/eba-publishes-results-of-the-basel-iii-monitoring-exercise-as-of-end-2012 Around a third of the 170 banks surveyed by the EBA failed to meet the very weak Basel target of a 3-per-cent equity buffer, with a combined capital shortfall of €133 billion. When in October 2011 EU leaders did agree to force banks to boost their capital buffers somewhat, they unfortunately botched the decision, as Chapter 4 explains. At the end of 2012, the EU's forty-two biggest banks still funded their assets with more than 97 per cent debt.

76 The FPC determined that banks' capital positions, as of end-2012, were overstated by £52 billion. This was attributed to under-provisioning for expected credit and trading book valuation losses (£30 billion) and conduct costs (£10 billion), and the overstatement of capital ratios resulting from an aggressive use of risk weights

which they are implicated, notably the Libor scandal, where banks conspired to rig the benchmark interest rate. Yet the FPC decided that banks needed to raise only an additional £27 billion in capital – far short of what they will eventually need to comply with the new global requirements set in Basel, which themselves are hardly stringent.[77] So while watchdogs may now be barking, they still don't have much bite. RBS, Lloyds and Barclays have smaller capital buffers than other huge US and EU banks.[78] Considering banks' huge balance sheets are still financed overwhelmingly with debt, this leaves very little margin for error. Only in 2014 will public stress tests of British banks' ability to cope with severe shocks take place. Let's hope they will be rigorous.

In the eurozone, governments pledged in June 2012 to create a common banking supervisor, a responsibility that the ECB is finally due to assume in late 2014, albeit only for bigger banks, as will be discussed in Chapter 5. The hope is that the ECB will be more independent than national bank supervisors and more effective than the toothless EBA. Before the ECB takes on its new oversight role, it is due to conduct a review of the quality of banks' assets. The EBA will follow through with what it promises will be rigorous stress tests.

(£12 billion). International Monetary Fund, United Kingdom 2013 Article IV Consultation, July 2013

77   The FPC's target was an end-2013 benchmark of a 7 percent fully-loaded Basel-III common equity tier 1 capital ratio, computed after making appropriate adjustments for expected loan losses and conduct costs over the next three-years, and for prudent risk weights. Systemically important banks will ultimately need to hit a 9.5-10 per cent ratio.

78   International Monetary Fund, United Kingdom 2013 Article IV Consultation, July 2013, Figure 5.

Credit crunch

Meanwhile, zombie banks continue to drain life out of European economies. In Britain, banks' outstanding loans to businesses fell by 5.4 per cent – £25 billion – in 2013.[79] In the eurozone as a whole, bank credit to businesses fell by 3 per cent in 2013[80] – with a collapse of credit in southern Europe, notably Spain.[81]

When challenged, bankers typically claim that they would like to lend more, but that fewer borrowers want to borrow more. In other words, they argue that the real problem is not a lack of supply of credit, but rather an absence of demand. For sure, some businesses' demand for loans has fallen: with a weak economic backdrop, companies may not want to borrow more. But if credit supply was truly bountiful and the main problem was inadequate demand, one would expect interest rates on new business loans to be low. In many countries, they aren't. Even though official interest rates are near-zero in both Britain and the eurozone, the cost of bank credit to small and medium-sized businesses – which, unlike big companies, cannot bypass banks and borrow directly from investors by selling corporate bonds – is often painfully high. Whereas in France a small business would have to pay a bit over 2 per cent a year for a small short-term loan, that rises to around 5 per cent in Ireland and Spain and more than 6 per cent in Portugal and Greece.[82]

---

79   Bank of England, Bankstats (Monetary & Financial Statistics) December 2013, Table A8.1 Monetary financial institutions loans to non-financial businesses http:// www.bankofengland.co.uk/statistics/Pages/bankstats/2013/Dec13/default.aspx

80   ECB, MFI loans to non-financial corporations, annual growth rate at end of December 2013. That average masks big differences across countries.

81   http://www.bde.es/webbde/es/estadis/infoest/e0806e.pdf

82   Eurozone figures are from ECB, MFI Interest Rate Statistics, loans for new business to non-financial corporations, up to €1 million, up to 1 year, December 2013. France is 2.15 per cent, Germany 2.26 per cent, Italy 4.34 per cent, Spain 4.79 per cent, Ireland 4.16 per cent, Portugal 5.90 per cent and Greece 6.06 per cent. http://

In part, this is because banks' funding costs – their own cost of borrowing – are higher in southern Europe than in northern Europe. Weak German banks can borrow cheaply because they enjoy the backing of the creditworthy German government; weak Portuguese banks can't because the Portuguese government is dependent on EU funding and cannot be relied on to stand behind them. But this merely underscores the fact that banks' weak balance sheets are restricting the supply of credit, a fact that is masked by government guarantees in northern Europe.

Over and above differences in funding costs, banks are now charging much fatter margins on loans to new business borrowers. Banks argue that they need to do so because the risks of lending have increased. That is true, up to a point. But even creditworthy businesses are being denied loans. In Britain, an independent study for the government by the National Institute of Economic and Social Research (NIESR) found that, controlling for relevant risks, it is harder for small and medium-sized businesses to obtain bank finance than before the crisis and that rejection rates for loans and overdrafts have increased, especially for less risky borrowers.[83] In the eurozone, hardly any smaller businesses in Germany are denied credit, while many more Italian and Spanish ones are.[84]

When challenged again, bankers change their story and say they can't lend more because of tighter regulations, notably requirements

---

www.ecb.europa.eu/stats/money/interest/interest/html/interest_rates_2013-12. en.html

83   Department for Business Innovation and Skills, "Evaluating Changes in Bank Lending to UK SMEs over 2001–12 – Ongoing Tight Credit", April 2013 https://www.gov.uk/government/uploads/system/uploads/attachment_data/ file/193945/bis-13-857-evaluating-changes-in-bank-lending-to-uk-smes-2001-12. pdf

84   International Monetary Fund, *Global Financial Stability Report*, April 2013

that they "hold" more capital. But this is nonsense, as Anat Admati and Martin Hellwig point out in their brilliant book, *The Bankers' New Clothes: What's Wrong with Banking and What to Do About It.*[85] Far from restricting lending, additional capital – shareholders' equity – is a means of funding it. Regulators can ensure that banks don't *choose* to meet higher capital requirements by restricting lending by insisting that they raise specific amounts of capital, rather than reach a particular ratio between equity and assets.

The real problem is that both British and eurozone banks still have lots of bad loans on their books and many more that they don't admit to. In Britain and elsewhere, many loans to commercial property developers, households with mortgages and smaller businesses are unlikely to be repaid in full, but banks are pretending that the loans remain sound – and because interest rates on existing (as opposed to new) loans are low, borrowers are able to keep servicing them. Banks don't want to admit to these problem loans, still less make provisions for likely losses on them, because they don't want to have to raise extra loss-absorbing capital, which would reduce returns on equity, the basis on which bonuses for senior managers tend to be paid. Markets realise that many banks are in a worse state than they claim: their stockmarket value is often (much) less than the book value of their shares on their balance sheet. But unfortunately, financial regulators and the government have not forced them to come clean, still less to plump up their inadequate capital buffers, in part because they have bought the bankers' lie that this would curb lending and hence stifle growth. In fact, the opposite is true: zombie banks are keeping unviable businesses afloat while depriving viable ones of the credit they need to grow. In any case, banks can – and should – be forced to boost their capital buffers in ways that do not hit lending to the real

85   Anat Admati and Martin Hellwig, *The Bankers' New Clothes: What's Wrong with Banking and What to Do About it*, Princeton: 2013

economy: by issuing new shares, retaining profits rather than paying them out as dividends and bonuses, selling off foreign assets and reducing lending within the financial system.

Drowning in debt

Policymakers' second big mistake is the failure to recognise that many of the debts run up in the bubble years and earlier decades cannot be paid in full – and that it is cruel and counterproductive to pretend otherwise. In large part, this is the flipside of the banking problem – many of the debts are in the form of bank loans or bonds owned by banks; banks are loath to recognise losses; regulators are reluctant to force them. But some of the debts are owed to other financial players, such as hedge funds, and investors, such as pension funds and insurance companies. This debt overhang is another big impediment to growth.

Many households in countries that have suffered a housing bust – such as Spain, Ireland and the Netherlands – have mortgages that exceed the value of their property, as do some in depressed parts of Britain. So long as interest rates remain low, banks are willing to show forbearance and borrowers still have an income, they may be able to make the mortgage payments. But being tied to a particular property prevents people from moving to take advantage of better job opportunities, while their unpayable debt burden depresses their spending. It would be better to write down debts across the board, in a way that allows families to remain in their homes and provides banks with an upside if house prices recover. One way is to create economy-wide mechanisms that allow banks to swap their bad mortgage debts for an equity stake, with mortgage-holders paying rent on the proportion of the property owned by the bank. Likewise, the IMF has advocated creating economy-wide mechanisms for writing down unpayable corporate debts while giving viable companies the scope to remain in business. While the failure to tackle the overhangs of household and corporate debt is impeding the recovery in many countries, so too is the failure to deal decisively with Greece's unsustainable government debt, as subsequent chapters will explain.

Investment and reform

In crafting economic policy, policymakers need to do three things: deal with the excesses of the past, address pressing current problems and build a bridge towards future growth. The first two mistakes involve failing to deal with the mistakes of the past: broken banks and excessive debts. The third concerns failing to build a secure bridge from the present to the future.

European economies need a viable growth strategy. In the short term, they need to support spending (demand) while the private sector and the financial sector are reducing their debts ("deleveraging"). In the longer term, they need to find new sources of growth. The pre-crisis model – whereby some economies relied on debt-fuelled consumption and housing bubbles, while others relied on exporting and lending to them – has broken down. Trying to revive it would be crazy, although the British government is trying its best to. Europe also needs to adapt to three big changes in the economic landscape. One: the rapid development of China and other emerging economies, which now account for more than half of the world economy for the first time since the Industrial Revolution as well as for the bulk of global growth. Two: the speedy deployment of new technologies, notably digital ones such as the internet, new manufacturing processes such as 3-D printing, and new energy sources such as shale gas and solar power. Three: the rapid onset of demographic challenges as European societies age and local workforces begin to shrink.

Often, policymakers and pundits focus on one at the expense of the other. Paul Krugman, a brilliant Nobel-winning economist who blogs for the *New York Times*, focuses almost exclusively on short-term demand issues and seems dismissive of longer-term structural challenges. On the other hand, the German government and its handmaidens in Brussels tend to neglect short-term demand and focus almost entirely on the long term instead. Others frame the issue as a tension between short-term needs and longer-term aims. But all of this is misleading. Neglecting the short term leads to longer-term damage: investment opportunities forgone, businesses not started, skills lost, lives stunted. Ignoring the longer term stores up even bigger problems for the future. The best strategy is to find measures that support demand in the short-term while helping the economy to adjust to longer-term challenges.

Unfortunately, both Britain and the eurozone have failed miserably at this. They have failed to tackle banking problems and excessive private-sector debts. They have done too little to boost investment and implement reforms to open up healthier future growth. And at a time when the private sector was cutting back and non-Europeans were not in a position to take up all the slack, they embarked on premature, front-loaded, slash-and-burn fiscal austerity.

When the world economy went into freefall after the chaotic collapse of Lehman Brothers, the leaders of the Group of Twenty (G-20) most important economies in the world agreed in London in April 2009 to embark on a big fiscal stimulus to support growth.[86] This was a success, not least thanks to bold pre-emptive action by the Chinese government. But after Greece's public-debt problems led it to seek an EU-IMF loan in April 2010, eurozone governments took fright at rising debt levels and slammed on the brakes. Britain followed suit after David Cameron's Conservative-Liberal coalition government took

---

86   G-20 Leaders' Statement, London, 2 April 2009

office in May. At the G-20 summit in Toronto in June 2010, governments committed to halve fiscal deficits by 2013.[87]

EU governments persuaded themselves that a collective lurch towards austerity would restore "confidence" and boost growth. But as Chapter 3 explains, this was a delusion. Premature tax rises and spending cuts killed off a nascent recovery and plunged economies back into recession. Instead of restoring "confidence", austerity shredded it. It has done so much damage to the economy that public debts are actually higher as a share of GDP than they would otherwise be.[88] Indeed, it may be pushing some southern European governments into a debt trap – and ultimately, insolvency. Far from stabilising public finances, excessive collective austerity has destabilised them.

In the case of Britain, this is a wholly unforced error. Contrary to the irresponsible, politically expedient claims by George Osborne in 2010, Britain was never in danger of becoming the next Greece. Investors never lost their appetite for UK government bonds – and in any case the Bank of England was buying them with gay abandon through QE and stood ready to buy even more if necessary. In the eurozone, austerity was imposed by the European Commission in Brussels under strong pressure from the German government in Berlin and the ECB in Frankfurt. Eurozone policymakers now argue that markets forced their hand, but that is misleading. While it is true that investors subsequently panicked, they did so primarily because of calamitous mistakes by eurozone policymakers, as Chapters 2 to 4 explain. As panic spread, policymakers argued that rising government bond yields in many countries were an accurate reflection of their deteriorating creditworthiness – and that in any case, the ECB

---

87   G-20, Toronto Summit Declaration, 27 June 2010 http://www.g20.utoronto. ca/2010/to-communique.html

88   See, for instance, Dawn Holland and Jonathan Portes, "Self-Defeating Austerity?", *National Institute Economic Review* no. 222, October 2012, pages F4-F10

did not have the right to act like a normal central bank and intervene to stabilise the situation. In other words, they argued that it was both right and necessary that governments tighten their belts. But in the summer of 2012 the ECB did finally act. The European Commission subsequently eased the pace of austerity, without an adverse market response. Thus in the eurozone too the lurch for austerity was a collective unforced error by eurozone policymakers.

Different paths to failure

While both Britain and the eurozone have been too passive towards banks and private-sector debt and premature in embarking on austerity, in other respects they have followed different strategies. Britain has pinned its hopes on easy money and a cheap currency while doing little to remedy the economy's longstanding structural weaknesses: its underinvestment in skills, infrastructure, housing and business capital more generally and its unhealthy reliance on a dysfunctional financial sector. In effect, the British government has assumed that low interest rates and QE would together boost investment and that a weaker currency and flexible labour markets would automatically shift the economy towards broad-based export-led growth. But in practice, banks have refused to lend, companies have been loath to invest and exports have stagnated, as Chapter 7 explains. When growth finally resumed in 2013, it was again based almost exclusively on higher consumption by debt-laden households.

The eurozone has given more emphasis to reforms to address its structural weaknesses than Britain has, while the ECB has been more passive than the Bank of England and the euro's exchange rate has bobbed up and down.[89] Economic reforms are essential and long overdue: Italy and Portugal failed to grow even in the bubble years and Spain had high unemployment even at the height of its construction boom. Reforms have yielded some positive results: even without

---

89   http://www.ecb.europa.eu/stats/exchange/effective/html/index.en.html

a weaker currency, Spanish exports have soared. But efforts have been patchy and often misdirected, while the results have often been disappointing so far.

Many governments have not reformed enough. Berlin has become complacent: Germany has done least to reform its hidebound economy since the outbreak of the crisis, according to the Organisation for Economic Co-Operation and Development (OECD). Italy is another disappointment. Hailed as a saviour when he replaced Berlusconi as prime minister in late 2011, Mario Monti missed a golden opportunity to shake up Italy's sclerotic labour market and inject competition into its many ossified industries and professions. By focusing on austerity in an unreformed economy, he caused a deep recession – and when he turned to reforms, his authority was spent. Worse, reform is now associated with recession. With luck, the new government led by thirty-nine-year-old Matteo Renzi that took over in February 2014 will shake things up.

Others have pursued the wrong priorities. Reforms have tended to focus on boosting "competitiveness" in southern Europe, mostly through wage cuts, when they ought to have promoted competition to boost productivity across Europe as a whole. In effect, under instructions from Berlin, EU policymakers have tried to reshape the eurozone along German lines. This has often had a perverse impact. For a start, it is not true that wages in southern Europe are too high – rather, Germany's are artificially low, as Chapter 2 explains. Second, whereas depressing wages has given German exports an artificial lift, southern European companies that don't face much competition have often pocketed the lower wage costs as fatter profits instead of cutting their prices. In any case, though, it is neither desirable nor feasible for the rest of Europe to emulate Germany, as Chapter 8 explains. Instead of producing the same old things at lower wages, economies need to move up the value chain, producing new and better things for more. Worse, pursuing German-style wage compression has crunched domestic spending and exacerbated southern Europe's debt problems. So instead of the immiserating and self-defeating pursuit of "competitiveness", the way forward for southern Europe is to invest more and boost productivity by promoting competition. Longer term, the priority ought to be to make all European economies more adaptable, dynamic and decent through reforms that ADD UP, as Chapters 9 to 12 set out.

To their credit, Portuguese shoemakers ignored the advice from Brussels and Berlin to slash wages. After years of losing sales to lower-cost places such as China and Turkey, they have invested in going upmarket. They have been so successful that exports have soared, while wages and employment have risen. "The secret of our success is very simple," said Joaquim Moreira da Silva, owner of J. Moreira, a Portuguese company that sells women's shoes for as much as €400 a pair. "We invest in quality, comfort and a product that is different from others out there."[90]

A final mistake has been to assume that reforms to boost the supply side of the economy in the longer term could substitute for short-term measures to boost demand. Even in good times, most reforms take time to bear fruit. Often, in fact, their initial impact is negative. For example, making it easier to hire and fire workers will lead to a shake-out of unproductive workers, pushing up unemployment, worsening public finances (as tax revenues fall and spending on benefits increases) and depressing the economy, because the newly unemployed workers will spend less. Eventually, those workers will be redeployed to more productive uses – but in a recession when demand is depressed, credit is crunched and barriers to starting new businesses are high, this will take much longer than usual. That's why measures to boost investment are so crucial. Yet until

---

90   http://online.wsj.com/news/articles/SB10001424052702303630904579419381 868559314?mod=WSJUK_hps_MIDDLEFourthNews&mg=reno64-wsj

June 2012, eurozone policymakers did nothing to boost investment; on the contrary, governments slashed capital spending. In effect, then, the eurozone's economic strategy has amounted to depressing the economy right now and hoping for faster growth at some point in the future. But crushing current demand and boosting future supply is not a growth strategy, it's an anti-growth strategy.

In short, neither Britain's policy mix (austerity plus QE plus devaluation), nor the eurozone's (austerity plus reforms to boost "competitiveness" in southern Europe) has been successful.

Productivity peril

Europe's balance-sheet crisis – broken banks, excessive debts, austerity without investment – is the main cause of its immediate problems. But a more enduring failing is that Europe's economies are not dynamic and adaptable enough. They don't innovate enough, they aren't entrepreneurial enough and they find it difficult to cope with and adjust to change. Many of these weaknesses are longstanding, but were papered over by easy credit and, in some cases, government borrowing. They have been exacerbated by the dramatic rise of China and other emerging economies over the past decade and the explosion of new technologies, notably digital ones, which have highlighted Europe's failure to adapt. They stand to get worse as the population ages and, in some places, starts to shrink. While some countries are in worse shape than others and their problems differ, nearly all suffer from sluggish productivity growth and inadequate investment.

Until the mid-1990s, most advanced European economies were catching up with the US, but since then progress has stalled. Living standards in Europe fall well short of those in America. In 2012 Britons were 28 per cent poorer than Americans – as measured by gross domestic product per person, adjusted for differences in purchasing power – while people in the eurozone were 30 per cent worse off. Except for Luxembourg and Switzerland, both tax havens, and oil-rich Norway, all European countries were poorer than America. The best performers otherwise were Austria (15 per cent poorer) and Sweden (16 per cent); figures for a selection of other countries are in the footnotes.[91]

The gap between average incomes in the US and Europe can be broken down into three factors. In some cases a smaller share of the European population is employed; they tend to work fewer hours; and they generally produce less per hour. Most of the reason why Britons are 28 per cent poorer than Americans is because they are 24 per cent less productive. While workers in the eurozone are 17 per cent less productive than Americans, nearly half of the gap in living standards is due to fewer people working, for fewer hours.[92]

---

91   OECD, breakdown of gross domestic product per capita in its components, 2012. As a percentage of the US, GDP per person was 85 per cent in Austria, 78 per cent in Belgium, 82 per cent in Denmark, 74 per cent in Finland, 70 per cent in France, 80 per cent in Germany, 49 per cent in Greece, 73 per cent in Iceland, 84 per cent in Ireland, 64 per cent in Italy, 171 per cent in Luxembourg, 83 per cent in the Netherlands, 127 per cent in Norway, 49 per cent in Portugal, 62 per cent in Spain, 84 per cent in Sweden, 104 per cent in Switzerland, 72 per cent in the UK and 70 per cent in the eurozone. GDP overstates the incomes of Irish residents by around 20 per cent.

92   *Ibid.* Compared with the US, labour utilisation was 1 per cent higher in Austria, 19 per cent lower in Belgium, 11 per cent lower in Denmark, 2 per cent lower in Finland, 23 per cent lower in France, 11 per cent lower in Germany, 5 per cent lower in Greece, 8 per cent higher in Iceland, 27 per cent lower in Ireland, 9 per cent lower in Italy, 43 per cent higher in Luxembourg, 10 per cent lower in the Netherlands, 8 per cent lower in Norway, 4 per cent lower in Portugal, 16 per cent lower in Spain, 2 per cent lower in Sweden, 18 per cent higher in Switzerland, 3 per cent lower in the UK and 12 per cent lower in the eurozone. Compared with the US, gross domestic product per hour worked was 16 per cent lower in Austria, 4 per cent lower in Belgium, 7 per cent lower in Denmark, 24 per cent lower in Finland, 7 per cent lower in France, 9 per cent lower in Germany, 46 per cent lower in Greece, 35 per

It is perfectly reasonable for Europeans to choose to work shorter hours as they get richer: the aim of economic activity is to enhance not your income but your welfare – and that includes enjoying more leisure time. Unless work is the only thing you enjoy, there is little point in working all your waking hours, never seeing your friends and family and ending up the richest person in the cemetery. That said, working less is an issue if individual decisions are skewed by taxes, benefits and regulations. People might choose to work less because taxes on labour income are punitive – or more, in order to achieve their desired income. In any case, the lower taxes on working are, the less distorted people's decisions will be.

A bigger issue is that far fewer people work in some European countries than elsewhere. For now, this divergence is not due to de-mography.[93] The main problem is that a smaller share of the work-ing-age population is employed. Some European countries do much better than America. In Iceland and Switzerland, the employment rate was just shy of 80 per cent in 2012, followed by Norway and the Netherlands, where three in four people of working age work. Then comes a cluster of northern European countries – Sweden, Germany and Denmark – in the low 70s. Britain is at 70.1 per cent, the US at 67.1 per cent. But in Mediterranean countries, employment rates are dismal, ranging from 63.9 per cent in France to 51.3 per cent in

cent lower in Iceland, 11 per cent higher in Ireland, 27 per cent lower in Italy, 28 per cent higher in Luxembourg, 6 per cent lower in the Netherlands, 35 per cent higher in Norway, 47 per cent lower in Portugal, 22 per cent lower in Spain, 15 per cent lower in Sweden, 14 per cent lower in Switzerland, 24 per cent lower in the UK and 17 per cent lower in the eurozone.

93   In both Europe and America, around two-thirds of the population are aged 15–64 and so deemed to be of working age. Given that it is increasingly important to get a university degree or a vocational qualification, and that people need to work a bit longer as we live longer, the working-age population probably ought to be re-defined as 18–69 or even 21–69.

Greece. For sure, the recession has made matters worse in many countries.[94] But even at the height of the boom in 2007, employment rates in Mediterranean countries were low.[95] That economies fail to make full use of everyone's talents and efforts is both unfair and hugely wasteful.

The biggest issues are Europeans' lower hourly productivity than Americans' and their measly productivity growth so far this century. Some outliers have higher measured productivity than America, but that is an artefact of resource rents. On paper, Norwegians are 35 per cent more productive than Americans because their vast oil output, which has soared in value over the past decade, divided by relatively few Norwegians makes output per hour look high. But in other sectors their productivity lags. The Irish are officially 11 per cent more productive than Americans in terms of GDP per hour worked, because GDP includes the output of companies attributed to Ireland for tax purposes. But since GNP, the output produced by Irish residents, is roughly 20 per cent lower than GDP, they are actually less productive. All other Europeans are bested by Americans. The top performers are Belgium, where people are only 4 per cent less productive than Americans, followed by the Dutch (6 per cent less), the French and the Danes (7 per cent less). A note of caution is needed, though. In countries where labour use is low and only more productive people work, average productivity will appear higher than in countries where many more people, including less productive ones, are employed. Given Belgium's employment rate was a mere 61.8 per cent in 2012, average Belgian productivity would doubtless be much lower if more people worked. Ditto in France, where the employment rate is scarcely

94   The figures are 61.8 per cent in Portugal, 56.8 per cent in Italy and 55.4 per cent in Spain.

95   The figures were 65.6 per cent in Spain, 64.3 per cent in France and 61.4 per cent in Greece.

higher. So only the Dutch and the Danes are roughly on a par with Americans, with the Germans somewhat behind. In other countries, the figures range from worrying – Swedes are 15 per cent behind – to poor: Spaniards, Britons and Italians all lag by more than 20 per cent.

Worse, Europeans are scarcely upping their game. Productivity growth – making more with less – is the key to higher living standards. In the pre-crisis years (2002–7), labour productivity growth averaged a mere 1.3 per cent a year in the eurozone.[96] Roughly speaking, that means wages can only rise by a similar amount. At that pace, over a working lifetime – say, forty-five years – average wages could rise by around three-quarters; not catastrophic, but far less than Europeans have grown accustomed to. Over the same period, productivity growth in the US averaged nearly 2 per cent a year – allowing wages to rise by nearly 150 per cent over a working life. Some European countries appeared to be doing even better: Britain managed just shy of 2.5 per cent a year, Greece a bit over 3.5 per cent. But then the crisis hit and performance plunged. In the US, productivity growth slipped to 1.5 per cent in 2007–12 – and Europe's slowed to a snail's pace. In many countries, including Britain, productivity has actually fallen.[97] The best of a bad bunch were the supposedly siesta-loving Spanish, with 2 per cent (although that is partly the result of soaring unemployment).

For sure, those were particularly bad years. But if you look at a ten-year average from 2002–12 that includes both boom and bust,

---

96   OECD, labour productivity growth in the total economy: Labour Productivity Growth (Compendium 1.4). Figures for 2002–7 were Austria 2 per cent, Belgium 1.3 per cent, Denmark 1.6 per cent, Finland 2.8 per cent, France 1.2 per cent, Germany 1.7 per cent, Greece 3.6 per cent, Iceland 3.4 per cent, Ireland 1.8 per cent, Italy 0.3 per cent, Netherlands 2 per cent, Norway 0.7 per cent, Portugal 1.6 per cent, Spain 0.8 per cent, Sweden 2.7 per cent, Switzerland 1.2 per cent, UK 2.5 per cent, US 1.9 per cent and eurozone 1.3 per cent.

97   Productivity has also fallen in Belgium, Finland, Greece, Italy, Luxembourg, Netherlands, Norway and Switzerland.

productivity growth is lower than America's 1.7 per cent in every significant European economy. (The only exception was Ireland, which managed 2.4 per cent, although this was partly one-off catch-up growth.) Both Britain and the eurozone averaged a mere 0.9 per cent. Greece (1.2 per cent) was ahead of Germany (1 per cent). Italy was zero.[98] All of this leaves very little scope for wage increases. Moreover, in many European countries, especially Germany, workers' pay has failed to keep pace with their productivity gains. German wages have stagnated for fifteen years, while the bottom third of the workforce have got poorer.[99]

It gets worse. Unless European economies can get more people to work, or bring in immigrants, the EU's workforce is set to shrink by over 0.6 per cent a year over the next decade.[100] So if each European worker produces only 0.9 per cent more each year and the number of workers falls by some 0.6 per cent, the economy could grow by less than 0.3 per cent a year. In effect, it would stagnate.

---

98   Calculations from OECD, labour productivity growth in the total economy, average 2002–12. Austria 1.3 per cent, Belgium 0.5 per cent, Denmark 0.9 per cent, Finland 1.1 per cent, France 0.7 per cent, Germany 1 per cent, Greece 1.2 per cent, Iceland 2 per cent, Ireland 2.4 per cent, Italy 0 per cent, Netherlands 0.9 per cent, Norway 0.1 per cent, Portugal 1.6 per cent, Spain 1.4 per cent, Sweden 1.5 per cent, Switzerland 0.6 per cent, UK 0.9 per cent, US 1.7 per cent and eurozone 0.9 per cent.

99   Federal Statistical Office of Germany, index of real earnings, January 2010 = 100. Index for 1999 and 2000 is 102.1; index for 2007 is 98.2; index for 2012 is 101.7. Kaja Bonesmo Fredriksen, "Income Inequality in the European Union", OECD Economics Department Working Papers No. 952, 2012 http://dx.doi.org/10.1787/5k9bdt47q5zt-en

100   Philippe Fargues and Ashley McCormick, "Ageing of skills and complementary immigration in the EU, 2010–2025". Draft paper prepared for discussion at the MPC Annual Conference (EUI, Florence, 21 June 2013).

The end of growth?

Radical greens who have long wanted an end to growth may rejoice. But since the rest of the world economy would still be expanding, it doesn't follow that the global environment would improve. Moreover, as recent years have showed, the politics of a zero-growth economy would most likely be poisonous. Instead of each pursuing a share of a growing pie, people would be fighting over the scraps. For anyone on the left (as most greens purport to be), that ought to be alarming. The poor and the weak would suffer. But perhaps the biggest battle would be generational: between young workers struggling to earn more and pensioners claiming a large share of the spoils. We can already see a foretaste of that generational conflict today and it isn't pretty.

None of this is inevitable. Faster productivity growth and higher immigration would transform the picture; more babies wouldn't make a difference for at least two decades. But the barriers to dynamism and change are many. Europe fails to make the most of all its talents, not least those of the young and the old, women and immigrants. It invests too little, often badly.[101] Markets are often run for the benefit of cosseted insiders rather than striving outsiders. Harmful regulations ossify economies and stunt enterprise. A cultural conservatism that is suspicious of change, hostile to diversity and deeply pessimistic about the future hampers innovation, investment and growth.

The biggest underlying problem is the capture of governments by vested interests and self-serving elites who appropriate value created by others rather than creating it themselves – call it crony capitalism. Most European countries have an overmighty and dysfunctional

---

101   Business investment (gross fixed capital formation by non-financial corporations) averaged 22.3 per cent of GDP in the eurozone in 1999–2001 and 18.9 per cent in Britain. In 2011 to Q3 2013, it averaged 19.8 per cent in the eurozone and 14.3 per cent in Britain. Personal calculations from Eurostat, gross investment rate of non-financial corporations. Code: nasq_ki

financial sector that benefits from taxpayer bailouts and subsidised borrowing, extracts value from companies and households, and does a poor job of channelling savings to productive investments. Big landowners in rigged property markets benefit from vast subsidies from the EU's Common Agricultural Policy in rural areas and capture the value created by others' investment and hard work in urban ones. To varying extents, incumbent companies – both big and small – benefit from rules that limit competition from upstarts. In many countries, insiders on permanent work contracts are privileged at the expense of young people, newcomers and other outsiders who languish on temporary contracts or unemployed. Public-sector bodies are often run for the benefit of the people who work there rather than the patients, students and other citizens they are meant to serve. Politicians and technocratic elites often serve their own interests rather than advancing the common good. Each of these, in effect, steals from others, both by grabbing an outsized share of the existing pie and by limiting how fast the pie grows. Eventually, in the absence of reform, vested interests clog up the economy so much that the pie stops growing, as the late Mancur Olson explained in his magisterial work, *The Rise and Decline of Nations*.[102]

Some economies are so hidebound that they failed to grow even when credit was booming: Portugal frittered away its borrowing on imports. With its corrupt administration and cartelised markets, Italy's sclerotic economy has stagnated for the best part of fifteen years. Greece's economy is dominated by a handful of superrich families and a grotesquely corrupt and dysfunctional state that operates a parasitic patronage system. While the problems in southern Europe are well-known, northern Europe is deeply flawed too. France is being strangled by taxes and regulations imposed by a gargantuan state that allocates 57 per cent of national income, often badly; one small

---

102   Mancur Olson, *The Rise and Decline of Nations*, Yale: 1984

business owner compares hiring a worker to marriage: a contract for life that can only be broken in exceptional circumstances and at great expense. Germany's economy is dominated by its mercantilist exporters which artificially hold down wages, while its politicised banking sector fritters away the resulting excess savings, its service sectors are hidebound and entrepreneurial Germans flock to the US to start a business. Britain has been hijacked by its outsized financial sector, which prioritises short-term speculation over long-term investment, and big landowners who profit immensely from property booms and restrictions on new development, while driving up everyone else's cost of living. We need a European Spring to begin to change all that.

Before coming back to these longer-term issues, let's focus on more immediate ones. This chapter has argued that Britain and the eurozone face a similar predicament. Why, then, did the eurozone suffer a devastating financial panic between 2010 and 2012 while Britain didn't?

2

A FIASCO MADE IN FRANKFURT, BRUSSELS AND BERLIN

A tragedy in five acts

> *By deciding that the crisis was largely fiscal, policy makers could ignore the truth that the underlying cause of the disarray was irresponsible cross-border lending, for which suppliers of credit are surely as responsible as users. If the culpability of both sides – lenders and borrowers – had been understood, the moral case for debt write-offs would have been clearer.*
>
> Martin Wolf, chief economics commentator,
> *Financial Times*[103]

Lazy. Feckless. Profligate. Thieving. Those are just some of the terms of abuse hurled at Gipsies, who have long been scapegoats in Europe for all manner of ills. Similar venom has recently been

---

103   http://www.ft.com/cms/s/0/b31dd248-d785-11e2-a26a-00144feab7de.html

directed at a different set of GIPSIs – Greece, Ireland, Portugal, Spain and Italy – the countries that have suffered the brunt of the crisis in the eurozone, and on which it has been blamed. But is it really all their fault?

As Chapter 1 explained, the crisis in both Britain and the eurozone is due to an orgy of bad lending by a dysfunctional financial system that caused huge property bubbles and a dangerous build-up of debt both within the financial sector and in the economy at large, primarily among households. When the bubbles burst, households, companies and the financial sector all tried to reduce their debts at once, causing spending to plunge and government borrowing to soar. From 2010 on, governments in both Britain and the eurozone reacted similarly, seeking to tackle the symptoms of the crisis – big public deficits – rather than its causes: balance-sheet problems in both the financial sector and the private sector. Yet their paths subsequently diverged. Britain stagnated, while the eurozone suffered an existential financial panic in 2010–12. Why?

Critics of the euro blame the single currency itself. They argue that the euro is destined to fail because its component economies are too dissimilar and sharing a currency first pushes them further apart and then makes it harder for them to bounce back. In contrast, Berlin, Brussels and Frankfurt blame policy mistakes in southern Europe: a lack of discipline over government borrowing and wages that weakened public finances and undermined economies' "competitiveness". (This geographic split is not exact: Ireland, for these purposes, is bracketed with southern Europe. An alternative split between "core" and "periphery" is also problematic, since Italy, a founding member of the European club, would need to be classified as peripheral, while Finland, a relative newcomer that is on the northeast edge of Europe, would be categorised as part of the core.)

This chapter will explain why neither of those two narratives is convincing. It will argue instead that the reason why the crisis mutated from a chronic, British-style deleveraging and economic adjustment problem into an acute financial and sovereign-debt crisis is because of five catastrophic policy mistakes made in Frankfurt, Brussels and Berlin. These exposed design flaws and political constraints that amplified those mistakes and thus made the euro increasingly unstable – until finally the ECB acted as a circuit breaker in the summer of 2012. Now that the eurozone is no longer wracked by acute panic, the crisis has again entered a chronic phase.

The crisis in the eurozone is a tragedy in a prologue and five acts. The prologue is the pre-crisis years, when the problems built up, as outlined in Chapter 1. Act One is the initial stage of the financial crisis, from the summer of 2007, when problems first emerged in eurozone banks, to late 2009, when the extent of Greece's sovereign debt problems were revealed. Big mistakes were made during this period, not least governments' decision to backstop all banks' debts, but the eurozone remained a stable system. Act Two is the period from early 2010, when the creditors of an insolvent Greece were bailed out by the EU and the IMF, to July 2011, when the crisis became systemic, during which the eurozone was progressively destabilised. Act Three is the following twelve months when Italian, Spanish, Belgian and even French government bond yields spiked as the eurozone became unstable and fragmented (see Chapter 4). Huge mistakes were made, notably the threat to force Greece out of the euro, fuelling outright panic, punctuated by sticking-plaster solutions. Act Four is the period from July 2012, when Mario Draghi, Trichet's replacement as ECB president, finally pledged that the ECB would do "whatever it takes" to save the euro, until when I am writing, early 2014, which has seen the panic abate and tentative crisis solutions proposed but no breakthrough, while economies fester and societies fracture (see Chapter 5). Act Five, the dénouement, is still unwritten.

The origins of the euro

As far back as the 1960s, Europe's leaders were already hatching plans for economic and monetary union.[104] The plans finally came to fruition in the 1990s when EU leaders agreed at Maastricht in 1992 to create a common currency by the end of the decade. Their motives were partly economic. A single currency was deemed necessary to complete Europe's newly established single market. Businesses couldn't treat the European market as one if their investment plans risked being blown off course by currency swings, while consumers couldn't fully benefit from competition if prices weren't readily comparable across borders. Sharing a currency would also promote financial integration. Investors could diversify their portfolios across the single-currency area without the risk of adverse exchange-rate moves, enabling them to earn higher returns for any given amount of risk. Companies would benefit from a wider pool of capital, allowing them to raise both equity and debt more cheaply. Eurozone financial institutions would increasingly replace national ones. Economies as a whole could borrow more readily from foreigners, enabling all countries to smooth over temporary difficulties more easily and poorer ones that invested wisely to catch up with richer ones more quickly.

Countries also decided to merge their money in order to insulate themselves against currency crises. These had periodically struck Europe since the breakdown of the Bretton Woods system of exchange rates pegged to the US dollar in the early 1970s. Its replacement in Europe, the exchange-rate mechanism (ERM) of the European Monetary System (EMS), involved trying to limit

---

104 At the European Summit in The Hague in 1969, the heads of state and government of the European Community agreed to prepare a plan for economic and monetary union. The Werner Report was drawn up by a working group chaired by Pierre Werner, Luxembourg's prime minister and minister for finances, and presented in October 1970. http://en.wikipedia.org/wiki/Werner_Plan

currencies' fluctuations around pegs to Germany's Deutsche Mark. But after European governments lifted capital controls in the 1980s, allowing money to flow freely in and out of the economy, the ERM became increasingly vulnerable to destabilising speculation. In 1992 currency after currency was forced to devalue. That September, sterling was forced out of the ERM on Black Wednesday. In 1993 EU governments decided to greatly widen the bands within which currencies could fluctuate. In effect, the ERM had all but broken down. The crisis convinced EU governments that they had to press on with their plans for a common currency.

The main motive for creating the euro, however, was political. Sharing a currency was seen as a step towards "an ever closer union among the peoples of Europe", the objective set out in the Treaty of Rome in 1957, to which all EU members have signed up. France's president, François Mitterrand, also wanted to bind a reunified Germany more tightly into Europe and end the humiliating hegemony of the Deutsche Mark, which stripped French policymakers of monetary autonomy. Germany's deeply pro-European Chancellor, Helmut Kohl, was happy to agree so long as the new currency was modelled on German lines. A set of conditions, the Maastricht criteria, would determine which countries could join: low inflation, a budget deficit that did not exceed 3 per cent of GDP, government debts that did not exceed 60 per cent of GDP or were falling towards that level fast enough[105], low long-term interest rates[106] and a stable exchange rate. To curb excessive public borrowing once countries shared a currency, governments subsequently committed to continue observing the 3-per-cent deficit and 60-per-cent debt limits. These fiscal rules

---

105 If the debt-to-GDP ratio exceeded the 60 per cent limit, it should at least have "sufficiently diminished and must be approaching the reference value at a satisfactory pace".

106 More precisely, ten-year government bond yields close to the EU average.

were enshrined in the Stability and Growth Pact, which the European Commission was tasked with monitoring and enforcing. In the event that a government ran into difficulties, other EU governments were forbidden from taking on their debts while the European Central Bank was banned from financing them directly.[107] It was hoped that, together with the Stability and Growth Pact, this "no-bailout clause" and the ban on "monetary financing" would ensure that markets kept government borrowing in check.

Several countries made heroic efforts to ensure they were among the founding members of the euro. Italy, Spain, Portugal and Belgium all slashed their budget deficit in the latter half of the 1990s, as did France, whose exclusion from the first wave of euro entry was in

---

107   The no-bailout clause was initially in the 1993 Maastricht Treaty and later in the 2009 Lisbon Treaty that encompasses and amends the Maastricht Treaty. Article 125.1 of the Lisbon Treaty states: "The Union shall not be liable for or assume the commitments of central governments, regional, local or other public authorities, other bodies governed by public law, or public undertakings of any Member State, without prejudice to mutual financial guarantees for the joint execution of a specific project. A Member State shall not be liable for or assume the commitments of central governments, regional, local or other public authorities, other bodies governed by public law, or public undertakings of another Member State, without prejudice to mutual financial guarantees for the joint execution of a specific project."

The ban on "monetary financing" is in Article 123 of the Lisbon Treaty: "1. Overdraft facilities or any other type of credit facility with the European Central Bank or with the central banks of the Member States (hereinafter referred to as 'national central banks') in favour of Union institutions, bodies, offices or agencies, central governments, regional, local or other public authorities, other bodies governed by public law, or public undertakings of Member States shall be prohibited, as shall the purchase directly from them by the European Central Bank or national central banks of debt instruments. 2. Paragraph 1 shall not apply to publicly owned credit institutions which, in the context of the supply of reserves by central banks, shall be given the same treatment by national central banks and the European Central Bank as private credit institutions."

any case politically inconceivable. But the debt criterion was fudged. When the first selection of euro members was made in March 1998 on the basis of 1997 figures, Belgium had an extremely high level of public debt (122.2 per cent of GDP), albeit falling. Italy's debt (121.6 per cent of GDP) was almost as high and edging down. Strictly speaking, even Germany shouldn't have qualified: its public debt was above 60 per cent of GDP (61.3 per cent) and *rising*.[108]

On 1 January 1999, eleven countries – Austria, Belgium, Finland, France, Germany, Ireland, Italy, Luxembourg, the Netherlands, Portugal and Spain – irrevocably locked their exchange rates. Greece failed to make this initial cut. But in 2000 the rules were bent to admit Greece. The European Commission decided, and EU leaders agreed, that "Greece has achieved a high degree of sustainable convergence by reference to all four criteria."[109] But that wasn't true. Greece had been rejected only two years earlier because its inflation, budget deficit, public debt and bond yields were all too high.[110] So it fiddled its figures in order to make the cut – and the European Commission was fooled.[111] As a result, Greece was among the twelve countries that

---

108   Germany was given a derogation, ostensibly because its rising debt was due to pay for the costs of reunification since 1990. European Commission, Directorate General for Economic and Financial Affairs, "Convergence Report 1998" http://ec.europa.eu/economy_finance/publications/publication8013_en.pdf

109   European Commission, "Proposal for a Council Decision in accordance with article 122(2) of the Treaty for the adoption by Greece of the single currency on 1.1.2001" http://ec.europa.eu/economy_finance/publications/publication8888_en.pdf

110   http://ec.europa.eu/economy_finance/publications/publication8013_en.pdf

111   The Commission thought that Greece's deficit had fallen to 1.6 per cent of GDP in 1999 and would decline to 1.3 per cent in 2000; it subsequently turned out that Greece's deficit was 3.1 per cent in 1999 and 3.7 per cent in 2000. As for Greece's public debt, the Commission thought that it edged down to 104.4 per cent in 1999 and would continue declining in 2000, but it actually soared that year.

swapped their old national banknotes for freshly printed euro ones and newly minted euro coins on 1 January 2002. Since then, six other countries have joined: Slovenia (2007), Cyprus and Malta (2008), Slovakia (2009), Estonia (2011) and Latvia (2014). All other EU countries are committed to joining the euro except Britain and Denmark, which have formal opt-outs, and Sweden, which is deliberately failing to meet the entry criteria.

Euro benefits

The euro has delivered many of its promised economic benefits. It has boosted trade. By lowering the cost and reducing the risk of trading across borders, it has enabled a wider range of firms to export a broader range of products, making consumers better off. Estimates of the boost to trade vary; perhaps the most authoritative study, by Richard Baldwin and others, reckons the euro increased it by 5 per cent between 1999 and 2006.[112] The euro has also stimulated cross-border business investment, notably in manufacturing, enabling firms to merge and restructure their activities across national lines, while also attracting increased investment from outside the eurozone. Studies agree that the euro has boosted foreign direct investment (but differ as to how much).[113] No doubt the euro has also generated some other positive financial flows across the eurozone, allowing investors to diversify their portfolios and earn higher risk-adjusted returns,

---

Old figures are from European Commission, "Convergence Report 2000" http://ec.europa.eu/economy_finance/publications/publication8912_en.pdf New figures are from European Commission, AMECO database

112   Richard Baldwin, Virginia DiNino, Lionel Fontagné, Roberto A. De Santis and Daria Taglioni, "Study on the Impact of the Euro on Trade and Foreign Direct Investment", *Economic Papers* 321, European Commission Directorate-General for Economic and Financial Affairs, 2008 http://ec.europa.eu/economy_finance/publications/publication12590_en.pdf

113   *Idem.*

particularly on equity investments. But because the euro's launch co-incided with the biggest financial bubble in history across the Western financial system, those positive flows were swamped by misdirected cross-border bank lending. And when European banks came unstuck, it turned out that they were still national after all.

Sharing the euro has also protected its members against damaging exchange-rate instability, notably in 2008 and 2009, as the chapter will explain. In a world where febrile currency markets trade an astonishing $5.3 trillion (£3.3 trillion) *each day*, dwarfing world trade, volatile exchange rates all too often disrupt economic activity, amplifying and even creating shocks, rather than damping them.[114] Like high inflation, currency volatility gums up price signals, distorting businesses' investment decisions. Currency misalignments can be even more damaging: witness how the pound's prolonged overvaluation in the pre-crisis years destroyed much of British industry. Since currency moves are unpredictable, foreign-exchange markets cannot be relied on to deliver those that policymakers want or economies "need". Even when the currency does move in the desired direction, it doesn't necessarily help the economy as much as policymakers hope, as Britain's poor export performance since the pound's plunge in 2008 shows (see Chapter 7).

Suboptimal?

While the euro has boosted trade and investment and limited currency instability, critics blame it for the crisis in the eurozone and generally believe it is destined to fail, for a variety of reasons. Some put it crudely: "having different countries share a currency will never work." A more sophisticated version of this argument is that the eurozone is not an "optimum currency area": national economies are too

---

114   http://www.bis.org/publ/rpfx13fx.pdf Converted at average 2012 exchange rate of £ = $1.5851

different in structure and cyclical behaviour to cope with a one-size-fits-all monetary policy; they lack a common budget to cushion individual economies against shocks that affect them differently to others; and without their own currency, they are not flexible and integrated enough to adjust to such shocks.[115] Others go further and assert that a fiscal union (a common eurozone budget or common debt issuance) is essential and only possible in a single state, so that a monetary union cannot work without "political union" – some form of European government – which they deem either unfeasible or undesirable or both.

Undeniably, the eurozone is not an optimum currency area. National economies are very different in structure – Greece is nothing like Germany; France bears little resemblance to Finland – as are regions within them: Milan specialises in fashion, Frankfurt in finance, Porto in footwear. Their economic cycles have often been out of synch: nearly everyone grew strongly in 2000 and 2006–7, but between those years Germany, Italy and Portugal stagnated, while Spain, Ireland and Greece boomed, with France in between. Stagnant economies might have benefited from lower interest rates, booming economies from higher ones. The one-size-fits-all interest rate doubtless caused some divergence in inflation rates too. Between 1999 and 2007, consumer prices rose by an average of 2.2 per cent a year in the eurozone as a whole – somewhat less in Germany (1.7 per cent) and France (1.9 per cent), fractionally more in Italy (2.4 per cent), somewhat higher in Portugal (3 per cent), Spain (3.2 per cent), Greece (3.3 per cent) and Ireland (3.4 per cent).[116] Since it is normal for prices to rise faster in poorer countries as they catch up with richer ones – as Ireland and Spain both did in the pre-crisis years, even after stripping

---

115   See, for instance, Paul Krugman: http://krugman.blogs.nytimes.com/2012/06/24/revenge-of-the-optimum-currency-area/

116   Personal calculations from Eurostat, all-items harmonised index of consumer prices (HICP) 2005 =100. Code: prc_hicp_aind

out the impact of the financial bubble – this divergence is less problematic than it may seem. Eurozone economies are also less integrated than they ought to be. Some, such as the Netherlands, trade a lot with the rest of the eurozone; others, such as Greece, do not. Their trade and investment ties would be much greater if the single market in services was completed. Contrary to popular perception, labour mobility within the eurozone remains low. Economies are also much less flexible than they ought to be, with the notable exception of Ireland. Self-evidently, the eurozone lacks a common budget, while the EU's does not act as an economic stabiliser. But did any of that cause the crisis?

No. With global credit booming and investors blind to risk (as Chapter 1 explained), neither the change in local interest rates, nor membership of the euro, nor even the extent of foreign borrowing were the critical factors in determining credit growth across countries, but rather which banks were willing and able to lend – and which local counterparties were willing and able to borrow. Thus while the fall in interest rates on joining the euro in 1999 generally boosted credit growth in southern Europe, it didn't in Italy, where credit was tightly controlled. Credit growth was particularly boisterous in the Netherlands, where interest rates didn't fall on joining the euro and which was a net lender to foreigners throughout the pre-crisis period.[117] Denmark, outside the euro, also had a credit boom while continuously being a net lender to foreigners. Banks in countries with a current-account surplus (post-2001 Germany, pre-2005 France, the Netherlands) were willing and able to lend to foreigners, as were banks in countries with a current-account deficit (Britain and post-2004 France). Household credit is tightly restricted in France, so French banks mostly lent overseas. German households didn't want to borrow and German companies didn't need to, so German banks

---

117 Eurostat, private credit flow in per cent of GDP, non consolidated, annual data. Code: tipspc10

mostly lent overseas too. Credit was easy in Britain and households were happy to borrow so both foreign and local banks lent to them, while also lending abroad. Despite easy credit conditions, the Spanish and Irish governments resisted the temptation to borrow, while the Greek authorities didn't.

Often, countries outside the euro borrowed more than those inside it. Between the creation of the euro and the peak of the bubble in 2007, household debt rose by more (as a share of disposable income) in Britain than in Spain.[118] In 2004–7, the years when the financial sector was awash with cash and investors spoke of a "wall of money", private-sector credit growth was faster in Iceland (outside the euro) than Ireland (inside it). It was higher in countries pegged to the euro – notably Denmark, Bulgaria, Latvia and Estonia – than in those that would doubtless have been pegged to the euro had they not joined it, such as Greece and Portugal.[119] The countries that recorded the biggest current-account deficits at their peak – those that ran up the biggest annual borrowing from foreigners – were all outside the euro: Bulgaria (30 per cent of GDP), Iceland (28 per cent), Latvia (22 per cent) and Estonia (17 per cent).[120]

Did members of the euro fare worse when the bubble burst in 2007–8? No. When banks stopped lending, first to each other and then to the rest of the economy, and cross-border lending came to a sudden stop, the adjustment was brutal for many economies outside

---

118 OECD, debts of households and NPISHs as a share of gross disposable income. Between 2000 and 2007, this rose by 58 percentage points in Spain and 61.8 percentage points in Britain.

119 Personal calculations from Eurostat, private credit flow in per cent of GDP, non consolidated, annual data. Code: tipspc10. In 2004–7, credit grew by a total of 76.2 per cent in Greece, 80.8 per cent in Portugal, 120.4 per cent in Denmark, 145.6 per cent in Bulgaria, 191.6 per cent in Latvia and 198.9 per cent in Estonia.

120 Dan O'Brien pointed this out in a letter to the *Financial Times* on 25 May 2012. http://www.ft.com/cms/s/0/9f8dbe06-a4ea-11e1-9a94-00144feabdc0.html

the eurozone that were reliant on fickle foreign finance. Both countries whose currency floated – such as Iceland, Hungary and Romania – and those pegged to the euro, notably Estonia, Latvia and Bulgaria, suffered more than euro members. Within two years, Latvia swung from borrowing net a quarter of its annual income from foreigners to lending net a seventh of its much-diminished income to them: a swing in its current account of nearly 40 per cent of GDP![121] Iceland's current-account deficit shrank by 13 per cent of GDP between 2008 and 2009.[122] Romania and Hungary suffered a much larger current-account adjustment and recession in 2008–9 than Portugal, a similarly sized and likewise external-credit-fuelled economy.[123] Some non-euro economies collapsed. Iceland's shrank by 13 per cent in a bit under three years, Estonia's by a fifth in two years, Latvia's by a quarter in a slightly shorter period.[124] Cut off from market funding, Iceland

---

121   Eurostat, net lending/borrowing, current prices, percentage of GDP, quarterly, seasonally adjusted and adjusted by working days. Code: namq_inc_c In Q2 2007, Latvia had a current-account deficit of 24.7 per cent of GDP; by Q2 2009, it had a surplus of 14.3 per cent of GDP.

122   Eurostat, net lending/borrowing, current prices, annual. Code: nama_inc_c

123   Eurostat, net lending/borrowing, current prices, annual. Code: nama_inc_c Hungary's current-account deficit of 5.9 per cent of GDP became a 3 per cent surplus in 2010, an adjustment of 8.9 per cent of GDP, and GDP fell by 8.4 per cent from its peak in Q2 2008 to its trough in Q3 2009. Romania's deficit of 11 per cent of GDP shrank to 3.6 per cent the following year, an adjustment of 7.4 per cent of GDP, and GDP fell by 9 per cent from its peak in Q3 2008 to its trough in Q1 2010. Portugal's current-account deficit shrank by 2.4 per cent of GDP between 2008 and 2010, from 11.4 per cent to 9 per cent, and GDP fell by 4.1 per cent from its peak in Q4 2007 to its trough in Q1 2009.

124   Personal calculations from Eurostat, gross domestic product at market prices, volumes, index 2005=100. Code: namq_gdp_k From its peak in Q3 2007 to its trough in Q2 2010, Iceland's GDP by 13.1 per cent. From its peak in Q4 2007 to its trough in Q4 2009, Estonia's GDP fell by 19.2 per cent. From its peak in Q4 2007 to its trough in Q3 2009, Latvia's GDP fell by 24.6 per cent.

was forced to resort to a loan from the IMF (and in desperation also sought one from Russia). Latvia, Hungary and Romania, all members of the EU but not the euro, had to obtain loans from both the EU and the IMF. Even Poland had to seek an IMF credit line. Outside the EU, Armenia, Belarus, Georgia, Serbia and Ukraine also all needed IMF help.

Eurozone economies fared better because they could still rely on funding from the European Central Bank. Banks that could no longer borrow from each other or markets obtained liquidity from the ECB instead. The ECB was also able to arrange swap lines with the US Federal Reserve to provide dollar loans to eurozone banks that needed them. It cut official interest rates, providing further relief. Since eurozone governments were seen as safe ports in a storm, they were able to continue borrowing cheaply and provide a fiscal stimulus to limit the slump. Thus in Act One of the crisis, the euro acted as a shock absorber for member economies.

Contrast Ireland's initial experience with Iceland's. When Iceland's banks collapsed in September 2008, the country was cut off from global markets, saw interest rates skyrocket to 20 per cent, had to seek an IMF rescue loan and imposed capital controls to stop cash draining out of the economy. But when Ireland's banks collapsed, its membership of the euro provided valuable breathing space: the government was able to continue borrowing from international markets and interest rates fell. Unfortunately, the Irish government squandered this advantage through its disastrous decision to guarantee all the debts of its collapsing banking system – thereby making taxpayers foot the bill for the huge losses of scoundrels such as Sean FitzPatrick at Anglo Irish Bank. More generally, euro membership protected countries from the currency crisis that they would doubtless otherwise have faced during the panic in late 2008 and early 2009. Many countries outside the euro suffered as panicky investors sought refuge in safe havens such as the dollar and the euro, forcing them to raise interest rates and slash government spending in a slump. Even Denmark had to raise interest rates for a time to protect its currency instead of cutting them to prop up demand. In short, the euro was initially a stabilising force – and as this chapter will explain, it was subsequently destabilised largely by policy mistakes, rather than because it wasn't an "optimum currency area".

Has membership of the euro made it harder for economies to adjust, though? After the bubble burst, economies that had previously relied on debt-fuelled consumption needed to shift towards more export-led growth. Euro-sceptics argue that such an adjustment can happen much more readily with one's own currency, which can fall in value, making a country's products cheaper for foreigners and thereby boosting exports. But it hasn't turned out that way for Britain. Despite a huge fall in the pound's value since 2007, Britain's exports were only 0.6 per cent above their pre-devaluation peak in late 2013 – while, without the purported benefit of devaluation, Spanish exports rose by a sixth over the same period.[125] Arguably, sterling's devaluation has not only failed to promote Britain's economic adjustment, it has actually delayed it. Unlike in Spain, policymakers have not felt a need to implement difficult reforms to promote export-led growth. Whereas Spanish companies have been forced to up their game and seek out

---

125   According to the Bank of England's effective exchange-rate index (code: XUMABK67), sterling's trade-weighted value declined by 26.7 per cent between July 2007 and March 2009. As recently as March 2013, it was still down by 24.8 per cent. It has since recovered somewhat, but by January 2014, the pound was still 18.8 per cent weaker than in July 2007. Despite this huge depreciation, the volume of UK exports in the third quarter of 2013 was only 0.6 per cent higher than its pre-devaluation peak in the second quarter of 2008. Over the same period, without devaluation, Spanish exports rose by 16.3 per cent. Source: personal calculations from Eurostat, exports of goods and services, seasonally adjusted and adjusted data by working days, volumes, index 2005=100. Code: namq_exi_k

new foreign markets, British ones have had the option to sit back and pocket the gains from a weaker currency as fatter margins. Thus while a weaker currency can sometimes help – think of Britain's experience after it was ejected from the ERM in 1992 – it is no panacea. As Spain's experience shows, countries can also adjust within the eurozone – and could do much better if policies elsewhere in the eurozone were different. It often seems as if British critics' obsession with the euro's perceived flaws is a form of displacement activity, given how poorly the UK economy and its not-so-precious pound have performed in recent years. In any case, the key to southern Europe's (and Britain's) long-term success is not cutting the cost of its traditional exports in a vain attempt to compete with China, but moving up the value chain – producing different and better things. That requires productivity-enhancing reforms and investment, not devaluation.

Even so, is the euro destined to break up because it isn't an optimum currency area? No. In the real world, currency areas are rarely optimal. Italy manifestly wasn't when it used the lira: while the north of the country boomed, the south stagnated. Yes, northern Italians were taxed to subsidise southerners, but this arguably entrenched the problem rather than solving it. Did anyone argue that Sicily should have its own currency? No, they said Italy needed to reform. Britain is not an optimum currency area either. Global London's finance-fuelled economy has little in common with the economies of Wales, Northern Ireland or the North of England. But do the huge divergences between them warrant them having separate currencies?

No, because the decision to share a currency is primarily political. London and Northern Ireland share a currency not because they form an optimum currency area but because history happens to have thrown them together in a single state. Likewise Piedmont and Sicily in Italy. Conversely, politically disparate places that happened to form an optimum currency area – say Russia and Saudi Arabia, both oil-dominated economies – would be unlikely to share a currency simply on that basis. In each case, a shared history – or in the euro's case, a desired destiny – would be the overriding factor.

Europe's monetary union is a key element of the political project set out in the Treaty of Rome. So while euro-sceptics are, of course, entitled to argue that they don't want Britain to be part of the euro because they don't share the political vision of a more united Europe, they should not dismiss the perfectly legitimate political aspiration of many other Europeans to share a currency (if not a single state), which is no more absurd than the UK's own monetary union.

Of course, if the economic consequences of a political decision are disastrous – or if political priorities change – it may be reversed. Scotland may vote for independence and end up with a different currency. Greeks may decide that the euro is destroying their economy and they would be better off leaving – or choose to stick with it. They might feel that they now hate the Germans so much that they don't want to be tied to them through a shared currency. Or they might continue to feel that the euro is a badge of their modernity and Europeanness that draws a line under their unhappy history of civil war and dictatorship and sets them apart from their previous Turkish colonial masters and their unstable Balkan neighbours. In any case, neither politics nor optimum-currency-area theory imply that a common currency area that is suboptimal – be it the eurozone or the UK – is destined to break up. The component parts might muddle along in an imperfect currency union (as in Britain, where little is done to tackle the north-south divide) or there might be efforts to remedy its deficiencies (as there are in the eurozone, as we shall see).

In short, the euro itself did not cause the financial excesses in the pre-crisis years, which occurred across the Western financial system. Indeed, in Act One of the crisis, after the bubble burst, it acted as a shock absorber. Nor has the euro prevented its member economies from adjusting. While it might fail, it is not destined to. Last but not least, the vicious interaction between a banking crisis and a bond-market panic that tore the eurozone apart between 2010 and 2012 was largely due to avoidable policy mistakes in Frankfurt, Brussels and Berlin, as we shall see.

What really went wrong

It was only in Act Two of the crisis after the bailout of Greece's creditors in 2010 and even more so in Act Three after the summer of 2011 that the euro became an unstable system that amplified shocks rather than damping them. This destabilising shift is largely due to a succession of catastrophic policy mistakes which exposed some of the euro's design flaws and revealed political constraints that have so far prevented a solution to the crisis. Had these policy mistakes not occurred, the eurozone would, like Britain, have faced balance-sheet problems, primarily in the financial and the private sector, as well as an economic adjustment problem, but not an existential financial panic.

The five policy mistakes were as follows. One: the decision that national governments would continue to stand behind every bank, tying their fates together. Two: the decision to lend to an insolvent Greece in 2010, rather than write down its debts, under the pretence that the financial stability on the eurozone needed safeguarding, creating a "euro crisis". Three: the collective lurch into premature, front-loaded, slash-and-burn – and therefore self-defeating – austerity. Four: the threat to write down the debts of governments that encountered temporary difficulties to borrow, triggering panic. Five: the threat to force Greece out of the euro, sparking speculation the euro would break-up.

These five policy mistakes highlighted design flaws and political constraints that amplified those mistakes and thus made the euro increasingly unstable. The decision to stand behind all the banks exposed a design flaw that the eurozone and other EU countries shared – the absence of national and Europe-wide mechanisms for restructuring and winding down banks in an orderly way – and damaging political constraints: a desire to protect the narrow interests of the banking sector (and its creditors) and an unwillingness to face up to and deal with past mistakes. The Greek fiasco highlighted another design flaw – the absence of a mechanism for the orderly restructuring of sovereign debt in the eurozone (and globally for that matter) – and a political constraint: a fear of debt restructuring, out of a misguided desire to protect the banking sector, a mistaken belief that it would lead to a Lehman-style crisis and a moralistic view that debt contracts are sacrosanct. The panic in sovereign bond markets that resulted from the five policy mistakes revealed a major design flaw: that the ECB was not explicitly mandated to be a lender of last resort to governments in the EU treaties. It also revealed two important political constraints: a deep reluctance of the ECB to intervene to stabilise sovereign bond markets and a perception that a central bank that jealously guards its independence was in fact a prisoner of German politics.

The overarching error was a misdiagnosis of the crisis as being primarily about excessive government borrowing and a lack of "competitiveness" in southern Europe for which the solution was immediate austerity and wage cuts. In fact, with the notable exception of Greece, it was primarily a banking crisis associated with excessive private borrowing for which the solution was bank restructuring, debt write-downs and policies to support investment and economic adjustment. As a result of these five catastrophic policy mistakes, however, the crisis evolved into a "doom loop" that dragged weak banks, weak governments and weak economies down together, exacerbated by self-defeating austerity and amplified by a systemic, self-fulfilling panic that governments would be unable to refinance their debts, forced to default and the euro would break up.

Mistake one: the banks

Fragile to start off with, punctured by losses on bad loans in the bubble years, the eurozone's tightly interconnected banks stopped lending to each other when the crisis struck, forcing the ECB to step in. The banking system was both the root cause of the crisis in the eurozone and its transmission mechanism, while its political clout has been one of the main obstacles to resolving the crisis. As Chapter 1 explained, the first huge mistake – which Britain made too – is that governments have tried to prop up nearly every failing bank at taxpayers' expense while failing to force them to face up to their losses. Within the eurozone, the decision that banks would be supported by individual national governments has proved catastrophic.[126]

In most eurozone countries, banks' balance sheets dwarf national economies. In the US, whose financial system relies more on capital markets, total bank assets amounted to €8.6 trillion in

---

126   The decision was taken at a meeting of the leaders of Britain and the eurozone at the Elysee Palace in Paris on 12 October 2008 and was entrenched in the European Council, "Declaration on a concerted European Action Plan of the Euro Area Countries", 14 October 2008, 14239/08, in particular, section 9: "So as to allow financial institutions to continue to ensure the proper financing of the Eurozone economy, each Member State will make available to financial institutions Tier 1 capital, e.g. by acquiring preferred shares or other instruments including non dilutive ones. Price conditions shall take into account the market situation of each institution involved. Governments commit themselves to provide capital when needed in appropriate volume while favouring by all available means the raising of private capital." Also, point 11: "Governments remain committed to support the financial system and therefore to avoid the failure of relevant financial institutions, through appropriate means including recapitalization."

2011 – equivalent to 78 per cent of GDP.[127] In the EU, in contrast, total bank assets were a whopping €46.8 trillion – or 370 per cent of EU economies' combined annual output. Within the eurozone, bank balance sheets range from a hefty 86 per cent of GDP in Slovakia to an astronomical 2,430 per cent of GDP in Luxembourg.[128] Clearly, if governments backstop undercapitalised banks many times larger than the economy, any significant fall in the value of banks' assets threatens to drag down governments with them.

To make matters worse, those bank assets are often the bonds of the government backstopping them. For instance, in mid-2010 Italian government bonds accounted for 12.5 per cent of local bank assets.[129] So if those bonds lost a tenth of their value, Italian banks would take a hit equivalent to 1.25 per cent of their assets. That would wipe out more than half of their capital if their assets were financed with 2 per cent equity and 98 per cent debt. Rising government bond yields would also squeeze banks by raising their funding costs. Together, that would deal a further blow to Italian government bonds, because it could prompt panic selling by banks and would increase the risk

---

127   High-Level Expert Group on Reforming the Structure of the EU Banking Sector, chaired by Erkki Liikanen, 2 October 2012, http://ec.europa.eu/internal_market/bank/docs/highlevel_expert_group/report_en.pdf

128   *Ibid*, Table A1.2: total number and assets of monetary financial institutions by country (March 2012) Bank assets are equivalent to 202 per cent of GDP in Greece, 263 per cent in Italy, 331 per cent in Germany, 340 per cent in Portugal, 348 per cent in Spain, 412 per cent in the Netherlands, 423 per cent in France, 734 per cent in Cyprus, 796 per cent in Malta and 799 per cent in Ireland. In Britain, they are a whopping 569 per cent of GDP.

129   International Monetary Fund, *Global Financial Stability Report*, October 2010. Table 1.1. Sovereign Market and Vulnerability Indicators. Domestic government bonds accounted for 9 per cent of Greek banks' assets, 7.1 per cent of German ones', 6.7 per cent of Spanish ones', 4.9 per cent of Portuguese ones' and 4.5 per cent of French ones'.

that banks would receive a government bailout. Britain was fortunate in this regard: domestic government bonds accounted for only 1.3 per cent of UK banks' assets.

To add insult to injury, the doom loop between distressed banks and weak sovereigns drags down economies too. Rising government bond yields push up interest rates for bank borrowers. Distressed banks stop lending, pushing economies into recession. Struggling governments may raise taxes or cut spending, dealing a further blow. A weaker economy, in turn, further corrodes both banks' balance sheets (as more households and businesses are unable to repay their loans) and governments', as tax revenues fall and social spending rises. A banking crisis combined with a government backstop is thus a toxic mix.

Banks in other eurozone countries were affected too, because they had lent to southern Europe or were exposed in other ways, notably through credit default swaps and other derivatives contracts. At the end of the first quarter of 2010, French banks had a €780.4 billion exposure to Greece, Ireland, Italy, Portugal and Spain; German banks a €557.8 billion exposure; Spanish banks a €134.5 billion foreign exposure, primarily to Portugal; Italian banks a $66.3 billion exposure; and other eurozone banks a €396.2 billion exposure. Non-eurozone banks were exposed too: to the tune of €387.4 billion in the case of British banks, predominantly to Ireland, and a total of €493.8 billion for US ones.[130] Those foreign banks' balance sheets took a hit as the value of their government bond holdings fell and as their loans to

---

130   Bank for International Settlements, *Quarterly Review*, September 2010. Foreign exposures to Greece, Ireland, Portugal and Spain, by bank nationality, end-Q1 2010, converted from US dollars to euros at exchange rate on 31 March 2010 of €1 = $1.3468. Figures for exposures to Italy added from BIS database, using figures for Q4 2010 for exposures to derivatives contracts, guarantees extended and credit commitments in the absence of figures for Q1 2010.

companies and households turned sour. But they were also among the prime beneficiaries, along with other creditors, of the government backstopping of failed banks. For example, had Irish banks defaulted on all their debt at the end of September 2010, German banks would have lost €42.5 billion, British ones €27.5 billion and French ones €12.3 billion.[131]

When Ireland was forced to seek a loan from the EU and the IMF in November 2010[132], the Irish government sought to backtrack on its foolish promise, made in the heat of the post-Lehman panic in October 2008, to guarantee all Irish banks' debts. Had it succeeded, the doom loop would have been greatly weakened. Instead, eurozone

---

131   Bank for International Settlements, *Quarterly Review*, March 2011. Foreign exposures to Greece, Ireland, Portugal and Spain, by bank nationality, end-Q3 2010, converted from US dollars to euros at exchange rate on 30 September 2010 of €1 = $1.36.15

132   After the market for unsecured interbank lending in Europe dried up, nearly all lending between banks was done with collateral, ie, through "repo" contracts. Much of this repo lending was through third-party clearers such as LCH.Clearnet, which has a clear set of rules on the setting of margins for collateral. Even direct over-the-counter (OTC) repo lending is done using the LCH margin requirements as a reference. In other words, LCH sets the benchmark for the interbank repo lending. When setting margin requirements on sovereign bond collateral, LCH looks at the yield of that sovereign's ten-year bond relative to a basket of AAA-rated eurozone sovereigns. If the spread rises above 450 basis points for more than a couple of weeks, they demand a higher margin. When LCH raised the margin requirements on Irish debt, Irish banks (and other banks with Irish bonds) suddenly had to find much more collateral in order to fund themselves. This is equivalent to having a sudden outflow of deposits. So when LCH raised the collateral requirements on Irish bonds, Irish banks suffered a liquidity crisis. While Irish banks could still go for funding to the ECB (which had not changed its collateral requirements), the ECB was not keen on providing additional funding. Since the Irish banks had a guarantee from the Irish government, this liquidity crisis forced the Irish government to seek a loan from the EFSF.

policymakers, notably ECB President Trichet, outrageously black-mailed the Irish government into making good on its guarantee, by threatening to cut off liquidity to the Irish banking system – in effect, threatening to force it out of the euro. Thus, having exhausted the borrowing capacity of the Irish government, the creditors of Irish banks could now call on loans from other eurozone governments, along with Britain's, Sweden's and the IMF. This was a flagrant abuse of power by an unelected central banker whose primary duty ought to have been to the citizens of countries that use the euro – not least Irish ones. Bleeding dry Irish taxpayers to repay foreign debts incurred by Irish banks to finance the country's property bubble was not only shocking unjust. It was a devilish mechanism not for safeguarding financial stability in the eurozone – which would be the ECB's defence for its actions – but rather for amplifying instability. It entrenched governments' backstopping of bank debts, sparking fears about countries that had experienced an Irish-style bank-financed property bubble, notably Spain. And it threatened to drag even countries with a reasonably sound banking system, such as Italy, into the doom loop if the situation deteriorated.

This doom loop was amplified by the other four big policy mistakes, which destabilised the bond yields of vulnerable sovereigns, worsening the banking crisis, and so on. But eurozone leaders didn't even officially recognise the problem until their June 2012 summit.[133] Even now they have yet to sever the link. In any case, these government guarantees for an unrestructured banking system have already done irreparable damage: the lost output and jobs in recent years. They have also enabled the creditors of failed banks to sell their bonds at a much higher price than otherwise, receive interest on all their remaining ones and be paid in full for those that came due. Thus by March

---

133   "We affirm that it is imperative to break the vicious circle between banks and sovereigns." Euro Area Summit Statement, 29 June 2012

2013, German banks had reduced their exposure to Spanish, Irish, Portuguese and Greek banks to €48.3 billion from €127.6 billion three years earlier; French banks had reduced their exposure to €31.5 billion from €75.7 billion; British ones to €32.2 billion from €58.4 billion; and US ones to €23 billion from €43.3 billion.[134] In effect, Europe has been hit by the biggest bank heist of all time. European taxpayers have been robbed blind by banks' creditors and the policy-makers who connived in it.

Mistake two: Greece

The second catastrophic policy mistake was how eurozone policymakers handled Greece's insolvency. When Greece's new socialist (Pasok) government led by George Papandreou took office in October 2009, it revealed that the previous conservative (New Democracy) administration had cooked the books: the government's deficit and debt were much higher than previously claimed. Under EU pressure, it embarked on massive austerity to try to right its public finances. But realising that Greece was insolvent, markets refused to continue funding it, so Papandreou sought an emergency loan from the EU and the IMF.

Since the Greek government was *insolvent*, its debts ought to have been written down to a sustainable level.[135] Like many other governments around the world, it could then have obtained an IMF loan to tide it over while it got the economy and public finances back on

---

134 Bank for International Settlements, *Quarterly Review*, March 2011. Foreign exposures to Greece, Ireland, Portugal and Spain, by bank nationality, end-Q1 2010, converted from US dollars to euros at exchange rate on 30 September 2010 of €1 = $1.3468 and Bank for International Settlements, international bank claims consolidated – ultimate risk basis, end-Q1 2013, converted at exchange rate on 31 March 2013 of €1 =€1.281

135 By insolvent, I mean that it was highly implausible that the future path of Greek GDP growth and interest rates would permit the Greek government to raise enough tax revenues to repay its debts in full.

track. Instead, eurozone policymakers decided to pretend that the Greek government was merely going through temporary difficulties borrowing from the market – that is, *illiquid*. And because policymakers – in particular the ECB's Trichet – did not want to hand a country in the eurozone over to the IMF, while the no-bail-out clause in the EU treaties forbade eurozone governments from lending to Greece, they devised a seemingly ingenious but actually catastrophic ruse. They claimed that a solvency crisis in a small country in southeastern Europe was actually a crisis that threatened financial stability in the eurozone as a whole – and therefore required exceptional measures to safeguard the single currency.[136] The no-bailout clause was thus circumvented, with EU governments first lending bilaterally to Greece, together with the IMF, and then creating two temporary funds – the European Financial Stabilisation Mechanism (EFSM) and the European Financial Stability Facility (EFSF) – and finally a permanent one, the European Stability Mechanism (ESM), for future rescues. The ECB connived in this deception by creating its Securities Markets Programme in order to buy Greek government bonds, again under the pretence that Greece was illiquid rather than insolvent – a

---

136   In February 2010, EU leaders stated that "Euro area Member states will take determined and coordinated action, if needed, to safeguard financial stability in the euro area as a whole. The Greek government has not requested any financial support." (Statement by the Heads of State or Government of the European Union, 11 February 2010.) In March, they stated that they stood ready to provide bilateral loans, with the IMF, subject to strict conditionality and at non-concessional rates. "Euro area member states reaffirm their willingness to take determined and coordinated action, if needed, to safeguard financial stability in the euro area as a whole, as decided on the 11th of February. As part of a package involving substantial International Monetary Fund financing and a majority of European financing, Euro area member states are ready to contribute to coordinated bilateral loans." (Statement by the Heads of State and Government of the Euro Area, 25 March 2010.)

mistake that would later make the ECB even more implacably opposed to a write-down of Greek debt.

At a stroke, eurozone policymakers created a "euro crisis" – with investors naturally looking for which country might be the next Greece. On a scale of 0–100, where 100 is the peak search interest, web searches for "euro crisis" on Google spiked from 2 in January 2010 to 11 in February when eurozone governments first declared themselves willing to lend to Greece to "safeguard financial stability in the euro area as a whole". They then soared from 11 in April to 52 in May when the Greek loan was announced, with a peak of 100 being reached in November 2011. The fact that people suddenly perceived a Greek government-debt crisis as a "euro crisis" once EU leaders branded it as such is telling. Astonishingly, searches for "euro crisis" were higher in May 2010 than in July 2012, when it had genuinely become a euro crisis and Draghi felt obliged to make his pledge to do "whatever it takes" to save the single currency. Policymakers also shredded their credibility, because they made claims about Greece that were palpably untrue, and therefore undermined confidence in everything else they subsequently said. Greece's debts were subsequently written down twice in 2012, but remain unbearably large.

The sums didn't add up

While it isn't always immediately clear whether a borrower is experiencing temporary difficulties or is unable to repay its debts, Greece was undeniably insolvent in May 2010. By that I mean, it was extremely implausible that the future path of Greek economic growth and interest rates would permit the government to raise enough tax revenues to repay its debts in full – and the common assumption that it was insolvent made a recovery impossible. The government had a huge stock of debt – 115 per cent of GDP in 2009 (subsequently revised up to 130 per cent) – to which it was rapidly adding: its deficit that year was 13.5 per cent of GDP (revised up to 15.5 per cent shortly after the EU-IMF programme was agreed).[137] The country as a whole had huge foreign debts – they exceeded the value of its overseas assets by 86 per cent of GDP – and it was adding to them fast: its current-account deficit was 11 per cent of GDP.[138]

Even under the heroically optimistic assumptions of the initial EU-IMF programme for Greece – which involved lending the government €110 billion, nearly half the country's national income that year, conditional on massive front-loaded austerity, root-and-branch economic reforms and a strategy to backstop the banking system – public debt was forecast to soar to 155–160 per cent of GDP as tax rises and spending cuts deepened the recession. The plan envisaged a fiscal squeeze of 18 per cent of GDP over 2010–14. It included a brutal front-loaded tightening of 8 per cent of GDP in the first year – four times greater than George Osborne's austerity measures in Britain in 2011–12![139] But it was predictable that massive austerity would plunge the economy into a much deeper recession than the programme assumed, causing debt to skyrocket as tax revenues collapsed, social spending soared and the economy shrank. It was also obvious that the return of "confidence" on which a private-sector investment boom – and hence a speedy recovery – was predicated wouldn't happen in a depressed and hidebound economy with a broken banking system and a huge debt overhang. The programme devised by the Troika – the

---

137   Excluding interest payments, Greece's primary deficit was 10.5 per cent of GDP.

138   International Monetary Fund, Greece 2013 Article IV Consultation, IMF Country Report No. 13/154 http://www.imf.org/external/pubs/ft/scr/2013/cr13154.pdf

139   European Commission Directorate General for Economic and Financial Affairs, "The Economic Adjustment Programme for Greece", *European Economy* Occasional Papers 61, May 2010 http://ec.europa.eu/economy_finance/publications/occasional_paper/2010/pdf/ocp61_en.pdf

European Commission, the ECB and the IMF, who together were put in charge of Greece's destiny – forecast that the economy would shrink by 5½ per cent between 2009 and 2012; it actually slumped by 17 per cent.

IMF officials were convinced that Greece was insolvent, but were overruled by their boss, Dominique Strauss Kahn, who had ambitions to be the next French president and did not want to confront the eurozone policy establishment or impose losses on French banks. After Strauss Kahn was forced out by a sex scandal in 2011, he was replaced by Christine Lagarde, who has heeded her officials' advice more. In 2013 the IMF officially recognised that Greece's debts ought to have been restructured in May 2010 (and that EU officials were both inexperienced and incompetent). I said so at the time, not least when I first met President Barroso in Brussels on 15 October 2010, as well as in print.[140]

In case you aren't persuaded by the numbers, remember that a government's solvency depends on its ability to raise taxes, which ultimately depends on its citizens' willingness to pay them. Had Greece been a country where default was perceived as a national disgrace and where its billionaire ship-owners felt such a sense of civic duty that they (and poorer citizens) were willing to buy "patriotic" bonds at low interest rates and pay a solidarity wealth tax for many years to help right the Greek ship, it might have been different. But in a country with a corrupt and dysfunctional government, where the rich and powerful often avoid tax entirely, where the poor people who can't avoid paying it rightly perceive it as theft, and where paying more taxes to repay debts incurred to stuff the pockets of politicians and the other parasites who fed off the system – worse, debts owed largely

---

140   Philippe Legrain, "This is primarily a crisis of the banking system, not the euro", Eurointelligence, 11 January 2011 http://www.philippelegrain.com/this-is-primarily-a-crisis-of-the-banking-system-not-the-euro/

to foreign creditors – therefore seemed not patriotic but stupid, it was obvious that Greece was insolvent. Only a liar or an idiot with a spreadsheet would say otherwise.[141]

Spreading panic, not calming it

Some senior EU officials were clueless enough to believe, even much later, that Greece could pull through without a debt write-off. Cannier ones will point to many other things that went wrong after May 2010 – economic reforms stalled, political turmoil erupted, the wider crisis worsened – which they can blame for Greece's programme going off track. But that won't wash: even if those other bad things hadn't happened, the original programme assumptions were unrealistic. The final fallback is to argue that even if Greece was insolvent in 2010, writing down its debts at the time would have been catastrophic – for the rest of the eurozone. As European Commission spokesman Simon O'Connor (a decent guy whose job is to act as the mouthpiece for others) said in response to the June 2013 IMF report arguing that Greece's debts should have been written down in 2010: "The report argues that an upfront debt restructuring in 2010 would have been desirable. We fundamentally disagree. The report ignores the interconnected nature of the euro area member states. Private debt

---

141 According to calculations in February 2011 by Bruegel, a Brussels-based think tank, the primary surplus required to reduce Greece's debt/GDP ratio from the 2014 level to 60 per cent by 2034 was 8.4 per cent of GDP under optimistic assumptions about growth and interest rates and 14.5 per under more cautious assumptions. Yet over the past fifty years, no OECD country (except Norway, thanks to its huge oil surpluses), has sustained a primary surplus above 6 per cent of GDP, so it is wholly unrealistic to believe Greece could. See Zsolt Darvas, Christophe Gouardo, Jean Pisani-Ferry, André Sapir, "A comprehensive approach to the euro-area crisis: Background calculations", Bruegel, 24 February 2011, Table 8, Panel B

restructuring would have certainly risked systemic contagion at that stage."[142] Translation: it would have created a Lehman-style panic.

Assume, for the sake of argument, that a Greek debt restructuring really would have created a wider panic. It is still breathtakingly cynical – some would say callous – to, in effect, lock the Greek people in a debtors' prison for the "greater good". If you're going to do that, you owe it to the prisoners to at least provide them some comfort. You might lend them money on concessional terms and go easy on austerity until the situation has calmed down enough for them to be released from their confinement. When the time finally comes to forgive some of their debts, you owe it to them to be generous and release them from prison once and for all. But the EU not only lent to Greece on punitive terms and inflicted massive suffering on ordinary Greeks, greatly aggravating their problems. It has also prolonged the misery by so far failing to reduce Greece's debts enough to make them "sustainable" – that is, able to be repaid in full.

In any case, the argument that a Greek restructuring would have caused a Lehman-style panic is misconceived. There is a world of difference between the chaotic collapse of a sizeable, complex, global investment bank to which countless counterparties may (or may not) be exposed and the orderly restructuring of the smaller, simpler debt of a government in south-east Europe to which far fewer counterparties were exposed, more transparently. While Lehman collapsed chaotically overnight, the FDIC closed down hundreds of other banks in an orderly fashion, without Lehman-style consequences. Offering Greece's creditors new bonds of lesser value that were likely to be repaid in full in exchange for old ones that the government was incapable of repaying (and markets were pricing as such) would have given them much

---

142 http://www.reuters.com/article/2013/06/06/eu-imf-greece-idUSL5N0EI1XF20130606

greater certainty.[143] Nor can one compare a global investment bank's very complex balance sheet and huge derivatives exposures to many counterparties, to the Greek government's much simpler liabilities, with a relatively small amount of credit default swaps (contracts that insure holders against a borrower's default) written on them. Yes, after a Greek restructuring, some banks would have needed recapitalising, but since markets were already pricing in a write-down, their balance sheets were impaired in any case. Last but not least, whereas investors didn't know which banks were exposed to Lehman and so lost confidence in all of them, exposures to Greek debt were known after the first EU bank stress tests in 2009 and could have been publicised. Far from sparking panic, then, tackling the debt overhang could have reduced uncertainty and therefore stabilised markets.[144]

Eurozone policymakers' handling of Greece was so inept that they spread panic rather than quelling it. Pretending that Greece was solvent didn't fool investors. Claiming that "the need to safeguard financial stability in the euro area as a whole" required this pretence didn't reassure investors; it terrified them. Their train of thought was

---

143 The new bonds could have delayed or lower interest payments, delayed or reduced principal repayments or some combination of these four, to suit investors' preferences. They could also be backed by collateral and sweetened with GDP warrants to provide some upside.

144 The argument that restructuring Greek debt would undermine or even destroy the euro was also made. Yet previous experience of restructurings in monetary unions in the Caribbean and Africa suggests otherwise. Three of the six members of the East Caribbean Currency Union underwent a default and debt restructuring in recent years, without putting the ECCU at risk. Nor did the 1998 and 2009 restructurings of Cote d'Ivoire, the largest economy of the West African Economic and Monetary Union, endanger the Central African Franc. According to the IMF, "there is no evidence that past restructurings of individual member countries threatened the viability of the currency union." See Udaibir Das, Michael Papaioannou, and Christoph Trebesch, "Sovereign Debt Restructurings 1950 - 2010: Literature Survey, Data, and Stylized Facts", IMF Working Paper 12/203, 1 August 2012

predictable: If policymakers are lying to us about Greece, what else might they be hiding? If the financial stability of the eurozone as a whole is at a risk, which country is next? Who is exposed to them? And so on.

Unsurprisingly, the bond yields of vulnerable governments spiked after the Greek bailout. Irish ten-year yields leapt from 4.66 per cent on 11 May 2010 to 5.72 per cent on 17 June. Since German ten-year yields fell from 2.95 per cent to 2.67 per cent over the same period, the spread between Irish yields and German ones – a measure of the perceived riskiness of Irish bonds – widened by 134 basis points (1.34 percentage points) to 305 basis points. Portuguese and Spanish spreads widened by a similar amount.[145] Yields in Italy, whose banking system and economy had avoided the bubble, remained stable at around 4 per cent, despite its very high level of government debt.[146] This initial impact greatly understates the destabilising impact of the many twists and turns of the Greek saga over the next few years, all of which followed on from this original mistake. Far from rescuing Greece and containing the crisis, the EU-IMF programme heaped misery on ordinary Greeks and spread panic.

Another bank bailout

The main beneficiaries of the Greek bailout were the foreign banks and investors that foolishly lent too much too cheaply to the Greek government and should have suffered the consequences of their mistakes. At the end of March 2010, foreign banks owned €68.7 billion of Greek government bonds; French banks had a €20 billion exposure,

---

145 Portugal's yields rose from 4.82 per cent to 5.71 per cent over the same period, with spreads widening by 112 basis points to 304. Spanish 10-year yields jumped from 3.97 per cent to 4.84 per cent, with spreads widening by 116 basis points to 218.

146 Figures are from ft.com, data archive, bonds and rates, ten-year government spreads. The FT sources the data from Thomson Reuters.

German ones €17.2 billion.[147] So if Greece had written off half its debt in early 2010, French banks would have lost €10 billion – and perhaps more, since their overall exposure to the Greek economy was much greater.[148] No wonder Trichet, Strauss-Kahn and Sarkozy were so adamant that the pretence of Greece's solvency had to be maintained. By the end of 2011, foreign banks had slashed their exposure to Greek government bonds to €17.6 billion.[149] French banks had cut their exposure to €5 billion, German ones to €5.2 billion.[150] Thanks to the EU-IMF loans, banks were able to sell their Greek bonds at a much higher price than otherwise, received interest on all their remaining ones and were paid in full for those that came due. The Greek bailout, in effect, was the second hold-up of the biggest bank heist of all time.

This opaque, indirect bank bailout will end up costing European taxpayers much more than an immediate debt write-down would have done. Had Greece's debt been restructured in early 2010, the losses might have led some French and German banks to seek further

---

147 Other (non-Greek) eurozone banks had a €20.1 billion exposure to Greek government debt at the end of March 2010. US banks' exposure was €4 billion and UK ones' €2.7 billion.

148 Since French banks had an overall exposure to the Greek economy of €82.9 billion, German banks €37.9 billion and other non-Greek eurozone banks €43.3 billion, they might have suffered even greater knock-on losses from a Greek write-down. US banks had a total exposure to Greece of €30.6 billion and UK ones €12.3 billion. Bank for International Settlements, *Quarterly Review*, September 2010. Foreign exposures to Greece, Ireland, Portugal and Spain, by bank nationality, end-Q1 2010, converted from US dollars to euros at exchange rate on 31 March 2010 of €1 = \$1.3468.

149 Bank for International Settlements, international bank claims, consolidated – ultimate risk basis, exposure to Greek public sector, by nationality, converted at €1 =\$1.2952 on 31 December 2011

150 US banks' exposure to Greek government bonds had fallen to €0.6 billion and UK ones' to €1.4 billion.

aid from the French and German governments. Since Sarkozy and Merkel were committed to propping up "their" banks, those banks doubtless would have obtained an injection of public money. That is regrettable, but at least it would have been a transparent transfer for which Sarkozy and Merkel could be held accountable. It would also have worked out cheaper than continuing to lend on an open-ended basis to an insolvent Greece – loans that will ultimately have to be written off. As we shall see, Greece's debts have soared since 2010, because the debt overhang and the massive austerity have crippled the economy. But they are now mostly owed to the EU and the IMF. In effect, Greece's creditors have been bailed out by eurozone taxpayers, whose governments have tried to pass on as much of the burden as possible to Greek taxpayers, but who will ultimately have to bear much of it themselves.

The political impact of the Greek bailout has been poisonous. German taxpayers fume that their taxes are being lent to supposedly lazy, greedy and corrupt Greeks who would doubtless not repay them. Hard-pressed Greeks, suffering one of the worst depressions of all time, lash out at Germany for the harsh austerity it has imposed. Because Greece's debts remain too high, future debt relief will involve the very transfers to Greek taxpayers that Germans resent. German taxpayers should not be angry at Greeks for this: they should be furious at the banks and other creditors that were bailed out and at Trichet, Strauss-Kahn and the other policymakers who made it happen – including Merkel for acquiescing to it.

Far from safeguarding the stability of the euro, the Greek tragedy has torn the EU apart. It has shredded support for the EU, because Greeks' fervent desire to be European has been abused to impose iniquitous terms on them. It has created hysteria among Germans that foreigners are trying to grab their money, making them suspicious of risk-sharing arrangements – not transfers – to safeguard the euro's long-term stability, as Chapter 6 will discuss. And because breaking the no-bailout rule made the German government feel like it was potentially on the hook for the debts of southern European governments, it has demanded ever tighter EU fiscal rules to try to restore control, undermining democracy and support for the EU.

The Greek fiasco was financially destabilising, economically calamitous, politically polarising and morally despicable – and the worst was yet to come. It also determined eurozone policymakers' diagnosis of the crisis and their policy response. In essence, they decided that all of southern Europe was like Greece and that the solution was to be more like Germany.

False narrative

It won't surprise you that the ECB in Frankfurt, the European Commission in Brussels and Angela Merkel's government in Berlin don't blame themselves for the destabilisation of the eurozone after Greece's public debt problems emerged in late 2009. Instead, they blame the crisis primarily on a lack of discipline in certain member countries where the government borrowed too much and businesses failed to keep a tight lid on costs. As a result, they argue, the eurozone ended up with ballooning public debts in southern Europe and large divergences in "competitiveness" between north and south.[151] When the crisis struck, markets were apparently no longer willing to finance the resulting budget and current-account deficits. Hence the flawed crisis response that eurozone leaders intoned like a mantra from early 2010 onwards: fiscal consolidation (austerity) to restore growth plus structural reforms (mostly wage cuts) to boost "competitiveness".

Listen to Wolfgang Schäuble, Germany's finance minister, in June 2010: "To the question of what caused the recent turmoil in

---

151 "Competitiveness" is a nebulous and misleading concept, as will be discussed later in the chapter.

the eurozone, there is one simple answer: excessive budget deficits in many European countries."[152] Or in October 2011, by which time policy-induced panic was raging in the eurozone: "Governments' public debts and deficits are too high because their public sectors spend too much, get too little and their economies lack competitiveness. That is why immediate fiscal consolidation and structural reforms in highly indebted countries are of the essence."[153] Or, if you can bear it, read the conclusions of the regular meetings of EU and eurozone leaders from 2010 on, which echo that message in terse language.[154]

Since Berlin's argument that governments borrowed too much in the pre-crisis years is an implicit criticism of the European Commission, which was meant to enforce the EU's fiscal rules, the Brussels twist on this narrative emphasises the fact that in 2003 and 2004 France and Germany drove a coach and horses through the Stability and Growth Pact in order to escape censure for their profligacy at the time. In both cases, though, Berlin, Brussels and Frankfurt absolve themselves of blame and single out southern sinners instead. While this official narrative has been revised somewhat since 2010 as eurozone policymakers have slowly grasped the real problems, it remains prevalent, not least in Germany. As Chancellor Merkel said upon her re-election in September 2013, "What we have done, everyone else can do." Crucially, this flawed analysis determined policy decisions in Acts Two and Three of the crisis and continues to shape them now.

---

152   http://www.bundesfinanzministerium.de/Content/EN/Reden/2010/2010-06-24-handelsblatt.html

153   http://www.bundesfinanzministerium.de/Content/EN/Reden/2011/2011-10-17-london.html

154   http://www.european-council.europa.eu/council-meetings/conclusions

Greece was an exception

The big mistake that Berlin, Brussels and Frankfurt made was to think Greece's specific problems applied more generally. The Greek government did borrow too much – and lied about it – albeit abetted by financial markets that judged lending to Greece to be as safe as lending to Germany, a mistake validated by the ECB's collateral rules and the Basel capital-adequacy rules, both of which deemed Greek bonds to be "risk-free". For other crisis victims, the picture looks very different. In the pre-crisis years, Ireland averaged a big budget surplus between 1999 and 2007 and Spain a slender one.[155] Italy's public borrowing averaged less than the Stability and Growth Pact limit of 3 per cent of GDP.[156] Portugal was twice brought to book for running an excessive deficit and then deemed to have got its fiscal house in order – but still suffered a government debt crisis.[157] In contrast, the two governments that were let off the hook for their excessive borrowing in 2003 and 2004 – France and Germany – have been largely unscathed. Since Greece is the only crisis victim that indulged in excessive public borrowing that went unpunished during the pre-crisis years, stricter enforcement of the EU's fiscal rules would not have prevented the crisis.

Turning to public debt, Ireland's and Spain's was very low in 2007, the year the financial crisis struck, as Chapter 1 explained.[158] Portugal's

---

155   Personal calculations from European Commission, AMECO database, general government net lending/borrowing, per cent of GDP at market prices. Ireland averaged a surplus of 1.6 per cent of GDP between 1999 and 2007, Spain a surplus of 0.2 per cent of GDP.

156   *Ibid.* Italy averaged a deficit of 2.9 per cent of GDP.

157   Portugal was disciplined for an excessive deficit in 2002, deemed to be in compliance with EU rules by 2004, and then again subject to the excessive deficit procedure from 2005 to 2008.

158   European Commission, AMECO database, general government consolidated gross debt as a percentage of GDP at market prices. Ireland's was 25 per cent of GDP, Spain's 36 per cent.

was only fractionally higher than Germany's.[159] So neither deficits nor debt levels are good predictors of the countries that suffered a sovereign debt crisis. Italy's admission to the euro was green-lighted in 1997 even though it had a public debt of 122 per cent of GDP, but over the following decade its debt fell by 19 percentage points. So one can argue that Italy shouldn't have been admitted in the first place, but not that it ran up huge debts once it joined.

For the most part, then, the large budget deficits and high public debts in the eurozone in early 2010 were consequences of the crisis – the counterpart of the collapse in private spending and the result of bank bailouts – not the causes of it; figures for various countries are in the footnotes.[160] Clearly, government borrowing needed to be brought down eventually, but at the time it was propping up demand, preventing a depression. Thus except in Greece and to a lesser extent Portugal, it was largely a symptom of the crisis, not a cause. But instead of tackling the root causes of the crisis in the banking sector and the resulting build-up of excessive private-sector debt, policymakers made a series of devastating policy mistakes that made matters much worse, not least a lurch towards collective front-loaded austerity,

---

159   Portugal's was 68 per cent in 2007, Germany's 65 per cent.

160   By 2009, the year when Greece's debt problems emerged, when economies had plunged into deep recession after the bubble burst and Lehman Brothers collapsed, Greece had a deficit of 15.6 per cent of GDP, Ireland 13.9 per cent, Spain 11.2 per cent, Portugal 10.2 per cent and Italy 5.5 per cent. At the same time, France's was 7.5 per cent, Germany's 3.1 per cent – and Britain's 11.5 per cent. European Commission, AMECO database, general government net lending/borrowing, per cent of GDP at market prices. As for public debt, it was 129.7 per cent of GDP in Greece, 116.4 per cent in Italy, 83.7 per cent in Portugal, 64.8 per cent in Ireland and 53.9 per cent in Spain. At the same time, Belgium's was 95.7 per cent, France's 79.2 per cent, Germany's 74.5 per cent – and Britain's 67.8 per cent. European Commission, AMECO database, general government consolidated gross debt as a percentage of GDP at market prices.

as Chapter 3 explains. Having sparked panic in government bond markets, policymakers wrongly interpreted rising yields as signalling Greek-style debt problems that required ever greater austerity until finally the ECB halted the panic in 2012.

The ant and the grasshopper

What about the "competitiveness" argument? At a conference in Brussels in May 2012, Thomas Steffen, one of Schäuble's deputies at Germany's finance ministry, illustrated Berlin's view by referring to the fable of *The Ant and the Grasshopper*.[161] A grasshopper has spent the summer singing while the ant worked to store up food for winter. When winter arrives, the grasshopper finds itself dying of hunger and begs the ant for food, offering to repay it with interest by the summer. The ant asks "What were you doing all summer?" to which the grasshopper replies that it was singing. "Very well, then dance now." Steffen intended to contrast German prudence with Mediterranean recklessness. But ironically he instead highlighted why Berlin's view of the crisis is incorrect. For a start, the comparison is economically illiterate, because "prudent" German ants do not literally pile up surplus food for future use, but rather lend out their surplus savings to "reckless" Spanish grasshoppers. It is impossible for everyone in a financial system to be a (net) saver at once – ants need grasshoppers – and catastrophic if everyone tries to be. The comparison also highlights how German officials see the crisis as a morality play, with virtuous Germans rewarded and irresponsible southerners punished – but that is not true either. German bankers are at least as culpable as Spanish households – if not more so. In any case, Steffen's black-and-white morality is a poor guide to economic policy. Last but not least, it is not even true that Germany has excess savings because Germans are prudent: rather it is mostly because German wages have been

---

161   Brussels Economic Forum, 31 May 2012

artificially held down, boosting corporate surpluses, while investment has plunged, as we shall see.

"Competitiveness" is a nebulous concept which means different things to different people. But when Schäuble and other German officials talk about it, they tend to mean three ant-like qualities: wage restraint, strong export growth and a current-account surplus (being a net lender to foreigners). They associate these with the reforms of Merkel's predecessor, Gerhard Schröder, to Germany's hidebound labour markets between 2003 and 2005. Conversely, "uncompetitive" grasshoppers pay themselves too much, splurge on imports, price their exports out of world markets, run current-account deficits and are thus net borrowers from foreigners. As Schäuble put it, "In the 'boom' phase, several of its [the eurozone's] members let labour grow expensive and their share of world trade shrink. As the bust came, jobs vanished and public finances deteriorated."[162] Hence the Berlin-Brussels prescription: tighten your budget belts and cut wages to curb imports and boost exports, so as to pile up surpluses rather than deficits. In other words, be more like Germany.

Rewind to 1998, the year before the euro's launch. At the time, Italy had a current-account surplus, as did Ireland.[163] Spain was in balance. Greece had a small deficit (1.3 per cent of GDP) and Portugal a hefty one (5.3 per cent). So by that measure southern Europe was "competitive" at the time, except for Greece and Portugal. Germany too was slightly "uncompetitive": it had a deficit of 0.7 per cent. Fast forward to 2007, just before the crisis struck. By then, all of southern Europe had a very large current-account deficit – 5.5 per cent of GDP in Ireland, 8.9 per cent in Portugal, 9.6 per cent in Spain and 15.4 per

162   http://www.ft.com/cms/s/0/e88c842a-1c67-11e3-a8a3-00144feab7de.html

163   Italy's current-account surplus was 2 per cent of GDP, Ireland's 1.7 per cent.

cent in Greece – except Italy.[164] Germany, in contrast, had a whopping €183 billion current-account surplus – equivalent to 7.5 per cent of its GDP and 2.1 per cent of the eurozone's.[165]

These figures are indisputable. But why did these deficits emerge? Did wages rise too fast in southern Europe, making their exports uncompetitive, as the Germans argue? Or was southern Europe swamped by capital inflows, notably from Germany, mostly in the form of bank lending that financed property bubbles in Spain and Ireland, consumer loans in Portugal and government borrowing in Greece? Let's look at the data.[166]

Were wage increases in southern Europe excessive in the pre-crisis years? Berlin and Brussels point out that in euro terms the cost of the labour needed to produce a unit of output soared in southern Europe in the pre-crisis years, while it fell in Germany – and blame southern Europe for letting their nominal unit labour costs get out of line with Germany's (see figures in footnotes).[167] But those figures are misleading and their analysis is flawed.

If workers' pay had risen faster than their productivity – and thus grown excessively – the share of national income going to labour would have risen. In fact, far from workers in southern Europe

---

164 Eurostat, net lending/borrowing, percentage of GDP, annual. Code: nama_inc_c Italy's deficit was a mere 1.2 per cent of GDP, lower than France's

165 Eurozone GDP in 2007 was €8,902.8 million, Germany's was €2,428.5 million

166 See also José Luis Diaz Sanchez and Aristomene Varoudakis, "Tracking the causes of Eurozone external imbalances: New evidence", Vox.eu, 6 February 2014. http://www.voxeu.org/article/causes-eurozone-external-imbalances

167 European Commission, AMECO database, nominal unit labour costs: total economy (ratio of compensation per employee to real GDP per person employed). Between 1998 and 2007, nominal unit labour costs rose by 22.4 per cent in Italy, 25.7 per cent in Greece, 27 per cent in Portugal, 30.7 per cent in Spain and 34.1 per cent in Ireland, while they declined by 1.1 per cent in Germany. For comparison, figures are 9.9 per cent for Finland, 15.2 per cent for Belgium and 17.0 per cent for France.

making businesses uncompetitive by grabbing a bigger share of the pie, the share of national income paid out in wages fell in every southern European country, dramatically so in Spain.[168] So if someone was being greedy, it generally wasn't workers. Nor does the fault lie with governments for piling additional costs on top of wage rises: changes in real unit labour costs mirror those in the wage share of GDP.[169] Most of the divergence in economy-wide nominal unit labour costs is because inflation in southern Europe was higher, not due to a lack of wage discipline.

A big chunk of the divergence, though, is due to excessive German belt-tightening. Astonishingly, German wages not only failed to keep pace with productivity gains in the pre-crisis years, they actually fell. After inflation, Germans earned 4 per cent less in 2007 than they did

---

168 European Commission, AMECO database, adjusted wage share: total economy: as percentage of GDP at current factor cost (Compensation per employee as percentage of GDP at factor cost per person employed.) In Italy the labour share of GDP fell from 63.0 per cent in 1998 to 62.1 per cent in 2007. In Ireland it edged down from 57.7 per cent to 57.3 per cent. In Portugal, it declined from 66.8 per cent to 65.9 per cent. In Greece, it fell from 64.5 per cent to 60.4 per cent. And in Spain, it slumped from 65.8 per cent to 61.6 per cent. Over the same period, the labour share of GDP fell from 62.6 per cent to 60.7 per cent in Finland, from 66.3 per cent to 65.6 per cent in France, from 70 per cent to 67.1 per cent in Belgium, from 66.9 per cent to 64.3 per cent in the Netherlands and from 68 per cent to 62 per cent in Austria. In Britain, it edged up from 69.8 per cent to 70.3 per cent.

169 European Commission, AMECO database, real unit labour costs: total economy. Irish workers' productivity gains outstripped increases in labour costs by a total of 2.4 per cent between 1998 and 2007. Real unit labour costs also fell in Italy, by 0.8 per cent, by 3.1 per cent in Portugal, 4.9 per cent in Greece and 6.9 per cent in Spain. In Finland real unit labour costs fell 2.3 per cent between 1998 and 2007, in France by 0.4 per cent, in Belgium by 3.2 per cent, in the Netherlands by 4.2 per cent and in Austria by 8.1 per cent. In Germany they fell by 7.6 per cent. In Britain, they rose by 1.5 per cent.

in 1999.[170] Germans often argue that this fall in wages is a good thing, because after the post-reunification boom in the early 1990s wages had got too high, because global competition, not least from China, has increased, and because lower wages have boosted employment. There is some validity to those arguments; after all, at the turn of the century high-cost, high-unemployment Germany was widely written off as the "sick man of Europe". But while some wage restraint may have been necessary, Germany has overdone it. The share of German output paid out in wages plunged from 66.8 per cent in 2000 to a historic low of 61.2 per cent in 2007.[171] This excessive wage *Disziplin* is not desirable – and to the extent that this has caused a problem for southern Europe, Germany is to blame.

It is a fallacy that countries ought to maximise their "competitiveness" by holding down wages. By that false logic, it is unreasonable – even dangerous – to expect Germany to become less "competitive" by paying Germans higher wages commensurate with their increased productivity. How would it help southern Europe, it is argued, if Germany abased itself to their level? No – everyone else ought to be more like Germany. As Schäuble himself put it: "Yes, we have to avoid overly large imbalances between member states. But no, this cannot take the form of successful countries voluntarily limiting their competitiveness. The only workable course is for those countries in

170   Federal Statistical Office of Germany, index of real earnings, January 2010 = 100. Index for 1999 and 2000 is 102.1; index for 2007 is 98.2; index for 2012 is 101.7.   https://www.destatis.de/DE/ZahlenFakten/GesamtwirtschaftUmwelt/ VerdiensteArbeitskosten/RealloehneNettoverdienste/RealloehneNettoverdienste. html For a fuller discussion see DIW Berlin, "Real Wages in Germany: Numerous Years of Decline", No 28/209, Volume 5, 23 October 2009. http://www.diw.de/ documents/publikationen/73/diw_01.c.342371.de/diw_wr_2009-28.pdf

171   European Commission, AMECO database, adjusted wage share: total economy: as percentage of GDP at factor cost (Compensation per employee as percentage of GDP at factor cost per person employed).

the eurozone who are somewhat weaker, to become stronger. We can help them, but we cannot do their job. One does not resolve one's own problems of competitiveness by asking others to become less competitive."[172] But Schäuble's argument is not just logically flawed – it is impossible for all countries to pile up surpluses, since for every lender there must be a borrower – it is dangerous.

From the standpoint of the owner of a German business, trying to keep wage costs to a minimum may make sense. But for society as a whole, "wage costs" are not a bad thing that needs to be minimised. On the contrary: insofar as they are justified by productivity, wages ought to be as high as possible. Countries are not companies. Policymakers should be seeking to raise living standards, not to maximise "competitiveness".

If policymakers aim to maximise "competitiveness" by squeezing wages, they are in effect seeking to maximise corporate surpluses at the expense of people's living standards, which is cruel and perverse. If wages are depressed, consumer spending will be curbed too – unless workers are willing and able to borrow more. If consumer spending is weak, companies that serve the domestic market are likely to invest less, further depressing domestic demand. So an economy where wages are squeezed must rely on exports to grow – and since consumer demand is weak, imports are likely to be low too. So such a mercantilist economy will tend to run large trade surpluses: it will earn more from foreigners in exports than it pays out in imports. That, in turn, means that it must lend those surplus savings to foreigners. In Europe, this tends to happen through the banking system. If German banks lend too much money to economies in southern Europe, this is likely to result in inflation – pushing up nominal unit labour costs. If German banks lend that money badly, not only will German savings

---

172 http://www.bundesfinanzministerium.de/Content/EN/Reden/2011/2011-09-27-berlin.html

be wasted, an economic and financial crisis will eventually occur when the mistakes are realised. Sound familiar? Between early 2002 and early 2008, German banks' total lending to eurozone countries for which the BIS has statistics soared by more than €500 billion, from €580 billion in March 2002 to €1,092 billion in March 2008. Lending directly to southern Europe soared by €352 billion, from €225 billion to €577 billion.[173]

To recap, it was German wage restraint, not wage growth in southern Europe, that was excessive, and inflation, partly due to capital inflows from Germany, drove an even bigger wedge between them. Let's now go one step further and question whether it is really true that southern Europe became "uncompetitive" in the pre-crisis years. In other words, were southern European exports priced out of global markets or not?[174]

Uncompetitive?

Imagine a German company, call it Strengen Gmbh, which was sickly in 1998 but has since cut its wage costs to the bone. Compare it to a Spanish one, call it Siesta S.A., which was doing fine in 1998 but has since squeezed wages less and has also been hit by higher inflation. Strengen likes to slate Siesta for slacking, but is that necessarily true? If Siesta was super-competitive in 1998, it may simply have become less so over the subsequent nine years. Siesta also got a boost when borrowing costs fell at the euro's launch, whereas Strengen's

---

173   Bank for International Settlements, International bank claims consolidated, immediate borrower basis (Figures on an ultimate risk basis, which are only available from March 2005 on, are identical). Southern Europe is Greece, Ireland, Italy, Portugal, Spain

174   See also Guillaume Gaulier, Daria Taglioni, Vincent Vicard, "Tradable sectors in Eurozone periphery countries did not underperform in the 2000s", Vox.eu, 19 July 2012. http://www.voxeu.org/article/tradable-sectors-eurozone-periphery

cost of capital was already low. Since inflation in Spain was subsequently higher than in Germany, Siesta even benefited from negative real interest rates, whereas Strengen had to pay higher, positive ones. If Siesta was wise, it used this cheap capital to invest in fancy new machinery that economised on labour. Thus even though Siesta's labour costs rose faster than Strengen's, its overall costs may not have risen as fast. Even if its costs did rise faster, Siesta might have come up with snazzy new products, more appealing branding or better after-care service for which its customers are willing to pay a premium. Strengen should know all about that: when the Deutsche Mark was revalued in the 1960s and 1970s, it continued to boost sales because its high-quality products were such a hot ticket.

Siesta might in fact be competitive after all – but lumping it together with a bunch of underperforming companies might obscure that. Think of America's consumer-electronics industry: overall, it is not globally competitive, but one company – Apple – is extremely so. The same applies in Spain, where companies such as Inditex, which owns Zara and other fast-fashion clothing stores, are global superstars, while many smaller companies are laggards. Clearly, the Spanish economy would perform better if the inefficient firms improved (or closed), but it might still be a successful exporter thanks to that handful of superstars.

Looking at an economy-wide average, which also includes the public sector and companies that scarcely compete with foreigners, such as local restaurants and hairdressers, is even more misleading.[175] Imagine the pay of Irish civil servants doubles without their productivity increasing. Economy-wide unit labour costs will rise. But the picture in the export sector may be very different. While nominal unit labour costs across the Irish economy soared by 34.1 per cent across

---

175 They can be traded, of course, to the extent that tourists or visiting business-people buy a haircut or restaurant meal.

the whole economy between 1998 and 2007, apparently undermining "competitiveness", in the manufacturing sector, they fell by 3.5 per cent over the same period.[176]

How, then, have southern European firms actually fared in global markets? According to the simplistic headline figures used by the European Commission and the German government, Spain became "uncompetitive" in the pre-crisis years. Yet between 1998 and 2007, a period when China was conquering market share from nearly everyone, Spain's share of global exports remained stable, with a dip from 2.35 per cent in 1998 to 2.13 per cent in 2000, followed by a rebound to 2.26 per cent.[177] Greece, a supposedly "uncompetitive" basket case, increased its share of world exports by half over that period, from 0.26 per cent to 0.39 per cent.[178] Ireland's export share edged up from 1.1 per cent to 1.2 per cent. Portugal's fell from 0.5 per cent to 0.43 per cent. By that metric, the economies that lost most ground in the pre-crisis years are France (whose share of world exports plunged from 5.31 per cent in 1997 to 4.02 per cent in 2007) and Italy (down from 4.54 per cent to 3.53 per cent) – as well as Britain, down from 5.54 per cent to 4.21 per cent. So the "competitiveness" story does have a semblance of truth for France, Italy and Portugal, but not for Spain, Greece or Ireland.

This fall in French, Italian and Portuguese export market share is due to a variety of reasons, but not excessive wage increases. One big

---

176 European Commission, AMECO database, nominal unit labour costs: manufacturing. Over the same period, nominal unit labour costs in manufacturing rose by 52.7 per cent in Greece, 19.9 per cent in Spain, 16.7 per cent in Italy and 10.5 per cent in Portugal, while they fell 15.7 per cent in Germany.

177 Eurostat, Export market shares. Code: tipsex20. Euro nominal effective exchange rate available from http://www.ecb.int/stats/exchange/effective/html/index.en.html

178 *Ibid.*

reason is the rapid rise of China and other emerging economies such as India, Brazil and Turkey. Competition from China hit the industries that Italy and Portugal specialise in, notably lower-end manufacturing. Unfortunately, those countries have not done enough to shift towards more sophisticated, higher-value production. Germany, though, has been lucky. Its exports to China have soared, not because its companies have suddenly become more nimble and innovative, but because it happened to specialise in the capital goods and engineering products that China needed at that stage of its breakneck industrial development. It remains to be seen how well Germany will fare as China shifts to more consumption-driven and services-led growth. And as Chinese industrial exports become more sophisticated, will Germany be dynamic and adaptable enough to face up to Chinese competition? In the few areas where German businesses have faced the full brunt of Chinese competition, notably solar panels, they too have failed to up their game and have resorted to appeals for EU protectionism instead.

Despite the lucky boost from China, Germany's share of world exports actually edged down from 9.1 per cent in 1998 to 9.07 per cent in 2007 – with a dip to 7.98 per cent in 2000 followed by a rebound. This rebound overstates Germany's export performance because it coincides with the decision by many German firms to shift part of their production chain to countries in central and eastern Europe. For instance, cars made in Germany now contain many parts made in Slovakia, Hungary and elsewhere; when they are exported, the total value of the car is ascribed to Germany, when only part of it was made there. According to estimates by the OECD and the World Trade Organisation, the share of domestic value-added in German exports fell between 2000 and 2008, whereas it rose for Spain.[179] So

---

179   The domestic value-added content of German exports fell from 75.6 per cent in 2000 to 72.2 per cent in 2008; Spain's rose from 73 per cent to 75.1 per cent. http://www.oecd.org/sti/ind/TiVA_GERMANY_MAY_2013.pdf

the increase in the value-added of German exports – which is a better measure of success – was smaller than its export figures suggest, while the Spanish increase was larger. Remember too that Germany's export success has been inflated by artificially holding down wages, which doesn't make it richer. In short, the conventional view that Germany is "competitive" and Spain isn't is false.

This may seem like an extended diversion. But it is incredibly important because pundits pontificate, Schäuble and others make speeches and the European Commission dictates policy based on the premise that economies as a whole are "uncompetitive" and so need across-the-board wage cuts – when in fact their assumptions and therefore their conclusions are often spurious. It is neither desirable nor feasible for everyone to try to be like Germany. Unnecessarily slashing wages across southern Europe isn't just cruel; it is self-defeating, since it makes it even harder to pay back their large debts – and ultimately pushes them towards default. Rather, it is in the interests of both German workers and southern ones that German wages rise. Moreover, a sustained rise in living standards depends on productivity growth, not "competitiveness". So the real long-term issue for Europe is not that some economies are "uncompetitive", but rather that all of them are not dynamic and adaptable enough, as the dismal productivity figures in Chapter 1 highlighted.

To sum up: yes, people and policymakers in southern Europe are partly to blame for their own misfortune. Households shouldn't have borrowed so much. Governments should have done more to curb financial excesses and more to make their economies more dynamic and adaptable. But the official EU narrative that blames the crisis primarily on policy mistakes in southern Europe is incorrect. Only the Greek government (and to some extent the Portuguese one) borrowed too much in the pre-crisis years. Southern Europeans didn't pay themselves too much. The export flops were France, Italy and Portugal, not Greece, Spain or Ireland. The huge current-account deficits across southern Europe (except Italy) mostly reflect bad cross-border lending, notably by German banks, not a loss of "competitiveness". Last but not least, the devastating panic that was to tear apart the eurozone between 2010 and 2012 is mostly a result of disastrous mistakes and misguided priorities in Frankfurt, Brussels and Berlin. This chapter discussed the first two mistakes: backstopping the banks and pretending Greece was solvent. The third was the lurch towards austerity across the eurozone, which was ratcheted up as the panic spread, amplifying the doom loop with catastrophic consequences, as the next chapter explains.

3

THE AUSTERITY DELUSION

All pain, no gain

It is an error to think that fiscal austerity is a threat to growth.
Jean-Claude Trichet, president of the European
Central Bank, 2010[180]

The data also supports, in my view, the fundamentals of our crisis response: a policy mix where building a stability culture and pursuing structural reforms supportive of growth and jobs go hand in hand.
Olli Rehn, EU commissioner for economic and
financial affairs, 2013[181]

Where they make a desert, they call it peace.
Tacitus, 98 AD

---

180   http://www.ecb.int/press/key/date/2010/html/sp100713.en.html
181   http://blogs.ec.europa.eu/rehn/recovery-is-within-reach/

From the window of the office in Brussels where I worked for the past three years, you can see the brutalist Justus Lipsius building where EU leaders hold their regular summits. It is there, after feasting on fine food and wine, that they agreed in June 2010 that what Europe really needed as it struggled to recover from a devastating financial crisis was massive fiscal austerity. New boy David Cameron heartily concurred. Fortunately, the budget cuts spared the new £280 million Europa building – described as a "jewel box" by European Council President Herman Van Rompuy – being erected next door, where EU leaders will meet in future. Not to be outdone, that May Jean-Claude Trichet unveiled plans for a dazzling new ECB skyscraper in Frankfurt that would cost €850 million. "We must ensure that construction costs remain within the estimated budget," the ECB president intoned. Cost overruns have since swelled the budget to at least €1.2 billion.[182]

Elsewhere in Europe, the consequences of slashed budgets are evident. Hungry Spanish children faint at school.[183] Young people queue up with their kids at soup kitchens.[184] Middle-aged Portuguese women resort to washing clothes outdoors, rubbing the garments in cold water on an ancient stone sink.[185] Patients, many of them elderly, pile up on trolleys in a crammed hospital ward at Athens' biggest hospital.[186] Malaria has even made a return.[187] As German Chancellor Angela

---

182   http://www.nytimes.com/2012/09/21/business/global/for-the-euro-a-costly-shelter-from-the-storm.html: http://www.spiegel.de/international/business/cost-overruns-and-delays-plague-ecb-skyscraper-project-in-frankfurt-a-930352.html

183   http://www.thelocal.es/20131010/spains-starving-school-kids-shock-europe

184   http://www.aljazeera.com/indepth/features/2012/11/20121115125033836440.html

185   http://www.bbc.co.uk/news/business-24915845

186   http://www.enetenglish.gr/?i=news.en.article&id=1574

187   http://www.theatlantic.com/international/archive/2013/05/malaria-and-hiv-spike-as-greece-cuts-healthcare-spending/275836/

Merkel put it, southern European debtor countries must "atone for past sins".[188]

Those who really ought to atone for their mistakes are eurozone policymakers, not least Merkel herself. They misdiagnosed the Greek government's debt problems as symptomatic of a wider fiscal crisis and prescribed immediate, front-loaded, slash-and-burn austerity across the eurozone without tackling its real problems. Instead of curing the patients, these quack doctors made them sicker.

Lurching into collective austerity at a time when households didn't want to spend, banks didn't want to lend, companies didn't want to invest and foreigners weren't in a position to take up all the slack was bound to have disastrous consequences. At a time when both the private sector and the financial sector as a whole were desperately trying to reduce their debts, the public sector should rather have supported demand in a way that encourages the necessary economic adjustment – notably by combining reforms with productive investment – while setting out a credible framework for stabilising public finances in a fair and growth-friendly way after the crisis has passed.

Let me be clear, lest I am caricatured. I have no objection to limiting public borrowing in good times. On the contrary, it is not just financially prudent, it is democratically desirable: if politicians want to spend money, they ought to convince voters of the need to do so. Even in bad times, fiscal reform is a good thing: cutting wasteful spending while increasing investment that boosts future growth and tax revenues; raising taxes on harmful things, such as carbon emissions, while lowering those on helpful ones, notably work. The point is not to maintain particular budget items but to sustain demand and promote adjustment. So

---

188   http://www.nybooks.com/articles/archives/2013/aug/15/new-german-question/

my objection is not to the principle of cutting public borrowing, but rather to the timing, pace, nature and scope of austerity.

Austerity was premature because it began when economies were still weak – and as Keynes rightly said, "The boom, not the slump, is the right time for austerity at the Treasury."[189] Front-loading it magnified that mistake: for example, the original EU-IMF programme for Ireland in November 2010 involved a front-loaded squeeze of 3.8 per cent of GDP in 2011.[190] So too did the slash-and-burn tactics, with desirable investment bearing the biggest cuts, the poor often hit hardest and already high taxes on labour raised to punitive levels. Worse, all eurozone economies (and Britain) pursued austerity at once, amplifying the damage because one country's depressed domestic market was another's emaciated export market.

This headlong rush to austerity caused deep recessions in many countries, preventing households from reducing their debts, deterring companies from investing and pushing up public borrowing. Indeed, austerity has often been self-defeating, raising government debt as a share of GDP higher than it otherwise would have been. In other words, far from stabilising public finances, it destabilised them. Only after the ECB stepped in and austerity was eased did economies recover somewhat.

Costs and benefits of borrowing

Eurozone policymakers justified their lurch to austerity on four grounds: an absolutist view that government borrowing is bad and

---

189   John Maynard Keynes, *Collected Writings of John Maynard Keynes*, vol 21. Palgrave Macmillan: 1937

190   European Commission Directorate General for Economic and Financial Affairs, "The Economic Adjustment Programme for Ireland", *European Economy* Occasional Papers 76, February 2011 http://ec.europa.eu/economy_finance/publications/occasional_paper/2011/pdf/ocp76_en.pdf

so should be reduced; an empirical argument that reducing borrowing would boost "confidence" and thus restore economic growth; the assertion that curbing borrowing was "responsible" because government debts were too high; and a fallback that policymakers had no choice because markets forced their hand. None of these justifications stands up to scrutiny.

Government borrowing entails both costs – the direct cost of the finance itself and the wider ones it may impose on the rest of the economy – and risks, notably that it may provoke a crisis. Worse, its proceeds may be wasted: frittered away on pre-election handouts and tax cuts, squandered on the pet projects of egomaniac leaders, misdirected to the creditors of bailed out banks, and so on. But government borrowing can also provide big benefits – especially in a slump, when it is vital to prop up spending and enable households to reduce their own debts. Better still, a well-designed fiscal stimulus can put a floor under a collapsing economy, prevent it getting stuck in a rut and even shove it towards a healthy growth path. So the absolutist view in effect implies that you think public debt is so wicked that it should be reduced, and eventually eliminated, no matter what suffering this might cause.

Consider what would happen if governments always had to balance their budget, as some argue they ought to. In a recession, tax revenues fall and social spending rises as people lose their jobs, so a balanced-budget rule would entail governments raising taxes and cutting spending in bad times, exacerbating the downturn. Conversely, by cutting taxes and raising spending in good times, governments would add fuel to the boom. Thus a simple balanced-budget rule is destabilising: it amplifies both booms and busts. So the perceived benefit of preventing governments from borrowing must be set against the costs to households and businesses of a more unstable economy that lurches between feast and famine.

A more intelligent rule might stipulate that governments balance their budget over the economic cycle. That would give them leeway to borrow in downturns, while repaying debt in upswings. In effect, it would enable government to smooth consumption patterns – by propping up the spending of those who lose their jobs in a recession without immediately taxing those still in work more, for instance – thereby helping to stabilise the economy too. However, governments can quite easily game such rules and borrow more than they ought to by stretching their definition of the economic cycle (as Gordon Brown did when he was Britain's finance minister from 1997 to 2007).

Worse, governments may "bribe" voters by continually borrowing more to fund higher spending than they can raise in taxes, at the cost of ever-rising debt. The French government, for instance, has never run a surplus since 1974; gross public debt has risen from a post-war low of 20 per cent of GDP in 1980 to 90 per cent in 2012.[191] That is a compelling argument for creating flexible mechanisms (not rigid rules) to constrain future government borrowing – and a crisis may be the ideal time to muster political support to do so. But while it may be desirable for governments to commit to be more prudent in future, that doesn't imply they ought to curb their borrowing immediately in a recession, thereby aggravating it.

A further reason why governments might legitimately wish to borrow is to spread over time the cost of long-term investments, especially those that boost future growth and tax revenues. For example, if a government is planning to build a high-speed rail network that will provide benefits for decades to come, it makes sense to spread the costs over time. So an even smarter rule would enable governments to borrow to invest throughout the economic cycle. The danger, though, is that governments will reclassify all sorts of other spending

---

191   http://epp.eurostat.ec.europa.eu/cache/ITY_PUBLIC/2-22042013-AP/EN/2-22042013-AP-EN.PDF

as investment in order to borrow more – and that their investments will deliver poor returns. That is a good reason to try to find ways to keep governments honest – for example, by establishing an independent fiscal authority to monitor public accounts and budget decisions. Better still, to make a clear distinction between current spending and investment, governments ought to shift from drawing up public accounts on a cash basis – incomings and outgoings each year – to a balance-sheet basis. New Zealand's public accounts are a model in that respect: they distinguish clearly between revenues and spending that are recurring and those that are exceptional; they separate current spending from capital spending and other items, such as loans to students, that bring in future revenues; and they set out the overall impact on the government's assets and liabilities.[192] To try to improve the quality of investment decisions, governments can also delegate them to a public investment bank that operates at arm's length from government, as the European Investment Bank does at EU level. What governments shouldn't do is slash public investment in a recession, as most EU ones have done. On the contrary, it is precisely in a slump when the private sector does not want to invest, construction workers lie idle and funding is cheap that governments ought to invest more.

The confidence trick

What, though, of the notion that far from depressing the economy, cutting spending and raising taxes in a slump would bolster "confidence" and actually boost growth? ECB President Trichet and other eurozone policymakers repeatedly made that argument. "It is an error to think that fiscal austerity is a threat to growth," Trichet told *Libération* newspaper on 8 July 2010. "At present, a major problem is the lack of confidence on the part of households, firms, savers and

---

192   See, for example, http://www.treasury.govt.nz/government/financialstatements/monthend/pdfs/fsgnz-11mths-may13.pdf

investors who feel that fiscal policies are not sound and sustainable. In a number of economies, it is this lack of confidence that poses a threat to the consolidation of the recovery. Economies embarking on austerity policies that lend credibility to their fiscal policy strengthen confidence, growth and job creation."[193] Or as he put it more bluntly in a television interview, austerity is "good for confidence, consumption and investment today."[194]

Keynes famously said that "Madmen in authority, who hear voices in the air, are distilling their frenzy from some academic scribbler of a few years back."[195] In this case, eurozone policymakers were echoing arguments peddled to them only a few months back by Harvard economist Alberto Alesina, who was invited to present his views to EU finance ministers at their meeting in Madrid in April 2010 and who also influenced Trichet. Alesina argued that "Many even sharp reductions of budget deficits have been accompanied and immediately followed by sustained growth rather than recessions even in the very short run. These are the adjustments which have occurred on the spending side and have been large, credible and decisive."[196] His theoretical arguments were four-fold. One: tax increases or spending cuts perceived to be permanent may make people feel richer, and therefore more willing to spend, if they remove the danger of sharper and more costly fiscal adjustments in future. Two: if investors believe the borrowing cuts are credible and avoid a default on government debt, they may be willing to lend more cheaply – and if that feeds through to lower interest rates for households and companies, it may boost

---

193   http://www.ecb.int/press/key/date/2010/html/sp100713.en.html

194   http://www.cnbc.com/id/38987325/Austerity_Equals_Confidence_Trichet

195   John Maynard Keynes, *The General Theory of Employment, Interest and Money*, 1936, chapter 24, concluding notes.

196   Alberto Alesina, "Fiscal adjustments: lessons from recent history", paper prepared for the Ecofin meeting in Madrid, 15 April 2010

consumption and investment. Three: lower interest rates may drive up the prices of bonds and shares, making people feel wealthier and "triggering a consumption/investment boom". Four: cutting the number of government jobs will put downward pressure on wages, "increasing profits, investment and competitiveness". He bolstered his theoretical arguments by pointing to evidence from several European countries documented in a paper he co-wrote.[197] So influential was Alesina's presentation that it was quoted in EU finance ministers' conclusions.

Alesina's methodology and findings were quickly debunked by an IMF paper in September 2010.[198] Yet even at the time the argument was preposterous. It is one thing to show that a few small, open economies that cut government borrowing by spending less recorded positive growth – when interest rates also fell, the currency depreciated and their export markets were buoyant. It is quite another to posit that if the entire eurozone slashes government spending at a time when the private sector is trying to pay down debt, banks won't lend and its main trading partners, notably Britain and the US, are in a similar situation, the economy will grow. Were overindebted Spanish households whose houses were plunging in value really going to suddenly feel "confident" and go on a spending spree because the government slashed spending and put people out of work, reducing how much they spent and therefore how much others could spend too?

197　Alberto Alesina, Silvia Ardagna, "Large Changes in Fiscal Policy: Taxes Versus Spending", NBER working paper 15438, October 2009 http://www.nber.org/papers/w15438.pdf They cite twenty-six episodes of purportedly expansionary fiscal adjustments: Finland in 1973, 1996, 1998 and 2000; Greece in 1976, 2005 and 2006; Ireland in 1976, 1987, 1988, 1989 and 2000; the Netherlands in 1996; New Zealand in 1993 and 1994 and 2000; Norway in 1979, 1980, 1983 and 1996; Portugal in 1986, 1988 and 1995; Spain in 1986 and 1987; and Sweden in 2004.

198　International Monetary Fund, *World Economic Outlook*, October 2010, Chapter 3: "Will It Hurt? Macroeconomic Effects of Fiscal Consolidation". See also *The Economist*'s discussion: http://www.economist.com/node/17147618

Were debt-laden Portuguese companies to which banks wouldn't lend and which faced falling demand for their products suddenly going to invest because the government axed spending, further reducing demand for their products? Were struggling British and American consumers and companies suddenly going to buy more eurozone products because governments there had fired lots of workers? In that context, the suggestion that slashing government spending was going to boost growth was nonsense on stilts. Yet, like a nasty mind-rotting virus, the voodoo-economic notion of "expansionary fiscal austerity" infected eurozone policymakers, who were particularly susceptible to arguments that seemed to confirm their pro-austerity bias, and it was reflected in the austerity plans that the European Commission demanded of eurozone governments.[199]

"Your sons and daughters"

What, though, of the argument that government debt was so high that it would be irresponsible to borrow more? As ECB President Trichet put it in September 2010, "it is an elementary recommendation to care for your sons and daughters and not overburden them."[200] That didn't stop Trichet and other eurozone policymakers deciding to overburden Greek sons and daughters in May 2010, lumbering Irish ones with the debts of the country's bankrupt banks in November 2010 and repeating the Greek mistake in Portugal in May 2011. Nor

---

199   For example, the Spanish government's "Stability Programme" of April 2011 planned a fiscal squeeze of 4.9 per cent of GDP in 2011 and 2012. Astonishingly, it was assumed that this massive austerity would coincide with faster economic growth. This, in turn, would stabilise public debt in 2013. In fact, the lurch towards austerity plunged the economy into deep recession, punching a hole in both banks' balance sheets and the government's. "Stability Programme for Spain, 2011–2014" http://ec.europa.eu/europe2020/pdf/nrp/sp_spain_en.pdf

200   http://www.cnbc.com/id/38987325/Austerity_Equals_Confidence_Trichet

was there any austerity for Trichet himself: his basic salary was increased to €367,863 in 2010.[201] Even so, was it sound advice for other eurozone economies?

Along with Alesina's claptrap, another flawed economic study that was influential with eurozone policymakers, notably European Commission fiscal enforcer Olli Rehn, purported to show that the economy grinds to a halt once public debt exceeds 90 per cent of GDP.[202] Since government debt in the eurozone as a whole was nearing that apparent threshold in 2010 – and had exceeded it in several countries – this appeared to warrant immediate, front-loaded austerity.[203] But the "findings" in the paper published in January 2010 by Harvard economists Carmen Reinhart and Kenneth Rogoff were always dubious – and they were later discredited.[204]

---

201   http://www.ecb.int/pub/pdf/annrep/ar2010annualaccounts_en.pdf

202   For example, in a speech to the Council of Foreign Relations in Brussels on 1 June 2011, Olli Rehn said "Carmen Reinhart and Kenneth Rogoff have coined the '90 per cent rule', that is, countries with public debt exceeding 90 per cent of annual economic output grow more slowly. High debt levels can crowd out economic activity and entrepreneurial dynamism, and thus hamper growth. This conclusion is particularly relevant at a time when debt levels in Europe are now approaching the 90% threshold, which the US has already passed." http://europa.eu/rapid/press-release_SPEECH-11-407_en.htm Even in February 2013, when the devastating consequences of austerity were apparent, Rehn wrote to EU finance ministers stating that "it is widely acknowledged, based on serious academic research, that when public debt levels rise above 90 per cent they tend to have a negative impact on economic dynamism, which translates into low growth for many years. That is why consistent and carefully calibrated fiscal consolidation remains necessary in Europe." http://ec.europa.eu/commission_2010-2014/rehn/documents/cab20130213_en.pdf

203   Eurostat, general government consolidated gross debt. Code: tsieb090. In the eurozone as a whole this was 85.4 per cent of GDP in 2010, 87.3 per cent in 2011 and 90.6 per cent in 2012.

204   Carmen Reinhart and Kenneth Rogoff, "Growth in a Time of Debt", NBER working paper 15639, January 2010

Reinhart and Rogoff found that high public debt was associated with slow growth but did not establish that the former caused the latter. While high debt may lead to slow growth, it is more plausible that slow growth leads to high debt, and that a third factor may determine both. That is obvious in Europe today: in both Spain and Britain, for example, the recession caused public debts to soar, rather than public debts causing the recession. The underlying causes for both the recession and the rise in public debts are the financial crisis and the build-up of excessive private-sector debts. More generally, another study finds that high public debt is strongly correlated with weak growth in the past but only weakly correlated with weak growth in the future – as one would expect if weak growth was causing the high debt, rather than vice versa.[205]

Nor did Reinhart and Rogoff establish a mechanism through which high debt supposedly slows growth. If growth really collapses once public debts exceed 90 per cent of GDP, there would have to be a trigger and such a calamity ought to be obvious from the data – yet no such causal mechanism has been found.[206] In the United States, there is no evidence of the triggers that might cause a slowdown, such as a spike in interest rates. In the case of the eurozone, the official line is that a nebulous "lack of confidence" was to blame: witness the abrupt rise in Italian sovereign yields between 2010 and 2012. But that is sloppy reasoning. Italy's public debt has exceeded 90 per cent of GDP for many years. Why did sovereign yields soar only between 2010 and 2012? Now, even though Italian public debt has soared to 130 per cent of GDP and beyond, sovereign yields are falling. So even in the eurozone, there is no evidence of such an abrupt causal mechanism.

---

205   http://www.nextnewdeal.net/rortybomb/guest-post-reinhartrogoff-and-growth-time-debt

206   A point eloquently made by Adam Posen here: http://www.ft.com/cms/s/0/a6d94b02-a774-11e2-9fbe-00144feabdc0.html

Last but not least, circumstances differ. Reinhart and Rogoff lump together many different episodes of high debt – in economies big and small, in those with developed and less developed financial systems, with an open capital account and a closed one, with fixed exchange rates and flexible ones, in countries that had suffered a financial crisis and those that hadn't, and so on – yet there are good reasons to think that economies will cope differently with high debts in different circumstances. In particular, high debts are more likely to harm growth when private investment is vigorous, but not when it is depressed and borrowing more to make productive public investments will actually boost growth.

In addition to those three big reasons for doubting Reinhart and Rogoff's findings, a paper published in April 2013 showed that their results are based on shoddy methodology.[207] These errors drastically distorted their results. Whereas Reinhart and Rogoff claimed that the average growth of economies with debts exceeding 90 per cent of GDP was *minus* 0.1 per cent, it was in fact *plus* 2.2 per cent. Indeed, an OECD study of twenty economies over the same period finds that growth is higher in economies with debts of more than 90 per cent of

---

207   Thomas Herndon, Michael Ash and Robert Pollin, "Does High Public Debt Consistently Stifle Economic Growth? A Critique of Reinhart and Rogoff", 15 April 2013. The paper finds that Reinhart and Rogoff excluded data on some high-debt countries with decent growth immediately after the Second World War – the US and the UK; used an eccentric weighting scheme in which a single year of bad growth in one high-debt country (New Zealand) counts as much as multiple years of good growth in another high-debt country; and made a basic coding error in their Excel spreadsheet that excluded several data points. Since there weren't that many occasions when countries had public debts of more than 90 per cent of GDP between 1946 and 2009, the findings are easily swayed by the availability (or unavailability) of data for certain countries, the choice of which countries to include (or not), and how their performance is weighted. http://www.peri.umass.edu/fileadmin/pdf/working_papers/working_papers_301-350/WP322.pdf

GDP than in those with debts of 60–90 per cent (and highest in those with debts of less than 60 per cent).[208]

What might seem like an obscure academic debate is of huge political significance because Olli Rehn, his officials and others often used the Reinhart-Rogoff findings to justify the premature, front-loaded, across-the-board fiscal austerity imposed in the eurozone. Perversely, the misguided fear that high debts would stifle growth led to massive austerity that caused economies to slump and debts to soar.

While government borrowing does impose a burden on "sons and daughters" – the interest payments on the loan and the future taxes needed to ultimately repay it (assuming it is not perpetually refinanced) – it also benefits them, not least if they are just out of school, can't find a job and face being scarred for life by years of unemployment, and even more so if the funds are borrowed cheaply and invested productively in projects that boost future growth and tax revenues. (Indeed, to the extent that the government bonds are bought by domestic residents, both debts and assets are being handed down to "sons and daughters".)

One calculation by Brad DeLong and Larry Summers finds that on plausible assumptions, government borrowing pays for itself in a slump when resources lie idle – especially when interest rates are very low but even when they are pretty high – notably by averting the scars on future growth of having workers unemployed for years, with their skills going rusty and their future employability ebbing away.[209] Yet

---

208   B. Égert, "Public Debt, Economic Growth and Nonlinear Effects: Myth or Reality?", OECD Economics Department Working Papers, No. 993, 2012. http://dx.doi.org/10.1787/5k918xk8d4zn-en

209   Brad DeLong and Lawrence Summers, "Fiscal Policy in a Depressed Economy", Brookings, 20 March 2012 http://www.brookings.edu/~/media/Files/Programs/ES/BPEA/2012_spring_bpea_papers/2012_spring_BPEA_delong-summers.pdf

astonishingly, Trichet argued on the contrary that in the worst crisis since the 1930s governments needed to embrace austerity to have the space to respond to potential future emergencies.[210] As Martin Wolf, the chief economics commentator for the *Financial Times*, has insightfully remarked: "Too often, fiscal conservatives sound just like the revolutionaries who were prepared to sacrifice present generations for what turned out to be imaginary future benefits."[211]

Everyone can't save at once

When the economy is at full tilt, government borrowing has an additional cost: since the domestic supply of loanable funds is limited, it crowds out borrowing by the private sector and risks inflation. The possibility of crowding out places the bar much higher: governments should only borrow to invest in projects that yield higher returns than the private sector can achieve. But if a country is small and foreigners have surplus funds that they are willing to lend to both the government and the private sector, there may not be much crowding out. Indeed, in a slump when the private sector as a whole is trying to save to reduce its debts, not borrow, there is no crowding out at all. On the contrary, by borrowing more, the government can enable the private sector to realise its desire to save more – and thus pay down its debts without defaulting.

If both the government and the private sector try to save more at once, they can only succeed if foreigners are willing to borrow more from them. But if the world's second-biggest economy tries to save more, along with Britain and others, their desired savings will greatly exceed desired borrowing by other foreigners – notably China – even once global interest rates have fallen to zero, especially if they too are

---

210   http://www.ecb.int/press/key/date/2010/html/sp101012.en.html

211   http://blogs.ft.com/martin-wolf-exchange/2012/07/30/accelerating-private-sector-deleveraging/

wary of borrowing too much.[212] In that case, since actual saving must equal actual borrowing, neither the private sector nor the government will be able to fully realise their desire to save more. Rather, by trying to save more and therefore spending less, they will deepen the slump, since their reduced spending is someone else's reduced income. As incomes fall, some are forced to save less than they wanted in order to meet their current spending needs. Others – in particular, those who lose their jobs – may be forced to borrow or run down their savings. Falling incomes also depress tax revenues and boost social spending, notably on unemployment benefits, which in turn forces the government to borrow more. In short, if everyone tries to save more at once, their efforts will fail and everyone ends up poorer. That is a good description of the eurozone from 2010 to 2013. Despite the private sector's efforts to save more and pay down debt, its debts scarcely fell. Despite governments' efforts to save more, public borrowing didn't fall much. And this collective effort to save more perversely caused such a deep recession that public debt skyrocketed as a share of GDP.

Strikingly, in the United States, where fiscal policy accommodated the private sector's desire to save – and where debt write-offs have been significant – households' debt fell from 130 per cent of their incomes in 2007 to 105 per cent at the end of 2012. In contrast, in the eurozone, where governments tried to save at the same time as the private sector – and where bankruptcy law is much more punitive – households' debt rose from 100 per cent of their incomes to almost 110 per cent.[213]

When confronted with the evidence that its austerity policies have been a disaster, the European Commission usually blames governments for failing to comply with its instructions or events outside its

---

212   Global risk-free interest rates, that is. There will still be a premium on top of that for credit risk and other risks.

213   International Monetary Fund, *World Economic Outlook*, April 2013, Figure 1.4

control. But in the case of Portugal, those excuses won't wash. Under EU tutelage since June 2011 when it received a €78 billion EU-IMF loan, its government can't be accused of shirking on austerity and reform. On the contrary, Vitor Gaspar, finance minister from June 2011 until July 2013, was more German than the Germans in his commitment to "no-pain-no-gain" austerity. His efforts were repeatedly praised by Merkel, Schäuble and the Commission.[214] Since Portugal has mostly borrowed from the EU and the IMF, its interest rates have largely been set in Brussels, not in the markets. So this "model pupil" is the perfect testing ground for whether austerity works.

In June 2011, when Olli Rehn and his henchmen grabbed the reins, Portugal's economy was stagnant, with a budget deficit of 9.1 per cent of GDP the previous year, public debt of 93 per cent of GDP and private-sector debt of 249.5 per cent of GDP.[215] They prescribed a massively front-loaded fiscal squeeze of 10.8 per cent of GDP[216] in order to reduce government borrowing to 3 per cent of GDP in 2013,

---

214 For example, on a supportive visit to Portugal in November 2012, Angela Merkel praised Lisbon for the "courageous way" it had implemented deficit-reduction measures, saying there was "at the moment no reason to renegotiate" the adjustment programme. http://www.ft.com/cms/s/0/fedad66a-2ca2-11e2-9211-00144feabdc0.html

215 The economy shrank by 0.1 per cent in Q2 2011. Public borrowing and debt figures from European Commission Directorate General for Economic and Financial Affairs, "The Economic Adjustment Programme for Portugal", *European Economy* Occasional Papers 79, June 2011 http://ec.europa.eu/economy_finance/publications/occasional_paper/2011/pdf/ocp79_en.pdf Private-sector debt figures are for Q4 2010 from Eurostat, private sector in per cent of GDP, non consolidated, quarterly data. Code: tipspd30

216 The fiscal tightening in Portugal was 5.9 per cent of GDP in 2011, 3 per cent in 2012 and 1.9 per cent in 2013.

the arbitrary deadline set by eurozone leaders.[217] By their reckoning, the economy would shrink by 4 per cent over 2011–12, stabilising public debt in 2013 at 108.6 per cent of GDP.[218]

In fact, massive austerity plunged the economy into a deep recession – a fall of 6 per cent within a year and a half.[219] Unemployment rocketed to 17.4 per cent, throwing three in eight Portuguese "sons and daughters" out of work.[220] As a result of the slump, the government failed to get its borrowing down much. So it massaged the figures[221] and tightened the screws further, while a much less am-

---

217   Statement by the Heads of State or Government of the Euro Area and EU Institutions, 21 July 2011. Section 11: "Public deficits in all countries except those under a programme will be brought below 3% by 2013 at the latest." This builds on European Council Conclusions, 24/25 March 2011, EUCO 10/1/11 REV 1. Section 3:"In particular, Member States will present multi-annual consolidation plans including specific deficit, revenue and expenditure targets, the strategy envisaged to reach these targets and a timeline for its implementation. Fiscal policies for 2012 should aim to restore confidence by bringing debt trends back onto a sustainable path and ensuring that deficits are brought back below 3 % of GDP in the timeframe agreed upon by the Council. This requires in most cases an annual structural adjustment well above 0.5% of GDP. Consolidation should be frontloaded in Member States facing very large structural deficits or very high or rapidly increasing levels of public debt."

218   http://ec.europa.eu/economy_finance/publications/occasional_paper/2011/pdf/ocp79_en.pdf Table 6

219   Eurostat, GDP and main components - volumes, gross domestic product at market prices, index, 2005 = 100, Code: namq_gdp_k Change between Q2 2011 and Q4 2012.

220   "Sons and daughters" are unemployment among those aged 15-24, which was 38.3 per cent at the end of 2012, according to Eurostat.

221   Borrowing was so far above its target in 2011 that the government cheated, using one-off accounting tricks to massage the figure down. It made a one-off transfer of banks' pension funds to the public social-security system, reducing the deficit by 3 per cent of GDP that year.

bitious deficit target was set. In 2011–12, spending was slashed and taxes were raised by an enormous 10.1 per cent of GDP, reducing the deficit by a mere 3.4 per cent of GDP.[222] That isn't responsible, it's barbaric. Meanwhile, public debt soared to 131.3 per cent of GDP by mid-2013,[223] while private-sector debt rose too.[224] Gaspar's commitment to the Berlin/Brussels orthodoxy was unwavering. But fervour is not necessarily the route to salvation: if you worship a false god, you actually end up in hell.

Two things then changed. In the summer of 2012, the ECB finally stepped in to halt the panic ripping the eurozone apart. And Portugal eased off on austerity: the fiscal squeeze in 2013 halved and the deficit target was set at 5.8 per cent of GDP, the same as in 2012.[225] When the economy then perked up, eurozone officials had the gall to claim this as evidence that austerity worked. Austerity has also destabilised Italy's public finances, plunging the economy into a recession from which it had not escaped by the end of 2013, as the footnotes detail.[226]

---

222 European Commission Directorate General for Economic and Financial Affairs, "The Economic Adjustment Programme for Portugal Seventh Review – Winter 2012/13", Occasional Papers 153, June 2013, Table 2.2

223 Eurostat, government debt in per cent of GDP - quarterly data. Code: tipsgo20

224 Private-sector debt rose to 255.6 per cent of GDP at the end of 2012. Eurostat, private sector in per cent of GDP, non consolidated, quarterly data. Code: tipspd30

225 European Commission Directorate General for Economic and Financial Affairs, "The Economic Adjustment Programme for Portugal Eighth and Ninth Review", Occasional Papers 164, November 2013, Table 2.1

226 In 2011 Italy's economy was stagnant with a high but stable level of public debt and a moderate budget deficit; excluding interest payments, the government was running a surplus of 1.3 per cent. Then, in 2012 Monti's government tightened fiscal policy by 2.1 per cent of GDP. The impact was brutal: after growing by 0.4 per cent in 2011, the economy shrank by 2.4 per cent in 2012. As a result, government borrowing didn't fall much: the deficit narrowed from 3.7 per cent of GDP in 2011 to 3 per cent in 2012. Public debt shot up from 121 per cent of GDP in 2011 to 127

What about Latvia, which is often held up as a model of successful austerity for the rest of the eurozone? It may be feasible for a tiny open economy to turn itself around in 2009–10 by slashing government spending and raising taxes because it could fill the gap through higher exports to its much larger trading partners whose economies happened to be buoyant at the time.[227] But such a strategy can scarcely succeed for a continent-sized economy, especially when demand is weak in most of its major trading partners. To suggest otherwise is merely a version of the Alesina fallacy.

Counting the cost

How harmful has austerity been across the eurozone? It's impossible to be sure, because the eurozone suffers from several problems and it is hard to disentangle, for instance, the depressing impact of austerity from the throttling effect of the credit crunch. For what it's worth, the IMF calculates that in 2010–11 a fiscal squeeze of 1 per cent of GDP depressed the economy by between 0.9 per cent and 1.7 per cent.[228] That is much more than in normal times, when it might shrink the economy by 0.5 per cent. Research by Jonathan Portes, formerly the head of the UK's Government Economic Service and now director of the National Institute of Economic and Social Research, and his colleague Dawn Holland finds that the fiscal squeeze across the eurozone and Britain has been so harmful that it actually caused govern-

---

per cent in 2012. In 2013, the economy continued to shrink, while public debt rose above 130 per cent of GDP.

227   Latvia's main export partners with buoyant economies at the time were Russia, Germany, Poland and Sweden.

228   International Monetary Fund, *World Economic Outlook*, October 2012. Box 1.1: "Are We Underestimating Short-Term Fiscal Multipliers?" That said, one can always poke holes in small-sample cross-country regressions, which are unlikely to take account of the many local factors in each country that may distort the results.

ment debt to rise as a share of GDP.[229] They reckon that the planned austerity in 2011–13 increased Greek government debt by more than 30 per cent of GDP! A 2013 study by a European Commission official using the Commission's official economic model comes to similarly damning conclusions.[230]

The bottom line is that front-loaded austerity in the eurozone has been irresponsible and destabilising. Could eurozone policymakers have known this in advance? Yes. Many people warned that austerity would be self-defeating. Had Olli Rehn spent less time lapping up Reinhart and Rogoff and rather read research published in April 2010 by, among others, two of the leading economic historians of the Great Depression – Barry Eichengreen of the University of California, Berkeley and Kevin O'Rourke of All Souls College, Oxford – he would have learned that in the 1930s, the period that most closely resembles our own, experience across twenty-seven economies suggests that a fiscal squeeze of 1 per cent of GDP caused the economy to contract by 1.6 per cent.[231]

---

229 Dawn Holland and Jonathan Portes, "Self-Defeating Austerity?", *National Institute Economic Review* No. 222, October 2012, pages F4–F10. For instance, by their reckoning, a planned attempt to raise taxes and cut spending by a total of 10 per cent of GDP in Greece between 2011 and 2013 would shrink the economy by 13 per cent. That, in turn, would slash tax revenues and swell social spending so much that the government's deficit would shrink by only 2 per cent of GDP. Portes and Holland estimate that across the eurozone, planned austerity for 2011–13 shrank the economy by 4 per cent and pushed up debt as a share of GDP by more than 5 percentage points, while in Britain it crunched the economy by 5 per cent, pushing debt up by nearly 5 per cent of GDP.

230 Jan in 't Veld, "Fiscal consolidations and spillovers in the Euro area periphery and core", *European Economy*, Economic Papers 506, October 2013 http://ec.europa. eu/economy_finance/publications/economic_paper/2013/pdf/ecp506_en.pdf

231 Miguel Almunia, Agustin Benetrix, Barry Eichengreen, Kevin O'Rourke and Gisela Rua, "From Great Depression to Great Credit Crisis: Similarities, Differences

Did the European Commission change course when the damage to the economy became apparent? Not for a long time, because it was rigidly committed to bringing government borrowing down to 3 per cent of GDP by 2013 come what may. So when economies contracted more than it had expected, causing borrowing to remain stubbornly high, more austerity was imposed to try to make up the difference. In effect, eurozone governments were chasing their tail in a downward spiral.[232]

Clearly, the lurch towards austerity was a catastrophic mistake. It is a travesty that the unelected policymakers at the ECB and European Commission have not suffered any consequences for inflicting so much misery on Europeans today while increasing the debt burden on "your sons and daughters" tomorrow. Unlike ordinary Europeans, they have jobs for life, automatically uprated salaries and gold-plated pensions. Only when they feared that their money in the bank might

---

and Lessons," *Economic Policy* 25, 2010 See also http://www.voxeu.org/article/gauging-multiplier-lessons-history

232   The belief in Brussels was that governments had to be held to their nominal deficit targets to maintain "credibility", but in practice sticking to unachievable targets shreds credibility. Only in March 2012 did EU leaders first recognise the need to allow automatic stabilisers to work. European Council, Conclusions, 1/2 March 2012, Section 8: "Fiscal consolidation is an essential condition to return to higher growth and employment. It must be differentiated according to Member States' circumstances. All Member States should continue to respect their commitments under the rules of the Stability and Growth Pact, which allow the automatic stabilisers to work around the agreed path of structural fiscal adjustment, while ensuring the long-term sustainability of public finances. Countries that are part of an assistance programme should stick to the targets and structural reforms agreed in the programme. Similarly, Member States under market pressure should meet agreed budgetary targets and stand ready to pursue further consolidation measures if needed. While pursuing consolidation efforts, particular care must be given to prioritising expenditure that constitutes an investment in future growth, with a particular emphasis on education, research and innovation."

not be safe, notably in late 2011, did the crisis actually affect them personally. One reason, indeed, why technocratic rule is so dangerous is that policymakers are detached from the people who are affected by their decisions and unaccountable to them for their mistakes. But am I being unfair? Are panicky markets actually to blame for forcing policymakers' hands?

The austerity bias

The swing towards austerity actually started long before the bond-market panic. Ireland's efforts to reduce government borrowing began as early as 2008.[233] At an EU level, policymakers were looking forward to reversing their post-Lehman fiscal stimulus as early as June 2009, when the outlook was still bleak and bond markets subdued.[234] By September, EU leaders were already on the starting blocks.[235] In late October, the new Greek government revealed that its public finances were in much worse shape than the previous government had admitted. By December, EU leaders were already planning a front-loaded fiscal squeeze, even though markets were prepared to lend to all euro-zone governments except Greece and Ireland on nearly as good terms

---

233   http://www.oecd.org/gov/budgeting/47840807.pdf

234   European Council Presidency Conclusions, 18/19 June 2009, 11225/2/09 REV 2. Section 12: "It is important that consolidation keeps pace with economic recovery. There is a clear need for a reliable and credible exit strategy, inter alia by improving the medium-term fiscal framework and through coordinated medium-term economic policies."

235   European Council, "Agreed Language for the Pittsburgh G-20 Summit", 17 September 2009. Section 2:"Fiscal policies must progressively be reoriented towards sustainability. Exit strategies need to be designed now and implemented in a co-ordinated manner as soon as recovery takes hold, taking into account the specific situations of individual countries."

as to Germany.[236] Both Spain and Italy tightened in 2010 without market pressure.[237]

In March 2010 – before Greece got its EU-IMF loan in May and well before bond yields rose more generally – EU leaders adopted an economic strategy that mirrored Germany's moves at the beginning of the century: fiscal austerity plus reforms to boost "competitiveness".[238] While this was partly a flawed response to a misdiagnosed fiscal crisis – European officials should have realised that the eurozone was not Latvia – some policymakers had long been looking to tighten the screws and seized on the Greek situation as a pretext.

Those policymakers who have only a basic grasp of economics tend to operate according to rules of thumb – for instance, that too much government borrowing is a bad thing – and are naturally sceptical of arguments that times are different, especially when they lack confidence in their ability to assess whether things really are. Moreover, until 2012 most eurozone leaders were from conservative

236   European Council Conclusions, 10/11 December 2009, EUCO 6/09. Section 8: "In this context, the European Council reiterates its conclusions from 20 October on fiscal exit strategy and recalls that the strategy will include a consolidation of well beyond the benchmark of 0.5 per cent of GDP per year combined with structural reforms underpinning long-term fiscal sustainability. Fiscal consolidation should start in 2011 at the latest, earlier in some Member States where economic circumstances make this appropriate, provided that the Commission forecasts continue to indicate that the recovery is strengthening and becoming self-sustaining." Spreads over 10-year Germany yields were less than 1 percentage point, except for Greece (247 basis points) and Ireland (189 basis points) on 9 December 2009, on the eve of the European Council meeting, according to data from Thomson Reuters on ft.com

237   http://www.slideshare.net/oscarm/spain-economic-policy-and-2010-funding-strategy

238   European Council Conclusions, 26 March 2010, EUCO 7/10. Section 2: "Restoring macroeconomic stability and returning public finances on a sustainable path are prerequisites for growth and jobs." They also launched Europe 2020, a ten-year plan to coordinate national reform programmes to meet EU target.

parties that are sceptical of Keynesian policies, which they associate with higher spending and therefore bigger government at all times. But while it is deplorable that EU governments have often borrowed and spent too much even in good times – which is not Keynesian at all – that is very different from temporarily higher borrowing to limit a slump.

This anti-Keynesian bias is particularly prominent among German politicians. Mainstream German economic thinking – known as ordoliberalism – involves an important role for the state in promoting a "social market economy" (*SozialeMarktwirtschaft*) but is emphatically anti-Keynesian (or indeed pre-Keynesian) in that it neglects the demand side of the economy, implicitly assuming that supply creates its own demand. Many Germans also have a moralistic dislike of borrowing; tellingly, the German word for debt, *Schuld*, also means guilt (or sin). Moreover, having previously "done their homework", to use Chancellor Merkel's favourite expression – and to their mind been successful as a result – many Germans struggle to grasp that such a strategy cannot succeed for everyone at once, still less that it hasn't actually been that successful for them, since it has resulted in stagnant living standards and squandered savings. On the contrary, they tend to dismiss objections as an unwillingness to endure the hard work and suffering necessary for redemption. As a creditor country, imposing austerity was also seemingly in Germany's self-interest, since if successful, it would increase the chances that German banks and investors got back more of the money that they foolishly lent to southern Europe in the bubble years – and later the money that their taxpayers forked out too. Ironically, because its prescription was flawed, Germany stands to make greater losses as borrowers are unnecessarily forced to default.

As for the European Commission officials whose main responsibility was to enforce EU fiscal rules, they were predisposed – like a hammer that perceives everything to be a nail – to see every problem as fiscal and lacked the mental flexibility to appreciate that exceptional times required different policies. They also relished the increased attention and power that a lurch towards austerity gave them. Many were indifferent to the social consequences of austerity since their overriding priority was to do what they thought necessary to save the euro – and in any case they are not accountable for their mistakes. Thus while market pressure may have contributed to the lurch towards austerity, markets were pushing at an open door.

In June 2010, fired up with the fervour that austerity would be expansionary, EU leaders pledged to "achieve budgetary targets without delay" and to tighten EU fiscal rules.[239] By then, both Portugal and Ireland needed to pay some three percentage points a year more than Germany to borrow for ten years and Spain nearly two percentage points more, but other eurozone governments were largely unaffected. The dash for ever-tighter fiscal rules gave the European Commission, egged on by the German government, new tools to enforce austerity on recalcitrant governments.[240] (These changes to the "economic

239   European Council Conclusions, 17 June 2010, EUCO 13/10. Section 2: "Member States are determined to ensure fiscal sustainability and achieve budgetary targets without delay. They will continue to adopt a differentiated speed in fiscal consolidation taking both fiscal and non-fiscal risks into account. Several Member States have recently strengthened and frontloaded budgetary consolidation. All Member States are ready, if necessary, to take additional measures to accelerate fiscal consolidation. Priority should be given to growth-friendly budgetary consolidation strategies mainly focused on expenditure restraint. Increasing the growth potential should be seen as paramount to ease fiscal adjustment in the long run." See also section 11

240   See, for instance, European Council Conclusions, 23 October 2011, Section 4: "The European Union now has more powerful tools to enhance its economic governance and to ensure that the required measures are taken to pull Europe out of the crisis: the Europe 2020 strategy continues to guide the Union and the Member States in promoting the delivery of growth-enhancing structural reforms; the European

governance" of the eurozone will be discussed at greater length in Chapter 6.) In short, then, while rising bond yields may subsequently have convinced policymakers to accelerate the pace of austerity, they already had their foot on the pedal beforehand.

Even after bond yields spiked, policymakers could have responded differently. They could have warned that a generalised lurch towards austerity was unwise and tried to persuade markets that there was a better alternative. They didn't. As I know from private conversations with senior eurozone policymakers, they genuinely believed, and still do believe in many cases, that it was the right course of action. So even if policymakers were doing what they thought markets demanded, they were at the very least willing accomplices. Does Trichet celebrating the joys of austerity sound like someone forced to say what he thought markets wanted to hear?

Nor did markets force policymakers to impose brutal austerity on Greece, Portugal and Ireland once they were primarily funded by the EU and the IMF. Clearly, this would have been less severe had policymakers written down Greek and Portuguese debts and not forced Ireland to take on all its banks' debts. In the case of Italy and Spain, even if panic did eventually force the hands of policymakers

---

semester will help ensure that they remain on track in implementing these reforms in a coordinated manner; and the Euro Plus Pact will achieve a new quality of economic policy coordination amongst the participating Member States. The package of six legislative acts on economic governance agreed last month will allow a much higher degree of surveillance and coordination, necessary to ensure sustainable public finances and avoid the accumulation of excessive imbalances. The European Council emphasises its determination to implement this new framework in order to ensure that it is fully and effectively applied. In this context, we welcome the intention of the Commission to strengthen, in the Commission, the role of the competent Commissioner for closer monitoring and additional enforcement." None of this was relevant to solving the crisis.

in 2011, markets certainly weren't baying for governments to slash investment.[241]

The European Commission's imposition of austerity in the Netherlands was even more absurd. In May 2012 Brussels insisted that the Dutch government tighten fiscal policy in a recession, even though its bond yields were at record lows, its public debt was scarcely above the EU limit and comfortably below Germany's, and it was a net lender to foreigners, with a huge current-account surplus of 7 per cent of GDP.[242]

Nor was there market pressure on Germany and other northern European countries – including Britain – to embrace austerity. On the contrary, they benefited from ultra-low interest rates as capital fled southern Europe. Since early 2012 Germany has been able to borrow for ten years at negative interest rates, after allowing for inflation, and it faced very low interest rates before that. It was an ideal opportunity to invest in upgrading the country's rundown infrastructure, in the clean energy needed to realise Merkel's desired "energy transition" (Energiewende) and more generally in future growth. This would also have helped offset the squeeze on demand in southern Europe – by

---

241   In January 2012, EU leaders advocated "smart fiscal consolidation preserving investment in future growth", but this was too little, too late. Statement of the members of the European Council, 30 January 2012. Later, they amplified on this. European Council Conclusions, 1/2 March 2012, Section 8: "While pursuing consolidation efforts, particular care must be given to prioritising expenditure that constitutes an investment in future growth, with a particular emphasis on education, research and innovation."

242   http://ec.europa.eu/europe2020/pdf/nd/csr2012_netherlands_en.pdf Interestingly, Dutch ten-year yields rebounded from an all-time low of 1.68 per cent on 30 May, when the austerity measures proposed by the European Commission were endorsed by EU leaders, to a bit over 2 per cent three weeks later, perhaps because markets realised the fiscal squeeze was counterproductive. http://www.bloomberg.com/quote/GNTH10YR:IND/chart

providing a growing market for southern European exports and those of other countries to which southern Europe might export, a role that southern Europe played for Germany in the pre-crisis years. Instead, Germany adopted austerity too.[243] Merkel's unforced error has done great damage not just to southern Europe but also to Germany itself.

Last but not least, market pressure did not preclude offsetting measures to boost growth at a European level – for example, a big capital increase for the European Investment Bank that would enable it to lend more to small businesses, fund venture capital for start-ups and create pan-European transport, energy and broadband networks. I lobbied for that throughout 2011 and managed to get it into President Barroso's State of the Union speech in September. I also pitched it to François Hollande's team in early 2012 when they were looking for ideas to boost growth. It was finally picked up by EU leaders in June 2012 after President Hollande's election. Unfortunately, the EIB has yet to make full use of its capital increase, as Werner Hoyer, its German president, has prioritised plumping up its buffer against losses over lending more.

Clearly, then, the collective lurch towards austerity was as much a political choice as a consequence of market pressure. Worse, that market pressure was not, for the most part, a reflection of fiscal profligacy by national governments, but rather a panic that eurozone policymakers created – and which the ECB could and should have stopped long before it finally did.

---

243 Germany tightened fiscal policy by 1.3 per cent of GDP in 2011 and a further 0.5 per cent of GDP in 2012.

4

PANIC!

How the euro came close to collapse

Credit event or selective default or default, we say 'no', full stop.
Jean Claude Trichet, president of the European
Central Bank, on Greece's debt, 2011[244]

*The question is whether Greece remains in the eurozone, that
is what we want. But it is up to the Greek people to answer
that question.*
Nicolas Sarkozy, president of France, 2011[245]

With its famous race course, casino and seaside promenade, the pic-
turesque Norman town of Deauville has long been a playground for
the international jet set. French high-society families have houses
there. Foreigners flock to its luxury hotels. Coco Chanel opened her

---

244 http://www.ecb.int/press/pressconf/2011/html/is110707.en.html
245 http://www.ft.com/cms/s/0/c47bc3f4-0605-11e1-ad0e-00144feabdc0.html

first boutique in the town. And now the French government hosts international summits there. But for that reason Deauville now has a much more negative connotation. It is there that Angela Merkel took a fateful walk on the beach with Nicolas Sarkozy in October 2010 and convinced him to make a terrible mistake that would spread panic across the eurozone.

To her credit, Angela Merkel had never wanted to bail out Greece. After all, Germany had insisted on the no-bailout rule before joining the euro because it did not want to be lumbered with the debts of profligate governments, in the hope that the rule would ensure markets disciplined government borrowing, along with the EU's fiscal rules. But she was persuaded that it was necessary to avert a Lehman-style panic, not least by the French (including Trichet and Strauss-Kahn) as well as by powerful German banks. Soon, though, it became apparent that Greece was a bottomless pit and buyer's remorse set in. So in an effort to avoid future Greek-style bailouts, she seized the opportunity of a one-on-one meeting with the French president to get him to agree that any government requiring a loan from the future ESM – the eurozone's permanent crisis-lending mechanism, which was at that time due to come into being in 2013 – would have to restructure its debts and make the private sector take a hit.[246]

---

246 Franco-German declaration, 18 October 2010. Section 2 states: The amendment of the Treaties will be restricted to the following issues: The establishment of a permanent and robust framework to ensure orderly crisis management in the future, providing the necessary arrangements for an adequate participation of private creditors and allowing Member States to take appropriate coordinated measures to safeguard financial stability of the Euro area as a whole. This was confirmed, in even more cryptic fashion in the European Council Conclusions of 28/29 October 2010, Section 2: "Further to the report of the Task Force, and in order to ensure balanced and sustainable growth, Heads of State or Government agree on the need for Member States to establish a permanent crisis mechanism to safeguard the financial stability of the euro area as a whole and invite the President of the European Council

Now that is a fine principle when a government is insolvent, as in the case of Greece. But it is dangerously destabilising when a government is merely illiquid, as future borrowers from the ESM would ostensibly be. After all, if a government is facing temporarily funding difficulties – for example, because of a bond-market panic – but is willing and able to pay its debts in full, there is no reason why its creditors should take a hit. In effect, then, Deauville involved the opposite mistake of the Greek bailout: Greece was treated as illiquid when in fact it was insolvent; now Merkel proposed to treat illiquid governments as if they were insolvent. Worse, pre-announcing that bondholders will take a hit is an invitation to panic and this precipitated the run on Ireland in late 2010. This policy mistake was reversed in December 2011, when eurozone leaders decided that debt restructuring would be imposed only in the event that a government's debts had been assessed as unsustainable, in line with IMF practices.[247] But

to undertake consultations with the members of the European Council on a limited treaty change required to that effect, not modifying article 125 TFEU ("no bail-out" clause). The European Council welcomes the intention of the Commission to undertake, in close consultation with the President of the European Council, preparatory work on the general features of a future new mechanism, i.a. the role of the private sector, the role of the IMF and the very strong conditionality under which such programmes should operate."

247   This was actually pre-agreed at a Merkel-Sarkozy summit on 5 December 2011 and then rubber-stamped by eurozone leaders more generally on 9 December. Statement by the Euro Area Heads of State or Government, 9 December 2011. Section 15: "We agree on the following adjustments to the ESM Treaty to make it more effective:

• Concerning the involvement of the private sector, we will strictly adhere to the well established IMF principles and practices. This will be unambiguously reflected in the preamble of the treaty. We clearly reaffirm that the decisions taken on 21 July and 26/27 October concerning Greek debt are unique and exceptional; standardised and identical Collective Action Clauses will be included, in such a way as to preserve market liquidity, in the terms and conditions of all new euro government bonds."

by then the damage was done: the vicious circle between weak banks and weak sovereigns was in full swing and policymakers' pledges had lost all credibility.

This failure to draw a clear line between insolvent and illiquid borrowers is a recurring theme of the crisis. Having muddied the waters by falsely claiming Greece was only illiquid, eurozone leaders implicitly recognised that Greece was insolvent by starting the process of restructuring its debts in July 2011 – while insisting that Greece was an exceptional case. But having shredded their credibility, why should anyone believe their protests that other governments, for instance Spain's, were only illiquid – even when that happened to be true? Worse, because of Deauville, even if investors did genuinely believe that Spain was merely illiquid, they feared that it would be treated as if it were insolvent.

Predictably, Deauville inflated the yields of governments threatened with insolvency, such as Ireland and Portugal, but also those, such as Italy and Belgium, that might become illiquid. Irish ten-year yields soared from 6.08 per cent on 18 October 2010 to 9.45 per cent on 29 November, when its EU-IMF loan was announced, with spreads over Germany widening by 303 basis points to 671.[248] Portuguese yields jumped from 5.57 per cent to 7.29 per cent over the same period, Spain's from 4.02 per cent to 5.50 per cent.[249] Italy's and Belgium's were destabilised too.[250] As with the Greek tragedy, this initial impact understates the cumulative impact of Deauville over time.

---

248   Ft.com, data archive, bonds and rates, ten-year government spreads. The FT sources the data from Thomson Reuters.

249   Portuguese spreads widened by 135 basis points to 454. Spanish spreads widened by 113 basis points to 276.

250   Italian ten-year yields rose from 3.74 per cent to 4.68 per cent; spreads widened by 59 basis points to 194. Belgian ten-year yields rose from 3.22 per cent to 3.88 per cent; spreads widened by 30 basis points to 113

By late 2010, then, all the ingredients for a nasty systemic crisis were in place. By backstopping huge distressed banks that owned lots of government bonds, fragile governments created a devastating doom loop between weak banks, weak governments and weak economies. First the Greek bailout then the Deauville declaration further destabilised government bond markets, weakening banks' balance sheets even more. That in turn hit the economy as banks cut credit and governments squeezed spending and raised taxes, dealing another blow to both banks' and governments' accounts.

From unthinkable to inevitable

In early 2011, with the Greek economy performing much worse than the initial EU-IMF programme had assumed and public borrowing still stubbornly high, the EU gradually had to face up to reality. Under German pressure, EU loans to Greece had initially been at punitively high rates. This was based on a moralistic desire to punish errant governments, an understandable wish to deter others from borrowing too much in future and a belief that a hefty premium was needed to cover the risk that the loan would not be paid back. But crises are not morality plays and the right way to deter governments from borrowing too much in future is a combination of good governance, market pressure (sorely lacking during the bubble years), voters' prudence and external surveillance. The purpose of an emergency loan is to assist a government that cannot borrow from private investors while it puts its fiscal house in order. Since Greece already was insolvent, lending to it at punitive rates simply compounded its misery. In March 2011 the terms of the EU loans were relaxed a little.[251]

---

251   The interest rate was reduced by one percentage point and the length of the loan extended by seven-and-a-half years. Conclusions of the Heads of State or Government of the Euro Area, 11 March 2011

In the EU institutions, a sovereign debt restructuring was still viewed as unthinkable. In the markets, it was seen as inevitable. So long as worried investors were willing to lend to Greece only at prohibitively high interest rates – if at all – it would remain dependent on EU-IMF loans. So whenever Greece needed more money, the EU had to decide whether to lend even more or to accept reality and reduce Greece's debts. Yet as bailout fatigue set in, further EU loans were increasingly unacceptable in creditor countries – the anti-bailout True Finns won a fifth of the vote in the Finnish elections in April 2011 and the German Bundestag was increasingly reticent too – so both politics and economics suggested that a restructuring would happen sooner rather than later.

Debate ensued about how to tackle Greece's debt burden. To avoid immediately lending more to Greece, various German voices proposed postponing Greece's debt repayments. This became known as "reprofiling" in EU jargon – which, it was asserted, could not in any way be construed as a default. Others advocated a "voluntary" rollover of Greece's debts – that investors should "voluntarily" agree to buy new Greek bonds once theirs matured, in effect postponing the moment when Greece had to pay them back. Clearly, these two options were tantamount to the same thing, yet farcical theological arguments ensued about whether one or the other would provoke Armageddon.[252] Neither of these options, of course, would reduce

---

252 When Germany proposed a "reprofiling" of Greek bonds – extending their maturity by a number of years – the ECB screamed that this would cause a Lehman-style meltdown. When it was suggested instead that investors agree to purchase new Greek bonds when theirs mature – on a "voluntary" basis, of course – the ECB said that this was acceptable. But there was scarcely any difference between these two proposals. In effect, both a "reprofiling" and a "debt rollover" result in a maturity extension – and neither is "voluntary".

In early June 2011, Greek ten-year bonds yielded over 16 per cent. That is the price at which the market was voluntarily willing to lend. Clearly, though, the rolled-over

Greece's unbearable debt burden; they merely extended the suffering and postponed the day of reckoning. The next big idea was therefore a "voluntary private sector involvement": another euphemism suggesting that bondholders would willingly take losses without this – heaven forbid – triggering a formal default.

Many eurozone policymakers, not least at the European Commission, were viscerally opposed to admitting that Greece was insolvent, partly because of genuine misconceptions, but also because they didn't want to lose face. EU economics chief Olli Rehn warned that a Greek restructuring risked a "Lehman Brothers catastrophe".[253] But the hardest of the hardliners was the ECB, which was deeply compromised by its own mistaken purchases of Greek government bonds. I remember Trichet hammering his vehement opposition to Greek restructuring with a Thatcher-like *"non, non, non"* at a seminar

---

bonds would pay less than this, since Greece cannot afford to borrow large sums at 16 per cent. What, then, might induce an investor to "voluntarily" lend at less than 16 per cent? A small carrot was the offer of preferential terms, perhaps preferred status or regulatory forbearance for banks. A big stick was the fear that Greece would otherwise default and investors would incur big losses on their other holdings of Greek sovereign and bank debt. In other words, such a debt rollover would hardly be "voluntary". For what it's worth, credit rating agencies signalled that they would consider both as "credit events", resulting in a downgrade of Greek debt to default-like levels.

Thus, the ECB's position was absurd. On the one hand, they (and then Olli Rehn) claimed that a reprofiling, restructuring or any other debt exchange that resulted in losses for creditors would lead to a Lehman-style meltdown. On the other, they said that a debt rollover that was tantamount to reprofiling was fine. Either the ECB was correct that reprofiling would lead to Armageddon, in which case so would a not-so-voluntary debt rollover. Or their claim that restructuring would cause a meltdown was actually nonsense, and their acceptance of a rollover was a tacit admission of that.

253   http://au.ibtimes.com/articles/158655/20110607/euro-rallies-on-trichet-endorsing-debt-rollover-plan-for-greece.htm

hosted by former European Commission President Jacques Delors in early 2011. Senior ECB officials warned darkly that a debt write-down would trigger disaster[254] – and that they themselves would do so if democratically elected policymakers dared to disobey them – thus sparking the very panic that they claimed to want to avert. Placing its own narrow interests as a creditor ahead of its wider duty to eurozone citizens was a gross dereliction of duty. Threatening to pull the plug on Greek banks by refusing to accept Greek bonds as collateral was deeply irresponsible. But while it would have been difficult to go ahead with a Greek debt restructuring without the ECB's cooperation, it was not impossible.[255]

---

254 For example, in late April 2011, Jürgen Stark, the ECB's chief economist, warned on German television that "In the worst case, a debt restructuring of a eurozone member could put the consequences of Lehman's bankruptcy in the shade." http://www.ft.com/cms/s/0/a0c9fee0-70ef-11e0-962a-00144feabdc0.html

255 A restructuring of Greek debt would be likely to trigger a selective default (SD) or default (D) rating from rating agencies – and the ECB had stated that it would not accept bonds rated SD or D as collateral for providing liquidity to banks, even though it had repeatedly changed its criteria for acceptable collateral after insisting that it couldn't and wouldn't. It is unlikely that Trichet would have gone through with his threat to deny liquidity to Greek banks – in effect, causing Greece's banking system to collapse, forcing it out of the euro, and creating panic across the eurozone. Assuming, however, that the ECB did not back down, several options existed.

To overcome the ECB's refusal to accept bonds rated SD or D as collateral, all that was needed was a temporary fix, because Greek bonds would only briefly be in default. In previous restructurings, agencies reassigned normal ratings to sovereigns as soon as their debt stock was reduced. So Greece would be likely to have an SD rating for at most two weeks and after that an investment grade of BBB or higher. If its new bonds were collateralised by AAA EFSF/ESM bonds, they would be rated even higher. In either case, the new bonds would be acceptable as collateral by the ECB. One option would be to provide alternative collateral for the brief period when countries were in selective default. EFSF collateral or some other temporary collateral could be lent to Greece for two weeks and this could be used to obtain liquidity

Preposterously, Lorenzo Bini Smaghi, the arch-austerian Italian member of the ECB governing board who was exiled to Harvard after his compatriot Mario Draghi took over from Trichet as ECB president in November 2011, argued that bleeding Greeks dry was actually in their own interests, because restructuring government debt would be even more costly for them.[256] His arguments were based

---

from the ECB. Another option would be for the national central bank to provide temporary liquidity through the Emergency Liquidity Assistance (ELA) facility. The Irish central bank had already provided ELA to Irish banks using different collateral rules and haircuts from the ECB. This route would not be possible if the ECB objected even to national central banks taking on the risk. A third option would be to arrange bridging loans from a consortium of large, well-capitalised eurozone banks that have plenty of collateral with which to access tens of billions of euros from the ECB's unlimited 3-month liquidity operation. Even if they lent these funds on at an interest rate of say 50 per cent – ie, 1 per cent a week – for two weeks the overall impact on the cost of borrowing for Greek banks would be small and hence affordable. Clearly, then, a restructuring was possible even against the wishes of the ECB.

256   See, for example, Lorenzo Bini Smaghi, "Private sector involvement: From (good) theory to (bad) practice", speech at the Reinventing Bretton Woods Committee, Berlin, 6 June 2011. http://www.ecb.int/press/key/date/2011/html/sp110606.en.html

Bini Smaghi argues that restructurings have typically been "disorderly, harmful and fraught with difficulties". But a comprehensive IMF study (Udaibir Das, Michael Papaioannou, and Christoph Trebesch, "Sovereign Debt Restructurings 1950 - 2010: Literature Survey, Data, and Stylized Facts", IMF Working Paper 12/203, 1 August 2012) argues that this isn't necessarily so. Indeed, once the decision to restructure Greece's debt was taken, this took only a few months and did not have the catastrophic impact Bini Smaghi and others predicted. The restructuring was relatively easy to do, since most Greek bonds were issued under Greek law, so their terms could be rewritten at will by the Greek parliament.

Bini Smaghi also argued that "private investors are likely to penalise a country which has a history of restructuring and to demand higher risk premia." In fact, markets have short memories – and once a country's debts are lower, investors are more willing to lend to it, because the risks of default are lower. The IMF paper on six decades

on the false premise that the Greek government was solvent, and so had a choice. Even so, it was ludicrous to suggest that restructuring Greece's debts would do more damage to the economy than the debt overhang, the crippling fears of a Greek default and euro exit, and the resulting investment slump. Bini Smaghi also argued that respect for debts contracts was a key principle and that "the payment of debts should be enforced, through sanctions if need be." Indeed, if only the ECB had gunships at its disposal, it could have sent them to shell the port of Piraeus.

Many others took a moralistic view that debt contracts were sacrosanct. But they aren't. Money is lent in the expectation of it being returned with interest, but with the risk that it won't. That is why lenders charge a risk premium. Sometimes people default on their mortgages. Sometimes companies go bankrupt. And sometimes governments don't pay their debts in full. (In fact, governments do this all the time: they erode their debts through inflation and, in the case of foreign creditors, currency depreciation – as anyone who holds a US Treasury bond knows all too well.) It is perfectly normal for the banks and other investors who lent too much, too cheaply to pay the price for their mistakes – and only fair that they share the pain. So while it was often argued that writing down Greece's debts would encourage Greeks to be even more reckless in future, this ignored that for governments to pay off the creditors of an insolvent borrower would encourage even greater state-sponsored recklessness by bankers. Capitalism without risk of loss is like power without accountability: it corrupts absolutely.

---

of sovereign debt restructurings finds that "capital exclusion periods are brief, effects on the cost of borrowing are temporary and small." Most countries are able to borrow from capital markets again within one or two years after undergoing a debt restructuring. In the case of Uruguay in 2003, it took only a month. There is every reason to believe that Greece could have returned to the markets within a relatively short space of time after a big enough restructuring – something that is highly unlikely while its debts remain unsustainably high.

Another common argument in EU policy circles was that debt restructuring would let the Greek government off the hook for reform. But leaving aside whether all the proposed reforms were desirable, Greece would still have been reliant on EU-IMF loans with strict conditionality and need to squeeze its budget to stabilise its outstanding debt. "Reform fatigue" is more likely to set in if countries are stuck in a debt trap with no light at the end of the tunnel.

A final argument was that it would be better to delay restructuring until 2013, once the eurozone's permanent rescue mechanism, the ESM, was up and running, by which time financial markets would, with luck, have stabilised. In part, this was based on the flawed premise that it was better to delay recapitalising banks. Muddling through was also mistaken because it increased Greece's debt, shifted it from private investors to the EU and IMF and imposed huge economic and political costs. Above all, the premise that the situation would settle down while Greece festered was false.

On the contrary, throughout the crisis the failure to tackle Greece's unbearable debts once and for all has been destabilising. As the overoptimistic assumptions of the EU-IMF programmes confronted reality and the economy nosedived, a hole would open up in Greece's finances. Each time, variants of the same debate would ensue. Would eurozone governments and national parliaments, notably the German Bundestag or the Finnish Eduskunta, agree to throw good money after bad by lending more? Would the IMF pull the plug, as its rules stipulate, in the absence of certainty that Greece's funding for the next twelve months was assured? Would the Fund continue to bend its own rules that prevent it lending to insolvent governments by conniving in the fiction that Greece's debts were sustainable? Might it be time to alleviate Greece's debt burden, by forcing losses on private bondholders or easing the terms of EU loans? Or might the Greek government throw in the towel and chaotically default, potentially forcing the country out of the euro and starting a domino process across southern Europe that would cause the single currency to implode?

In June 2011, eurozone leaders officially recognised that Greece would need additional EU-IMF loans and a debt restructuring.[257] They called for "voluntary private sector involvement...while avoiding a selective default" – a twisted piece of jargon which meant that owners of Greek government bonds should "voluntarily" agree to exchange them for less valuable ones so that the pretence that Greece had not defaulted could be maintained and credit default swaps (contracts that pay out in the event that a borrower defaults) wouldn't be triggered. While there were incentives to exchange one's bonds – notably that unlike the old ones issued under Greek law, the terms of which could be easily rewritten by the Greek parliament, the new ones would be issued under English law – there was also a threat that bondholders might otherwise get a worse deal.

In July, eurozone leaders agreed to offer Greece a second EU-IMF loan programme on much better terms than the first.[258] The

---

257   European Council Conclusions, 23/24 June 2011, EUCO 23/1/11 REV 1. Section 15: "The euro area Heads of State or Government agree that required additional funding will be financed through both official and private sources. They endorse the approach decided by the Eurogroup on 20 June as regards the pursuit of voluntary private sector involvement in the form of informal and voluntary rollovers of existing Greek debt at maturity for a substantial reduction of the required year-by-year funding within the programme while avoiding a selective default."

258   Statement by the Heads of State or Government of the Euro Area and EU Institutions, 21 July 2011. Section 3: "We have decided to lengthen the maturity of future EFSF loans to Greece to the maximum extent possible from the current 7.5 years to a minimum of 15 years and up to 30 years with a grace period of 10 years. In this context, we will ensure adequate post programme monitoring. We will provide EFSF loans at lending rates equivalent to those of the Balance of Payments facility (currently approx. 3.5 per cent), close to, without going below, the EFSF funding cost. We also decided to extend substantially the maturities of the existing Greek

new plan was predicated on Greece conjuring up €50 billion in privatisation revenues by 2015 – as if a desperate seller in a depressed economy could get a decent price for distressed state assets that could end up denominated in devalued drachmas. Cunning bankers conned naïve EU negotiators into a debt exchange that offered them much more generous terms for their Greek bonds than they could get on the open market – in effect, another bailout.[259] Eurozone leaders insisted that this debt write-down was an "exceptional and unique solution"[260] – but by then markets didn't believe a word they said. Fortunately, this outrageous debt exchange never happened.

In October 2011, eurozone leaders agreed to seek a "deeper private-sector involvement".[261] The IMF, now run by Christine

---

facility. This will be accompanied by a mechanism which ensures appropriate incentives to implement the programme." In effect, the longstanding German view that official lending should be at punitive rates had lost out to the IMF view that it should be as cheap as possible.

259   They got to swap bonds that were trading at less than 50 cents on the euro for new ones that give 79 cents or more: in effect, a bailout.

260   Statement by the Heads of State or Government of the Euro Area and EU Institutions, 21 July 2011, Section 6.

261   Euro Area Summit Statement, 26 October 2011. Section 12: "The Private Sector Involvement (PSI) has a vital role in establishing the sustainability of the Greek debt. Therefore we welcome the current discussion between Greece and its private investors to find a solution for a deeper PSI. Together with an ambitious reform programme for the Greek economy, the PSI should secure the decline of the Greek debt to GDP ratio with an objective of reaching 120 per cent by 2020. To this end we invite Greece, private investors and all parties concerned to develop a voluntary bond exchange with a nominal discount of 50 per cent on notional Greek debt held by private investors. The Euro zone Member States would contribute to the PSI package up to 30 billion euro. On that basis, the official sector stands ready to provide additional programme financing of up to 100 billion euro until 2014, including the required recapitalisation of Greek banks. The new programme should be

Lagarde, took a much tougher line in the debt-exchange negotiations. In principle, Greece could simply have imposed a deep restructuring through a vote in parliament. But the ECB's insistence that it be "voluntary" gave bondholders huge bargaining power.[262] Finally, in March 2012, the debt exchange was completed and the second, €130 billion EU-IMF loan programme for Greece signed off. Bondholders who had not taken the opportunity to sell over the previous two years took big losses (but still did well considering).[263] Credit-default swaps were triggered. Was there a Lehman-style panic? No. Did the world end? No. Did Rehn, Bini Smaghi or Trichet apologise? Of course not.

Unfortunately, all this fuss didn't deliver a lasting solution. The debt write-down was not big enough to make Greece's debts sustainable and the economy continued to sink. Indeed, Greece ended 2012 with public debts of 175.8 per cent of GDP – higher than in 2011, even after the write-down![264]

---

agreed by the end of 2011 and the exchange of bonds should be implemented at the beginning of 2012. We call on the IMF to continue to contribute to the financing of the new Greek programme."

262   For example, on 7 July 2011, Trichet said: "I have already said what our message for those who are in charge was, and that message was: no credit event, no selective default, no default. That is the message of the Governing Council." http://www.ecb.int/press/pressconf/2011/html/is110707.en.html The ECB could have been protected from losses by the EFSF buying its Greek bonds at their purchase price and then swapping them with Athens for a direct loan.

263   Private investors swapped roughly €206 billion of old bonds issued under Greek law for new bonds issued under English law together with EFSF notes and GDP warrants. The face value of the bonds was roughly halved; the net present value of the new bonds was around 75 per cent lower.

264   Eurostat, general government gross debt (Maastricht debt) in per cent of GDP - annual data. Code: tipsgo20

Act Three: it's systemic

Throughout the crisis, eurozone policymakers have been several steps behind. By June 2011, they had got Greece, Ireland and Portugal on EU-IMF programmes. They were finally starting to tackle Greece's debts. They had launched a broader push towards austerity and tighter fiscal rules that they thought would reassure markets and stabilise public finances. So they thought they could contain the crisis to those three small economies. In any case, they had set up a €440 billion crisis-lending fund, the EFSF, big enough to handle the next possible crisis victim, Spain, if it too got cut off from markets. So policymakers thought they had everything under control.

Behind the scenes, though, the Deauville-amplified doom loop was destabilising government bond yields, inflicting bigger losses on the eurozone's often-distressed banks. Suddenly, in July, the crisis took a virulent new turn as Italian yields soared, sparking a wider sell-off. Italy's near-€2-trillion bond market – the eurozone's largest and the world's third-biggest – was too big to fail, but also too big for even Germany to bail out. Thus Plan A – try to contain the crisis to Greece, Ireland and Portugal, and muddle through until 2013 in the hope that things would improve by then – had clearly failed. It was no longer a crisis in specific euro member states; it was a systemic crisis that threatened the eurozone – and the global financial system – as a whole. Act Three had begun.

Ever since Deauville, Italian bond yields had been creeping up. By the end of June 2011 ten-year yields had reached 4.88 per cent. Then in July they soared, hitting 6.13 per cent on 2 August.[265] Spanish ten-years leapt from 5.45 per cent to 6.45 per cent over the same period.[266] Belgian yields were close behind, and even France was starting to be dragged into the crisis. As investors panicked, they sought

265   http://www.bloomberg.com/quote/GBTPGR10:IND/chart
266   http://www.bloomberg.com/quote/GSPG10YR:IND/chart

refuge in the perceived safety of German Bunds: yields plunged from a post-Deauville high of 3.43 per cent on 6 April to 2.42 per cent on 2 August and to a low of 1.64 per cent on 23 September.[267] Since German yields collapsed, the rise in Italian, Spanish and other spreads was huge. Astonishingly, in the midst of this bond-market panic, the ECB decided to raise interest rates on 13 July, for the second time that year.

July 2011 was a particularly anxious month for global bond markets because the US government and Congress were also engaged in a game of chicken over whether legislators would raise the government's debt ceiling – the maximum it could borrow – or force a default in the world's biggest bond market, where US Treasury bonds were supposedly a "risk-free" asset. A deal was finally reached at the last minute, but on 5 August US debt lost its AAA-rating when it was downgraded a notch by Standard & Poor's, a credit rating agency. Ironically, such was the turmoil in the eurozone that US Treasury yields actually fell after the news.

In a systemic crisis, one can always point to local triggers as the proximate causes of turmoil. In Italy, Silvio Berlusconi was at war with his finance minister, Giulio Tremonti, not least because the former wanted tax cuts and the latter austerity measures. Soaring yields were seized on by the pro-austerity brigade as requiring a tightening of the screws in Italy; some also blamed the mere suggestion of "voluntary public sector involvement" in Greece in June. But Italy's situation had little in common with other crisis-hit economies. As Gregorio de Felice, chief economist at Intesa Sanpaolo, an Italian bank, remarked at the time: "Italy has good fundamentals. There is no property bubble, no financial bubble, the total debt did not increase during the crisis."[268] Even with a stagnant economy, the Italian

267   http://www.bloomberg.com/quote/GDBR10:IND/chart

268   http://www.ft.com/cms/s/0/20695168-a977-11e0-bcc2-00144feabdc0.html

government had a primary surplus: its revenues more than covered its spending, excluding interest payments. So it hardly needed an immediate dose of austerity and there was no fundamental reason for the soaring yields. Many investors were perplexed and thought the market reaction greatly overdone.[269] That's because the primary cause of the panic was not Italy but the instability of the system itself, which amplified the impact of any bond-market sell-off through a series of negative feedback loops.

Until that summer, Italian banks had generally been in decent shape. But because of their large holdings of Italian government bonds, falling bond prices dealt them a nasty blow.[270] Because other eurozone banks also held lots of Italian bonds, they too took a hit, sparking panic sales, causing them to cut off credit to businesses, and prompting fears that their own government would feel obliged to bail them out – but might not be able to.[271] Once bond yields began rising, it became rational to sell because of fears that if others wouldn't lend, governments would be forced to default. Italy was particularly vulnerable because its refinancing and other borrowing needs exceeded other eurozone governments' willingness or ability to lend. Because of these interconnections and negative feedback loops, individual governments' actions could not hope to stabilise the system. The ECB needed to step in as lender of last resort.

---

269   See, for instance, http://www.ft.com/cms/s/0/20695168-a977-11e0-bcc2-00144feabdc0.html

270   Italian banks' holdings of Italian government bonds accounted for 13.2 per cent of their assets. International Monetary Fund, *Global Financial Stability Report*, September 2011, Table 1.2

271   At the end of June 2011, French banks' exposure to Italian government bonds was €73.6 billion, German banks' €32.8 billion, Belgian banks' €11.1 billion, Spanish banks' €7.7 billion; UK ones' was €2 billion and US ones' €8.9 billion. Bank for International Settlements, international bank claims, consolidated, ultimate risk basis, converted at €1 = $1.4495

Lender of last resort

Governments are continually issuing new bonds and refinancing old ones. So they are always at risk that lenders will take fright, drive up interest rates and ultimately refuse to lend altogether. Such a crisis may take two forms. A solvency crisis occurs when investors demand much higher interest rates to compensate for the increased risk that a government may be unwilling or unable to pay back its debts and therefore may choose or be forced to default. Greece suffered a solvency crisis; Ireland was pushed towards one by its guarantee of all bank debts. A liquidity crisis occurs because something triggers panic among bond investors that becomes self-fulfilling: if many people think bond prices are going to fall and so sell, bond prices fall, which in turn encourages others to sell, and so on. Spain, Italy – and for a while, Belgium and France too – suffered a liquidity crisis. In effect, a panic is like a bubble in reverse: whereas a bubble is a rush to buy assets at ever higher prices driven by excessive optimism that can prove self-fulfilling for a long while, a panic is a dash to sell assets at ever lower prices driven by excessive pessimism that can also prove self-fulfilling. But a bond-market panic is particularly pernicious because it can force even a solvent government to default, because it may not be able to raise funds quickly enough to meet its obligations. In that respect, a bond-market panic is like a bank run, where a dash for cash by depositors (or a refusal of other lenders to refinance its debts) can force even a solvent bank that can't raise funds fast enough to fail.

Bank runs used to be common and crippling until the central bank began stepping in as a "lender of last resort", providing solvent banks with liquidity (cash loans secured against their assets). This not only ensured that solvent banks wouldn't be felled by a liquidity crisis; it also stopped most bank runs from happening altogether, since depositors knew that the central bank stood ready to lend if necessary. For the same reasons, the central bank also typically acts as a lender of last resort to the government. The first central banks – Sweden's Riksbank, which was founded in 1664, followed soon after by the Bank of England in 1694 and later by the Banque de France in 1800 – were set up precisely to manage governments' finances and to lend to them if necessary. Even the Deutsche Bundesbank, which is peculiar in many respects, is authorised to buy German government bonds and did so in the 1970s. However, the ECB is not mandated in the EU treaties to be a lender of last resort to governments. Worse, it claimed that it was legally unable to perform that essential function; both Trichet and Draghi insisted to President Barroso that the ECB could only intervene if the EU treaties were changed. This legal figleaf was a cover for political expediency: the desire by Trichet and then Draghi to advance their austerity agenda and the kow-towing of a supposedly independent European central bank to German political sensitivities.

In the absence of a lender of last resort, eurozone governments issue bonds in a currency that they do not control, as Paul de Grauwe of the London School of Economics brilliantly observed. In that sense, they have become like emerging economies that until recently could only borrow internationally in foreign currency. That makes them vulnerable to panic among investors, who may suddenly stop funding them.[272] This is a major flaw in the global financial system. As I argued in *Open World: the Truth about Globalisation*, in the absence of a provider of emergency liquidity with deep enough pockets, economies need to be wary of borrowing too much from foreigners and impose capital controls to protect themselves if necessary.[273] But within the eurozone, capital controls are meant to be illegal, while one of the major selling points of the single currency is that it ought to allow poorer countries to borrow freely from richer

272   Paul De Grauwe, "The European Central Bank: Lender of Last Resort in the Government Bond Markets?", CESifo Working Paper No. 3569, September 2011

273   Philippe Legrain, *Open World: The Truth About Globalisation*, Abacus: 2002

ones to fund catch-up growth and should promote integrated financial markets more generally. So by refusing to act as a lender of last resort, the ECB was not only threatening to allow eurozone governments to be forced unnecessarily to default, it was undermining the very basis of financial integration within the eurozone.

Policymakers could not claim ignorance about this. De Grauwe, a leading expert on the economics of monetary union, published his paper pointing out that eurozone governments were vulnerable to self-fulfilling panics in May 2011.[274] Soon after, I had a long discussion with him. When the panic became systemic in July 2011, I began insisting that only unlimited intervention by the ECB could halt it – as De Grauwe himself stressed in an article in the *Financial Times* on 4 August.[275]

After using soaring bond yields as leverage to secure commitments from Berlusconi that he would press on with austerity measures and structural reforms, the ECB did eventually buy Italian bonds – a whopping €36 billion in the space of two weeks – but it repeatedly emphasised that purchases would remain limited. This was counterproductive. While potentially unlimited intervention deters selling because investors know the ECB always stands ready to buy, temporary, limited intervention simply encourages investors to sell risky bonds before the ECB stops buying.[276] Perversely, these limited purchases

---

274 Paul de Grauwe, "Governance of a Fragile Eurozone", CEPS Working Documents, 4 May 2011 http://www.ceps.eu/book/governance-fragile-eurozone

275 Paul de Grauwe, "Only the ECB can halt eurozone contagion", *Financial Times*, 4 August 2011 http://www.ft.com/cms/s/0/4fd2a0c8-be10-11e0-ab9f-00144feabdc0. html#axzz1Tlg8yiSY Later that year, I was finally allowed to publish my own article arguing as much. Philippe Legrain, "The ECB Fear Factor", Project Syndicate, 13 December 2011 http://www.project-syndicate.org/commentary/the-ecb-fear-factor

276 While the ECB succeeded in pushing yields down temporarily, it failed to end the panic. Investors feared that yields would rise again once these limited interventions were over, and because some acted on those fears, yields duly rose again.

cost much more than the threat of unlimited intervention would have. A credible threat of unlimited intervention need not require the ECB to buy a single bond.

Blind alleys

With the ECB refusing to act as a lender of last resort and eurozone policymakers in any case persuaded that the solution was ever more austerity, Spain and Italy risked being cut off from market funding. While the EFSF had just about enough money for Spain, its limited funds couldn't stretch to Italy. So the prospect of a disorderly default in Italy loomed – and with it potentially the collapse of the euro. This sparked a desperate search for alternatives to ECB intervention, all of which were either politically impossible or financially unworkable.

Some argued that the solution was Eurobonds – that governments should be able to borrow by issuing bonds that were joint and severally guaranteed by all other eurozone governments. Proposals for Eurobonds were dressed up in highfalutin language about deeper integration, solidarity and fiscal union, but the underlying argument was that if Italy could issue bonds guaranteed by German taxpayers, it would have no problem borrowing at much lower interest rates. Unsurprisingly, Germans were none too keen on this idea. But if the ECB refused to blink, it seemed just about conceivable that the prospect of the imminent collapse of both the euro and six decades' efforts to embed Germany in a more integrated Europe might bounce Chancellor Merkel into it. That might have ended the panic, but it would have been politically devastating. The crisis had corroded the trust that such a joint venture would require. Introducing Eurobonds immediately

---

http://www.ecb.int/press/pr/wfs/2011/html/fs110816.en.html and http://www.ecb.int/press/pr/wfs/2011/html/fs110823.en.html

might have proved so politically toxic that it killed support for the euro. Since their issuance would require a change not just to the EU treaties but also to the German constitution, a pledge to introduce them might not even have been credible enough to arrest the panic. Another proposal was to create a debt-redemption fund, but this faced similar obstacles.[277]

Still others proposed ingenious schemes that, in effect, involved unlimited ECB intervention in an indirect way – for instance, giving the future ESM a banking licence. This would allow it to buy, say, Italian government bonds, use them as collateral to obtain cash from the ECB and thus buy more bonds. It seemed clever but was hardly likely to be more acceptable to the ECB than direct intervention.

Eurozone policymakers, meanwhile, latched on to ever more harebrained schemes that would purportedly allow the EFSF's meagre resources to magically multiply. In July 2011, they agreed to allow the EFSF to buy government bonds in the secondary market, as the ECB was already doing.[278] Clearly, limited intervention by the EFSF wasn't going to be any more successful than the ECB's. In October, leaders

---

277   http://www.voxeu.org/article/european-redemption-pact

278   They also allowed the EFSF to lend on a precautionary basis and to lend to governments to recapitalise banks. Statement by the Heads of State or Government of the Euro Area and EU Institutions, 21 July 2011. Section 8: "To improve the effectiveness of the EFSF and of the ESM and address contagion, we agree to increase their flexibility linked to appropriate conditionality, allowing them to:
- act on the basis of a precautionary programme;
- finance recapitalisation of financial institutions through loans to governments including in non programme countries ;
- intervene in the secondary markets on the basis of an ECB analysis recognizing the existence of exceptional financial market circumstances and risks to financial stability and on the basis of a decision by mutual agreement of the EFSF/ESM Member States, to avoid contagion."

agreed on two schemes to try to make the EFSF's resources stretch further – one hopeless and the other dangerous.[279] The hopeless one was to send the begging bowl around Asia and the Middle East to invest in unfortunately named "special purpose investment vehicles" (spivs) that would in turn buy Italian and other troubled bonds – in essence, still limited intervention but on a bigger scale. Unsurprisingly, the Chinese were not won over. After all, would you put money into a venture in which the salesman himself doesn't want to invest more?

The dangerous idea was that the EFSF should offer bondholders a guarantee that it would bear the first losses in the event of a default. This ludicrous idea was bound to fail for lots of reasons (see footnotes for details).[280] Worse, far from limiting panic, it spread

---

279   Euro Summit Statement, 26 October 2011. Section 19: "We agree on two basic options to leverage the resources of the EFSF:

• providing credit enhancement to new debt issued by Member States, thus reducing the funding cost. Purchasing this risk insurance would be offered to private investors as an option when buying bonds in the primary market;

• maximising the funding arrangements of the EFSF with a combination of resources from private and public financial institutions and investors, which can be arranged through Special Purpose Vehicles. This will enlarge the amount of resources available to extend loans, for bank recapitalization and for buying bonds in the primary and secondary markets."

280   The proposal to make the EFSF a bond insurer would not work and would actually be dangerous for several reasons. First, its resources were limited: out of its €440 billion, some €200 billion were already committed to Greece, Ireland and Portugal – and even levered up five times, its resources were still limited. Second, unlike the ECB, which can provide liquidity for free, it would have to cover its funding costs – at least 3 per cent. Third, because it operated by unanimity and was hostage to political constraints in member states, EFSF guarantees could only ever be conditional. Fourth, it was fragile. Logically, Italy and Spain could not guarantee themselves or each other – and if the crisis spread to Belgium and even France, the EFSF would implode: the call on its resources would increase, while its firepower would decrease. The EFSF's AAA-rating also relied on France's threatened AAA-rating. If France lost its AAA, either the EFSF would have to accept a lower AA

it.[281] Promising to take the first hit in the event of default greatly increased the risk of losses for the EFSF – and the eurozone

---

rating, or the remaining AAA-countries would have to increase the size of their guarantees, or the firepower of the EFSF would fall further.

Worst of all, levering the EFSF could trigger a French and even a German down-grade, because it greatly increased the risk that AAA-countries' guarantees would be called on. When the EFSF lent to a government that subsequently haircut its debt by 20 per cent, EFSF guarantors lost only if the EFSF-held bonds were included in the restructuring, and then by only 20 per cent. But if the EFSF guaranteed the first 20 per cent of losses, EFSF guarantors automatically lost 100 per cent of their exposure in the event of a restructuring. Since markets and rating agencies think ahead, this increased risk of losses raised the yields of EFSF guarantors and was likely to lead to a French downgrade, and perhaps even a German one, as S&P had signalled. This would be politically devastating and cause the EFSF to implode. In short, because the EFSF's resources were limited, costly, conditional and fragile, it could not pro-vide a credible commitment that illiquid governments would always be funded and thus remain solvent. As such, it would not stabilise market expectations: rational investors would continue to have an incentive to shun Italian and Spanish bonds, and speculators would have an incentive to bet heavily on that basis.

281   Such was the Byzantine complexity of the first-loss-guarantee and SPIV pro-posals that it was easy to forget what the real priority was: convincing investors that Italian, Spanish, Belgian and French bonds were safe. To do so, policymakers needed to halt what amounted to a run on their bonds. Put yourself in the shoes, for a moment, of a typical bond investor who buys Italian bonds because he thinks they are safe. What signal does providing a 20 per cent or 33 per cent first-loss guarantee send? It makes you think that the risk of Italian default is real. Then you think: Is the guarantee credible? Will it be big enough? Do I want to worry about all these risks when what I am looking for is a safe investment? The answer, typically, will be no, no and no, because the EFSF has limited firepower, conditional on unanim-ity, dependent on France's threatened AAA which the leverage scheme makes even more fragile.

Of course, the guarantee and SPIV might attract a different type of investor – one willing or able to take more risk. But risk demands a reward – higher yields than those on a safe investment – especially because the risks involved are new, hard to assess and contingent on unpredictable political decisions. All of this would raise long-term

governments that guaranteed EFSF loans. If that led credit-rating agencies to strip France of its vulnerable AAA-rating, the EFSF's lending capacity would implode. In effect, the EFSF, whose ability to borrow cheaply to lend to stricken governments depended on guarantees from stronger ones, was a bit like a rope holding together a convoy of mountain climbers. It was effective at catching the fall of the smaller climbers at the rear, but as bigger climbers started to lose their footing too, they threatened to drag everyone else down with them.[282]

---

funding costs. Crucially, it also defeated the purpose of the exercise, which is not to protect investors against losses on a risky investment but to convince them that it is safe.

Because the first-loss-guarantee/SPIV proposal solely involved intervention in the primary market, it would also fragment bond markets into old bonds (which would have no guarantee) and a variety of new bonds (which would have guarantees of varying sizes and credibility). This complexity and fragmentation, in turn, would do lasting damage to sovereign bond markets, draining liquidity and deterring investors who want a safe, simple investment. For those investors who were willing to buy new Italian bonds with a limited guarantee, it would reduce the appeal of uninsured bonds, both Italian/Spanish and Belgian/French. In effect, it would be likely to drive up spreads on uninsured Italian, Spanish, Belgian and French bonds – increasing contagion rather than calming it, and damaging banks' balance sheets. In short, not only would the first-loss-guarantee/SPIV scheme not work, it would be likely to spread contagion and do lasting damage to eurozone sovereign bond markets.

282   The sums involved were large but bearable when only small countries – Greece, Ireland and Portugal – were in play. The second programme for Greece amounted to €164.5 billion: €144.7 billion from the EFSF and €19.8 billion from the IMF. Ireland's loan was €67.5 billion: €22.5 billion from EU governments through the EFSM, €17.7 billion from the EFSF, €3.8 billion (£3.2 billion) bilaterally from the UK government, €600 million bilaterally from the Swedish government, €400 million bilaterally from the Danish government, and €22.5 billion from the IMF. Portugal's was €78 billion: €26 billion from EU governments through the EFSM, €26 billion from the EFSF and €26 billion from the IMF. In total, then, the loans amounted to €310 billion.

In November, before the crazy EFSF first-loss scheme was ever used, French bond yields soared. France's debt was no longer deemed safe, so its guarantees to Spain and Italy were worthless – nor did the EFSF itself even seem like a safe investment any more. The nail in the coffin came in January 2012 when France (and Austria) were downgraded, killing the first-loss idea and sparking a big debate about the role of credit-rating agencies.[283]

---

283 Undeniably, rating agencies' judgments are often flawed. During the bubble years, they validated the misplaced belief among investors and central bankers (notably Greenspan and Trichet) that both American mortgage bonds and Greek government bonds were safe. Wise independent investors pay little heed to their judgments. Yet rating agencies' judgements carry undue weight because of their quasi-regulatory role and the fetishising of AAA-ratings by politicians – Sarkozy wore France's AAA as a badge of honour and eurozone policymakers were determined that the EFSF should have a AAA-rating. Policymakers therefore largely have themselves to blame for rating agencies' exalted role: if one seeks external validation from their (often ill-deserved) positive judgements, one must accept that their negative judgements will sting more too.

The proper policy response is not to shoot the messenger. Michel Barnier's suggestion that ratings be banned in periods of market turmoil was an absurd, unenforceable and counterproductive violation of freedom of speech; would you buy bonds whose ratings the European Commission had banned? The right response is to remove rating agencies' privileged regulatory position, while encouraging greater competition, and thus a greater diversity of opinions. Rating agencies' quasi-official role in regulations should be removed or replaced by appropriate alternatives, as the US's Dodd-Frank Act requires. For instance, while pension funds will naturally take account of the perceived riskiness of investing in various assets, legislation should not compel them to buy, or prevent them from buying, bonds with a certain rating. Likewise, central-bank counterparty rules should not take account of ratings. And the Basel rules should be reformed (again). They have had a noxious effect during the boom (when they encouraged banks to buy lots of sovereign bonds because these were zero risk-weighted) and again during the bust (when sovereign downgrades have exacerbated a vicious circle of margin calls and selling). More fundamentally, we need to get away from the idea that there is a single correct

Mayhem

Just when you thought things couldn't get any worse, they did. As a result of their previous losses, many eurozone banks were under-capitalised while others were insolvent but propped up by government guarantees and regulatory forbearance. Soaring government bond yields over the summer punched an even bigger hole in banks' balance sheets, including in ones that had previously come through the crisis relatively unscathed. Newly installed at the IMF, Christine Lagarde sounded the alarm in late August, saying eurozone banks should be forced to raise fresh capital.[284] Eurozone policymakers accused her of sparking panic, but that was nonsense. Bank share prices were already collapsing. Markets were refusing to lend to many banks, forcing them to rely on ECB funding. The fear that weak banks might need government bailouts was adding to the sovereign-bond panic. Seemingly unaware that government guarantees were increasingly worthless and were dragging down governments with banks, eurozone leaders agreed in October 2011 to offer fresh guarantees for bank debt.[285] They also decided to force banks to increase their capital buffers to 9 per cent by the end of June 2012.[286]

---

assessment of creditworthiness: a multiplicity of views and methodologies is welcome. And to overcome the conflict of interest at the heart of rating agencies, investors, rather than (private) issuers, should pay for ratings, as they did prior to the 1970s. Policymakers should stop fetishising a AAA rating, giving undue credence to rating agencies' judgements.

284   http://www.ft.com/cms/s/0/9f857244-d0d0-11e0-8891-00144feab49a.html

285   Statement of EU Heads of State or Government, 26 October 2011. Section 2: "Guarantees on bank liabilities would be required to provide more direct support for banks in accessing term funding (short-term funding being available at the ECB and relevant national central banks), where appropriate."

286   Based on sovereign debt valuations on 30 September 2011. *Ibid*, Section 5: "Financing of capital increase: Banks should first use private sources of capital, including through restructuring and conversion of debt to equity instruments. Banks

A capital increase was long overdue. Unfortunately, policymakers botched the move. Instead of stipulating that banks raise a specific sum of capital, they told them to hit a higher ratio of capital to assets. Since bank share prices were low and earnings meagre, banks opted to shrink their assets rather than raise additional capital. But since banks' assets are primarily their loans to households and companies along with their government bond holdings, this led to a massive credit crunch and firesales of government bonds. By January 2012, EU leaders realised their mistake, but the damage was already done.[287] Smaller businesses were hit hardest.[288] Worse, policymakers were about to make an even bigger mistake.

---

should be subject to constraints regarding the distribution of dividends and bonus payments until the target has been attained. If necessary, national governments should provide support, and if this support is not available, recapitalisation should be funded via a loan from the EFSF in the case of Eurozone countries."

287 Statement of the Members of the European Council, 30 January 2012, Section 7: "It is vital to take measures to prevent the present credit crunch severely limiting the ability of enterprises to grow and create jobs. The recent measures taken by the ECB as regards long-term lending to banks help very much in that respect. National supervisors and the EBA must ensure that bank recapitalisation does not lead to deleveraging which would negatively affect the financing of the economy. Supervisors should ensure a rigorous application by all banks of EU legislation restricting bonus payments.

288 EU leaders' package of measures to help SMEs was only a sticking plaster. See *Ibid*, Section 8: "The 23 million European SMEs are the backbone of Europe's economic success and a key provider of employment. We therefore agree on the following urgent measures to be implemented by June:

• better mobilising structural funds by speeding up the implementation of existing programmes and projects, where appropriate re-programming monies and rapidly committing monies not yet allocated to specific projects, concentrating on growth enhancement and job creation;

• strengthening EIB support for SMEs and infrastructure; the Council, the Commission and the EIB are invited to consider possible options to enhance EIB

Mistake five: threatening to force Greece out of the euro

What is there about international summits in France? The fifth huge policy mistake was the threat to force Greece out of the euro, initially made at the G20 summit in Cannes in early November 2011. With the economy collapsing, unemployment soaring and Greeks in uproar at the brutal austerity imposed on them by the EU and the IMF, prime minister Papandreou felt obliged to promise a referendum on the country's second EU-IMF loan programme, announced back in July but still not formally agreed. Merkel and Sarkozy responded by publicly threatening to force Greece out of the euro.[289] Papandreou backed down and resigned – in effect, bundled out of office by Merkel and Sarkozy – and was succeeded by a more obedient technocrat-led coalition. Even so, Merkel and Sarkozy opened the floodgates for a tidal wave of comments by politicians and policymakers about the merits of Greek euro exit – or Grexit, as Willem Buiter of Citi termed it. For many months, senior German policymakers and others argued that forcing Greece out would actually be a good thing because it would signal to other recalcitrant southern European countries that unless

action to support growth and to make appropriate recommendations, including possibilities for the EU budget to leverage EIB group financing capacity;

• rapidly examining the Commission's proposals on a pilot phase for the use of "project bonds" to stimulate private financing of key infrastructure projects;

• ensuring better access to venture capital across Europe by agreeing the EU passport by June;

• promoting the role of the Progress Microfinance Facility in support for microenterprises;

• making renewed efforts to improve the environment in which SMEs operate, in particular as regards the reduction of unjustified administrative and regulatory burdens as well as by ensuring that all actions at the European Union level fully support economic growth and job creation."

289   Sarkozy said: "The question is whether Greece remains in the eurozone, that is what we want. But it is up to the Greek people to answer that question." http://www.ft.com/cms/s/0/c47bc3f4-0605-11e1-ad0e-00144feabdc0.html

they implemented the austerity and reform programmes mandated by Berlin and Brussels they too would be expelled. Legally, there are no provisions in the EU treaties for leaving the euro. But nor was there any legal impediment to countries reintroducing their own national currency, either as a replacement for, or in parallel with, the euro. In practice, just as the ECB successfully blackmailed Ireland, so Greece (and others) could be threatened with exit.

If the EU and the IMF cut off lending to a government that needed to borrow but could not do so from markets – call it Greece – it would have to default either on its debts or on its domestic obligations: stop paying public-sector salaries, pensions and so on, or pay them in IOUs instead. If Greece defaulted on its debts, local banks that owned lots of Greek government bonds would become insolvent (unless the bonds they held were exchanged for new ones on which the government chose not to default) and so would be ineligible for ECB funding. Even if they remained solvent, the ECB could refuse to accept Greek government bonds as collateral for short-term liquidity. To avoid the collapse of its banking system, Greece would be forced to declare a bank holiday, impose capital controls and redenominate accounts in a currency that it could create at will. Alternatively, Greece could choose to continue paying its debts and "default" on its domestic payments. Since it could not borrow, it would need to stop any euro outgoings that exceeded its current revenues. If it stopped paying salaries and pensions, this brutal fiscal squeeze would throttle the economy. If it paid them in IOUs – which could potentially be tradable, and hence become a parallel Greek currency – the impact would be almost as severe, since the IOUs would be almost worthless, presaging hyperinflation if they subsequently became the Greek currency. It is questionable whether the ECB actually would have cut off Greek banks, breaking up the euro and spreading panic – but the threat was deemed credible and never tested.

While eurozone policymakers would doubtless argue (as always) that their actions were necessary to safeguard the stability of the euro by bringing Greece into line, they actually had the opposite effect, creating a doom loop on steroids. The euro had previously been perceived as an irreversible currency union – like the United States, where nobody thinks that a default by the state of California or the city of Detroit will lead to it abandoning the dollar. Instead, the euro became, in effect, a system of fixed exchange rates that is extremely costly – but not impossible – to break. In the exchange-rate mechanism (ERM), which preceded the euro, speculation about devaluation was expressed as pressure on a currency peg (as during the ERM crisis in 1992–3); now it was expressed as pressure on sovereign bond yields and bank funding costs as capital fled vulnerable eurozone economies to Germany. This capital flight caused interest rates to soar and credit to contract across southern Europe, deepening the recession. Such was the demand for the perceived safety of German assets that Berlin was able to borrow at deeply negative interest rates. Even dodgy German banks that enjoyed a government guarantee were awash with cash. Because of the ratchet effect of the doom loop, capital flight weakened banks, government and the economy in succession, increasing the perceived probability that the euro would break up and exacerbating the negative feedback loop. What was that about the Greek bailout averting a Lehman-style panic? In fact, the tug of war since that fateful mistake in May 2010 had even more devastating consequences.

In effect, a Greek euro was no longer equivalent to a German one. Greek euros risked being redenominated into depreciating drachmas, while German ones might become appreciating Deutsche Marks. Since Greek euros could still be converted into German ones at par, banks, companies and people rushed to do so. Not just Greek euros, in fact, but Portuguese, Spanish, Italian, Irish, Belgian and even French ones too. Bank deposits drained out of southern Europe and poured into Germany. Investors rushed to dump assets that might be redenominated – not least government and bank bonds. Banks scrambled to limit their exposure to southern Europe: foreign banks refused to lend to local ones, which refused to extend new loans or roll over existing ones. National regulators banned banks from lending to vulnerable economies – in effect, imposing capital controls within the eurozone. Companies reorganised their operations, trying to match incomings and outgoings for each national economy – unravelling the single market. Lawyers pored over contracts to determine how they might be affected by euro break-up and sought to rewrite them to mitigate its impact. Officially, the euro still existed. In practice, it had fragmented along national lines.

More mayhem

By November 2011, the euro's days seemed numbered. The banking system was on the brink of meltdown. Banks could not obtain funding, had largely stopped lending to each other, and were scrambling to sell assets and cut credit lines in order to raise cash, reassure nervous investors and meet the EBA's 9 per-cent capital ratio. Even EU officials feared for the safety of their savings in the bank. Panic stalked sovereign bond markets. On 9 November, the ECB finally reversed its July interest-rate rise. Even so, Italian ten-year yields, which spiked to 7.5 per cent, closed higher that day. An Italian default seemed imminent. Amid the turmoil, Silvio Berlusconi was bundled out of office, victim in effect of an ECB-led coup. His successor, Mario Monti, a technocratic former European Commissioner, promised to stop the rot. But tellingly, the panic deepened, because it had little to do with how committed to austerity the Italian prime minister was. The hope, though, was that Monti's sobriety would make it politically easier for the ECB to intervene. The election of an austere right-wing government in Spain on 20 November didn't reassure markets either. French yields also soared, only days after a new austerity package had been announced, as did Belgian ones. It wasn't clear whether Germany and the ECB wanted the euro to survive in its current form or would be willing to do enough to prevent its break-up.

On 1 December Draghi hinted that, following agreement on a "fiscal compact", "other things might follow", triggering a burst of hope. EU leaders duly complied, agreeing eight days later to a compact that would entrench stringent limits on government borrowing in national constitutions. While David Cameron "vetoed" the deal after his bid to get special treatment for the City of London was given short shrift, other EU governments proceeded without him. With Britain marginalised, the eurozone crisis had now become an EU one too.

Merkel was delighted by the new fiscal straightjacket. Others hoped that Berlin might reciprocate with a roadmap towards Eurobonds. Above all, they hoped the ECB would finally step in. But on 15 December, Draghi disingenuously said that his comments had been misinterpreted. Thus up to twenty-six countries had agreed to a dangerously one-sided fiscal pact without securing either a German commitment for a roadmap to Eurobonds or ECB intervention to stop the run on eurozone government bonds.

Truce
The ECB did, however, buy some time. A week earlier, it had announced that it would provide banks with unlimited liquidity (cash loans) for up to three years in exchange for a much wider range of collateral. In the mayhem, this announcement was initially overlooked. But once the first three-year "long-term refinancing operation" (LTRO) took place on 21 December, this eased banks' funding problems and eventually halted their increasingly desperate firesales of government bonds. It was an astonishing value judgement, though,

that the ECB was willing to provide €1 trillion in 1-per-cent loans to eurozone banks but wasn't willing to come to the aid of elected governments.

For a few months, the LTROs dampened the negative feedback loops. From early January 2012 to a bit beyond 29 February, the date of the second LTRO, Italian spreads fell a lot and Spanish ones a little.[290] Investors were relieved that a euro collapse had been avoided for now. Initially, panicky banks deposited a large share of the €489 billion that they borrowed on 21 December back with the ECB. But as confidence began to return, they also bought short-term Italian and Spanish bonds, which paid a higher return. More unexpectedly, the LTROs also contributed to a dip in longer-term yields.[291] Under strong pressure from national capitals, domestic banks which knew that a sovereign default would sink them decided to "double down" and gamble on redemption: if the government defaulted, they would be bankrupted in any case; if it pulled through, they would profit handsomely. Others joined in on a speculative basis. Just as the panic was self-fulfilling, so was the rally. A vicious circle turned into a virtuous one. But the LTROs tied the fates of banks and governments even closer together – buying time at the expense of greater future fragility.

Worse, while the LTROs rehydrated liquidity-parched banks, these cheap ECB loans also propped up zombie and insolvent ones. Lending to an illiquid bank is like tiding over a viable business with cashflow problems; lending to an insolvent one is throwing good

---

290   Italian ten-year yields fell from 7.16 per cent on 6 January 2012 to 4.84 per cent on 10 March, with spreads narrowing by 253 basis points, from 530 basis points to 277. Spain's dropped from 5.72 per cent to 5.20 per cent, with spreads narrowing by 73 basis points, from 386 basis points to 313.

291   At a time when banks were trying to shrink and were being driven by investor pressure and EBA decisions to minimise their exposure to southern European sovereigns, buying longer-term Italian and Spanish bonds was both risky (because a rebound in sovereign yields would hit them hard) and costly.

money after bad, like a sugar daddy who bankrolls their protégé's loss-making venture. Unsurprisingly, then, this ECB funding scarcely improved credit conditions for European households and businesses: neither the cost nor the availability of credit to the real economy improved much.

The LTROs appeared to quell the crisis for the first three months of 2012 – and eurozone policymakers prematurely declared victory. As early as 6 February, European Council President Herman van Rompuy infamously said "the worst part is over."[292] On 22 March, ECB President Draghi echoed this, saying "the worst is over."[293] Ironically, his declaration marked the peak of the LTRO rally. As I warned at the time, in the absence of a credible guarantee that Italy would be able to refinance its debt and certainty that the euro was going to hold together, the situation remained precarious and sentiment could easily reverse itself. It did.

Panic redux

Panic returned in earnest in April 2012. As with Italy the previous summer, policymakers focused on the proximate cause – Spain's refusal to enact brutal austerity measures demanded by Germany and prescribed by the European Commission – rather than the underlying one: the systemic instability created by the negative feedback loops. Almost immediately, soaring Spanish yields sparked contagion to Italy and beyond. But if, as Brussels and Berlin insisted, the rise in Spanish yields was due to Madrid's reluctance to accept austerity, why was the panic transmitted to Italy? In what way was Monti less austere than before? In fact, investors were increasingly aware that

---

292   https://mninews.marketnews.com/content/update-eu-van-rompuyfacing-long-crisis-worst-part-over

293   To be fair, Draghi said "the worst is over, but there are still risks." http://in.reuters.com/article/2012/03/21/ecb-draghi-idINDEE82K0I720120321

the EU's crisis-resolution strategy was flawed. It was imposing huge pain without stabilising public debt, fomenting a growing political backlash and sparking fear rather than reassuring investors. Above all, policymakers were ignoring the real issues: the doom loop and the self-fulfilling panic.

The various interlocking strands of the crisis came to a head in June 2012. After inconclusive elections in May, Greece was due to hold a re-run on 17 June. Syriza, a far-left party that wanted to renegotiate the country's EU-IMF programme while remaining in the euro, looked set to win, with eurozone policymakers threatening to force Greece out if it did. That prospect was accelerating the slow-motion bank run across southern Europe, threatening a full-on stampede. Such was the fragmentation of eurozone financial markets that a creditworthy hotel in South Tirol (Italy) had to pay three percentage points more for a bank loan than its equivalent in North Tirol (Austria) – if it could borrow at all. In effect, the single market had shattered.

As well as a liquidity crisis, many banks faced a solvency crisis. In Germany, this was a slow-burning problem, because nobody doubted the government's willingness and ability to keep zombie banks afloat. But in Spain, it was pressing. With the 30 June deadline for raising banks' capital ratio to 9 per cent looming, many banks fell far short and couldn't raise additional equity from markets. One bankrupt bank alone, Bankia, an amalgam of stricken *cajas* (savings banks), had a €19 billion shortfall, though its chairman, former Partido Popular finance minister Rodrigo Rato, had still paid himself a no doubt wholly deserved salary of €2.3 million. Estimates of Spanish banks' capital needs were as high as €100 billion, or 10 per cent of Spanish GDP.[294]

---

294   It was impossible to determine an exact figure since it depended on how bad things might get – how much further property prices might fall, how much deeper the recession might get, how much higher sovereign yields might soar – and how big a safety margin banks were deemed to need.

But with Spanish ten-year yields soaring to 7 per cent and the ECB still refusing to intervene, Mariano Rajoy's government felt unable to borrow from the markets to recapitalise them and so was seeking EU help. A full bailout, however, would drain the EFSF/ESM's coffers, raising new fears about its inadequacy for dealing with the country next in line, Italy. Another option was to lend solely to recapitalise Spanish banks, while hoping that the government would be able to continue funding its other requirements from the markets.

A third option was for EU money to directly recapitalise the banks, as the IMF and the European Commission had proposed. This would break the link between weak banks and weak sovereigns: the burden of recapitalising local banks would not fall on Spanish taxpayers, eliminating the risk that their losses could drag down the state. Unsurprisingly, this was Madrid's preferred option, with strong support from Ireland and others hopeful that this could relieve pressure on their own taxpayers, but Germany was set against the idea. Injecting EU money into stricken Spanish banks would require external oversight to ensure that Madrid followed through with restructuring and resolving them. All this prompted a broader debate about the need for a eurozone "banking union" – a single bank supervisor, a common mechanism for restructuring or winding down failed banks and shared deposit insurance – which in turn seemed to imply closer fiscal integration too. The best option – requiring banks' bondholders to bail in bust banks, thus breaking the doom loop without burdening European taxpayers – sadly wasn't on the agenda; to do this, Spain could simply have passed a bank-resolution law modelled on German or British lines.

To make matters worse, massive austerity, a crippling credit crunch and existential worries about the euro's future had pushed the eurozone as a whole into recession since the start of the year, with southern Europe in a deep funk and even Germany struggling. The euro's days again seemed numbered.

False dawn

In the second half of June, things suddenly looked like they were falling into place. The threat of euro ejection scared Greeks into rejecting Syriza and electing New Democracy – ironically, the party whose mismanagement between 2004 and 2009 pushed Greece into insolvency – which formed a coalition that pledged to continue implementing the EU-IMF programme. Crucially, Germany then decided that it did wish to keep Greece in the euro after all.

On 29 June, eurozone leaders officially recognised for the first time the "imperative to break the vicious circle between banks and sovereigns".[295] They agreed to fast-track the creation of a single eurozone bank supervisor and for the ESM, whose creation had been brought forward to July 2012,[296] then to be able to recapitalise banks directly.[297] They also agreed to look again at Ireland's bank bailout and other similar cases. In the meantime they would lend to Spain to recapitalise its banks, with the suggestion that the burden would only temporarily fall on the Spanish government.[298]

EU leaders also called for a "specific and time-bound roadmap" towards closer monetary union by the end of the year, building on a report by Europe's four presidents (it has five, including the president

295 Euro Area Summit Statement, 29 June 2012.

296 In December 2011, eurozone leaders decided to bring forward the creation of the EFSF's permanent replacement, the ESM, to July 2012, phase in its capital contributions faster and provide a further €200 billion to the IMF. Statement of Euro Area Heads of State or Government, 9 December 2011

297 *Ibid.* "When an effective single supervisory mechanism is established, involving the ECB, for banks in the euro area the ESM could, following a regular decision, have the possibility to recapitalize banks directly."

298 *Ibid.* They also persisted with the wrongheaded notion that the EFSF/ESM's limited resources could stabilise sovereign bond markets, and hinted misleadingly at a role for the ECB. "We welcome that the ECB has agreed to serve as an agent to EFSF/ESM in conducting market operations in an effective and efficient manner."

of the European Parliament). The presidents of the European Council, the European Commission, the ECB and the Eurogroup (eurozone finance ministers) had sketched out how to complete the monetary union through closer integration in finance (a banking union) and budget-making (a fiscal union), closer economic-policy coordination (an economic union) and greater democratic legitimacy and accountability. In a nod to the newly elected President Hollande, who had pledged to end austerity and boost growth, they also adopted a "Compact on Growth and Jobs". While mostly a rehash of existing proposals, there was some recognition that investment in future growth should be spared from budget cuts. Importantly, it promised a boost equivalent to 1 per cent of EU GDP for investment to support demand and help reforms succeed, notably a capital increase for the European Investment Bank and tilting EU aid for poorer regions towards growth-boosting measures.[299]

Eurozone leaders were very pleased with themselves. Yet again, they thought they had done enough to quell the panic. But while Spanish ten-year yields fell by half a percentage point on 29 June, a week later they were back at 7 per cent. The knee-jerk reaction of the quack doctors at the European Commission was to demand further bloodletting, bullying Madrid into a further €65 billion – 6.5 per cent of GDP – austerity package on 11 July, including a three percentage-point rise in value-added tax (VAT) and cuts in unemployment benefit in a depressed economy where more than a quarter of the workforce were unemployed.[300] In the Brussels mythology of the crisis, this barbaric austerity brought Spanish yields down. In fact, yields continued to soar, topping 7.5 per cent until Draghi finally promised those

---

299   European Council Conclusions, 29 June 2012 http://www.consilium.europa. eu/uedocs/cms_data/docs/pressdata/en/ec/131388.pdf

300   http://www.reuters.com/article/2012/07/11/us-spain-economy-cuts-idUSBRE86A0CP20120711

magic words on 26 July – "Within our mandate, the ECB is ready to do whatever it takes to preserve the euro. And believe me, it will be enough."[301] – and Merkel publicly supported him.

No way to manage a crisis

Until the summer of 2012, eurozone policymakers' crisis response was generally inept, often misdirected and frequently outright destructive. "Safeguarding financial stability" meant sparing no taxpayer expense to pay creditors in full (then threatening to hit those they shouldn't) and papering over banking problems, while doing nothing to break the doom loop between vulnerable sovereigns, troubled banks and shrinking economies. Misdiagnosing the crisis led to a collective lurch towards slash-and-burn austerity and wage cuts rather than a focus on investment and productivity-enhancing reforms. Frankfurt, Brussels and Berlin bullied eurozone leaders into accepting a dangerously inflexible and undemocratic fiscal straightjacket. The excessively independent but politically compromised ECB bounced governments into austerity while refusing to act as a lender of last resort to them for far too long.

As a result of the five massive policy mistakes – backstopping the banks, the Greek fiasco, collective austerity, Deauville and the Grexit threat – and many smaller ones, by the summer of 2012 the eurozone faced a much deeper crisis than two years earlier. An economic and social crisis: shrinking (sometimes collapsing) economies, mass unemployment, household debts that falling wages made even more unbearable, the poor and vulnerable disproportionately hit by swingeing austerity. This was exacerbated by a devastating financial crisis that took several forms. A banking crisis: zombie banks curtailing credit to southern Europe, their losses deepening as shrinking economies turned more household and business loans sour, with their debts

---

301   http://www.ecb.int/press/key/date/2012/html/sp120726.en.html

threatening to sink the government – notably in Ireland and Spain – that backstopped them. A solvency crisis in Greece – prompting savage, devastating austerity, complicated by the fact that EU-IMF loans had substituted for private-sector ones and by the fear that Greece's default might entail its exit from the euro – as well as in Portugal and potentially in Ireland too. A liquidity crisis: a self-fulfilling panic that governments might not be able to refinance themselves at reasonable rates which, in the absence of an adequate lender of last resort, could lead to default, notably in Italy. And a currency crisis: a fear that one or more countries might leave the euro and that it might break up, causing investors to sell assets and curtail lending that risked redenomination into currencies that would depreciate and buy assets that might be redenominated into currencies that would appreciate – a problem across southern Europe and a boost for Germany and subsequently for France too. Worse, the combination of shrinking economies, self-defeating austerity, credit-crunched businesses and panicky high interest rates threatened to push even solvent governments such as Spain and Italy into a debt trap and ultimately default.

On top of that, there was an institutional crisis: the eurozone lacked a proper framework for resolving banks or restructuring sovereign debt, while the ECB's role as a lender of last resort to governments was undefined and contested. And there was also a deepening political crisis: absence of agreement on a solution to the crisis; doubts whether such an agreement was even possible; a lack of political leadership; a credibility gap, because policymakers kept saying they would do whatever it takes to resolve the crisis, but repeatedly failed to do so; growing conflict between member states; bailout fatigue in creditor countries and austerity fatigue in debtor countries; a mounting backlash against the EU itself.

A crisis that could have united Europe in tackling the excesses of the financial sector had instead fractured it. While this was partly due to conflicting narratives about what had gone wrong, it was also due to a battle over how the burden of losses from the crisis should be shared – among investors, bank shareholders, bondholders and tax-payers; and between creditor countries and debtor ones. Last but not least, it involved a game of chicken between the monetary authority (the ECB) and seventeen fiscal ones (national governments) over who took responsibility for resolving the crisis and what conditions were exacted in return. It was no way to manage a crisis.

5

IT'S NOT OVER

How to fix the crisis in the eurozone for good

> *Within our mandate, the ECB is ready to do whatever it takes*
> *to preserve the euro. And believe me, it will be enough.*
>
> Mario Draghi, president of the European Central Bank,
> 26 July 2012[302]

It is impossible to repair a rickety, half-built house during a hurricane. Rain lashes down, blinding those trying to put things right. Planks fly in every direction, knocking the builders off balance. While some struggle to reinforce the windows, the wind tears away the roof. Worse, the arrogant architects who assert that they know how to stabilise the situation repeatedly undermine the building's foundations with their successive mistakes. Eventually, the house becomes so dangerously unstable that it seems on the verge of collapse. Hurrah,

---

302 http://www.ecb.int/press/key/date/2012/html/sp120726.en.html

say the critics who believe it was a mistake to share a house in the first place; tear the edifice down, even if the residents and neighbours are crushed in the wreckage. Surely, though, it would be far better to shore up the house and then complete its architecture – but how? Finally, a sorcerer orders the wind and rain to stop. The spell works. Now what?

Act Four of the crisis – a respite from the lashing wind and rain – began on 26 July 2012 when Draghi dared the markets to defy him and they deferred to him. The threat of unlimited ECB intervention pushed down panic-driven yields on Spanish and Italian bonds, dramatically so at shorter maturities and significantly so at longer ones. Spanish two-year yields, which had topped 7 per cent on 25 July, fell back below 4 per cent over the next two weeks and were soon below 2 per cent. Italian two-year yields also plunged.[303] Even though the ECB was only proposing to buy bonds of a maturity between one and three years, Spanish ten-year yields fell from 7.41 per cent on 25 July to 4 per cent in early May 2013, while Italian ones fell from 6.45 per cent to below 4 per cent.[304] Thanks to the ECB, not self-defeating austerity, "confidence" suddenly returned to government bond markets. In the real world, nothing had changed – not a single bond had been bought. Yet in people's minds, everything had changed. In

---

303 Italian two-year yields, which had topped 5.3 per cent on 25 July, also soon fell to below 2 per cent.

304 Spanish ten-year yields fell to 6.93 per cent on 26 July. They fell further when Draghi detailed the actual OMT programme, from 6.42 per cent on 5 September to 6.06 per cent on 6 September and continued falling. Spanish spreads fell from 615 basis points on 25 July 2012, when Germany ten-year bonds yielded only 1.26 per cent, to 279 basis points on 3 May 2013. Italian 10-year yields fell to 6.04 per cent on 26 July, from 5.50 per cent on 5 September to 5.29 per cent on 6 September and then continued falling. Italian spreads narrowed from 519 basis points on 25 July 2012 to 257 basis points on 3 May 2013.

effect, the threat of unlimited ECB intervention through "outright monetary transactions" (OMT) acted as a circuit breaker in the negative feedback loop.

With threats to force Greece out of the euro also replaced by determination to keep it in, investors were reassured that crisis-hit governments would be able to continue funding themselves and that the euro would survive in its current form for now. This halted the devastating capital flight from southern Europe. Crucially, Draghi and Merkel had signalled that they were prepared to act to hold the euro together after all.

But while the ECB has acted as a circuit breaker, it is not fail safe. The belief (and relief) that the ECB's potential intervention is unlimited has stabilised markets, so it has not been tested.[305] But testing it would expose that because it is conditional, it is limited by politics.[306]

---

305   "No ex ante quantitative limits are set on the size of Outright Monetary Transactions." http://www.ecb.int/press/pr/date/2012/html/pr120906_1.en.html

306   "A necessary condition for Outright Monetary Transactions is strict and effective conditionality attached to an appropriate European Financial Stability Facility/ European Stability Mechanism (EFSF/ESM) programme. Such programmes can take the form of a full EFSF/ESM macroeconomic adjustment programme or a precautionary programme (Enhanced Conditions Credit Line), provided that they include the possibility of EFSF/ESM primary market purchases. The involvement of the IMF shall also be sought for the design of the country-specific conditionality and the monitoring of such a programme.

The Governing Council will consider Outright Monetary Transactions to the extent that they are warranted from a monetary policy perspective as long as programme conditionality is fully respected, and terminate them once their objectives are achieved or when there is non-compliance with the macroeconomic adjustment or precautionary programme.

Following a thorough assessment, the Governing Council will decide on the start, continuation and suspension of Outright Monetary Transactions in full

For a start, it is conditional on a government applying for an ESM programme – and other eurozone governments and parliaments approving it. So if a government refused, or was unable to obtain a parliamentary majority, to do so, the ECB would not, as it stands, intervene. That was a risk after Italy's elections in February 2013; had Berlusconi won and Italian yields soared, he might have refused an ESM programme and the ECB might not have intervened. The German Bundestag, or another national parliament, might also refuse to approve the programme. It is also conditional on a government sticking to the terms of that programme. Given that all governments have been unable to meet their unrealistic targets, this would be highly likely. While the programme might be adapted and the ECB might allow some leeway to make up lost ground, it would be trickier if a government stopped complying because of a political backlash. What would the ECB do then? Would it stop intervening and risk Italian yields soaring so high that it defaulted and was possibly forced out of the euro, or continue intervening and face German uproar and a loss of market credibility?[307] No doubt there would be a game of chicken (or cat and mouse) but this would be intensely destabilising.

OMT are also conditional on the continuing support of the ECB's Governing Council. In practice, that means they are limited to what is politically acceptable to those central bankers. For now, only Jens Weidmann, the head of Germany's Bundesbank – who

---

discretion and acting in accordance with its monetary policy mandate." http://www.ecb.int/press/pr/date/2012/html/pr120906_1.en.html

307 If, as Draghi has insisted, the OMTs are necessary in order for the ECB to fulfil its mandate – to ensure the "singleness of monetary policy" and ensure its transmission to the real economy, as he put it – wouldn't the ECB be breaching its mandate if, in effect, it decided not to implement its monetary policy in one part of the eurozone?

has called OMT "tantamount to financing governments by printing banknotes" – is opposed.[308] (Germany's Constitutional Court has also considered OMT's legality and in February 2014 referred the case to the European Court of Justice.[309]) But that might change if German politicians started screaming blue murder because the ECB was buying lots of bonds – and the fear that the ECB might halt OMT would in turn undermine them. So while many eurozone policymakers urged Spain and Italy to apply quickly for OMT, fortunately they refused to, primarily for reasons of national pride. Had they done so, OMT's flaws might quickly have been exposed, especially since markets were still very edgy in late 2012. Instead of OMT acting as a nuclear deterrent, market participants would doubtless have tested the terms of engagement, for instance, how high they could push yields before the ECB responded. Fortunately, the eurozone is still in the deterrent phase, but the peace might not last forever. Let's hope OMT are not tested to destruction. The only permanent solution is to change the ECB's mandate to officially make it a lender of last resort to governments.

The crisis isn't over

By quelling the panic, the ECB has given eurozone policymakers breathing space to put their house in order. In 2013 the European Commission also relaxed the brutal pace of austerity and gave governments a little

---

308   http://www.ft.com/cms/s/0/3651b028-f846-11e1-b0e1-00144feabdc0.html

309   http://www.ft.com/cms/s/0/3feab440-8fd5-11e3-aee9-00144feab7de.html

more scope to borrow to invest.[310] [311] Thanks to these moves, by early 2014 the eurozone economy had stabilised. With brazen cheek, eurozone policymakers now claim this as a vindication of their austerity policies, when in fact it was their relaxation and OMT that have helped.[312]

---

310   "In the preventive arm of the SGP, the Commission will consider allowing temporary deviations from the structural deficit path towards the Medium-Term Objective (MTO) set in the country specific recommendations, or the MTO for Member States that have reached it, provided that:

(1) the economic growth of the Member State remains negative or well below its potential;

(2) the deviation does not lead to a breach of the 3% of GDP deficit ceiling, and the public debt rule is respected; and

(3) the deviation is linked to the national expenditure on projects co-funded by the EU under the Structural and Cohesion policy, Trans-European Networks (TEN) and Connecting Europe Facility (CEF) with positive, direct and verifiable long-term budgetary effect.

This application of the provisions of the SGP concerning temporary deviations from the MTO or the adjustment path towards it is related to the current economic conditions of large negative output gap. Once these temporary conditions are no longer in place and the Member State is forecast to return to positive growth, thus approaching its potential, any deviation as the above must be compensated so that the time path towards the MTO is not affected. The above elements will first be implemented when assessing the national budgets for 2014 and the budgetary outcomes for 2013. They will be reviewed on a yearly basis in time for the submission of stability and convergence programmes. http://ec.europa.eu/commission_2010-2014/rehn/documents/letter_on_investment_clause_en.pdf

311   Spain and France were both given two more years (until 2016) to bring their government deficits below 3 per cent of GDP, Portugal an extra year (until 2015) and the Netherlands an extra year too (until 2014). http://europa.eu/rapid/press-release_MEMO-13-463_en.htm?locale=en

312   Eurozone policymakers still insist that bond spreads rose because markets accurately assessed a deterioration in governments' creditworthiness, which in turn justified the lurch towards austerity to bring spreads down again. But after the ECB announced that it would intervene on a potentially unlimited basis to stabilise government bond markets, spreads collapsed. Charts show a dramatic turning

Unfortunately, halting the panic has also taken the pressure off Germany and other recalcitrant eurozone governments to resolve the crisis. Almost immediately, Berlin backtracked on its June 2012 concessions and sought to delay, block and emasculate common efforts to clear up eurozone banks. More ambitious efforts to complete the eurozone's architecture ground to a halt (see Chapter 6).[313] As George Soros has remarked, Germany has done just enough to hold the euro together for now, but not enough to resolve the crisis, let alone make the eurozone thrive.

Economies remain in dire straits. The recovery is too weak to make much of make a dent in shockingly high unemployment, while Italy and Greece remain mired in recession. Wages are still falling. Household debts remain huge, while public ones are still rising. Zombie banks refuse to lend on good terms even to creditworthy companies. While big businesses can borrow cheaply by issuing corporate bonds – reducing the EU's overdependence on bank finance –

---

point, first when Draghi said he would do "whatever it takes" on 26 July 2012 and then when he fleshed out the details of the OMT on 6 September. While EU officials give some credit to the ECB for this, they disingenuously attribute it mostly to the "success" of austerity measures. Yet spreads plunged even in countries where public debt was still soaring. As De Grauwe rightly observes, "If anything, the fundamentalist school of thinking would have predicted that as the debt-to-GDP ratios increased in all countries, spreads should have increased rather than declined." Paul de Grauwe and Yuemei Li, "Panic-driven austerity in the eurozone and its implications", Vox.eu, 21 February 2013 http://www.voxeu.org/article/panic-driven-austerity-eurozone-and-its-implications

313　Remember the roadmap towards closer union that was promised by the end of 2012? Nothing much has come of it. Worse, Germany almost immediately tried to row back on what it had agreed in June 2012. It sought to delay the creation of a eurozone bank supervisor and limit its scope. It backtracked on the commitment to enable the ESM to directly recapitalise stricken banks. And it has sought to delay, block and emasculate the proposed common mechanism for winding down stricken banks. Moral hazard begins and ends in Berlin.

smaller (in other words, most) businesses are deprived of affordable credit. Interest rates on new business loans in southern Europe have scarcely fallen, while the supply of credit has collapsed.[314] "Everyone is saying that the crisis is over," says Jorge Fernández-Cid, the founder of a small Spanish advertising agency. "But this has not arrived at the level of businesses. The problem with this crisis is that there is no money."[315]

Looming deflation – a sustained period of falling prices – could exacerbate all these problems. Falling prices would cause people to postpone spending because they expect things to be cheaper in future, entrenching stagnation. Worse, whereas inflation erodes the value of debt, deflation would increase the eurozone's already huge debt burden. Falling prices would also increase real interest rates: since nominal interest rates are already near zero and can scarcely fall below, deflation raises the real cost of borrowing, crimping investment. Even very low inflation – the eurozone's was a mere 0.8 per cent in the year to February 2014 – is a drag. The chances of getting stuck in a deflationary debt trap are rising.

Yet again, eurozone policymakers have prematurely declared victory. Even though the ECB may have averted a financial heart-attack, the euro may yet succumb to slow economic strangulation that at some point proves politically unbearable in crisis-hit countries.

---

314   Banks' lending rates for small short-term loans to new business customers fell from 5.17 per cent in June 2012 to 4.79 per cent in December 2013 in Spain, 4.57 per cent to 4.34 per cent in Italy, 7.13 per cent to 5.90 per cent in Portugal and 4.51 per cent to 4.16 per cent in Ireland. Source: ECB, MFI Interest Rate Statistics, Loans for new business to non-financial corporations, up to €1 million, up to 1 year, December 2013 compared with June 2012 http://www.ecb.europa.eu/stats/money/interest/interest/html/interest_rates_2013-12.en.html

315   http://www.ft.com/cms/s/0/3d260e6c-956b-11e3-8371-00144feab7de.html

How to solve the crisis

Now that the ECB has addressed the cashflow (liquidity) problems that threatened to force both banks and governments into unnecessary default and alleviated fears that the euro was about to break up, the remaining problems revolve around distressed banks, excessive debts and weak economies. Muddling through will not solve these problems: the longer zombie banks and excessive debts are allowed to fester, the longer economies will be sickly.

Some believe the panacea is for southern European countries to reintroduce their own currencies. These would promptly depreciate, forcing them to default: a 25-per-cent depreciation would swell their euro-denominated debt burden by a third in their new currency; re-denominating it would constitute a default too. Reintroducing a currency in the midst of a crisis would also provoke chaos: bank runs, lost savings, mass bankruptcies. But in any case, is devaluation really the solution? It hasn't worked for Britain.

Another solution, suggested by George Soros as a fallback option, is for Germany (or all the creditor countries) to leave the euro.[316] The beauty of his proposal is that since southern Europe would keep the euro, it would not be forced to default, but that as the euro depreciated against the new Deutsche Mark, its debt burden in D-Mark terms would fall, imposing losses on Germany. Insofar as devaluation also enabled, say, Fiat cars to compete more readily with Volkswagens, boosting export earnings, the real burden of the debt for southern Europe would fall too. While less painful than the previous option of leaving the euro, it would not solve the problem on its own, for the same reasons as above.

Far from breaking up the euro, eurozone policymakers tend to think the panacea is closer integration. For sure, the eurozone's overall

---

316   George Soros, "Why Germany Should Lead or Leave", Project Syndicate, 8 September 2012 http://www.project-syndicate.org/commentary/why-germany-should-lead-or-leave-by-george-soros

vital statistics are fitter than those of many of its component parts. Its economy is flatlining.[317] Unemployment is a near-record 12 per cent, but not at the obscene levels in southern Europe. Government borrowing is manageable: 3.1 per cent of GDP in late 2013.[318] So if waving a magic wand could turn the eurozone into a single country, it would look better in many respects. Even so, the eurozone would still have a big zombie bank problem. While public debt, at 92.7 per cent of GDP, would be sustainable, private debt would still be extremely high.[319] After all, it's not just the economy-wide average that matters; it's who owes the debt and whether they can bear it. On its own, unifying the eurozone wouldn't fix Germany's Ländesbanks or the crushing debts of many Spanish households. Nor would it create growth, if other policies remained unchanged. So while closer integration *could* help in several ways, it is not a cure-all.

To put the crisis behind it, the eurozone needs to draw a line under the losses incurred so far, preferably share them out as fairly as possible, and stop adding to them. That means fixing the banks, writing down debts and pushing the economy towards sustained growth.

Fixing the banks

The starting point is to force banks to recognise their losses and dispose of their bad assets – and then recapitalise those with a viable business model and close down unviable ones. Before the ECB begins overseeing the eurozone's biggest banks in November 2014, it will review the quality of their assets. Its findings will feed into a fresh set of stress tests by the European Banking Authority of how EU banks – including British ones – might cope with a severe crisis.

---

317   In the year to the fourth quarter of 2013, eurozone GDP grew by 0.5 per cent.

318   http://epp.eurostat.ec.europa.eu/cache/ITY_PUBLIC/2-03022014-AP/EN/2-03022014-AP-EN.PDF

319   At the end of the third quarter of 2013.

The hope is that this exercise will be more honest and rigorous than the previous shams described in Chapter 1 – and that prompt and vigorous restructuring will ensue. After all, the premise for giving the ECB primary responsibility for overseeing major eurozone banks is that it is less captured by them than national supervisors are. Undoubtedly, the ECB has a strong incentive to do a proper job, since giving a clean bill of health to a bank that failed soon after would shred its reputation as a supervisor – and tarnish the credibility of its monetary policy too.

But there are also strong grounds for scepticism. Throughout the crisis, the ECB has tended to place the narrow interests of banks ahead of the welfare of Europeans in general. While a lenient probe threatens its future reputation, an honest one could tar its past record, notably because Draghi's cheap LTRO loans in 2011–12 undoubtedly propped up insolvent banks.[320] Moreover, if the ECB does go easy on banks, it can cover this up by keeping them afloat with abundant liquidity. In any case, banks and national supervisors may not be forthcoming , while the ECB is unlikely to know where the skeletons are and may lack the powers to compel them to come clean. If problems subsequently emerge, the ECB could then blame banks and national supervisors.

Even if the ECB is both willing and able to do a proper job, it will come under huge political pressure to paper over problems. It may cave in if there is neither the political will nor the cash to deal with any issues it uncovers. Imagine the ECB finds that Italian banks incurred huge losses during the recent recession. Suppose private investors don't want to put in extra capital and the government is unwilling to force bondholders to do so. The Italian government might not even feel able to borrow the necessary funds from markets, while

---

320 The ECB could, however, could blame its decisions on a lack of adequate information from banks and national supervisors.

the EU may be loath to lend it the cash. Would the ECB really provoke a crisis by being honest about Italian banks' balance sheets, or would it push the problem under the carpet? Tellingly, in the summer of 2013 Draghi privately wrote to the European Commission asking for a waiver from new state-aid rules that require bank creditors to be bailed in before public money is injected into banks. Or what if the ECB uncovered large losses at German banks? Ill-informed investors might still be prepared to fund those banks, especially if they assumed the German government stood behind them. Would the ECB dare defy Berlin, if told the situation was under control and warned that it would be reckless to destabilise the German banking system?

In any case, at Germany's insistence, the ECB will only directly supervise 130 or so of the many thousands of banks in the eurozone. Yet throughout the crisis, smaller banks (such as Belgium's Dexia), collections of smaller banks (such as Spain's *cajas*), and other banks that will fall outside the ECB's purview (notably Germany's smaller Ländesbanks) have repeatedly failed and caused much wider problems. Few would have defined Lehman as systemically important before its collapse. So the ECB's asset-quality review will at best provide only a partial picture of the health of the eurozone banking system. As for the feeble EBA, its previously shoddy stress tests do not augur well for its efforts in 2014.

Assume, though, for the sake of argument, that the ECB's asset-quality review and the EBA's stress tests are thorough and credible. The next step is forcing viable banks to raise fresh capital and restructuring or winding down unviable ones. That requires effective rules and the political will to enforce them. At the moment, there is a hodgepodge of national rules on bank resolution – some countries still lack any – and varying degrees of political willingness to enforce them. That is meant to change when common EU rules on restructuring and winding down banks are finally enacted – hopefully before the Parliament breaks for the European elections in May 2014.[321]

The proposed EU rules are a step forward. They stipulate that banks draw up annual plans for addressing balance-sheet problems, and that national supervisors set out how banks might be restructured and wound down in an orderly fashion, including by bailing in the creditors of failing banks (see footnotes for details).[322] But the new rules still leave responsibility for bank resolution – and great discretion – in the hands of national supervisors. So national practices will vary and supervisors will have plenty of scope to turn a blind eye to banks' problems, exclude creditors from bail-ins and agree to taxpayer bailouts. Worse, the rules won't come into force until 2016, so they are useless for dealing with the current crisis.

In July 2013, the European Commission finally published its proposals for a pan-eurozone mechanism for restructuring and resolving failing banks.[323] The aim was to have a single means of

---

321   Although EU leaders committed to do so at the G-20 summit in Washington DC back in November 2008, the European Commission delayed even publishing its proposals until June 2012. Only in July 2013 did EU finance ministers reach broad agreement on the draft directive. http://www.consilium.europa.eu/uedocs/cms_data/docs/pressdata/en/ecofin/137627.pdf

322   According to the Bank Recovery and Resolution Directive (BRRD), shareholders would take a hit first, followed by junior bondholders, then senior ones and finally uninsured depositors; deposits of less than €100,000 would be protected. Once losses of 8 per cent of total liabilities had been imposed, a resolution fund, ideally funded over time by banks, would step in to cover losses of a further 5 per cent of liabilities. If that was still not enough, taxpayer funds could be called on once all unsecured creditors had been bailed in.

323   http://europa.eu/rapid/press-release_IP-13-674_en.htm?locale=en Eurozone leaders had agreed to this in December 2012. European Council Conclusions, 13/14 December 2012, Section 11: "The Commission will submit in the course of 2013 a proposal for a single resolution mechanism for Member States participating in the

dealing with failing eurozone banks that operates independently of national governments and supervisors and minimises the burden on taxpayers, breaking the link between weak banks and weak sovereigns that caused the doom loop. But German opposition gutted the plans of their substance.[324] Berlin claimed that it wanted to avoid German taxpayers bearing the burden for bank losses in southern Europe – a seemingly reasonable argument. But the creation of a single bank resolution mechanism that made their creditors take a hit would actually limit taxpayers' exposure. The real reason why Berlin objected was to keep control over the fate of distressed German banks. As it stands, the scheme agreed by eurozone leaders in December 2013 is so devilishly complicated that it is unworkable, while national capitals will retain a veto over the fate of "their" banks. So the eurozone's banking union will exist on paper but not in practice.

Ultimately, the real problem is political. Governments could have decisively dealt with Europe's banking problems long before now without calling on taxpayer funds. Instead, they have tried to paper over problems and ultimately save every bank while safeguarding

---

SSM, to be examined by the co-legislators as a matter of priority with the intention of adopting it during the current parliamentary cycle. It should safeguard financial stability and ensure an effective framework for resolving financial institutions while protecting taxpayers in the context of banking crises. The single resolution mechanism should be based on contributions by the financial sector itself and include appropriate and effective backstop arrangements. This backstop should be fiscally neutral over the medium term, by ensuring that public assistance is recouped by means of ex post levies on the financial industry."

324 Berlin claimed that creating a pan-eurozone resolution mechanism would require a change in the EU treaties. This was both a delaying tactic (because such a change would take several years) and political blackmail (because other governments, notably France's, are reluctant to reopen the EU treaties and go through an arduous process of national parliamentary approval and in some cases a referendum).

their creditors. This denial, muddling through and bailout approach has not really changed – except in cases where governments have run out of money. So if a southern European country can no longer hide its banks' problems and its government is unable to rescue them, creditors are likely to take a hit, as they did in Cyprus. But in northern Europe, governments still stand four-square behind their banks. The upshot is that the eurozone as a whole is likely to struggle with a zombie banking system, with only patchy efforts to restructure banks in a fair way. Worse, the eurozone is set to remain fragmented between north and south, or "core" and "periphery". Northern Europe will have taxpayer-backed banks, while southern European ones will increasingly have to fend for themselves. That is a bonus for struggling southern European taxpayers, but implies that even sound banks could have funding costs that are higher than those of dodgy ones in northern Europe for the foreseeable future.[325] As a result, the cost of credit for businesses and households is likely to remain higher, crimping growth. A lasting division between a northern "core" and a southern "periphery" would entrench a quasi-imperialist system subordinating debtor countries to creditor ones.

Several stopgap solutions have been suggested to ease credit conditions for southern European businesses. Governments could pay smaller businesses money they owe them, as Italy's is, injecting working capital directly. Cheap ECB finance could lower banks' funding costs. This could specifically be targeted at boosting small-business loans if the ECB accepted a wider range of small-business loans as

---

325   As Martin Sandbu of the *Financial Times* pointed out to me in an email, in the longer term businesses in southern Europe could also borrow from capital markets or non-European banks instead. But for now most southern European businesses are small and wholly reliant on bank finance, and that is unlikely to change much in the near term. As for non-European banks, which international banks are in expansive mode these days? EU authorities, notably the ECB, are also unlikely to be keen on foreign-owned banks playing a big role in eurozone banking.

collateral, with lower haircuts. Credit guarantees from the European Investment Bank could reduce the risks of lending to smaller businesses, and hence lower the spreads banks charge. The EIB could also lend more to smaller businesses at lower rates, both directly and through intermediary banks. Most promisingly, efforts to revive the securitisation market for small-business loans – that is, the bundling together of packages of loans into bonds that banks can sell to investors – could be stepped up. Ultimately, though, banks' balance sheets need to be cleaned up, the debt overhang tackled and growth rekindled.

Until its banking problems are dealt with through a common, comprehensive and conclusive approach, the eurozone is likely to remain sickly. This long delay has also allowed the northern European creditors who financed southern Europe's bad lending to drastically reduce their exposure to losses. Justice will not be done.

Writing down debts

One side of drawing a line under past losses is cleaning up the banks. The other is writing down the excessive debts of households, companies and governments. Once banks have made provisions in their accounts for bad loans (or disposed of them), a vigorous, comprehensive approach to grant borrowers debt relief is needed.

Start with households. In Greece, nearly a quarter of mortgages are in long arrears, while in Ireland an eighth are – and only a fraction of those have been restructured.[326] Caroline Lennon, a public-sector

326 In Greece, 22.9 per cent of residential and commercial mortgages were in arrears of more than 90 days at the end of June 2013, out of a total of outstanding home loans amounting to €73 billion. http://www.ft.com/cms/s/0/62819704- 148c-11e3-b3db-00144feabdc0.html Figures for Irish mortgage arrears are from http://www.centralbank.ie/press-area/press-releases/Pages/ResidentialMortgageArrearsandRepossessionsStatisticsQ42013.aspx Only a quarter of mortgages that are in arrears of more than three months have been restructured.

worker, has seen the value of her home more than halve since she bought it in 2007, just before prices crashed. "Getting back to markets and emerging from the bailout [the Irish government graduated from its EU-IMF programme in December 2013] means very little to ordinary people because we will be paying for the crash for many years to come," said Lennon, who is struggling to repay a €320,000 loan on her home in County Carlow. "I am one of the lucky ones who kept their job. But my pay has been cut and there has been on top of that a substantial amount of pension cuts." She set up Irish Homeowners Unite, a campaigning group for distressed borrowers that advises households on their options. While the Irish government introduced new insolvency laws in 2013 that aim to make it easier for distressed homeowners to negotiate "sustainable" deals on their mortgages with lenders, that is not enough. Mortgage debts ought to be reduced through economy-wide debt-equity swaps. Where necessary, personal bankruptcy terms ought to be eased and the process streamlined.

Corporate debt has continued to soar in Ireland and Portugal and remains high in Spain.[327] The IMF reckons that up to 20 per cent of southern European companies' debts may end up in default: some 30 per cent in Italy, 41 per cent in Spain and 47 per cent in Portugal.[328] The Fund therefore proposes a move towards insolvency procedures along the lines of America's Chapter 11, which allows companies to continue trading while restructuring their debts, as well as economy-wide write-downs. Last but not least, unpayable government debts need to be reduced.

---

327   OECD Statistics Database, debt of non-financial corporations as a percentage of GDP.

328   International Monetary Fund, *Global Financial Stability Report*, April 2013. The assessment is based on firms whose interest expense exceeds gross earnings (EBIT).

Grim Greece

While Greece's public debt was restructured in March 2012, the government remains insolvent. Even before the year was out, eurozone governments made a further attempt to reduce Greece's debts, partly through a botched debt buyback.[329] EU governments also agreed to take losses on some of their own loans to Greece.[330] Germany's 2013 budget contains an item for €730 million in revenues foregone due to the debt relief granted to Greece. The once-unthinkable and still politically poisonous process of imposing losses on European taxpayers has begun.

Now the principle of taking losses on the EU's loans to Greece has been conceded, it would be best to press on. Delay builds up more debt (and hence greater future losses), inflicts more suffering and runs the risk of provoking a political meltdown and a chaotic Greek default. Greece's slump is already deeper and longer than Germany's in the 1930s.[331] At some point, the social fabric will rip – with unpredictable political consequences.

Just as Germany's unpayable Versailles Treaty reparations were salami-sliced down in the 1920s until eventually Hitler repudiated

---

329   Eurozone governments insisted Greece buy back some of the new bonds issued only in March, which had been trading for as little as 15 cents on the euro. Stupidly, they pre-announced their intention to do so, so prices shot up. Eventually, Greece managed to buy back €31.9 billion of its bonds for a third of their face value, reducing its debt by €20 billion. http://online.wsj.com/article/SB1000142412788732 4024004578173080175399670.html

330   Bond maturities were extended and interest payments both cut and deferred, reducing Greece's debt burden somewhat. But the face value of the bonds remains untouched, so the German government can claim that taxpayers are getting all their money back.

331   International Monetary Fund, *Greece 2013 Article IV Consultation*, IMF Country Report No. 13/154, page 7 http://www.imf.org/external/pubs/ft/scr/2013/cr13154. pdf

them, so Greece's debts have been cut twice, but not enough, with the likelihood that a future government will eventually default on them. Now that Greece has achieved a primary surplus, the political economy of austerity changes dramatically. Since Greece could suspend its debt payments and not need to borrow, the EU has much less leverage. Conversely, the continuing fiscal squeeze – the EU-IMF programme targets a primary surplus of 4.5 per cent of GDP by 2016 – primarily benefits hated foreign creditors. Thus the Greek government has a greater incentive to default and the threat to do so could be credible – but only if Greeks are willing to risk being forced out of the euro. (Alternatively, it could wait a while until it has a surplus excluding interest payments to foreigners and suspend payments only to them. This would protect Greek banks and make it harder for the ECB to justify cutting off their access to liquidity.) To the extent that EU governments want to avoid such a crisis, which could rekindle the financial panic in the eurozone, they have good reason to press on with Greek debt relief.

A bold, enlightened leader would make a virtue of a necessity. Forgiving Greece's debt could be portrayed as a grand gesture of European solidarity. One possibility would be to make debt relief conditional on implementing a reform programme, as was the case with the IMF-World Bank initiative for alleviating the debt of highly indebted poor countries (HIPCs). Another model is post-communist Poland in 1991. Then, debt forgiveness went hand-in-hand with drastic economic reforms and help in building a modern, efficient, honest state. In many respects, Greece is more like a transition economy than a struggling European one: its problems go far deeper than a lack of finance or export capacity. A Marshall Plan for Greece that mobilised EU investment could also help revive the economy and spark the private-sector investment boom that the EU-IMF programmes have singularly failed to stimulate. Is that too much to ask of Angela Merkel?

Losses for German and other European taxpayers – which, to repeat, are due to the failure to restructure Greece's debt in 2010, not Greeks themselves – would be easier to swallow if politicians were honest with voters and toned down their anti-Greek rhetoric. They should make a clearer distinction between the failings of the Greek political class (and the corrupt institutions they control) and the alleged cultural characteristics of the Greek people. Policymakers could also try to explain the country's plight and express some sympathy for the suffering of ordinary Greeks. Nasty Greek talk of Germans as Nazis could then hopefully be buried.

While the German government privately accepts that Greece's EU debts will have to be written down further, for now this looks likely to take place in an opaque, drawn out, ad hoc fashion. The IMF is already insisting on further debt relief to achieve the target of reducing Greece's government debt to substantially below 110 per cent of GDP by 2022, a level it deems sustainable.[332] Talk of a third EU-IMF loan package is in the air. But as the IMF rightly says, "If investors are not persuaded that the policy for dealing with the debt problem is credible, investment and growth will be unlikely to recover as programmed."[333]

Awash with funds but still in danger

The ECB has been so successful at calming global investors' nerves that they have poured funds into southern Europe's bond markets.

---

332 http://www.ft.com/cms/s/0/70b9d150-f9e4-11e2-b8ef-00144feabdc0.html

333 International Monetary Fund, *Greece 2013 Article IV Consultation*, IMF Country Report No. 13/154 http://www.imf.org/external/pubs/ft/scr/2013/cr13154.pdf

In early 2014, a sell-off in emerging economies – notably the so-called fragile five: Turkey, Brazil, India, Indonesia and South Africa – added to the perceived attraction of southern Europe for investors who want to earn higher returns than the measly ones they can obtain on "safe" investments such as US Treasuries. Ireland felt able to graduate from its EU-IMF loan programme in December 2013 and fund itself from markets without a safety net. By late February 2014, Ireland could borrow for ten years for 3.1 per cent, scarcely more than Britain, and down from 12 per cent three years earlier.[334] Portugal is tempted to take a similar leap when its programme ends in May 2014, weeks before the European elections. Its ten-year yields have fallen from double digits in early 2012 to below 5 per cent.[335] In late February 2014, Italy and Spain could both borrow for 3.5 per cent, as they could before the Greek crisis began in late 2009.[336]

Lower interest rates are welcome. While market conditions are favourable, governments should fund their borrowing needs in advance, as Ireland has done. But they should not be lulled into complacency, as eurozone officials have been. Sentiment can quickly reverse itself – emerging-economy bonds were until recently a hot ticket – not least as the US exits from QE and begins to normalise its interest rates. Moreover, as markets' willingness to lend to Greece as if it were Germany in the pre-crisis years shows, a wall of money can disguise longer-term solvency problems. Unless the feeble recovery strengthens and inflation picks up – which is unlikely without a change of policies – southern Europe could sink into a debt trap and ultimately default. The politics of prolonged austerity to pay off foreign creditors

are also poisonous and unpredictable. So huge are Portugal's debts –
public, private and foreign – that it already needs debt relief.[337] Ireland,
where a third of its massive government debt of €42,000 per man,
woman and child is the result of bank bailouts, ought to play hardball
with Brussels and Berlin to obtain debt relief for this unjust imposition.[338] The biggest worry is that prolonged stagnation could tip even
Italy into insolvency.

---

337   The IMF's assessment that Portugal's debts are sustainable is predicated on
optimistic assumptions about future growth and interest rates. If nominal GDP
growth disappoints, or interest rates spike again, debts will continue rising. As of
the first quarter of 2013, more than half of Portugal's debt was owed to the private
sector, nearly half of that to foreigners. Writing that down by three-quarters would
lop some 45 per cent of GDP off Portugal's public debt, to sustainable levels. See
also Barclays Economics Research, Portugal: More funding and debt relief needed,
14 August 2013

338   Ireland's GDP statistics are inflated by the profits of the many foreign companies operating there, which are lightly taxed. GDP figures are therefore a poor measure
of its economic performance and its debt sustainability. Gross national product –
the value of all the goods and services produced by Irish residents – is a better
measure, but it too is inflated (and current-account figures even more so) by profits
booked in Ireland for tax purposes by international companies that were actually
generated by operations elsewhere – which have been growing quickly, according to
John FitzGerald of Ireland's Economic and Social Research Institute. As a share of
GDP, Ireland's gross public debt was 117.6 per cent at the end of 2012. But as a share
of GNP, it was 143.5 per cent. Factor in Fitzgerald's adjustment for taxes booked in
Ireland and debt as a share of adjusted GNP is a whopping 151.9 per cent! Roughly a
third of that debt is due to the direct cost of Ireland's bank bailouts, so had the Irish
government not made its foolish pledge to guarantee all bank debts in late 2008 and
the ECB not forced Ireland to stick to it in late 2010, Ireland would now undeniably be solvent. As it stands, the hope that Irish taxpayers will be able (unfairly) to
pay back all the government's debts rests on the hope that economic growth will
be buoyant and interest rates low (which, in turn, depends on the assumption that
Ireland will remain solvent). With public borrowing forecast to be 7.5 per cent of

Policy shift

Fixing the banks and clearing the debt overhang would do wonders for crisis-stricken economies' prospects. So too would longer-term reforms to make all European economies more dynamic and adaptable, as Chapters 10 and 11 will detail. There is also plenty more that governments could do to boost growth and adjustment now.

Where possible, governments should support the economy until after households, businesses and banks have largely finished reducing their own debts. That is what Sweden, Norway and Finland all did after their own banking crises in the early 1990s (see Chapter 7). The surest way to repair public finances quickly is not to counterproductively pursue austerity at the same time as the private sector, but rather to fix the banks, clear the private debt overhang and boost productive investment.

While the eurozone's new fiscal straightjacket (see Chapter 6) greatly limits governments' room for manoeuvre, they could still shift their spending priorities and reform their tax systems in ways that support growth now and are also desirable longer term. For example, they could axe harmful subsidies[339] – such as the handouts the French government gave to Peugeot, a heavily loss-making carmaker, in 2013 or that Germany gives it to its coal industry each year – and plough

---

GDP in 2013 and a big fiscal squeeze still to come over the coming years, Ireland's hopes rest on a strong recovery in Britain, the eurozone and the US to boost exports.

339 While EU state-aid rules are meant to curb subsidies, these still accounted for 1.2 per cent of GDP in the eurozone in 2012 (and 0.6 per cent of GDP in Britain). There are plenty of corporate handouts to cut in Austria (3.5 per cent of GDP), Belgium (2.7 per cent), France (1.5 per cent), the Netherlands (1.3 per cent), Spain and Italy (1 per cent) and Germany (0.9 per cent). European Commission, AMECO database, Subsidies: general government ESA 1995, as percentage of GDP at market prices

the savings into higher public investment.[340] Countries could also create arms-length public investment banks for that purpose. Raising the pension age by three months a year while removing the disincentives to keep working could provide increased funding for education and training. Costly subsidies for renewable energy and environmentally dubious biofuels ought to be replaced with a tax on carbon consumption (see Chapter 10). Governments could then cut taxes on labour, creating jobs and boosting living standards.

At the EU level, the budget for 2014–20 agreed in 2013 was a missed opportunity to reorient the Union's spending priorities. While David Cameron trumpeted a headline cut in the budget, the real issue is how the money is spent. Scandalously, at a time of high food prices, wage cuts and economy-wide austerity, subsidies for European farmers – or to be more precise, handouts for European landowners and agribusinesses – are being maintained. This corporate pork is bad for growth, because a handout for agriculture is a tax on industry and services, not to mention consumers. Farm lobbies with their snouts in the trough will snaffle up €55.4 billion in 2014 alone.[341] In contrast, a piffling €1.4 billion is allocated to investment in transport, €0.5 billion to energy and a mere €70 million for the internet.[342] To make better use of the €44.7 billion for promoting development in poorer regions in 2014, some could be used to endow a regional development

---

340 Government investment has plunged from 4 per cent of GDP in 2010 to 1.4 per cent in 2013 in Spain and by similar proportions elsewhere in southern Europe. In Germany it has remained an extremely low 1.5 per cent. Public investment has fallen from 3.5 per cent of GDP in 2010 to 1.7 per cent in 2013 in Ireland and from 3.8 per cent to 1.8 per cent in Portugal over the same period. In Greece, it has fallen from 3.1 per cent in 2009 to 1.9 per cent in 2013. European Commission, AMECO database, gross fixed capital formation: general government ESA 1995, as percentage of GDP at market prices

341 http://register.consilium.europa.eu/pdf/en/13/st08/st08288.en13.pdf

342 *Idem*

bank (or to expand the European Investment Bank's activities) and disbursements frontloaded to stimulate growth. Last but not least, a further capital increase for the EIB tied to increased lending across the EU would help.[343]

Germany needs to adjust too

Germany and smaller creditor countries in northern Europe must also play their part. Germany's beggar-thy-neighbour policy of

---

343   An additional €10 billion capital increase for the EIB, together with instructions that this be used to boost growth, could be used to co-finance a further €120 billion of investment, equivalent to 1 per cent of EU GDP, building on the investment plan announced in June 2013. European Council Conclusions, 27/28 June 2013. Section 8a: "stepping up efforts by the EIB to support lending to the economy by making full use of the recent increase of EUR 10 billion in its capital. The European Council calls on the EIB to implement its plan to increase its lending activity in the EU by at least 40% over 2013-2015. To this effect, the EIB has already identified new lending opportunities of more than EUR 150 billion across a set of critical priorities such as innovation and skills, SME access to finance, resources efficiency and strategic infrastructures; expansion of joint risk-sharing financial instruments between the European Commission and the EIB to leverage private sector and capital markets investments in SMEs. These initiatives should ensure that the volume of new loans to SMEs across the EU is expanded, respecting the principles of financial soundness and transparency as well as the MFF ceilings. The Council, in consultation with the Commission and the EIB, will specify without delay the parameters for the design of such instruments co-financed by the Structural Funds, aiming at high leverage effects. The necessary preparations should be made to allow these instruments to begin operating in January 2014;
(c) increasing the EIF's credit enhancement capacity;
(d) gradual expansion of the EIB's trade finance schemes to favour SME business across the Union, especially in programme countries;
(e) strengthening of the cooperation between national development banks and the EIB to increase opportunities for co-lending and exchanges of best practices;
(f) developing alternative sources of financing in close cooperation with Member States

suppressing wages to boost exports (and compress imports) and its failure to invest enough are depressing the rest of the eurozone (and the world). Remember that after the crisis hit, the private sector in southern Europe desperately tried to save more. Following the lurch towards austerity driven by Brussels under orders from Berlin, so did governments. For this strategy to succeed, someone else has to borrow more (or save less). In particular, economies that are big net savers – countries whose savings greatly exceed investment and therefore have large current-account surpluses – need to play their part. Otherwise, the desire to save more cannot be realised and the result is a slump – and ultimately default on debts owed to German banks and taxpayers. Globally, China has played its part: its huge surpluses have shrunk a lot. Within the eurozone, Germany has actually made matters worse: its current-account surplus has swelled from 6 per cent of GDP in 2009 to some 7 per cent in 2013. In absolute terms, its surplus – $267.6 billion in 2013 – is now much bigger than China's.[344] Far from being an "anchor of stability" and a "growth locomotive", as finance minister Wolfgang Schäuble claims, in a world of deficient demand Germany is a destabilising force and a drain on spending, since it buys much less than it sells. In fact, its current-account surplus is the largest and most dangerously destabilising imbalance in the eurozone.

Unless Germany plays its part, southern Europe can only adjust against the rest of the world. (Contrary to the belief in Berlin that everyone should emulate Germany and run a current-account surplus, that is impossible unless we starting exporting and lending to Mars.) Were this strategy to succeed, the eurozone as a whole would be running a huge current-account surplus; it was already $288.7 billion in 2013. That would entail big deficits (and lower growth) in the US

---

344 *The Economist*, Trade, exchange rates, budget balances and interest rates, 8 March 2014. China's surplus was $188.6 billion over the same period.

and elsewhere, destabilising fragile emerging economies and risking a broader protectionist response.

Tackling Germany's surplus is not painful. It is in Germans' own interest to pay themselves wages commensurate with their productivity, invest more in future growth (not least in their often dilapidated infrastructure) and stop squandering their savings on bad loans abroad.[345] But if Germany's mercantilist policymakers refuse to do what's right for Germans, the European Commission must use its new powers to tackle dangerously excessive imbalances to force Berlin to act.[346] If the EU is a community of equals, not an instrument for imposing the writ of powerful creditor countries on debtors, its rules must apply to Germany too. American pressure could also make a difference. The US Treasury has criticised Germany's surplus, which could also become an issue in ongoing talks on an EU-US trade and investment deal. Since there are demands in the US Congress to tackle currency manipulation in future US trade deals, it is only a small step to requiring that Germany address its current-account surplus. After all, artificially holding wages below productivity is a manipulation of Germany's real exchange rate.

---

345   The federal budget was in deficit by 0.1 per cent of GDP in 2013. So even within the confines of the fiscal compact, it has scope to invest more and/or cut taxes. According to European Commission estimates, Germany will have a surplus, after allowing for the impact of the economic cycle, of 0.4 per cent of GDP in 2013. That is comfortably higher than the structural deficit of 0.5 per cent of GDP prescribed by the fiscal compact treaty. A fiscal boost of 1 per cent of GDP would inject €25 billion into the German economy and lift the rest of the eurozone too. Sources: http://www.bundesfinanzministerium.de/Content/EN/Pressemitteilungen/2014/2014-01-15-new-borrowing-in-2013.html and European Commission, AMECO database, structural balance of general government adjustment based on potential GDP

346   In late 2013, the European Commission launched an in-depth review of Germany's surplus that is due to report back in the spring of 2014.

Promote competition, not competitiveness

Provided they are combined with bank restructuring to restore credit to businesses and investment to support demand, the right reforms can unblock hidebound economies and open up future growth. Instead of a wrong-headed drive to push down wages to boost "competitiveness" – that is, corporate surpluses – the focus should be on root-and-branch reforms to make economies more adaptable, dynamic and decent – reforms that ADD UP (as Chapters 10–12 expand on).

Start with reforms that have no downside even in the short term, like making it easier to start a business. Many talented young people are unemployed and so have nothing to lose – and potentially plenty to gain – by trying their luck with a start-up. Apply those reforms across the eurozone, not just in southern Europe. Combine them with increased funding for venture capital, by giving tax breaks for start-up funds, as well as through the EIB's European Investment Fund.[347] Make it easier for small entrepreneurs by giving them a tax holiday for the first few years and exempt them from employment protection laws: someone who is taking the risk of starting a business cannot afford, in effect, to provide employment insurance to new recruits.

More broadly, prioritise measures to boost competition. Europe's much-vaunted single market exists only for goods. Services, which account for the bulk of the EU economy, remain overwhelmingly national. Citizens of the richer EU-15 countries buy 94 per cent of their services from firms based at home.[348] Segmented domestic markets lack scale, while a lack of competition and an excess of regulation stifle innovation and hence growth. Years after it was agreed in 2006, the EU's directive to create a limited single market in services has yet

---

347   http://www.eib.org/products/venture_capital/index.htm

348   John Springford, "How to build European services markets", Centre for European Reform, September 2012 http://www.cer.org.uk/sites/default/files/publications/attachments/pdf/2012/js_markets_sept12-6206.pdf

to be fully implemented.[349] France, Germany and Italy have opened up much less than Britain and Ireland.[350] Worse, there is little to stop governments erecting new barriers to replace the old ones they have torn down. If laggards caught up, this could boost EU GDP by 0.8 per cent within five years. In a paper for the Centre for European Reform, John Springford sets out good suggestions on how to speed progress and improve enforcement.[351]

Creating a genuine EU single market in services will take years, but some measures can be fast-tracked. Neelie Kroes, the EU's digital commissioner, is pressing on with creating a telecoms single market that includes abolishing roaming charges when you use your phone around the EU. Establishing a single EU energy market by building interconnections between national gas and electricity networks and injecting greater competition into energy supply and distribution would help lower energy costs and diversify Europe's supplies. Retail is also ripe for reform. It accounts for a bigger share of the economy than manufacturing and many more jobs. Opening it up is a great way

---

349   The services directive aimed to open up EU services markets in two ways. It enshrined services companies' freedom of establishment in another member state, by stopping host countries from demanding a more onerous registration process or more stringent regulation for foreign companies. Second, it made member states set up 'points of single contact', so companies entering the market do not have to register with multiple agencies. However, the services directive left governments too much discretion to decide what constitutes a barrier to establishment, or a barrier to the provision of services across borders. The reduction in barriers to entry has not been as expected.

350   European Commission, "The economic impact of the services directive: A first assessment following implementation", June 2012

351   John Springford, "How to build European services markets", Centre for European Reform, September 2012 http://www.cer.org.uk/sites/default/files/publications/attachments/pdf/2012/js_markets_sept12-6206.pdf

to get youth unemployment down.[352] Other restrictions, for instance, on shop-opening hours could also quickly be abolished, notably in Germany, to boost consumer spending (and give people more freedom to shop when they like).

Unfortunately, the Commission has done little over the past five years.[353] When my team put forward ambitious proposals, none were

---

352   Sometimes the retail sector is competitive; often it is not. Belgium is particularly bad. Supermarkets are shoddy and overpriced. One big barrier to entry is the availability of land: an intensely local issue that prevents an outsider like Britain's Tesco from injecting much-needed competition.

353   While the Commission has produced two Single Market Acts in recent years, these mostly collate existing, often minor initiatives. The Single Market Act, published in April 2011, collates twelve measures: common rules for venture-capital funds so they can readily provide finance to innovative businesses across the EU, streamlining the procedures for recognising the professional qualifications of mobile workers, creating a single European patent (everywhere except Spain and Italy), better redress for consumers whose rights have been violated, strengthening standardisation for services, identifying strategic projects to boost European transport and energy networks, mutual recognition of digital signatures, a European framework to boost social entrepreneurship, a revision of the energy tax directive, preventing abuse of posted workers' directive, reducing administrative burden for businesses, more open access to public procurement contracts. http://eur-lex.europa. eu/LexUriServ/LexUriServ.do?uri=CELEX:52011DC0206:EN:NOT   This   was followed by the Single Market Act II, published in October 2012, which also includes twelve measures under four headings. Transport and energy networks: opening up domestic rail passenger services to intra-EU competition, improving the single market for maritime transport, accelerating the creation of a Single European Sky and measures to make the application of existing EU energy legislation effective. Mobility: developing a fully-fledged cross-border and job recruitment tool, provisions to mobilise long-term investment funds, modernising insolvency procedures. Digital economy: making online payments services easier to use, more trustworthy and competitive; reducing civil engineering costs of broadband network investment, making electronic invoicing standard in public procurement procedures. Social entrepreneurship, cohesion and consumer confidence: improving product safety rules

taken up. The new Commission that takes over in November 2014 should be bolder. Part of the problem has been that EU internal market commissioner Michel Barnier thinks the single market is a "liberal" project and that he therefore needs to do "social" things. That is nonsense – the poor suffer most from a lack of competition, which inflates the cost of living and denies them choice (and hence power) – and besides it is others' job to focus on explicitly social matters. The bigger problem is that cosseted businesses, both big and small, want to fend off competition, while reactionary trade unions defend the narrow interests of existing members over those of workers in general (including the unemployed and potential future members).

Both national and EU trustbusters should be much more vigorous in tackling monopolistic practices. Hefty financial penalties should be complemented with criminal ones for complicit managers. The threat of prison is a far more effective deterrent than a corporate fine.

A blast of foreign competition would also do a world of good. Ideally, the EU would open up its markets unilaterally, since cheaper foreign products would be a boon to Europeans with shrunken wages and would spur local companies to up their game. Since politics typically precludes that, trade agreements that offer the prospect of better access to foreign markets are a good way of overcoming protectionist lobbies, but they take time to negotiate and implement. Some progress has finally been made through the World Trade Organisation. A deal agreed in Bali in December 2013 will streamline customs procedures. With luck, the WTO's new boss, Roberto Azevedo, will be able to reinvigorate a broader push to free up global trade. The fallback options are bilateral and regional. By giving preferences to some, such deals handicap others. That is unfortunate for consumers as well as for businesses that rely on imports of parts and components. It also

---

and their enforcement, improving access to bank accounts and reduce switching costs. http://ec.europa.eu/internal_market/smact/docs/single-market-act2_en.pdf

distorts trade. Since hundreds of such agreements are being negotiated, this creates a devilishly complicated web of overlapping rules that is a gift to lawyers and a burden on businesses. Still, they may be better than nothing. The EU's free-trade deal with South Korea, its first with an Asian country, entered into force in July 2011. EU exports to Korea have soared, while Hyundai cars and Samsung phones cost less in Europe than before.[354] The EU also concluded a deal with Canada in late 2013.

The biggest prize in the offing is a trade and investment agreement with the United States. Talks began in 2013 with the aim of concluding a speedy deal. One study reckons an ambitious and comprehensive agreement would boost the EU economy by €119 billion a year – boosting the income of a family of four by €545 a year.[355] Thorny issues abound, not least agriculture, but most are in services. The French government frets that French people will only watch Hollywood films unless it protects local ones. The US and the EU have taken different approaches to bank regulation since the crisis. The NSA spying scandal has made Europeans leerier of entrusting their data to American internet companies. Regulators on both sides of the Atlantic jealously guard their turf. Recognising each other's standards, let alone agreeing common ones, is a mammoth task, especially when the divergence is due to differing principles as well as protectionism. Put simply, the surest way to curb American businesses' enthusiasm is to portray the deal as a vehicle for imposing costly European-style regulation, while European consumer groups

354   Hyundai's Western European car sales soared from 362,110 in 2010 to 444,001 in 2012. http://worldwide.hyundai.com/WW/Corporate/InvestorRelations/IRActivities/SalesPerformance/EuropeRetailSales/index.html

355   Centre for Economic Policy Research, "Reducing Transatlantic Barriers to Trade and Investment: An Economic Investment", March 2013 http://trade.ec.europa.eu/doclib/docs/2013/march/tradoc_150737.pdf

and environmentalists would be up in arms if they thought it was a backdoor for lower American standards. In short, don't count on a quick deal, let alone an ambitious one.

With the Chinese economy adding the equivalent of another Italy to the world economy every two years and Chinese products increasingly popular with hard-pressed European consumers, the EU ought to be launching trade negotiations with China too.[356] This would make both strategic and economic sense. Since the United States seems to be trying to contain China commercially through its Trans-Pacific Partnership (TPP) with eleven other Pacific countries, the EU ought to signal that it favours constructive engagement. With luck, that in turn will help unblock global trade liberalisation efforts at the WTO.

At a time when domestic investment is in short supply, the EU should also make better use of its new powers to negotiate foreign investment deals. While President Barroso fended off pressure from corporatist commissioners, notably France's Michel Barnier and Berlusconi appointee Antonio Tajani, for the EU to screen foreign direct investment, as the US does through its Committee on Foreign Investment in the United States (CFIUS), the Commission has not been active enough in trying to boost investment. Investment talks with China have yet to make much progress. With Chinese companies keen to expand internationally to open up new markets, obtain rights to resources and acquire better technologies, and the Chinese state eager to diversify its huge portfolio of foreign assets away from low-yielding and depreciating US Treasury bonds, the EU should be welcoming Chinese investment with open arms. Britain has been laudably open – to Chinese money if not to Chinese tourists and students.

---

356 International Monetary Fund, World Economic Outlook database, April 2013. China's GDP in current dollars in 2013 is estimated at $9.02 trillion, rising to $11.02 trillion in 2015. This $2 trillion rise is almost identical to Italy's 2013 GDP of $2.08 trillion.

To sum up, thanks to the ECB, the eurozone has gained some breathing space to fix its problems. But it still needs to restructure its banks, write down excessive debts, boost investment and pursue reforms that promote competition, rather than competitiveness. Germany too must play its part. While the eurozone house is no longer battered by wind and rain, it is still not complete. The next chapter explains how that might be achieved.

6

GRAND DESIGNS

How to complete the half-built euro house

> *The European Union that will emerge from this process will be diametrically opposed to the idea of a European Union that is the embodiment of an open society. It will be a hierarchical system built on debt obligations instead of a voluntary association of equals. There will be two classes of states, creditors and debtors, and the creditors will be in charge. As the strongest creditor country, Germany will emerge as the hegemon. The class differentiation will become permanent because the debtor countries will have to pay significant risk premiums for access to capital and it will become impossible for them to catch up with the creditor countries.*
>
> George Soros, 2012[357]

---

357   http://www.nybooks.com/articles/archives/2012/sep/27/tragedy-european-union-and-how-resolve-it/

Europe is now defined by the constraints it imposes on governments, not by the possibilities it affords them to improve the lives of their people. This is politically unsustainable.

Kevin O'Rourke, professor of economic history at
All Souls College, Oxford, 2014[358]

The Western financial crisis has highlighted huge flaws in how our economies are run. Global finance runs amok, economies swing from bubble to bust and national governments struggle to cope. In many respects, the eurozone is a microcosm of this global system. The tensions between cross-border finance, interconnected economies and fragmented politics are replicated there. But whereas globally common rules are patchy, international institutions weak and democratic accountability sorely lacking, within the eurozone such governance is much more developed – for good and ill. The hope is that the eurozone might evolve into an enhanced and enlightened form of international economic cooperation. The danger is that it will become a glorified debtors' prison with a German jailer and Brussels-based guards.

To work well, eurozone governance needs to do four things. Try to prevent problems – financial crises, fiscal difficulties, economic slumps – from emerging. Limit their consequences when they do arise: avoid banks dragging down governments, prevent panic in government bond markets, keep job losses and suffering to a minimum. Resolve problems – tackle distressed banks, deal with excessive private and public debt, promote economic recovery – promptly, fairly and safely. Last but not least, ensure effective democratic accountability and choice.

Tackling these challenges may be trickier for the eurozone in some respects. When economies are out of synch, a shared eurozone

358   http://www.imf.org/external/pubs/ft/fandd/2014/03/orourke.htm

interest rate may be too low for booming ones and too high for slug-gish ones – and so drive economies even further apart. There is also a tension between the need for governments that share a currency to have greater fiscal flexibility and the fear that this might be abused at others' expense. And when economies irrevocably lock their ex-change rates, adjustments between them must happen in different ways. Most importantly, eurozone governments are vulnerable to panics because they are forced to borrow in a currency that they do not control.[359]

But in other ways, being part of the euro could make such prob-lems easier to address. A bigger economic entity has greater control over its destiny. Currency swings matter less to the eurozone than they do to Britain, let alone New Zealand. Together, eurozone gov-ernments have a better chance of bringing big cross-border banks to heel – and they can also have more influence in shaping global rules on finance and much else. As a political club, the eurozone may be able to establish fair and effective common rules and institutions that remain elusive globally. A recurring problem globally is that economic adjustment tends to be unbalanced and deflationary: in a slump debtor countries are forced to curb their spending but credi-tor ones are not compelled to increase theirs; within the eurozone, a means of forcing surplus countries to adjust already exists – it just needs to be applied. A mechanism for closing down cross-border banks is also within reach. Whereas creating a global lender of last resort remains a distant dream, all it takes in the eurozone is a change to the EU treaty. Last but not least, whereas EU policymaking can become more democratic by enhancing existing institutions, the gap between global decision-making and local democracy is much harder to bridge.

---

359   Arguably, this is true of all eurozone governments except Germany and per-haps France too.

Four dimensions

Strengthening the eurozone's architecture requires work on four interlocking planks: finance, fiscal matters, monetary policy and economic issues. In each, there are four key issues. To what extent does the eurozone need common rules, institutions and policies? What should those be? How do eurozone-only institutions interact with EU-wide ones? And how should democratic choice and accountability be ensured? How to improve democracy in the EU as a whole is tackled in Chapter 13.

Start with finance. The EU is meant to have a single market in financial services: money can move freely and financial institutions established in one EU country can operate across all twenty-eight. Britain's Barclays has branches in Spain. Spain's Santander has bought Abbey National and other British banks. Germany's Commerzbank has made lots of (bad) property loans in Spain, both directly and via local banks. In the pre-crisis years, many banks became ostensibly pan-European. But when the crisis hit, that turned out to be an illusion: banks fell back on various national governments for bailouts and prioritised domestic operations over foreign ones. Banks that seemed European while alive proved to be national when they became zombies. Worse, in the absence of a common "safe" asset such as eurozone bonds, eurozone banks tend to primarily hold the bonds of the government backstopping them. So as the price of German government bonds soared while that of Italian ones plummeted, German banks' balance sheets improved while Italian ones' deteriorated. As a result, banks' funding costs now vary widely according to those of the government backstopping them: a sickly German bank can borrow more cheaply than a healthy Italian one. Moreover, the single market in financial services has fragmented: most lending is now national again.

Since cross-border bank lending did more harm than good in the pre-crisis years, one option would be to try to keep banking mostly national. After all, even within the United States, most banking is local. But that would go against the spirit (and the treaty) of European integration and would be tough to enforce in practice. So the alternative is to try to make pan-European finance work better. To that end, the EU now has common regulation that establishes minimum standards – a "single rulebook" – for everything from insurance to hedge funds. Banks are now required to have slightly bigger capital buffers to absorb potential losses and larger reserves of cash and other liquid assets to deal with cashflow problems.[360] Those buffers against losses are meant to be greater for riskier assets, but government bonds are still deemed "risk-free". (An official expert group chaired by Erkki Liikanen, the governor of the Bank of Finland, has also opined on whether the structure of banks needs reform. Like the Vickers report in Britain, it stops short of recommending breaking up banks, suggesting instead that risky trading activities be ringfenced from retail banking. In 2014 the Commission published proposals that dilute Liikanen's recommendations; in any case nothing will happen until the next Parliament is in place.) Eleven countries (but not Britain) are planning to tax financial transactions. European watchdogs have also been created – the London-based European Banking Authority (EBA), the Paris-based European Securities and Markets Authority (ESMA) and the Frankfurt-based European Insurance and Occupational Pensions Authority (EIOPA) – along with a European Systemic Risk Board that is meant to take an overarching view. However, these European agencies are weak and oversight remains primarily national. Common rules for restructuring and winding down failed banks have been agreed, but these still leave national authorities ample discretion. All countries must guarantee bank deposits

---

360   The Capital Requirements Directive IV package http://ec.europa.eu/ internal_market/bank/regcapital/legislation_in_force_en.htm

up to €100,000 (£85,000), but national authorities' ability to make good on that promise varies.

Within the eurozone, all banks have access to liquidity (cash loans in exchange for collateral) from the ECB on equal terms – although in practice German government bonds can be pawned for more cash than Italian ones[361] – as well as additional liquidity from national central banks on varying terms. In November 2014, the ECB is due to become the primary supervisor of eurozone banks, as the previous chapter explained. A single resolution mechanism for restructuring and closing down failed banks that still involves a national veto is also due to be introduced. Proposals for shared deposit insurance have been shelved. Countries outside the eurozone can opt into this "banking union", but so far none have.

Is all this sufficient to restore cross-border financial flows across the eurozone and the EU? Will it ensure a level playing field? Does it do enough to prevent future crises, contain their impact and resolve them quickly, fairly and safely? More specifically, will it prevent governments bailing out banks and creating another doom loop? Will it ensure distressed banks are dealt with in a prompt and orderly way that minimises the burden on taxpayers and the disruption of credit to the economy? Does the eurozone's piecemeal banking union – only bigger banks handled at the eurozone level, with plenty of discretion for national authorities and no common deposit insurance – need to become more comprehensive? Last but not least, does it require a common "safe" asset – such as a commonly issued eurozone bond?

That question dovetails with the next area: fiscal matters. In the EU, almost all taxes, government spending and official borrowing are national. One exception is the EU budget, largely funded by customs duties and a share of domestic VAT revenues, which amounts to a

---

361 While the ECB widened its range of acceptable collateral for repo operations, deep haircuts were applied to southern European government bonds.

bit over 2 per cent of government spending in the EU. Another is the European Investment Bank, which has expanded its lending since the crisis to €65 billion–70 billion a year, co-financing projects worth a multiple of that.[362] Within the eurozone, the European Stability Mechanism (ESM) can also borrow to provide crisis loans to eurozone governments.

But while tax, spending and borrowing remain overwhelming national, eurozone governments' discretion is ever more tightly constrained by EU rules. You can take my word for it and jump two paragraphs, or read on if you are interested in the gruesome detail. In Euro 1.0, governments had plenty of autonomy within a loose framework of EU rules: deficits no greater than 3 per cent of GDP, public debt no more than 60 per cent of GDP (or declining towards that level), with the European Commission able to fine EU governments that failed to cut their excessive deficits – if a big enough majority of governments agreed. In 2005, the rules were tightened (and complicated). In Euro 1.1, governments were required to set a "medium term objective" for their underlying deficit (that is, stripping out one-off items and the impact of the economic cycle) – no more than 1 per cent of GDP – consistent with staying within the deficit and debt limits or achieving them promptly. In effect, in the pre-crisis years it was assumed that EU prodding and markets would together keep public borrowing in check, with the no-bailout rule and the ban on monetary financing as fail-safes to prevent one government's excessive borrowing becoming others' responsibility. But after markets' failure to keep Greece's borrowing in check was revealed in late 2009 and Chancellor Merkel made the mistake of putting German taxpayers on the hook for other governments' debts by bailing out Greece's creditors in 2010, Berlin and Brussels sought to assert much greater control over governments' borrowing.

---

362   The EIB lends primarily, but not exclusively, in EU countries.

The screws were first tightened with a six-pack of measures in December 2011.[363] Euro 2.0 required governments with underlying deficits that exceed their medium-term objective to reduce them by at least 0.5 per cent of GDP a year – and faster if their debts exceed EU limits. Those with debts greater than 60 per cent of GDP must reduce the excess by a twentieth each year.[364] Public spending not matched by revenues must not rise faster than the trend rate of economic growth. Bigger fines of up to 0.5 per cent of GDP can be imposed faster on recalcitrant governments – unless a big enough majority of EU leaders object. The ink was barely dry on Euro 2.0 when Berlin and Frankfurt demanded a separate set of torture instruments: the treaty containing a German-inspired fiscal compact that came into force in January 2013 (the one that David Cameron "vetoed").[365] Euro 2.1 involves even tighter rules (an underlying deficit target of no more than 0.5 per cent of GDP). These are to be enshrined in national – preferably constitutional – law (rather than interpreted by Brussels). Governments with excessive deficits must also commit to

---

363   These changes, which also include the introduction of the macroeconomic imbalances procedure, are known as the "six-pack" in EU jargon. http://europa.eu/rapid/press-release_MEMO-11-898_en.htm

364   On average over three years.

365   Under the Treaty on Stability, Coordination and Governance came into force on 1 January 2013, signatories have committed themselves to a medium-term objective (MTO) of a government budget with a structural (ie, cyclically adjusted) deficit no greater than 0.5 per cent of GDP. Under the rules of the Stability and Growth Pact, governments with a structural deficit greater than their MTO must close the gap by at least 0.5 per cent of GDP a year, with a faster pace of adjustment for governments with debts exceeding 60 per cent of GDP. Governments that have a deficit of more than 3 per cent of GDP or public debt exceeding 60 per cent of GDP that is not falling towards that level by at least one-twentieth averaged over three years are subject to further interventions under the Excessive Deficit Procedure. http://www.eurozone.europa.eu/media/304649/st00tscg26_en12.pdf

reforms to boost "competitiveness" and growth. And any government – guess which one Merkel had in mind? – can ask the European
Court of Justice to slap fines on their non-compliant peers. Not
thoroughly confused (or fast asleep) yet? It gets worse. Still not satisfied, the screws were tightened for a third time in May 2013.[366] Euro
2.2 requires governments to submit their draft annual budget to the
Commission and eurozone finance ministers the previous October.
The Commission can demand changes to budgets that it deems non-
compliant. It also can also impose tighter controls on governments
experiencing, or that it thinks are threatened by, financial difficulties,
forcing them to tackle the perceived problems and submit to regular
reviews by EU officials. It's actually even more complicated than that,
but I won't test your patience any further.[367]

These devilishly complicated rules give plenty of work (and power) to EU officials and impose a bureaucratic nightmare on eurozone
governments.[368] They are confusing for experts and baffling for ordinary citizens. Absurdly, they try to punish governments that have borrowed too much by imposing fines on them. But are they necessary
and sufficient to prevent fiscal problems from emerging? Do they give
governments enough flexibility to respond to downturns and fund
long-term investments? Are they compatible with greater democratic
accountability and choice? Is the way forward to build on the current
approach – ever tighter centralised rules that limit national governments' budgetary discretion – or adopt a more decentralised, flexible one? How should governments that become insolvent be dealt
with? To what extent should the eurozone share fiscal risks by issuing

---

366   http://europa.eu/rapid/press-release_MEMO-13-457_en.htm

367   http://europa.eu/rapid/press-release_MEMO-13-318_en.htm

368   See, for example, the notes to governments explaining what they must do
to comply: http://ec.europa.eu/economy_finance/economic_governance/sgp/pdf/
coc/code_of_conduct_en.pdf

common debt – and would it be better to issue Eurobonds guaranteed by all eurozone governments or create a common eurozone Treasury with tax-raising and borrowing powers? Last but not least, how does one prevent panic in government bond markets: will the ECB's ad hoc, conditional OMT policy suffice, should it be formally mandated as a lender of last resort to illiquid but not insolvent governments, or is there another alternative?

That brings us neatly to monetary policy. Most central banks now operate independently of governments day to day, but the ECB's autonomy is exceptional. It decides both what its target should be – it has settled on consumer-price inflation of close to but under 2 per cent – and how it wants to try to achieve it. It can even choose to do nothing when it fails to meet its target: even though inflation has plunged to below 1 per cent, threatening deflation, it is sitting on its hands. The ECB's deliberations are also the most secretive of all major central banks and it is scarcely accountable to elected authorities.

For now, reform of the ECB isn't even on policymakers agenda. What little debate there is – for example, whether to publish minutes of its meetings – takes place within the confines of its skyscraper in Frankfurt. Even so, should the ECB try to limit asset-price bubbles as well as curb consumer-price inflation – and if so, how? Like the US Federal Reserve, should it have a broader mandate of supporting growth and employment, not just keeping inflation low, especially in a downturn? Should it be more open and accountable?

Last but not least comes economic policy. Eurozone economies are very different, often ossified and not as integrated as they ought to be: the EU single market remains woefully incomplete and labour mobility low. Moreover, even very open and flexible economies such as Ireland's can get blown off course by a surge of foreign money that inflates a bubble and then inflicts a bust. The danger, then, is that economies will get out of joint and not be able to snap back.

To try to prevent and remedy that, the European Commission has acquired new powers to coordinate economic policies and has devised a scoreboard that seeks to provide an early warning of dangerous economic imbalances. It can also demand that governments try to correct excessive imbalances, such as soaring credit growth or huge current-account surpluses, with sanctions on recalcitrant ones, unless a big enough majority of EU leaders objects. In practice, though, such surveillance tends to be ineffective: none of the international institutions foresaw the financial crisis, let alone forestalled it.[369] And the EU's macroeconomic imbalance procedure is particularly flawed.[370] Its "early-warning system" is based on (sometimes very) old data to which it responds slowly.[371] It is dangerously unbalanced, since it is

---

369   Monitoring worrying imbalances seems like a good idea, but in practice such surveillance tends to be ineffective. It often raises false alarms – hence the joke that economists have predicted ten of the last three recessions. It often fails to warn (or warns too late) about big crises: the IMF missed the 1997–8 Asian financial crisis; the IMF, ECB and the European Commission were all blindsided by the current financial crisis and its eurozone offshoot. Even when risks are correctly identified, political interference and special-interest lobbying often ensure that concerns are watered down or ignored. Last but not least, the resulting policy recommendations may be flawed or not implemented.

370   The European Commission previously monitored imbalances through the EU's Broad Economic Policy Guidelines.

371   To have any hope of identifying problems in good time, an early-warning system ought to be based on current information and in particular on leading indicators – economic data that tends to provide early indications of future trends. Yet, astonishingly, the MIP scoreboard published in 2012 used 2010 data and in some cases, the average of the previous three years' data, ie, 2008–10 data. While the European Commission says it also takes into account more recent information, the scoreboard that purports to be a key basis for its judgements is hopelessly out of date. Moreover, if one allows up to a year for the in-depth review, European Council decision and design of a corrective action plan, implementing that plan might begin in 2013 and its impact be felt only in 2014 and beyond.

more lenient on current-account surpluses than on deficits and treats Germany's vast surplus equivalently to tiny Luxembourg's.[372] It is distorted by politics: hence why it goes easy on Germany. Above all, it is based on the misconception that economies are predictable and perfectible and policymakers omniscient.

Even so, is this enough to prevent parts of the eurozone getting too out of line with each other? Is there a danger, on the contrary, that the Commission will try to stamp out beneficial "imbalances" such as temporary foreign borrowing to cushion the blow of a recession or sustained capital inflows to finance productive investment and catch-up growth? What else might be done to make the eurozone operate more as one? Should governments be forced to sign contracts committing them to reform? Is there a case for mechanisms that might automatically offset temporary divergences, such as a eurozone-wide unemployment insurance scheme? What else could be done to make economies better able to adapt?

Four futures

So many questions, so many possible answers. There is a kaleidoscope of potential future institutional arrangements and policy settings in the eurozone, but only a few are politically possible or economically sensible. Broadly speaking, there are four possible futures for the eurozone: a Germanic eurozone, a technocratic one, a federal one and a flexible one. These are just archetypes; one could readily imagine

---

372 The Commission's definition of an excessive imbalance is one where "the degree of the macroeconomic imbalances is considered severe or may jeopardise the proper functioning of the Economic and Monetary Union". That is unarguably true of Germany's huge current-account surplus. For further details about the macroeconomic imbalances procedure, see http://europa.eu/rapid/press-release_MEMO-13-318_en.htm

variants of them, such as a flexible federal eurozone. What emerges in practice may be a messy political compromise between them.

At the moment, the eurozone is heading towards a Germanic eurozone. That is one whose rules, institutions and policies are shaped by Germany's idiosyncratic ideas and interests, rather than by a coherent vision of the interests of the eurozone as a whole. Officially, the German government supports "more European integration – a genuine transfer of sovereignty and a significant strengthening of European institutions" in financial, fiscal and other matters, as finance minister Wolfgang Schäuble has put it.[373] German officials even claim to favour a "political union", without defining it, before hastily and disingenuously adding that since others aren't willing to go that far, any steps towards it are not possible. But in practice, Germany tends to want more controls over others but not itself. So it wants rules that automatically curb governments that borrow too much (its budget is in balance), a move that also suits its interests as a creditor. But, convinced that it will always be strong and therefore a contributor rather than a beneficiary, it resists any form of risk-sharing – be it commonly issued debt or pan-eurozone unemployment insurance – which is viewed as a backdoor to open-ended German transfers to southern Europe. It has also sought to eviscerate moves towards a banking union and retain plenty of national discretion over its (often distressed) banks.[374] It believes that everyone else in the eurozone

---

373   Wolfgang Schäuble, "How to protect EU taxpayers against bank failures", *Financial Times*, 31 August 2012 http://www.ft.com/cms/s/0/d270a89e-f213-11e1-8973-00144feabdc0.html

374   For example, German finance minister Wolfgang Schäuble argued that "we cannot expect a European watchdog to supervise directly all of the region's lenders – 6,000 in the eurozone alone – effectively." But that is a bogus argument: Germany's financial supervisory agency, BaFin, supervises around 2,079 banks and 718 financial services institutions plus around 700 insurance companies, 25 pension funds, 5,900 investment funds and 77 asset-management companies – roughly 9,500

ought to be more like Germany and boost their "competitiveness" – which is neither feasible nor desirable – and wants the EU to impose pseudo-colonial "contracts" on recalcitrant governments,[375] while resisting any pressure to reform its own often-hidebound economy. Historical taboos – paranoia that even a little inflation could lead to hyperinflation which (it is wrongly believed) paved the way for Hitler – rule out ECB reform, a stance that also benefits German creditors. And so on.

While all governments generally pursue what they perceive as their own interests, it is one thing if Luxembourg does so and quite another if Germany does. What made the European club work well until recently was that Germany perceived its national interest as creating a more European Germany rather than a more Germanic Europe. In other words, it sought to embed itself in European institutions rather

---

entities in total – and Schäuble has never argued that BaFin is ineffective. So this was just a pretext for avoiding eurozone oversight of Germany's many smaller banks. Besides, it was never argued that the new eurozone supervisor should "supervise directly all of the region's lenders", but rather that it should have ultimate responsibility for supervising all of them, with many powers and tasks delegated to national supervisors. Ultimate responsibility means the right to receive any information it requests from national supervisors, the power to require banks to take whatever action it deems necessary to comply with banking regulations, the power to revoke a bank's licence and the power to demand that a bank's balance sheet be restructured and, if necessary, wound down.

375   See, for instance, European Council, Conclusions on Completing EMU, 18 October 2012. Section 13: "The smooth functioning of EMU calls for stronger and sustainable economic growth, employment and social cohesion and requires stronger coordination, convergence and enforcement of economic policy. In this respect, the idea of the euro area Member States entering into individual arrangements of a contractual nature with the EU institutions on the reforms they commit to undertake and on their implementation will be explored. Such arrangements could be linked to the reforms identified in the country-specific recommendations adopted by the Council and build on EU procedures."

than use those institutions to reshape Europe as it saw fit. Since the Second World War is long gone and Angela Merkel is no Adolf Hitler, Germany may now feel entitled to behave more like a "normal" country and define its interests in a more selfish way. But the bigger issue is how the European club can cope with a hegemonic Germany that has the power to impose its positions on others. That issue is particularly stark in the eurozone, from which Britain has excluded itself, in which France is enfeebled, where the European Commission is politically weak and which – crucially – is increasingly polarised between creditors and debtors. If rules, institutions and policies in the eurozone, which is meant to be a club of equals, increasingly become instruments for Germany as a creditor to impose controls on debtors, the eurozone is likely to remain an unhappy marriage that might eventually end in divorce. To put it differently, a Germanic eurozone is not a desirable future for the eurozone and I doubt it is ultimately a viable one either. If the German government wants the euro to survive and succeed – as I believe it does – it would be wise to take more account of the interests of the system as a whole, as the United States did during the Cold War in supporting an open multilateral trading system. For a more integrated eurozone to be both effective and legitimate, the new rules and institutional arrangements must reflect everyone's interests and apply equally to everyone.

Another possible future is a technocratic eurozone. This would involve a genuine, comprehensive banking union. It would also include tighter, centrally enforced fiscal rules that limit governments' discretion and a mechanism to limit macroeconomic imbalances – in the hope that these would prevent future crises. These would eventually be complemented by commonly issued Eurobonds that would pool fiscal risks across the eurozone and provide a safe asset for banks – in the hope that this would provide stable funding for governments and end the doom loop between banks and governments. The single market would be completed, domestic reforms implemented and economic policies more closely controlled from Brussels.[376] Reforming the ECB or establishing a mechanism for restructuring the debts of insolvent governments would remain taboo. Democratic accountability would remain limited and be primarily through the European Parliament.

A technocratic eurozone is preferable to a Germanic one. It would involve rules that apply to all – not least a genuine banking union – and the hope that they might be enforced impartially. A fiscal straightjacket would be more tolerable if complemented with commonly issued debt. A more integrated and competitive EU single market would be a boon. But the huge disadvantage of a technocratic eurozone is that it involves a big centralisation of powers in Brussels. That would give too much power to unelected, remote and often incompetent EU bureaucrats, place too many constraints on national governments' economic flexibility and varying political priorities, and as a result not be democratic enough. It is a fallacy that economies are predictable, mechanical systems that can be fine-tuned by an ever more elaborate system of rules and likewise that even wise

---

376   See, for example, European Council Conclusions, 13/14 December 2012, Section 12 a: "coordination of national reforms: the participating Member States will be invited to ensure, in line with Article 11 of the TSCG, that all major economic policy reforms that they plan to undertake will be discussed ex ante and, where appropriate, coordinated among themselves. Such coordination shall involve the institutions of the EU as required by EU law to this end. The Commission has announced its intention to make a proposal for a framework for ex ante coordination of major economic policy reforms in the context of the European Semester" and Section 12c: "the feasibility and modalities of mutually agreed contracts for competitiveness and growth: individual arrangements of a contractual nature with EU institutions could enhance ownership and effectiveness. Such arrangements should be differentiated depending on Member States' specific situations. This would engage all euro area Member States, but non euro Member States may also choose to enter into similar arrangements"

and impartial technocrats are best-placed to run economies centrally. They lack the information to do so properly. They are too detached from those who lives they seek to shape. And there is no single "right" way of doing things that they know best. Competing visions of what governments should (and shouldn't) do are the essence of politics, not a matter for arbitrary rules and technocratic enforcement. And without the possibility of throwing the rascals out and changing course, a technocratic eurozone would be abhorrently undemocratic.

A more ambitious vision is a federal eurozone – or at least a fiscally federal one. This would involve creating a common eurozone Treasury with a budget that automatically damped economic ups and downs across the eurozone and could also provide a discretionary fiscal stimulus if necessary. It would have tax-raising powers and the right to issue its own bonds, guaranteed not by national governments but by its tax revenues (or hypothecated ones from national governments).[377] The ECB would, in effect, agree to act as lender of last resort for this single fiscal authority, whose bonds would also serve as a common "safe asset" for eurozone banks, which would be regulated, supervised and resolved at eurozone level. The no-bailout rule would be restored and democratically elected national governments would regain much greater discretion over their budgets. Proper democratic accountability of the eurozone Treasury would be ensured through the European Parliament and, potentially, a committee of national parliamentarians.

A fiscally federal eurozone is greatly preferable to a technocratic one. It would create common supranational institutions where they are needed – a fiscal authority and banking authorities as equal counterparts to the overmighty ECB – while leaving ample discretion for

---

377   In effect, these would be like bonds issued by the German or Swiss federal governments, whereas Eurobonds would be equivalent to the Länder or Cantons issuing mutually guaranteed debt.

democratically elected national governments. It would also do away with the complex and over-stringent fiscal rules and meddlesome bureaucracy that are strangling the eurozone. As experience in the US, Germany, Switzerland, Canada and Australia shows, various forms of fiscal federalism can cope with a variety of circumstances and policy mistakes. Runs on national government bonds would be limited by the ECB continuing its OMT programme. Fiscal federalism has been championed by Shahin Vallée, the brilliant economic adviser to European Council President Herman van Rompuy.[378]

Unfortunately, it may not be politically feasible for now. While it does not require creating a federal state, it may be seen as a leap too far by increasingly EU-sceptic voters – although it is in fact much more respectful of national democracy than either a Germanic or a technocratic eurozone. Political leadership would be needed to explain its merits. Vigorous, open debates should ensue, preferably followed by referendums. The biggest obstacle may be national finance ministers and European Commission officials who feel threatened by it. For the former, fiscal federalism is a double-edged sword: they would no longer have to bow and scrape to Brussels and submit to Germanic fiscal torture, but they might feel upstaged by a eurozone finance minister. Shorn of their neo-colonial powers, hapless fiscal enforcers at the European Commission would have to put away their spreadsheets and go back to shuffling paper clips. They would doubtless fight a rearguard action, perhaps with German support, arguing that creating eurozone-only institutions would undermine the EU – an argument that might also resonate in Britain – when it is their bureaucratic power grab and policy mistakes that are doing so. As a fallback, they might be bought off by housing the new eurozone Treasury at

---

378 Shahin Vallée does not see the need for a committee of national parliamentarians; that is my idea.

the European Commission. While fiscal federalism may not yet be feasible, it ought at least to be a long-term goal.

That leaves a final option: a flexible eurozone. This would involve a genuine and comprehensive banking union, with tougher common rules, a truly independent single banking watchdog and an effective common mechanism for restructuring and resolving banks without taxpayers taking a hit. Even in a decentralised monetary union, financial issues cannot properly be handled locally. The no-bailout rule would be restored and national governments would have much greater freedom to respond to varying economic circumstances and changing political preferences, with the ECB mandated to act as a lender of last resort to illiquid governments and insolvent governments' debts promptly restructured under IMF direction prior to accessing IMF bailouts. Together with completing the single market, reforms would focus on making economies more dynamic and adaptable, not more "competitive". Collective decisions – whether by the Eurogroup, the European Commission or the ECB – would be much more democratically accountable, to both the European and national parliaments, while most decisions would remain in national hands.

The advantages of a flexible eurozone are clear: greater economic freedom for national policymakers, genuine responsiveness to changing political preferences, insolvent banks and sovereigns dealt with promptly and fairly. Is this more politically feasible than a fiscally federal eurozone? If Germany wouldn't accept a change to the ECB's mandate, a flexible Europe would be hostage to the ECB's willingness to continue with its ad hoc, conditional lender-of-last-resort role. Given the capture of governments by the banking system, it is also questionable whether a mechanism for resolving banks could operate independently and effectively; and whether eurozone governments would allow the IMF to oversee a restructuring of an insolvent government's debts. In practice, these processes might unfortunately prove messier and more political.

To sum up, a fiscally federal eurozone is probably the best long-term option, but may not be politically possible for now. If so, a flexible eurozone would be the best way of combining the economic and political flexibility needed for the euro to thrive with an overarching framework to hold it together. A Germanic eurozone with a technocratic edge is where we seem to be heading for now. But stripping national governments of their discretion over tax and spending decisions is likely to prove economically and politically unsustainable. This may ultimately cause the euro to disintegrate or, with luck, provide the political momentum to create a fiscally federal eurozone.

Reshaping the ECB

A big debate is also needed about the role of the ECB. It is the most powerful European institution. Like the US Federal Reserve and the Bank of England, it can print money at will – giving it near-magical powers so long as people believe the currency is valuable. Unlike those two institutions, it enjoys extreme independence – the right both to set its own target and decide how to achieve it – enshrined in an EU treaty that can only be revised if all EU governments, national parliaments and in some cases a popular vote agree. Yet it is scarcely accountable for its many mistakes and often deeply political actions.

Jean Claude Trichet was proud to point out that the ECB had delivered on its promise to keep consumer-price inflation near but below 2 per cent. He would boast that it had a better record than Germany's mighty Bundesbank did, albeit over a different period: the disinflationary Noughties rather than the inflationary post-war period.

Yet, as Chapters 1 to 4 explained, the ECB helped create the crisis, greatly exacerbated it and was often an obstacle to resolving it. During the pre-crisis years, it turned a blind eye to asset-price bubbles and financial excesses. It even encouraged the convergence of Greek and German government bond yields, and so must take a large share of the blame for the resulting crash. In May 2010 and subsequently, Trichet adamantly opposed a Greek debt restructuring and was prepared to threaten Armageddon to ensure his view prevailed. The ECB exacerbated this situation by buying Greek government bonds, giving it a vested interest to oppose a restructuring that would expose the foolishness of buying the bonds of an insolvent government and impose losses on it unless it got special treatment. Trichet threatened to force Ireland out of the euro to blackmail its government to stick to its unfortunate pledge to stand behind the debts of all Irish banks – locking in the "doom loop". Trichet and Bini Smaghi were the cheerleaders for massive, front-loaded and ostensibly "expansionary" austerity, which has caused so much suffering and destabilised public finances. Both Trichet and Draghi threatened to force Greece out of the euro in the event it defaulted, provoking panic across the eurozone.

The ECB's crisis response has also generally been poor. To its credit, it was quick to respond to incipient problems in the summer of 2007 by providing emergency liquidity to the financial system. But in the summer of 2008, when the crisis was already raging, it misinterpreted rising oil and commodities prices – a change in relative prices – as presaging generalised inflation and raised interest rates, only to reverse course drastically in September when Lehman Brothers collapsed.[379] It then repeated the mistake twice in 2011, when the panic in sovereign bond markets was already raging, raising interest rates on 13 April and 13 July – the latter, insanely, just after Italian bond yields had spiked.[380] In each case, the ECB obsessed about non-existent inflation

---

379   On 9 July 2008, the ECB raised its deposit rate from 3 per cent to 3.25 per cent and the interest rate on variable-rate tenders from 4 per cent to 4.25 per cent. http://www.ecb.int/stats/monetary/rates/html/index.en.html

380   On 13 April 2011, the ECB raised the interest rate on its fixed-rate tenders from 1 per cent to 1.25 per cent, and by a further 0.25 per cent on 13 July 2011. http://www.ecb.int/stats/monetary/rates/html/index.en.html

risks when the economy was collapsing and the financial sector was in crisis. As Oscar Wilde might have said, to strangle the economy with a rate rise once is unfortunate. Twice is carelessness.

Subsequently, the ECB has been too slow to cut interest rates, only trimming its benchmark rate to 0.25 per cent in November 2013. With deflation looming, it is again passive. Worse, official interest rates in Frankfurt have not fed through to the rates that a creditworthy company in Italy or household in Spain has to pay. To use the technical jargon, the monetary transmission mechanism is broken – and the ECB has done very little about it. Worst of all, while it has provided open-ended support to eurozone banks, many of them insolvent, it refused for a long time to come to the rescue of eurozone governments facing a liquidity crisis. Once the panic became systemic in the summer of 2011, the ECB took over a year to finally intervene to stabilise sovereign bond markets through the OMT, insisting all along that it was legally unable to act. Fears that intervening could prompt future recklessness were hardly grounds to stand by and watch the house burn down, especially since enforcing the EU's fiscal rules does not fall within the ECB's mandate.[381] Nor should a central bank which protests that its independence is sacrosanct be constrained by political pressure from Germany. This reckless game of chicken, designed to force governments to embark on massive austerity, caused huge suffering and pushed the eurozone to the brink of collapse.

So many mistakes in so little time – and with so little accountability for them. Faced with seventeen (now eighteen) separate fiscal authorities, the ECB refuses to cooperate with any of them, batting away the mere suggestion as an unacceptable invasion of its independence, while playing them off against each other. Yet in a slump, when inflation is not a threat, authorities need to

---

381 Others worried about inflation, even though the eurozone economy was stagnant and the money supply falling. In any case, any bond purchases could be sterilised by withdrawing money from the economy elsewhere.

work together to avert deflation. Worse, the ECB is scarcely accountable to democratic authorities: it deigns only to a "dialogue" with the European Parliament rather than hearings or testimony, and the Parliament cannot fire any board member who fails to perform. While refusing to cooperate with fiscal authorities and being scarcely accountable to democratic ones, the ECB repeatedly meddles in deeply political issues that have huge distributional consequences. By what right does an unelected central bank threaten dire consequences – even expulsion from the euro – if the Greek government restructures its debt, if the Irish one revokes a mistaken guarantee of bank bondholders or if Silvio Berlusconi, not my favourite politician but still at the time the democratically elected prime minister of Italy, fails to implement a list of fiscal reforms at a time when inflation was low? Since when does the ECB have a mandate for threatening governments if they don't engage in structural reforms, desirable as those reforms might be? It is also completely inappropriate that, together with the European Commission and the IMF, it is part of the Troika that imposes austerity and reform programmes on countries that have borrowed from the EU and IMF. The ECB cannot have it both ways: refusing any political accountability for its monetary and financial decisions while intervening at will in political and fiscal matters. Clearly, when its awesome power is put to good effect – as a lender of last resort to illiquid governments, for instance – it can be a force for good, but even so it urgently needs reform.

The ECB is buttressed by a secular religion which holds that central-bank independence is sacred and ought to be inviolate. It is particularly beloved by federalists because it is a truly supranational European institution. Yet the general principle in a democracy is that power is exercised by elected authorities. When democratic authorities delegate power to unelected ones, that power ought to be exercised openly and accountably. Surely the ECB ought to be judged by its results?

The conventional case for central-bank independence rests on three planks: common agreement that low inflation is a good thing; the absence of a trade-off between low inflation and other desirable goals such as low unemployment, high growth or financial stability; and the belief that independent central banks are better placed to deliver low inflation at lower cost than politicians are. Yet in practice, most people care as much, if not more, about low unemployment, rising living standards and stable credit as they do about low inflation – and the ECB should take this into account in its decision making. Focusing exclusively on keeping inflation (too) low has come at the expense of financial stability and living standards, while privileging creditors over debtors. At the very least, then, the ECB needs a broader mandate that takes account of both asset-price and consumer-price inflation, financial and price stability, as well as growth and employment. It also needs to be more accountable to democratic authorities – the European Parliament as well as a committee of national parliamentarians.

There also needs to be more cooperation between elected fiscal authorities and unelected monetary ones. Closer coordination would ensure better economic outcomes, while the ECB ought to take account of the views of elected governments. Such cooperation would be easier if a common eurozone Treasury were created. The ECB also ought to act as a lender of last resort for solvent governments, as central banks throughout history and around the world are. As it acquires new responsibilities for banking supervision, it is even more important that the ECB becomes properly accountable. Power corrupts; and a concentration of unaccountable power corrupts absolutely.

Some will say that it is taboo to question the mandate and conduct of the ECB. I strongly disagree. What the ECB does is far too important – and far too political – for it to be above democratic scrutiny. Central-bank independence is not an end in itself. On the contrary, it trades off a value we hold dear – democratic decision-making – for perceived greater gains. It surely ought to be conditional on the ECB actually making citizens of the eurozone better off. Unfortunately, central bankers seem to have forgotten that their role is to enhance the welfare of Europeans, not bask in their power, privilege the interests of the financial sector over those of ordinary people, pursue their political prejudices and refuse to be open and accountable to the citizens they are meant to serve.

7

NORDIC LIGHTS, BRITISH GLOOM

Why Britain's long-delayed recovery is dysfunctional

We want the words 'Made in Britain', 'Created in Britain', 'Designed in Britain', 'Invented in Britain' to drive our nation forward. A Britain carried aloft by the march of the makers. That is how we will create jobs and support families.

George Osborne, Chancellor of the Exchequer, budget speech, 2011

In 2012 Britain was 159th out of 173 countries ranked by investment as a share of GDP. Of the 14 farther down the table, seven were in sub-Saharan Africa. The only advanced economies were Malta, Ireland, Cyprus and Greece. Mr Osborne should not be comfortable in this company. If Britain is to remain a G20 economy, it must start investing like one.

The Economist editorial, 2013[382]

---

382   http://www.economist.com/news/leaders/21580466-why-being-159th-best-investment-no-way-country-sustain-recovery-lets-try

Partly due to its flawed design but largely because of policy mistakes and political capture, the eurozone has been a disaster in recent years. Its banking system is so huge and globally connected that the crisis threatened to drag the world economy down with it. Its economy is only a fifth smaller than America's, so its prolonged weakness has been a drag on global growth. Its neighbours in particular have suffered from lost exports, bank loans gone sour and damaging uncertainty. But while some have barely broken sweat, others have struggled and one country – Britain – has contrived to do worse than the eurozone in some respects. The British government has made many of the same mistakes as the eurozone – failing to clean up the banks, doing too little about private-sector debt and lurching into austerity – while failing to tackle the economy's deep-seated structural weaknesses and relying on an ineffective mix of loose monetary policy and devaluation to boost growth. By early 2013, five years after the UK economy collapsed, it was still more than 3 per cent smaller than its pre-crisis peak – a performance fractionally weaker than the eurozone's and worse than during the Great Depression of the 1930s.[383] But then the economy sprang to life, leading the government to claim victory. In fact, having failed to engineer a healthy recovery, the government is stoking up a pre-election housing bubble and a return to unsustainable debt-fuelled consumption at a time when banks remain rickety, household debts are already scarily high and real wages continue to fall. It is a disaster in the making.

Think Britain is a success? Compare its performance since the crisis to Switzerland's. Both have outsized banks whose assets total more than five times national income. Both suffered a wrenching

---

383   Eurostat, GDP and main components – volumes. Code: namq_gdp_k
Comparison between Q1 2008 and Q1 2013. UK GDP was 3.4 per cent lower, the eurozone's 3.3 per cent lower

financial crisis: Switzerland's biggest bank, UBS, came close to sinking it. Swiss exporters have had a torrid time. Exports to the eurozone are a much bigger share of the Swiss economy than they are of Britain's – and while UK exporters have enjoyed a much weaker pound, Swiss ones have struggled with a super-strong franc.[384] Yet in the five years from early 2008 in which the UK economy shrank by more than 3 per cent, Switzerland's grew by more than 5 per cent – and Britain's subsequent spurt of growth scarcely makes up for lost time.[385] Unlike Britain's, the Swiss authorities have forced their banks to shape up. Unlike Britain's, Swiss exporters have coped. So much for George Osborne's claim that foreigners are to blame for Britain's delayed and unbalanced recovery.

The best-performing European economy since the crisis has been Poland's, the only EU country to avoid recession. When it joined the EU in 2004 together with seven other former communist countries in central and eastern Europe (plus Cyprus and Malta), Poles were barely half as rich as the average European. By 2012 their living standards were two-thirds of those of a typical European.[386] They have caught up even more impressively with Britons: from two-fifths of the UK average to three-fifths in a mere eight years. At this rate, Brits will be soon be flocking as immigrants to Poland. Apart from Switzerland and post-communist economies that are still catching up with western

---

384   While UK exporters enjoyed a 25 per cent depreciation after 2008, Swiss ones had to cope with an appreciation of more than 15 per cent. As a perceived safe haven, the Swiss franc soared during the eurozone crisis until the Swiss National Bank intervened to cap its rise.

385   Eurostat, GDP and main components – volumes. Code: namq_gdp_k Comparison between Q1 2008 and Q1 2013. UK GDP was 3.4 per cent lower, Switzerland's 5.3 per cent higher

386   Eurostat, GDP per capita in PPS. Code: tec00114

Europe, the country that has fared best since the crisis is Sweden, followed by oil-rich Norway.[387]

Nordic warning

It didn't feel so at the time, but Nordic countries were lucky to have their banking crises long before the rest of the West did. Until the 1980s, borrowing had been frowned on in sober Scandinavia and governments tightly restricted it. But when the financial system was deregulated, the results were predictable. Like normally restrained Scandinavians letting rip on a weekend drinking binge, exuberant bankers tanked up on short-term debt and went on an a wild lending spree. Swedish financiers pumped up a huge housing bubble. Staid Finnish savings banks dished out rounds of corporate loans and placed leveraged bets on bubbly stockmarkets. Norwegian novices neglected basic credit controls.[388] Households and companies piled on debt, economies boomed and Scandinavians splurged. Bank supervisors turned a blind eye. So much for the notion that northern Europeans are inherently more prudent than southerners.

---

387   Sweden's economy grew by a total of 5 per cent between the first quarter of 2008 and the third quarter of 2013. Over the same period, Norway's grew by 4.6 per cent. Source: Eurostat, GDP and main components – volumes. Code: namq_gdp_k Denmark has struggled with its own banking crisis. Iceland remains deeply scarred from its huge financial bubble, which I described at length in *Aftershock*.

388   One bank let a firm selling yachts grant loans on its behalf. The firm could even grant loans to new customers on weekends when it was impossible to control their creditworthiness. Unsurprisingly, both the firm and bank soon went out of business, the latter by merging with a large commercial bank that was rescued by the government in 1991. See Erling Steigum, "Financial Deregulation with a Fixed Exchange Rate: Lessons from Norway's Boom-Bust Cycle and Banking Crisis", 2003. http://www.norges-bank.no/Upload/import/publikasjoner/skriftserie/33/chapter2.pdf

Then the bubbles burst and banks went bust. In the early 1990s, the Nordic three suffered the first systemic banking crises in advanced economies since the 1930s – a warning that went unheeded elsewhere in Europe.[389] Norway's economy scarcely shrank and bounced back quite quickly. Sweden suffered three years of shallow recession followed by a vigorous recovery once problems were addressed in 1992. Finland plunged into a deep funk, compounded by the collapse of the Soviet Union and with it Finnish exports, though it too rebounded after three years. Clearly, all three Nordic countries dealt with their banking crises much better than Japan, which suffered a bust around the same time and has yet to fully recover. They also outperformed Britain and the eurozone, which have been struggling for more than half a decade since their banking crisis began. Why?

In part, they were lucky. They were fortunate financially because even though governments provided an Irish-style guarantee to all bank depositors and creditors, banks' losses did not turn out large enough to sink the state. They were also lucky economically, because they had their crises out of synch with everyone else: as small open economies they were able to count on exports to revive growth. Sometimes it helps to fail first. But while each country dealt with its banks differently, they all did one big thing right. They didn't allow bad loans to fester and turn distressed banks into zombies – the terrible mistake that Japan, Britain and the eurozone have all made. Instead, they forced banks to own up to their losses, write them down and raise fresh capital, either privately or from the government, which restructured the balance sheets of failed banks. That decisiveness helped both bank credit and the economy to recover quickly.

With memories of the early 1990s banking crash still fresh, Nordic countries avoided the worst financial excesses of the Noughties.

---

389 The banking crisis started in the late 1980s in Norway and in the early 1990s in Finland and Sweden.

Whereas German banks helped finance southern Europe's bubble, Finnish ones stood aside. While some Swedish banks went on a lending spree in nearby Estonia, Latvia and Lithuania, they pulled through without government bailouts (although the Swedish government did contribute to the EU-IMF loan to Latvia in 2008).[390]

Bankster Britain

Britain was not so lucky. Egged on by low Bank of England interest rates, regulators that prided themselves on their light touch and a Labour government which viewed the City of London as the golden goose that could be plucked to boost welfare spending, Britain's outsized, precariously financed banks fuelled a domestic property bubble and piled into American subprime mortgages and exotic new financial contracts based on them. Some, intoxicated with dreams of global domination, went on an international buying and lending spree. Back home, banks' reckless lending, mostly against the perceived security of booming house prices, saw British households pile on record amounts of debt, rising from 108 per cent of their disposable income in 2000 to a whopping 170 per cent in early 2008.[391]

When the US housing bubble burst, bank lending froze and then UK house prices slumped too, one bank after another toppled. The first was Northern Rock, an overextended local bank that pumped out cheap, risky mortgages financed by short-term debt, which suffered a

---

390   They extended loans worth 20 per cent of Swedish GDP, pumping up local housing bubbles, with Swedbank and SEB in particular taking big risks. http://www.economonitor.com/analysts/2009/06/24/swedish-banks-could-they-get-burned-by-heavy-baltic-exposure/

391   Personal calculations from Office for National Statistics, net financial liabilities of households and non-profit institutions serving households (code: AF.L) divided by four-quarter moving sum of their gross disposable income (code: RPHQ). Figures are for Q1 2008, Q3 2013, Q1 2004 and Q1 2000.

run in September 2007 and was eventually nationalised in February 2008. Days after the collapse of Lehman Brothers in September 2008, HBOS, a retail bank similarly laid low by wild mortgage lending financed with fickle debt, was rescued through a government-brokered takeover by Lloyds TSB, a more conservative lender seduced by the prospect of dominating high-street banking. But swallowing HBOS dragged Lloyds down too: to save it from collapse the following month, the British government took a 43 per cent stake in the bank. Royal Bank of Scotland – which had grown so large that its assets were more than one-and-a-half times bigger than the British economy – was felled by all manner of mistakes, not least the hubris of its boss, Fred Goodwin, who overpaid for ABN Amro, a distressed Dutch bank, in 2007 *after* the crisis had begun. In October 2008, the British government took a majority stake in RBS, which subsequently rose from 58 per cent to 84 per cent, but without taking on day-to-day control over its management. Barclays was able to raise private capital and thus claim that it pulled through without government help, but that is untrue. Like other British banks, it benefited from open-ended government guarantees – and had prime minister Gordon Brown not rescued other British banks, Barclays too would have gone under. As in the eurozone, the British government in effect pledged taxpayers' future incomes as collateral to back its guarantee that banks' debts would be paid in full.

Fortunately, thanks to collective efforts by governments and central banks, the post-Lehman collapse of the global economy was arrested. Both the British economy and house prices stabilised in the latter half of 2009. Britain narrowly escaped Ireland's fate. It also avoided a eurozone-style doom loop. UK banks owned few British government bonds. More importantly, the Bank of England stood ready to act as lender of last resort to the government and was already buying large amounts of government bonds through its quantitative easing (QE) programme from 2009 on. Thus a run on UK government bonds was never likely – and could have been checked in any case.

Unfortunately, Britain's banking crisis continues to hold the economy back. The narrow debate about whether the government sells its stakes in Lloyds and Royal Bank of Scotland at a profit or a loss misses the wider point. They and other British banks have imposed – and continue to impose – a massively larger cost on everyone. As Chapter 1 highlighted, zombie banks are keeping unviable businesses afloat while depriving viable ones of the credit they need to grow.

Misrule Britannia

British Conservatives tend to look to Washington not Brussels for inspiration. Yet David Cameron's embrace of austerity on becoming prime minister in May 2010 was thoroughly European. Even the language of George Osborne's "emergency budget" in June 2010 echoes the austerian claptrap of EU leaders' summit conclusions: "The most urgent task facing this country is to implement an accelerated plan to reduce the deficit. Reducing the deficit is a necessary precondition for sustained economic growth. To continue with the existing fiscal plans would put the recovery at risk, given the scale of the challenge. High levels of debt also put an unfair burden on future generations."[392] Absurdly, while rejoicing that Britain was fortunate not to be in the euro, Osborne warned that it nonetheless risked a Greek-style crisis unless it adopted immediate austerity.

His aim was to bring public-sector net borrowing down from 11 per cent of GDP in 2009-10 (UK budgets are for financial years that run from April to March) to 1.1 per cent in 2015-16. Gross debt

---

392   HM Treasury, Budget 2010, 22 June 2010 http://www.direct.gov.uk/prod_consum_dg/groups/dg_digitalassets/@dg/@en/documents/digitalasset/dg_188581.pdf

would peak in 2012-13 and net debt in 2013-14.[393] How? By slashing spending and raising taxes somewhat, above and beyond the plans set out by the outgoing Labour government in March 2010 – a total of £130 billion (8 per cent of GDP) over five years. Since the new government could have scrapped its predecessor's fiscal plans rather than adding to them, it is responsible for the entire fiscal squeeze since June 2010. Like the eurozone, the UK government decided to front-load austerity, with the biggest hit occurring in 2011-12.[394] In total, the government planned to cut what it estimated as an underlying (structural) deficit of 8.7 per cent of GDP in 2009-10 to 0.3 per cent in 2015-16.[395] Despite this unprecedented fiscal squeeze, it expected the economy to recover steadily, with rising incomes enabling households to consume more while also saving more to pay down debt, and investment and exports also increasing.[396] Growth would come from a combination of exceptionally loose monetary policy and the expected boost to exports from a weaker pound.[397] Last but not least, the government pledged to slash net migration from "hundreds of thousands" to "tens of thousands", contradicting its claim that Britain was "open for business".

By November 2010, Osborne was crowing that "Britain is on course both to grow the economy and balance the books, something

---

393   *Ibid*, Table C6

394   *Ibid*, Table 1.1. This involved a squeeze of £8.9 billion in 2010-11, £32.1 billion in 2011-12, £25 billion in 2012-13, £24 billion in 2013-14, £23 billion in 2014-15 and £15 billion in 2015-16.

395   *Ibid*, Table C6

396   *Ibid*, Table 1.2 and Table C3. The government projected growth of 1.2 per cent in 2010, 2.3 per cent in 2011, 2.8 per cent in 2012, 2.9 per cent in 2013 and 2.7 per cent thereafter

397   Corporation tax was also cut, deregulation promised and minor measures to boost smaller companies access to finance announced.

that some people repeatedly said could not happen."[398] Unfortunately, neither of those claims was correct. Growth slowed in 2011 and then came to a halt in 2012.[399] In his first three years as finance minister, the UK economy grew by a mere 2.1 per cent in total.[400] According to the assumptions of the Office of Budget Responsibility, the official fiscal watchdog established by Osborne himself, austerity has shrunk the economy by 2.5 per cent – but as Chapter 3 discussed, the true impact is probably much greater. In any case, those three years of stagnation are largely due to Osborne's mistakes: not just austerity, but his failure to fix the banks, tackle private-sector debt, boost investment and implement necessary reforms.

With the economy so weak, the fiscal squeeze failed to reduce government borrowing much, as tax revenues flagged. Fortunately, Osborne did not chase his tail with even greater austerity, as eurozone policymakers did. To mask the gaping hole in its budget plans, the government fiddled the headline figures in 2012 with a one-off transfer of assets from the Royal Mail pension plan to the public sector. Since 2013 it has cheated on a regular basis by pocketing interest on the assets purchased by the Bank of England through QE. Even so, by the 2013 budget, the government had revised up its forecast for public borrowing in 2013-14 from 3.5 per cent of GDP to 6.8 per cent.[401] So Osborne was planning to borrow nearly double what he

---

398   George Osborne, Autumn Statement, 29 November 2010 http://www.publications.parliament.uk/pa/cm201011/cmhansrd/cm101129/debtext/101129-0001.htm#1011298000002

399   Eurostat, real GDP growth rate volume, percentage change on previous year, Code: tec00115. The UK economy grew by 1.7 per cent in 2010, 1.1 per cent in 2011 and 0.2 per cent in 2012.

400   Personal calculations from Eurostat, GDP and main components – volumes, comparison of Q2 2010 and Q2 2013. Code: namq_gdp_k

401   HM Treasury, Budget 2013, Table 1.5

had set out in the 2010 budget. Instead of peaking at 85.5 per cent of GDP in 2012-13, gross debt would top 100 per cent in 2015-16.[402] Even if those forecasts prove correct, stabilising public finances will have taken years longer – and been much more painful – than the government initially claimed.[403]

Even using Osborne's own figures and his chosen yardstick of deficit reduction, this is a dismal failure. Britain's broader economic performance has also been awful. While the good news is that the employment rate has edged up and the unemployment rate down, average wages fell by nearly 5 per cent in the three-and-a-half years after Osborne's emergency budget and by late 2013 2.3 million people remained out of work.[404]

Workers' productivity – the value of the output they produce each hour – has slumped.[405] Economists disagree about why. No doubt it is due to several factors. Some argue that firms hung on to surplus workers because it was costly to fire them and rehire them when demand picked up, but it seems implausible that businesses would hoard lots of labour for so long. Nor can this explain why there were so many new hires, no doubt because wages have fallen. On the supply side, sectoral issues, such as the decline in North Sea oil production,

---

402   Net debt would rise to 85.6 per cent in 2016-17, instead of peaking at 70.3 per cent in 2013-14.

403   HM Treasury, Budget 2013, Table 1.2. The Treasury forecasts growth of 1.8 per cent in 2013, 2.3 per cent in 2015 and 2.7 per cent or so thereafter.

404   According to the Office for National Statistics, average weekly earnings rose from £450 in June 2010 to £478 in December 2013. Over the same period, consumer prices rose by 11.3 per cent, so real wages fell by 4.5 per cent. Unemployment figures for the three months to November 2013.

405   Output per hour peaked at 103.5 (index 2010 = 100) in Q1 2008. It bottomed at 97.8 in Q4 2009, rose to 100.6 in Q1 2010 and has since fallen back to 98.9 in Q3 2013, 4.4 per cent lower than its pre-crisis peak. Office for National Statistics, labour productivity and unit labour costs, PROD01

make a difference. As banks have retrenched, measured productivity in the financial sector has also fallen, but since its output was overstated in the bubble years, some of this decline is more apparent than real.[406] More generally, firms have failed to invest enough and so the capital stock has depreciated. But the biggest reason for the fall in productivity results from the government's failure to fix the banks. Zombie banks have kept unproductive companies alive while failing to fund the investment of more productive ones.[407]

Meanwhile, household debt hit a new high of £1,430 billion in late 2013. Largely thanks to inflation, it has dipped to 141 per cent of disposable income – back to 2004 levels but still well above where it was before the bubble.[408] Britain's failure contrasts with the Nordics' earlier success. As an IMF study shows, they successfully cut household debt after their financial crises by allowing government spending to support the economy while people were tightening their belts. Rather than lurching into austerity, the Nordic countries only brought government spending down to pre-crisis levels ten years afterwards.[409]

---

406   See, for instance, http://www.bankofengland.co.uk/publications/Documents/quarterlybulletin/qb110304.pdf

407   See, for example, Ben Broadbent, "Productivity and the allocation of resources", speech at Durham Business School, 12 September 2012 http://www.bankofengland.co.uk/publications/Documents/speeches/2012/speech599.pdf

408   http://www.bbc.co.uk/news/business-25152556 Also, personal calculations from Office for National Statistics, net financial liabilities of households and non-profit institutions serving households (code: AF.L) divided by four-quarter moving sum of their gross disposable income (code: RPHQ). Figures are for Q1 2008, Q3 2013, Q1 2004 and Q1 2000.

409   International Monetary Fund, United Kingdom 2013 Article IV Consultation, July 2013, Annex 2

Export flop

As well as underestimating the harmful impact of austerity, Osborne overestimated the benefits of devaluation and loose monetary policy to an unreformed economy. Remember all the talk about "rebalancing" the economy away from debt-fuelled consumption towards investment and exports? In his March 2011 budget speech Osborne called for "a Britain carried aloft by the march of the makers".[410] Yet by late 2013 exports were lower.[411] Britain's share of world exports has fallen.[412] The trade deficit was bigger in 2013 than in 2011.[413] Far from fuelling an export-led recovery, net trade has been a drag on growth.

Worse, even at a time of depressed spending, the current-account deficit – net borrowing from foreigners – reached a record £59.2 billion in 2012, equivalent to 3.8 per cent of GDP, the highest since the Lawson boom in 1989.[414] By the third quarter of 2013, the gap had widened to 5.1 per cent of GDP![415] Since an export-stunted,

---

410   Or as the budget itself put it more prosaically "The Government's economic policy objective is to achieve strong, sustainable and balanced growth that is more evenly shared across the country and between industries. Creating lasting prosperity requires the economy to change and to rebalance from unsustainable public spending toward net trade and private-sector investment. This will support the UK's long-term economic potential and help to create new jobs." http://www.direct. gov.uk/prod_consum_dg/groups/dg_digitalassets/@dg/documents/digitalasset/ dg_196165.pdf

411   Eurostat, Exports of goods and services, seasonally adjusted and adjusted data by goods and services (code: namq_exi_k). In the third quarter of 2013 UK exports were 1.4 per cent lower than in the first quarter of 2011.

412   Eurostat, Shares of world exports. In 2010, Britain's share of world exports was 3.53 per cent; in 2012 it was 3.42 per cent. Code: tipsex20

413   Office for National Statistics, balance of trade in goods and services. Code: IKBJ. The trade deficit was £23.3 billion in 2011 and £29.9 billion in 2013.

414   http://www.ons.gov.uk/ons/dcp171776_318123.pdf

415   http://www.ons.gov.uk/ons/dcp171778_347294.pdf

consumption-led recovery will tend to widen the deficit, who knows how big the deficit might get. And as experience in southern Europe and many emerging economies shows, a reliance on fickle foreign finance can be dangerous.

The government's excuse is that the crisis in the eurozone has stunted UK exports. No doubt it has, but that is not the whole story. Even with a weaker pound, British exports have flatlined since 2008, whereas the eurozone's have risen. They have performed worse than, among others, those of France, Germany, Ireland, the Netherlands, Portugal and Spain – not to mention Switzerland.[416] Is it really plausible that the crisis in the eurozone has harmed Britain more than the eurozone itself?

As well as this cyclical problem, Britain faces deeper, structural challenges. Before it blew up the British economy, the financial sector squeezed talent and capital out of both industry and other service sectors. Instead of devising valuable new products and services, mathematics whizzes focused on new forms of financial speculation. The overvalued pound crushed manufacturing, which shrank from 20 per cent of the economy in 1997 to 12 per cent a decade later. Britain's industrial and skills base is now so shrivelled that it has been unable to benefit much from a cheaper pound. A broken banking system has also failed to fund promising new exporters. While the foreign-owned car industry and the pharmaceuticals and aerospace sectors have fared well, overall exports of Britain's higher-tech industries have been flat

---

416   The volume of UK exports in the third quarter of 2013 was 0.6 per cent higher than its pre-devaluation peak in the second quarter of 2008. Eurozone exports are up by 6.5 per cent over the same period. Source: personal calculations from Eurostat, exports of goods and services, seasonally adjusted and adjusted data by working days, volumes, index 2005=100. Code: namq_exi_k

in recent years.[417] A plunge in North Sea oil and gas production and the delay in developing alternatives such as shale gas have made matters worse. Britain remains unhealthily reliant on exports of financial services, for which demand has fallen.[418]

Worse, Britain has failed to tap into the boom in emerging economies. As a share of GDP, it exports less to emerging economies than any other of the Group of Seven (G7) largest advanced economies – and indeed less to China than any EU-15 country, including Greece.[419] Japan sends nearly a quarter of its goods exports to Brazil, Russia, India and China (the BRICs), Germany a tenth – and Britain only 5 per cent.[420] Worse, Britain's exports to the BRICs have grown more slowly in recent years than any other G-7 economy's.[421] That said, since Britain sends more of its exports to America, it will hopefully do better if the US recovery strengthens.

---

417 International Monetary Fund, United Kingdom 2013 Article IV Consultation, July 2013, Annex 3. Figure A3.8. Britain's exports of "high and medium-high technology industries" grew by an average of only 0.8 per cent between 2007 and 2011.

418 International Monetary Fund, United Kingdom 2013 Article IV Consultation, July 2013, Annex 3, Figure A3.9 and A3.10. Exports of financial and insurance services accounted for 10.2 per cent of Britain's exports in 2011 and fell by an average of 1 per cent between 2007 and 2011.

419 EU-15 countries are the (generally richer) 15 countries that were members of the EU before its eastward enlargement in 2004.

420 International Monetary Fund, United Kingdom 2013 Article IV Consultation, July 2013, Annex 3, Figure A3.6. In 2011, 23.2 per cent of Japan's goods exports went to the BRICs, 10.2 per cent of Germany's, 7.4 per cent of Italy's and 6.2 per cent of France's, but only 5.2 per cent of Britain's.

421 International Monetary Fund, United Kingdom 2013 Article IV Consultation, July 2013, Annex 3, Figure A3.7. Between 2007 and 2011, Britain's exports to the BRICs grew by 4.2 per cent a year, while France's grew by 5.9 per cent, Italy's by 6.7 per cent, Germany by 9.6 per cent, Japan by 10 per cent and the United States' by 11.4 per cent.

Sterling's devaluation has not only failed to promote Britain's economic rebalancing, it has most likely delayed it, as Chapter 2 explained.[422] Policymakers have complacently assumed that exports would automatically soar and neglected difficult reforms and investment to promote export-led growth. Instead of upping their game and seeking out new foreign markets, British companies have often sat back and enjoyed the gains from a weaker currency as fatter margins. Pocketing short-term profits may seem wise at the time, but longer term a failure to invest, innovate and expand can be catastrophic. In any case, in a global economy where businesses increasingly tap into international supply chains, any price advantage gained from a weaker currency is quickly eroded by the higher cost of imported raw materials, parts and components, and services. Moreover, higher-end companies increasingly compete on the basis of quality, technology and service, rather than price. The benefits of devaluation are massively oversold.

Money illusion
Investment has been woefully weak too. It collapsed by a quarter from mid-2007 to a mere 13.7 per cent of GDP in early 2013 – the lowest since records began in 1955 – and remains feeble.[423] As *The Economist* has pointed out, Britain's investment rate ranks 159th out of 173 countries in the world, behind Mali and barely above Greece.[424] Like in the eurozone, the government compounded the problem by slashing

---

422   See also Philippe Legrain, "Don't Blame the Euro Mess for Britain's Plight", *Wall Street Journal*, 21 October 2012 http://online.wsj.com/article/SB10000872396390 4444734804578066134006073180.html

423   Office for National Statistics, gross fixed capital formation (code: NPQR) divided by GDP at market prices (code: ABMI)

424   http://www.economist.com/news/leaders/21580466-why-being-159th-best-investment-no-way-country-sustain-recovery-lets-try

public investment by a quarter.[425] It blamed the crisis in the eurozone – again – and global uncertainty for undermining "confidence". But the real problems are closer to home: zombie banks that fail to provide credit to smaller businesses and weak demand that deters companies from investing.

The contrast with the US, which fixed its banks and maintained its fiscal stimulus longer, is stark. While bank lending to businesses initially fell further in the US, it started growing again three years later; in Britain it has continued to fall and is down by more than a fifth.[426] Meanwhile, UK banks are charging fatter margins on business loans, a strong sign that the supply of credit is impaired.[427]

The failure to restructure and recapitalise the banking system has hampered the authorities' attempt to stimulate the economy by monetary means. As early as March 2009, the Bank of England cut the interest rate at which it lends to banks to a record low of 0.5 per cent. By 2011 inflation averaged 4.5 per cent, so real interest rates were minus 4 per cent. One might have expected such exceptionally generous borrowing terms to have sparked a recovery. But they didn't, because when banks, households and companies all want to hoard money not part with it, monetary policy becomes largely ineffective. In a liquidity trap, it is like pushing on a string.

Normally, when the Bank of England cuts its bank lending rate, the rate at which banks can borrow more generally also falls.[428] Banks then tend to lend to people and companies more cheaply, which gen-

---

425   http://www.prospectmagazine.co.uk/economics/adam-posen-george-osborne/

426   International Monetary Fund, United Kingdom 2013 Article IV Consultation, July 2013, pages 77 and 78

427   *Ibid*, Figure A4.11 and Figure A4.24

428   More precisely, this is the rate at which the Bank of England lends to banks overnight secured against collateral.

erally encourages both to borrow more and in time to spend or invest more. Lower interest rates also tend to push up the prices of shares, bonds, property and other assets, making investors feel wealthier and therefore more likely to spend. And they generally push the exchange rate down, which may eventually boost exports and curb imports. But in a slump when banks are bust, investment opportunities meagre and most households don't want to borrow more at any price, each link through which lower Bank of England interest rates normally feed through to higher spending is impaired.[429] Only in 2013 did households suddenly stop saving and start splurging again.

Crucially, banks have charged smaller firms more, while refusing to lend to many of them.[430] While bigger businesses that can borrow from capital markets have replaced bank loans with cheaper corporate debt, smaller ones that do not have that option have been hit hard, especially since nearly half of credit to smaller firms is in the form of (extremely expensive) credit-card lending and overdrafts.[431] They have responded by trying to build up cash buffers and inventories, stifling investment and undermining productivity. Since small and medium-sized enterprises represent 99.9 per cent of businesses in

---

429   Near-zero interest rates lowered mortgage interest costs for existing borrowers, which has doubtless supported spending. They pushed and held down the exchange rate, but as we have seen this has not boosted exports. They also bid up asset prices, but this increased wealth on paper did not translate into higher spending until 2013.

430   Banks' funding costs – the rate at which they can borrow – have not fallen as much as official interest rates have, while they have widened the spreads they charge. Banks have also tightened their official lending criteria, swinging from recklessness to stinginess.

431   International Monetary Fund, United Kingdom 2013 Article IV Consultation, July 2013, Figure A4.14

Britain, account for 60 per cent of private sector jobs and 50 per cent of businesses' turnover, this has been a big brake on growth.[432]

A wise government would have forced banks to tackle their balance-sheet problems. Or it would have bypassed them by directing the banks that it nationalised (Northern Rock) or controlled (RBS) to lend more to creditworthy businesses. Instead, government efforts to boost bank lending have tried to tackle the symptoms of the problem rather than the cause, with predictably disappointing results. First came Project Merlin, a corporatist deal with Britain's four biggest banks in February 2011 that failed to boost lending. This was followed in March 2012 by the National Loan Guarantee Scheme, which sought to lower banks' funding costs but achieved little. Soon after came the third wheeze.[433] The Funding for Lending scheme allows banks to swap dodgy assets for UK government bonds and use those as collateral to borrow cheaply from markets, with banks charged a low fee if they maintain their lending and a higher one if they reduce it.[434] While the scheme has cut banks' funding costs, it has yet to feed through to lower lending rates for smaller businesses, still less higher lending volumes. In effect, it has fattened banks' margins and made it easier for them to continue rolling over impaired loans.

The Bank of England has also tried to bypass the banking system through QE: creating money to buy assets with the aim of driving down longer-term interest rates, pushing up asset prices and thereby encouraging consumers to spend and companies to invest. Between March and November 2009, the Bank of England spent £200 billion,

---

432   International Monetary Fund, United Kingdom 2013 Article IV Consultation, July 2013. Footnote 9, page 16

433   The Funding for Lending scheme was launched in August 2012 and subsequently extended to January 2015.

434   In April 2013, the terms were made more generous for banks that lent more and sooner to smaller businesses.

mostly on government bonds. Further waves of QE in the twelve months from October 2011 brought total purchases to £375 billion – around a quarter of GDP. When the Bank buys government bonds off investors, they can spend the proceeds, deposit them at the bank (hopefully boosting lending and spending) or use them to buy other assets. If the proceeds are used to buy domestic assets, that pushes up their price. That may make consumers feel wealthier and so willing to spend more. And it enables big companies to raise capital more cheaply and potentially use that to invest more. If the proceeds are used to buy foreign assets, the pound will decline, which may boost exports. Britain has also been affected by America's much more ambitious and extended QE. This has given a further lift to UK asset prices, while propping up the pound. But while QE has artificially inflated asset prices, this has scarcely boosted the economy. Bigger companies took advantage of lower interest rates to refinance themselves more cheaply, but didn't invest more. Nor did banks lend more, households spend more or exports rise. As Stephen King, the chief economist of HSBC, puts it, QE and other monetary drugs "are acting more as pain killers than as antibiotics. They make some of us feel a bit better but the economic results are, to say the least, disappointing."[435]

The problem isn't just that QE was never likely to work. It's that it can be dangerous. While providing liquidity was essential in the aftermath of Lehman's collapse, the US Federal Reserve and the Bank of England have since inflated asset-price bubbles in the hope that this prompts consumers to start spending again. But households need to reduce their debt, not spend more. The aim should be to stimulate investment and exports, not rekindle unsustainable consumption. Moreover, QE has mainly benefited the wealthy, who own the overwhelming majority of financial assets. A fairer and more effective

---

435   http://www.hsbcnet.com/gbm/global-insights/insights/2013/stephen-king-pain-killers-might-work-but-economies-need-antibiotics.html

monetary policy would bypass the financial system altogether: print money and send everyone a cheque of equal size. If the cash was spent, it would boost demand. If it was used to pay off debt, it would be a form of debt relief. Better still, policymakers ought to tackle excessive private debts directly and force banks to write them down.

In August 2013, the new governor of the Bank of England, Mark Carney, who had the good fortune to leave his job running Canada's central bank just as that country's housing bubble appears to be bursting, called time on QE and tried a new trick designed to give monetary policy more traction: "forward guidance".[436] He sought to reassure markets, businesses and the general public that he would not raise interest rates until the unemployment rate had fallen to 7 per cent – so long as this did not threaten to destabilise inflation or the financial system.[437] But although Carney had been lionised by Osborne – who hailed him as "the outstanding central banker of his generation", something his peers might dispute – markets were not impressed by his announcement.[438] Far from falling after he spoke, longer-term interest rates rose substantially. Even more

---

436 Forward guidance involves signalling what future interest rates are likely to be. But as Erik Nielsen, the chief economist of Unicredit, has pointed out, if a commitment to keep interest rates low is too weak and full of escape clauses, it is likely to have little effect on markets' expectations. On the other hand, a firm commitment to keep interest rates low come what may risks undermining a central bank's credibility, because if it is successful and stimulates the economy, the central bank will subsequently be torn between leaving rates low and risk inflation taking off or breaking its promise and losing credibility. See Erik Nielsen, "Bank of England Risks Blow to Credibility", *Financial Times*, 5 August 2013. http://www.ft.com/cms/s/0/052376f4-f91b-11e2-86e1-00144feabdc0.html

437 See http://www.bankofengland.co.uk/monetarypolicy/Pages/forwardguidance.aspx for further details.

438 http://www.independent.co.uk/news/uk/politics/george-osborne-hails-outstanding-banker-mark-carney-8352663.html

embarrassingly, Carney had to jettison the policy six months later. Unemployment had already fallen to 7.1 per cent – not thanks to his efforts, because monetary policy doesn't work that quickly, but because British consumers stopped saving and started spending again – prompting fears of higher interest rates. So Carney tried to reassure people that rate rises weren't in the pipeline after all. Outstanding, indeed.

Jumpstarting investment

Because Britain's broken banks have kept zombie companies alive while failing to lend to promising ones, the recovery has been stifled, seemingly justifying their caution. Meanwhile, even companies with piles of cash have not invested, for fear that demand would remain weak. Instead of trying to kickstart the economy onto a healthy growth path, the government dug a bigger hole by slashing public investment too. As a result, for several years the economy got stuck in a rut where weak demand led to low investment and hence to weak growth, which in turn seemed to justify low investment. What was needed was a jolt to jumpstart the economy.

With the private sector unwilling to invest even with near-zero interest rates, the government should have stepped in. Temporary tax credits that allowed non-financial businesses to write off all their investments against tax in the first year would encourage them to bring forward capital spending. Bypassing banks by creating a credit market for lending to smaller businesses would also help, an idea advocated by Adam Posen, a former member of the Bank of England's monetary-policy committee and now the president of the Peterson Institute for International Economics, the world's top think-tank on such matters.[439] A new British Investment Bank could finance productive

---

439   Britain lacks "the diversity of lending sources that the US and Germany have, with no small or community banks, a very high minimum company size required to

investment – for example, much-needed infrastructure improvements – and provide credit to smaller businesses, as the European Investment Bank does.[440] Britain needs better roads, more underpasses and bridges, a high-speed railway network, new Tube (metro) lines and a second Crossrail in London, greater airport capacity in the south-east of England, modernised ports, new power plants, a smart electricity grid, broadband infrastructure, water reservoirs – why not maglev trains and a Hyperloop to boot?[441]

Unfortunately, the government has so far failed to take advantage of this once-in-a-generation opportunity to borrow cheaply, invest and promote a healthy, investment-led recovery. Instead, it has prompted debt-laden households to start spending again by stoking up yet another housing bubble. Like a junkie doped up with steroids, the economy has staggered back to its feet – until the next stroke.

---

float corporate bonds, and tiny corporate paper and venture capital markets," Posen points out."Countries around the world are passing laws, issuing charters to specialised financial institutions, making markets to allow companies to borrow from the market by issuing bonds (in conjunction with the central bank), and encouraging new entrants to create just such infrastructures in their own economies. Both Latin American and South East Asian emerging markets have made huge strides in domestic credit and capital creation in recent years through such policy efforts. It is time the government learned from these initiatives, and benefited from the handbooks that the IMF and World Bank have written for how to do so." Adam Posen, "What next?", *Prospect*, January 2013 http://www.prospectmagazine.co.uk/economics/adam-posen-george-osborne/

440 *Ibid.* The Bank of England could buy the bonds of the new British Investment Bank, simultaneously providing more effective monetary stimulus and improving businesses' access to credit, as Adam Posen, a former member of the Bank of England's monetary policy committee, has advocated.

441 The government has already published a National Infrastructure Plan, but has so far done little actual investment. https://www.gov.uk/government/uploads/system/uploads/attachment_data/file/209279/PU1524_IUK_new_template.pdf

Bubble trouble

There is a healthy way in which housing could contribute to the economy's growth. Cracking open Britain's rigged and dysfunctional land market could unleash a construction boom to satisfy the huge pent-up demand for housing, boosting the economy as a whole.

The supply of property is restricted by planning regulations that strictly limit where new housing can be built. Local authorities have little incentive to open up land for development because they don't capture any of the increase in the value of the land. Building on a "green belt" around cities is especially tightly controlled. Big property developers with vast land banks also maximise their profits by limiting how many new properties they build each year – just as countries in the OPEC cartel maximise profits on their oil reserves by restricting how much they sell each year.

This artificial scarcity drives up land prices, especially when combined with rising demand: for living space from a rising and (until recently) richer population made up of many more smaller households, together with speculative demand in anticipation of price increases. Even in the slump, prices remained exceptionally high in proportion to average incomes, driving up rents too. In addition, foreign demand has sent prices soaring in central London in recent years, causing price rises to ripple out across and around the capital. For the global rich (and increasingly the prosperous middle classes too), London property is seen as a safe haven, not to mention a good investment in a time of depressed returns – and a status symbol to boot.

This racket is extremely lucrative for large landowners – both the hereditary ones who own vast swathes of Britain and property companies more generally – who have a vested interest to block reform. Land in Britain is distributed extremely unequally: a mere 0.3 per cent of the population owns 69 per cent of it.[442] Big hereditary landowners are a powerful lobby who are particularly well connected to the ruling Conservative Party; some continue to shape laws in the House of Lords.[443] Home-owners who have profited from tax-free property-price gains provide broader support for maintaining the artificial scarcity of property. "They may complain about their children being unable to buy a house, but at the same time will staunchly oppose new development," observes Simon Tilford of the Centre for European Reform, a London-based think-tank.[444]

Yet while individual home-owners are richer on paper, their apparent wealth is largely a delusion. They are no better off in terms of their ability to buy an equivalent home – and worse off, in terms of their ability to buy a bigger one. Only those who own several properties are clear beneficiaries. The property racket is, in effect, a tax on most people's living standards. The cost of everything sold in cities is inflated by the excessive cost of land. People are forced to spend an ever larger share of their disposable income on housing. High prices oblige people to make do with less living space: the average size of homes built in Britain is now the smallest in the EU and Britons have the least living space per person.[445] Many are forced to put up with long commutes because they can't afford to live near where they work. The biggest losers are the young and others who don't own a property. Many young people are forced to live with their parents for

---

442 Kevin Cahill, *Who Owns the World: The Hidden Facts Behind Landownership*, Mainstream, 2006

443 http://en.wikipedia.org/wiki/List_of_elected_hereditary_peers_under_the_House_of_Lords_Act_1999

444 Simon Tilford, "Why British prosperity is hobbled by a rigged land market", Centre for European Reform, 13 February 2013 http://centreforeuropeanreform.blogspot.co.uk/2013/02/why-british-prosperity-is-hobbled-by.html

445 *Idem*

longer, while couples rent for years before being able to afford their own place. It is hard to imagine a more unfair system than a rigged land market that robs the young and the poor to stuff the pockets of the old and the rich.

Britain's rigged property market is also a big impediment to growth. Banks deem it safer to lend vast sums to homebuyers to swap more or less the same set of properties at ever more inflated prices than to fund productive investment by businesses. Infrastructure investment suffers too, because the cost of land makes it so expensive. Artificially inflated property prices also act as a tax on growth. Businesses fork out an ever-greater share of their revenues on rent. Britain has the highest office rents in the EU: firms in Manchester pay more than in Frankfurt or Milan.[446] Potentially profitable new businesses are not created because the fixed cost of premises is prohibitive. The cost of housing in London and the south-east in particular deters people from moving there to fill job opportunities. Mark Carney, the Canadian governor of the Bank of England, demanded a £250,000 a year housing allowance to relocate to London from Ottawa; few will be able to obtain such largesse. Welfare recipients are discouraged from working (as they then lose access to subsidised housing). All of this crimps economic growth. "The UK's essentially rigged market for land and its restrictive planning system are as big an obstacle to economic growth as restrictive labour markets and protected professions are in southern Europe," Tilford rightly argues.[447]

A sensible government would do its best to expand the supply of property. But the current one's steps have been half-hearted and ineffective, perhaps unsurprisingly since so many of its members are property millionaires. As well as permitting the redevelopment of brownfield sites, which are often in places where people don't want

446   *Idem*

447   *Idem*

to live, the government ought to allow building on the (often ugly) green belt. Contrary to the myth that Britain is full up, only around 13 per cent of its surface area is built on, a lower proportion than in countries with a similar population density such as Germany, Belgium and the Netherlands. Increasing that by one to two percentage points would address the country's land constraints without concreting over England's "green and pleasant land". Likewise, allowing London to expand by two to three miles in each direction would solve its land-use problems. The government should also relax planning restrictions more generally.

There is also a desperate shortage of social and affordable housing. Instead of subsidising private landlords with housing benefit for poor tenants, the government should build more social housing. It could do so cheaply by purchasing industrial or rural land and then redesignating it as suitable for residential development. Selling a fraction of the rezoned land to private developers would more than pay for the new social housing.

Introducing a tax on land values (see Chapter 12) would give both landowners and local authorities an incentive to develop. Since landowners would pay tax on their unused land, they would have an incentive to build on it. Since local authorities would gain from rezoning agricultural land as residential and commercial, they would have an incentive to do so. Since rising land prices would boost revenues from land taxes, infrastructure investment would pay for itself.

Unfortunately, instead of freeing up the supply of property, the government is seeking to boost demand. Outside London, the property market has been subdued in recent years by more restrictive credit. Banks have asked for deposits of 20 per cent or more – equivalent to a year's pre-tax salary in the country as a whole and nearly two in London. They have also been more discriminating about whom they will lend to. But now the government's Help to Buy scheme enables home-buyers to borrow up to 95 per cent of the value of a property, with the government guaranteeing 20 per cent of the mortgage. More generally, every public statement by David Cameron and George Osborne about helping people to get on the "property ladder" signals that they wish to sustain the current system – and the resulting high prices – rather than reform it.

But with supply unchanged, an increase in the money demand for housing simply drives up prices. These are now rising fast and have surpassed their 2008 peak – dramatically so in London.[448] According to *The Economist*, they were already overvalued by more than a third in late 2013 – more than in any other major European country that it tracks.[449] The main beneficiaries of this new bubble are existing land-owners. Worse, the scheme exposes taxpayers to losses from a future property downturn that causes borrowers to default. As experience in the US shows, government guarantees on mortgage lending are dangerous and can be very costly. Osborne is mortgaging taxpayers' future incomes to try to buy himself re-election. He has all but given up on trying to rebalance the economy towards healthier investment- and export-led growth, choosing instead to stoke up an old-fashioned debt-fuelled housing boom. It is tragic.

These first seven chapters have focused on the long economic winter in the eurozone and Britain. The rest of the book looks at reforms to build a brighter future. Many people say Europe needs to take a page out of Germany's book. The next chapter questions that assumption.

---

448   http://www.economist.com/news/finance-and-economics/21592646-mone-tary-policy-may-call-end-house-price-party-castles-made-sand
449   *Idem*

PART II: SPRING?

8

THE EAGLE ALSO LANDS

Why Germany is not a role model for the rest of Europe

What we have done, everyone else can do.
Angela Merkel, chancellor of Germany, 2013[450]

If Germany's economic model is the future of Europe, we should all be quite troubled... The policy response to the eurozone crisis is likely to remain a programme to induce member states to follow Germany's path to competitiveness: cutting the cost of labour. Make no mistake; that has been the basis of the nation's export success in the past dozen years; and exports have been its sole consistent source of growth in that period. But low wages are not the basis on which a rich nation should compete.
Adam Posen, president of the Peterson Institute for International Economics, 2013[451]

450   http://www.theguardian.com/commentisfree/2013/sep/25/merkel-germany-europe-tortoise-us-china

451   http://www.ft.com/cms/s/0/4f975822-1405-11e3-9289-00144feabdc0.html

At the euro's launch in 1999, Germany was dismissed as the "sick man of Europe".[452] Bloated, over-taxed and over-regulated, its economy was stagnant, with four million unemployed. Some even compared it to Japan. In the pre-crisis years, it plodded on, outshone by fizzier growth in Britain and southern Europe. But after the crisis struck, it suddenly seemed like a success. Bouncing back quickly from the post-Lehman collapse, its economy grew by 8 per cent in two years.[453] With the West laid low by flashy but ultimately fragile financial engineering, a country renowned for its stable and solid industrial engineering looked like a winner. While others had built a house of cards based on debt, Germany had prudently saved. Whereas most of Europe seemed ill-equipped for a new world of global competition with China, German exports to the Middle Kingdom were booming. While unemployment has soared to record highs across much of Europe, Germany's jobless rate is lower than before the crisis.[454] In a time of fiscal incontinence, the German government has even balanced its budget. 2010 was a banner year for Germany, so its star shone brightest just as Greece sank and the policy response to the crisis in the eurozone was set. When panic subsequently ripped through the eurozone, Germany seemed like the safest of havens: investors were even willing to pay its government to take their money. As Europe's largest and most populous economy, its largest exporter and

---

452   http://www.economist.com/node/21552567

453   Eurostat, gross domestic product at market prices, volume, index 2005 =100. Seasonally adjusted and adjusted data by working days. Between Q1 2009 and Q1 2011 Germany's GDP grew by 8 per cent.

454   Whereas the jobless rate was 12 per cent in the eurozone in December 2013, it was only 5.1 per cent in Germany. http://epp.eurostat.ec.europa.eu/statistics_ explained/index.php?title=File:Unemployment_rates,_seasonally_adjusted,_ December_2013.png&filetimestamp=20140130142558

its biggest creditor, Berlin seems to hold all the cards. Many fear it, some loathe it, but few question its supremacy.

Politicians and pundits of all stripes have queued up to express admiration. Former US President Bill Clinton has praised it, as has Jeffrey Immelt, the chief executive of General Electric, a Republican.[455] "The German economy has been one of the wonders of the world over the last couple of years," opined the *New York Times* in February 2012.[456] Estonia's president, Toomas Ilves, was gushing: "Europe needs to set Germany as an example."[457] Vitor Gaspar, Portugal's finance minister from 2011 to 2013, was positively Teutonic in his embrace of austerity. President Sarkozy initially based his re-election campaign in 2012 on a pledge to reform France in Germany's image; he lost. The European Commission too embraces the notion that the rest of Europe needs to be more Germanic. In Britain, where admiration for the German model was once limited to centre-left thinkers such as Will Hutton who had little influence over Tony Blair's Labour government, even market-oriented Conservatives now look to the Rhineland model for inspiration. David Cameron says Britain needs a "Germanic approach to skills"; George Osborne concurs.[458] Labour leader Ed Miliband's economic strategy seems to consist of trying to emulate Germany. As Phil Collins, a columnist in *The Times*, put it, "Ed's plan for

---

455   http://www.spiegel.de/international/business/the-us-discovers-germany-as-an-economic-role-model-a-822167.html

456   http://www.nytimes.com/2012/02/17/business/global/the-rest-of-europe-vs-germany.html?pagewanted=all

457   http://www.baltic-course.com/eng/analytics/?doc=77419

458   Osborne said "We've under-valued vocational education, not like in Germany." http://www.thisisderbyshire.co.uk/Osborne-UK-skilled/story-18845737-detail/story.html

Britain: be more like Germany."[459] Intoxicated by all this flattery, one senior German politician quipped that "now all of a sudden Europe is speaking German."[460] With much of Europe laid low by the crisis, some Germans began to see Europe as a millstone and envision a global future for their country. Berlin-boosters boasted of even brighter days ahead. In their 2012 bestseller "Fat Years: Why Germany has a Brilliant Future", Bert Rürup, a former chairman of the German government's council of economic "wise men", and Dirk Heilmann, a journalist at *Handelsblatt*, predict that by 2030 Germany will become the world's richest large country in terms of income per head.[461]

Exuberance often comes before a fall. In 1989, when Japan's bubble was at its height and admiration for all things Nippon was laced with fear of its seemingly inexorable economic rise, a young journalist at *The Economist*, Bill Emmott, wrote a contrarian book entitled *The Sun Also Sets: The Limits to Japan's Economic Power*. His scepticism about Japan's apparent success proved prescient – and helped him to become editor. (Full disclosure: as editor, he hired me at *The Economist*.) Soon, the bubble burst – and Japan has since endured two decades of underperformance. The belief that Germany is a world-beater is even more misconceived. Germany may be Europe's biggest and most powerful economy, but it is not a very successful one, still less a model for others. So it is deeply worrying that it is using EU institutions to try to reshape Europe in its own image, while British politicians should temper their enthusiasm.

---

459   http://www.thetimes.co.uk/tto/opinion/columnists/philipcollins/article3285029.ece

460   http://www.theguardian.com/business/2011/nov/15/eurozone-crisis-britain-germany-tension

461   http://www.economist.com/node/21552567

Big is not always best

By European standards, Germany is certainly big. Its 82 million people (a quarter more than France and Britain)[462] produced an output worth €2.6 trillion (£2.1 trillion) in 2012 – 30 per cent more than France, a fifth of the EU total and 27.9 per cent of the eurozone's.[463] Germany weighs even more heavily in manufacturing: 30 per cent of EU value added.[464] It is an export powerhouse, second globally behind China, and accounted for 24 per cent of EU countries' foreign sales in 2012.[465] Remarkably, nearly half of EU exports to China come from Germany.[466]

Some of its companies are world-beaters. Its high-end cars – Volkswagen (which also makes Audi and Porsche), Mercedes-Benz, BMW – are prized around the world. The Volkswagen group, which also includes Bentley, Bugatti, Lamborghini, Seat and Skoda cars, Ducati motorcycles and MAN and Scania lorries, is the world's sixth most profitable business.[467] BASF is the world's top chemicals company, E-on the biggest listed electricity utility, Deutsche Post DHL the largest courier company. Siemens is Europe's number-one electrical engineering firm. Allianz is the world's third-biggest insurer.[468]

---

462   Eurostat, population at 1 January 2012. Gross domestic product at market prices (current prices), 2012 converted at Bank of England average 2012 exchange rate of £1 = €1.2337.

463   European Commission, AMECO database

464   Eurostat, national accounts by 10 branches, gross value added at basic prices, 2012. Code: nama_nace10_c

465   Eurostat, exports and imports by member states of the EU/third countries, current prices, 2012. Code: nama_exi_c

466   Eurostat. EU Trade -40- By SITC. In 2012 Germany's exports to China accounted for 46.3 per cent of the EU total.

467   http://money.cnn.com/magazines/fortune/global500/2013/full_list/

468   Allianz is Europe's second-biggest insurer, behind France's AXA. http://www.relbanks.com/top-insurance-companies/world

Deutsche Bank is a thinly-capitalised financial behemoth that is the world's largest foreign-exchange trader. Metro, a cash-and-carry group, is the world's fifth-biggest retailer, with Schwarz Gruppe, the owner of Lidl supermarkets, close behind. Sports fans swear by Adidas clothes and Puma shoes; posher ones sport Hugo Boss. Nivea cream is ubiquitous. That said, many German giants are big because their home market is Europe's largest, rather than because they are particularly successful. Lufthansa is Europe's biggest airline by passengers, but lags far behind Easyjet by profits.[469] Majority-state-owned Deutsche Bahn, which owns Arriva in Britain, is Europe's biggest railway operator, but far from its best.

While Germany has plenty of big companies, it is perhaps best known for its mid-sized ones, the *Mittelstand*. These are mostly manufacturers which focus on machinery, auto parts, chemicals and electrical equipment. Many have carved out specialised niches so narrow that they face little global competition. Their perceived virtues – notably the patient, long-term view that these often family-owned firms can take – contrast with the adrenaline-rush, rollercoaster ride of Anglo-American financial capitalism. The point is not to maximise short-term profit, says Markus Miele, a managing director at his eponymous firm, which makes high-end household appliances, but to aim at "where we want to be when we hand over to the next generation."[470]

Germany's economic model defies simple categorisation, allowing different types of people to like (and dislike) different things about it. Whereas free-marketeers tend to be fans of America's more unbridled capitalism and statists admire France's more dirigiste approach, aspects of the German model appeal to both conservatives and social democrats. Perhaps unsurprisingly, the architects of post-war Germany

---

469   http://centreforaviation.com/analysis/european-airlines-financial-results-in-2012-net-profit-of-biggest-13-down-72-for-the-year-102456

470   http://www.economist.com/node/21552567

reacted against both the failures of the free-wheeling interwar Weimar republic – first hyperinflation in 1923, then mass unemployment in the early 1930s – and the Nazis' economic interventionism. Their governing philosophy was based on a fear that freedom would be abused and hence a belief that both governments and markets should be constrained by tight rules. "If you don't have a set of rules then you have to improvise, and when you improvise you make mistakes," says Hans-Werner Sinn, one of Germany's best-known economists.[471] Misleadingly known as "ordoliberalism", this deeply conservative philosophy in fact privileges order over freedom. But this rules-based conservatism is embedded in a *SozialeMarktwirtschaft*, a "social market economy" that involves close coordination between businesses, unions and government, notably in setting wages and providing social insurance. Thus, for instance, collective bargaining between unions and companies sets industry-wide pay levels, while the government redistributes incomes. Designed to be a third-way between laissez-faire liberalism and social democracy, this Christian Democratic approach – call it capitalism with a social conscience – was taken up by the country's Social Democrats too once it became associated with Germany's post-war boom. Within this social market economy, German business is guided by a model of "stakeholder capitalism" which dates back at least to Bismarck, the country's first Chancellor after its unification in 1871, and which contrasts with Britain's and America's shareholder-focused variety. German companies have two levels of governance: management boards, responsible for day-to-day decisions, and supervisory ones, made up of big shareholders and other stakeholders: bankers, politicians and (more recently) trade-union representatives.

---

471   http://www.ft.com/intl/cms/s/0/4d3c0b1e-e38c-11e0-8f47-00144feabdc0.html

There is something for almost everyone to like. Hard-money types love how Germany's hostility to inflation is entrenched in the extreme independence of its central bank, the Bundesbank, on which the ECB was modelled. German orthodoxy believes in limiting budgetary discretion too – hence the EU's Stability and Growth Pact – and fiscal conservatives drool over its constitutional brake on public debt, which the fiscal compact treaty sought to export to the rest of Europe. But while Keynesians bemoan Germany's aversion to fiscal activism – the fiscal stimulus after Lehman's collapse was exceptional – the government is much more interventionist in other areas. Taxes and other government revenues gobble up 45.2 per cent of national income, much less than in France (51.7 per cent) let alone Denmark (56.1 per cent), but more than in Britain (42.2 per cent) and much more than in Spain (36.4 per cent) or Ireland (34.6 per cent).[472] Even at a time of low unemployment in Germany, social spending is a chunky 28.7 per cent of GDP, much less than in France (35.9 per cent), but more than in recession-hit Ireland (27 per cent) and Spain (27.8 per cent).[473] While government is boxed in by rules, so are markets. Product markets are highly regulated, limiting competition and thereby favouring established companies over potential challengers and producers' interests over consumers'. Labour markets are tightly regulated too, so companies cannot readily shed workers. While the German model has many fans, to my mind it is back to front: the government intervenes too little where it ought to (in macroeconomic policy) and too much where it shouldn't (by over-regulating product and labour markets).

---

472   European Commission, AMECO database, total revenue: general government ESA 1995, percentage of GDP at market prices in 2012

473   European Commission, AMECO database, social transfers in kind plus social benefits other than social transfers in kind, percentage of GDP at market prices in 2012

As a result, the economy is far too rigid and sluggish. It is good at cutting costs, but not at changing course.

Many foreigners admire its apprenticeships. These involve businesses, unions and local governments collaborating to provide highly specialised vocational training, a legacy of the medieval guild system. Young Germans are less keen on them: the number starting an apprenticeship has plunged to its lowest level since 1990 and many places go unfilled.[474] Sceptics question the value of such narrow training that may soon become outdated as technologies change and industries disappear. During the crisis, many praised and some copied its *Kurzarbeit* programme whereby the government subsidises the wages of employees who agree to work shorter hours. Sceptics pointed out that this protects specific jobs rather than overall employment and therefore impedes economic adjustment. Fans of shareholder capitalism love the fact that companies are meant to take account of a wider set of interests, not least those of workers. Close links between businesses and local banks also provide "patient" capital that allows companies to take a long-term view. There's a lot to be said for that. But Germany's cosy corporatism also privileges insiders, restricts competition and impedes change.

When perceptions of an economy improve, observers tend to attribute its apparent success to its prominent features, especially those they approve of. Since Germany has aspects that appeal to almost everyone, each can find confirmation for their preconceptions. But such logical leaps are often flawed. For a start, perceptions of success can be deceptive. Moreover, just because outsiders like an aspect of Germany's economy doesn't mean it has had a decisive influence in recent years. I happen to think Audi cars are great, but that doesn't mean Germany's automotive excellence explains its perceived outperformance; after all, Audi cars were already superb a decade ago.

---

474   http://www.ft.com/cms/s/0/3e680126-8db5-11e3-ba55-00144feab7de.html

Any improvement may have occurred not because of something you like, but despite it, or for other reasons entirely. For example, while Germany now has a balanced budget, its public debt was much higher in 2012 (81.9 per cent of GDP) than in 2000 (60.2 per cent of GDP).[475] Over the same period, public debt fell as a share of GDP in Belgium, Bulgaria, Denmark, Sweden and rose by a smaller share of GDP in Austria, Estonia, Finland, the Netherlands, Poland, Romania and Slovakia. Seventeen of the twenty-six other EU countries had lower debt as a share of GDP.[476] So Germany's perceived success can hardly be attributed to its public finances.

Moreover, while any improvement in Germany's performance may be due to the (potentially lagged) effect of changes within the country, it may also be due to changes in external conditions that happen to enhance the value of an existing feature of its economy – in other words, luck. So let's unpick each aspect of Germany's perceived success point by point.

A lost decade

Germany is certainly rich – as it was in 1999 when it was deemed to be the "sick man of Europe" – but it is not a world-beater. It is a bit more prosperous – measured by GDP per person adjusted for differences in purchasing power – than Britain and France, but poorer than thirteen

---

475   AMECO database, general government consolidated gross debt, percentage of GDP at market prices

476   Public debt was a lower share of GDP in Bulgaria (18.5 per cent of GDP), the Czech Republic (45.8 per cent), Denmark (45.8 per cent), Estonia (10.1 per cent), Latvia (40.7 per cent), Lithuania (40.7 per cent), Luxembourg (20.8 per cent), Hungary (79.2 per cent), Malta (72.1 per cent), the Netherlands (71.2 per cent), Austria (73.4 per cent), Poland (55.6 per cent), Romania (37.8 per cent), Slovenia (54.1 per cent), Slovakia (52.1 per cent), Finland (53 per cent) and Sweden (38.2 per cent).

other advanced economies, including Austria, Australia, Canada, the Netherlands, Sweden, Switzerland and the United States.[477]

Since the crisis, its economy has fared better than many. By late 2013, France's economy was still fractionally smaller than in early 2008, Britain's a bit more so. Southern European economies have fallen off a cliff. In contrast, Germany's was up by 2.6 per cent.[478] That is hardly enough to set the heart racing, but a snail's pace seems good considering.

Or does it? Switzerland has advanced by 6.4 per cent while Sweden has pulled ahead by 5 per cent. The US, the epicentre of the financial crisis, has also outperformed Germany: it is up 6.4 per cent.[479] Taking a longer view also changes your perspective. Since the turn of the century, Germany has been a laggard, not a leader. Between 2000 and 2012, it crawled ahead by only 14.3 per cent – a mere 1.1 per cent a year – level-pegging with France's 13.6 per cent. That is slower than those freewheeling Anglo-Americans – Britain (up 20.4 per cent) and the US (up 21.2 per cent) – not to mention those supposedly lazy Latins (Spain is up 21.2 per cent) and reckless Celts (Ireland is up 33.4 per cent). Among the seventeen countries in the eurozone, Germany came twelfth.[480]

---

477 International Monetary Fund, World Economic Outlook database, April 2013. GDP per capita in PPP terms 2012. The thirteen economies are: Austria, Australia, Canada, Hong Kong, Iceland, Ireland, Luxembourg, the Netherlands, Norway, Singapore, Sweden, Switzerland and the United States.

478 Eurostat, gross domestic product at market prices, volume, index 2005 =100, seasonally adjusted and adjusted data by working days. Change between Q1 2008 and Q3 2013.

479 Some central European economies, which still have plenty of catching up to do, have fared even better.

480 Calculations from International Monetary Fund, World Economic Outlook database, April 2013. Gross domestic product at constant prices, change between 2000 and 2012.

Long-term growth comes from a combination of productive investment and productivity gains – and on both those scores Germany's performance has been feeble. Investment plunged from 22.3 per cent of GDP in 2000 to a mere 17.2 per cent in 2012.[481] While Britain is even worse, Germany lags behind France, Spain, Sweden and even Italy.[482] Public investment is particularly feeble, at only 1.5 per cent of GDP in 2012, less than in Italy and Britain (2.1 per cent) and far behind France, the Netherlands and Sweden (3.5 per cent).[483] After years of neglect, infrastructure is crumbling. "Highway bridges are in such poor condition that lorries carrying heavy loads often have to make detours, while some transport infrastructure in waterways dates back to a century ago," points out Sebastian Dullien of the European Council on Foreign Relations.[484] In March 2013, the Kiel Canal, a vital trade artery, had to be closed temporarily because two of its locks were in such a state of disrepair.[485]

Worse, Germany has fallen behind in educating its workforce. It spends only 5.8 per cent of GDP on education and training, less than in France, Ireland, the Netherlands, Sweden, the United States and

---

481   International Monetary Fund, World Economic Outlook database, April 2013, total investment as a share of GDP.

482   Investment in Germany lags behind France (19.9 per cent of GDP), Spain (19.6 per cent), Sweden (18.5 per cent) and even Italy (17.6 per cent).

483   Public investment is particularly feeble, at only 1.5 per cent of GDP in 2012, less than in Italy (1.9 per cent) and Britain (2.1 per cent) and far behind France (3.1 per cent), the Netherlands (3.4 per cent) and Sweden (3.5 per cent). European Commission, AMECO database, Gross fixed capital formation: general government ESA 1995, percentage of GDP at market prices

484   http://ecfr.eu/content/entry/commentary_why_britain_should_not_view_germany_as_an_economic_role_model

485   http://www.ft.com/cms/s/0/b52a2d5e-25c6-11e3-aee8-00144feab7de.html

Britain (8.2 per cent).[486] Less than a quarter of Germany's workforce has a university degree, far fewer than in France, Spain, Sweden, Estonia, Ireland and Britain (34.7 per cent).[487] The divergence is particularly striking among younger workers aged 25–34. Fewer young Germans are graduates (29 per cent) than young Greeks (34.2 per cent).[488] Young Germans lag even further behind young Spaniards, Estonians, Danes, Dutch, French, Swedes and Britons (45 per cent).[489] "Germany has failed to invest in its public university system," observes Adam Posen of the Peterson Institute for International Economics.[490] In global rankings, the highest-rated German university is the Technical University of Munich, in fiftieth place.[491]

Start-ups are stunted. Contrary to the myth that Germany is a healthy, dynamic economy, it is harder to start a business there than

---

486   Germany spends only 5.8 per cent of GDP on education and training, compared with 6.5 per cent in France, 7 per cent in Ireland and the Netherlands, 7.1 per cent in Sweden, 7.7 per cent in the United States and 8.2 per cent in Britain. Eurostat, investments in education and training, total public expenditure on education as a per cent of GDP plus expenditure from private sources. Latest year: 2010 Code: educ_thexp

487   Eurostat, persons with tertiary education attainment by age and sex, per cent, aged 15-64, latest year: 2012 Only 24.1 per cent of Germany's workforce has a university degree, far fewer than in France (27.9 per cent), Spain (29.6 per cent), Sweden (30.1 per cent), Britain (34.7 per cent), Estonia (31.8 per cent) and Ireland (34.7 per cent).

488   *Ibid.* aged 25-34

489   Young Germans lag even further behind young Spaniards (39.3 per cent), Estonians (39.8 per cent), Danes (40.2 per cent), Dutch (41.5 per cent), French (42.9 per cent), Swedes (43.5 per cent) and Britons (45 per cent)

490   Adam Posen, "Germany is being crushed by its export obsession", *Financial Times*, 4 September 2013 http://www.ft.com/cms/s/0/4f975822-1405-11e3-9289-00144feabdc0.html

491   http://www.fuw.ch/article/germanys-complacency-problem/

in Sierra Leone, Iran, Moldova, Pakistan or Russia, according to the World Bank's Doing Business rankings; Germany ranks 106th in the world. Ireland towers over Germany, in tenth place globally. All the world-beating companies mentioned earlier in the chapter have been around for ages; there is no German Google. No wonder 50,000 German entrepreneurs have emigrated to Silicon Valley.

Low investment, decrepit infrastructure, a depreciating education system, a lack of enterprise – all are worrying indicators. But the proof of Germany's underperformance is its poor productivity growth: a mere 1 per cent a year over the past decade, less than in Greece.[492] To be a sustainable success, Germany needs much faster productivity growth. Without it, any growth is likely to be as ephemeral as southern Europe's bubbles.

Immiserating export growth

What little growth Germany has had has been driven primarily by exports, which nearly doubled between early 2000 and early 2013.[493] That is better than any other advanced European economy except Iceland. This growth has also been concentrated in manufacturing, which has shrunk in most advanced economies over the past fifteen years but expanded in Germany. Whereas in 1997, making things was almost as important to Italy's economy (20.9 per cent of GDP) as to Germany's (21.6 per cent), by 2012 it had fallen to 15.5 per cent of GDP in Italy and edged up to 22.4 per cent in Germany.[494] Over the

492   Calculations from OECD, labour productivity growth in the total economy, average 2002–12.

493   Eurostat, exports and imports by member states of the EU/third countries, volumes, seasonally adjusted and adjusted data by working days, index 2005=100. Code: namq_exi_k

494   Eurostat, national accounts by 10 branches, aggregates at current prices as a share of GDP. Code: nama_nace10_c

same period, British manufacturing slumped from 18.7 per cent of GDP to 10.1 per cent. But Germany's export boom is less impressive than it seems – and its reliance on manufacturing may turn out to be a weakness in years to come.

Germany's export growth over the past fifteen years has been flattered by its firms' outsourcing of production to central and eastern Europe, as mentioned in Chapter 2. Thus much of the value-added attributed to Germany is actually generated elsewhere. Germany has also been lucky. Its traditional exports – capital goods, engineering and chemicals – are precisely those that China has needed during its breakneck industrial development since the turn of the century. The euro has also been a huge boost. It has been much weaker than the Deutsche Mark doubtless would have been, inflating foreign sales. It has also prevented competitors in places such as Italy from devaluing to undercut German firms. Until the crisis struck, it also provided Germany with booming export markets in southern Europe. But since then, the recession in southern Europe has deprived Germany of an outlet for its exports. Now that China's economy is also slowing and shifting away from investment-led growth, Germany's export machine is stalling. In the year to the third quarter of 2013, its exports edged down, while Spain's soared.[495] Since the crisis, Germany's share of world exports has slumped from 9.07 per cent in 2007 to 7.92 per cent in 2012 – a record low.

Nor is Germany's dependence on manufacturing all it's cracked up to be. There is nothing special about making things. Is making cars more valuable than making people healthy? Is manufacturing washing machines more important than teaching? Is making pipes superior to

---

495 Eurostat, exports and imports by member states of the EU/third countries, volumes, seasonally adjusted and adjusted data by working days, index 2005=100 Code: namq_exi_k Between Q3 2012 and Q3 2013, German exports fell by 0.1 per cent, while Spanish ones rose by 4.7 per cent.

fitting or repairing them? Is producing computers more useful than programming them? Manufacturing is an even bigger share of the economy in the Czech Republic, Ireland and Hungary.[496] Does that make them more successful than Germany?

The important thing is not what people do, but whether it adds value. While that may come in high-tech manufacturing, it may also come from low-tech manufacturing, such as food processing, producing fine wine and cheeses (or profitable plonk). Mostly, though, the value added is in services. Jobs that cannot be mechanised or outsourced – everything from childcare and cleaning to retail and restaurant work – as well as ones in high-tech services such as telecoms, software and media.

Even in Germany, services account for well over three-fifths of economic activity, yet productivity in those sectors is often dismal.[497] Part of the problem is that its service sectors tend to be tied up in red tape. Regulation of professional services is stricter in Germany than in all but five of twenty-seven countries ranked by the OECD. According to a study for the European Commission of thirteen countries, Germany has more professions reserved to holders of professional qualifications than all but one. In the liberal professions, which account for a tenth of the economy, regulations dictate who may offer what sort of service, the charges allowed for professionals and how they may advertise. For example, only qualified pharmacists can own a pharmacy, and they are limited to four. Other shops may not

---

496   The share of manufacturing in GDP is even higher in the Czech Republic (24.7 per cent of GDP), Ireland (23.3 per cent) and Hungary (23.2 per cent).

497   Between 2000 and 2007, value added in market services grew by 2.2 per cent a year, compared with an average of 3.1 per cent in the OECD group of rich countries. In business services, productivity grew by 0.9 per cent a year in Germany between 2000 and 2008, against 1.7 per cent in the OECD http://www.economist.com/node/21547837

compete, even for non-prescription drugs. In many professions, investment by outsiders is restricted.

The weakness of German services is particularly worrying because its industry is unlikely to be able to defy gravity for much longer. Like agriculture before it, manufacturing tends to weigh less heavily in the economy over time – even in China, the workshop of the world. As technology improves, we can make better-quality goods more cheaply – think of flat-screen TVs. As people get richer, they devote more of their income to services – holidays, healthcare, home help – rather than spending it all on accumulating ever more stuff. So Germany's over-reliance on manufacturing is a vulnerability. Unless its economy can adapt, it would be hit hard by a fall in demand for its manufactures, not least as China moves up the value chain and starts to compete directly with higher-end German products. Germany's position is particularly precarious because it is reliant on four sectors – vehicles, machines, electronic devices and chemicals – for more than half of its exports.[498]

Rising energy prices pose an immediate threat to energy-intensive sectors such as chemicals. The price of electricity has already more than doubled since 2000.[499] It is now 40 per cent more costly for consumers and 20 per cent more expensive for industrial users in Germany than the EU average.[500] Because of the shale gas revolution in the US, German companies pay almost three times as much as their

---

498   http://www.economist.com/node/21552567

499   Power prices for industry have risen to €0.1487 (20 cents) per kilowatt-hour in 2013, from €0.0606 in 2000, while prices for private households climbed to €0.2873 from €0.1394 in 2000, according to Germany's energy and water industry association, known as BDEW. http://online.wsj.com/article/SB1000142412788732330850 4579087291213517538.html

500   http://www.ft.com/cms/s/0/b52a2d5e-25c6-11e3-aee8-00144feab7de. html#ixzz2g4GYC9IE

American competitors for electricity, according to a Siemens study. Worse, the government plans to phase out nuclear power and replace it with pricey renewable energy while spurning cheaper shale gas.

The economy's biggest weakness is that its earlier export boom was achieved on the backs of German workers. Remarkably, after inflation, wages in 2013 were lower than in 1999 – fourteen years and counting of stagnation.[501] Downward pressure on wages – which began with a tripartite agreement in 1999 between government, companies and unions[502] – and the absence of a legal minimum wage have resulted in some workers earning as little as €4 (£3.30) an hour. Around a quarter of the German workforce are paid less than two-thirds of the median wage, a higher proportion than in all seventeen European countries studied by Germany's Institute for Employment Research (IAB), except Lithuania.[503]

Pressing down on wages is not only self-defeating. It is unsustainable: there is only so long wages can held down in a democracy. And it is immiserating. "Dependence on external demand has deprived Germany's workers of what they have earned, and should be able to save and spend," Adam Posen rightly remarks. "This leaves them dependent on exports for growth, in a self-reinforcing cycle. Most importantly, this means they move down the value chain in relative terms, not up. The pursuit of the same policy by its European trading

---

501   Federal Statistical Office of Germany, index of real earnings, January 2010 = 100. Index for 1999 and 2000 is 102.1; index for 2007 is 98.2; index for 2012 is 101.7. https://www.destatis.de/DE/ZahlenFakten/GesamtwirtschaftUmwelt/VerdiensteArbeitskosten/RealloehneNettoverdienste/RealloehneNettoverdienste.html

502   Contrary to the belief that Gerhard Schröder's labour-market reforms in 2003–5 ushered in wage restraint, this began four years earlier, with a tripartite agreement in 1999 between government, companies and unions.

503   Comparable data were not available for the other 10 EU members. http://www.ft.com/cms/s/0/0bf80e46-0fc2-11e3-99e0-00144feabdc0.html

partners will reinforce those pressures. Wage compression will not be a successful growth strategy for Germany's or Europe's future."[504] To prosper in future, Germany's economy will need to adapt. Unfortunately, it is arthritic. Its service sector is hidebound, its start-ups stunted. Its businesses invest less than ever. And while Schröder's labour-market reforms helped create low-end jobs and nudge the long-term jobless back into work, they did not make Germany's labour market more flexible. In fact, it is harder to lay off a permanent worker in Germany than in any other OECD country.[505] Thus far from having a healthy, adaptable labour market that is a model for others, Germany has a rigid and downtrodden one. Nor are things improving: the OECD says that since 2007 Germany has brought in fewer pro-growth reforms than any other of its advanced-country members.[506]

---

504 Adam Posen, "Germany is being crushed by its export obsession", *Financial Times,* 4 September 2013 http://www.ft.com/cms/s/0/4f975822-1405-11e3-9289-00144feabdc0.html

505 According to the OECD: "Unlike in all other OECD countries, opposition from works councils can delay dismissals until a court ruling is made. This de facto lengthens the period of notice before a dismissal can become effective, particularly for longer tenure workers. Second, employers are not free to choose which worker to dismiss in the case of redundancy but social criteria must be applied and employers must show that the chosen workers could not be retained in another capacity. No other OECD country applies simultaneously both criteria and this combination potentially limits the ability of firms to quickly adapt to changing economic conditions." That said, "in the case of redundancy, employees are allowed to trade their right to contest the dismissal in court against a relatively high severance pay (and the right to claim unemployment benefits), provided this choice is made immediately after dismissal. In practice, mostly due to this provision, over 90 per cent of the cases are solved before being heard by a court, the largest proportion among OECD countries for which comparable data are available." http://www.oecd.org/els/emp/Country%20Notes-GERMANY.pdf

506 http://www.economist.com/news/special-report/21579145-ingredients-german-economic-success-are-more-complex-they-seem-dissecting

Germany also faces particularly bad demography, which will be a drag on future growth. Its population is the oldest in the EU, with an average age of forty-five, compared with forty in Britain and thirty-five in Ireland.[507] Its population is even projected to fall below Britain's and France's in the 2040s. In the absence of a productivity miracle, that implies a correspondingly smaller economy too. Immigration could help fill the gap, but that would require a sea change in legislation and public attitudes. One-fifth of Germany's residents – and one-third of its schoolchildren – has a migrant background, yet they are often treated as second-class citizens (if they are citizens at all).

Depressed demand, wasted savings

The upshot of an ageing economy where wages (and therefore consumption) are weak, investment is feeble and the government doesn't borrow is a huge surplus of savings – that is, a current-account surplus. This is often seen as a symbol of Germany's superior "competitiveness". But it is actually a sign of weakness. "The German economy cannot find enough useful investment opportunities at home for domestically-generated savings," observes Simon Tilford of the Centre for European Reform.[508]

As a result of its surpluses, Germany has become Europe's biggest net creditor. Back in 2000, Germany's foreign assets barely exceeded its foreign liabilities. By the end of 2012, its net international investment position had risen to a whopping €1,107 billion.[509] No other economy in Europe comes close: the Netherlands, in second

---

507   http://www.ft.com/cms/s/0/de58ad92-5828-11e3-82fc-00144feabdc0. html#axzz2m0oTD4a4

508   Simon Tilford, "Germany's brief moment in the sun", Centre for European Reform, June 2011

509   Eurostat, net international investment position, annual data, end 2012. Code: bop_ext_intpos

place, had net foreign assets of €281 billion.[510] Germany's net claims on foreigners are not just huge by European standards; they are hefty in global terms too. They amount to $1.5 trillion, almost as large as China's $1.7 trillion.[511] In contrast, most European economies are net debtors. Spain's foreign liabilities exceed its foreign assets by a whopping €941 billion.[512] It owes foreigners the equivalent of 91.4 per cent of its annual output – and Hungary, Ireland, Greece and Portugal owe more than their GDP.[513]

In a crisis, Germany's position as a net creditor gives it clout. But its loans to foreigners have often been badly invested, as we saw in previous chapters. A study by the DIW economic research institute in Berlin suggests that Germany lost €600 billion, the equivalent of 22 per cent of GDP, on the valuation of its foreign portfolio investments between 2006 and 2012.[514] Now that Germany is fearful of making losses on its loans to foreigners, it is particularly perverse to keep piling up surpluses that necessarily have to be invested abroad. Once it turns out that debtors cannot or will not pay – which Germany's refusal to contribute to European growth makes more likely – its huge foreign exposure will inflict hefty losses on Germany.

---

510 *Idem.*

511 Calculation based on year-end exchange rate of €1 = $1.3194. China figures from State Administration of Foreign Exchange, www.safe.gov.cn

512 Eurostat, net international investment position, end 2011. Far behind come Italy (€388 billion), France (€430 billion) and Britain (€174 billion).

513 Spain owes foreigners the equivalent of 91.4 per cent of GDP, Hungary 102.2 per cent, Ireland 108.2 per cent, Greece 114.5 per cent and Portugal 116.7 per cent. Eurostat, net international investment position as a percentage of GDP, end 2012. Code: tipsii10

514 http://www.diw.de/documents/publikationen/73/diw_01.c.425759.de/diw_econ_bull_2013-08-1.pdf See also http://www.economist.com/news/special-report/21579145-ingredients-german-economic-success-are-more-complex-they-seem-dissecting

Germany is not a model

Germany's economic model should not be emulated. It is not the success story it is portrayed to be. Nor, indeed, can it be copied at a continental level. Mercantilism is destructive when pursued by a single country, especially one that looms as large as Germany does in Europe. But it is impossible for the eurozone as a whole. The eurozone's economy is too big for the world to be able to absorb its current-account surpluses. Logically, it is impossible for everyone to run surpluses, since for every lender there must be a borrower.

Germany's brief moment in the sun looks like it is coming to an end. While it excels at incremental innovation and cost cutting, it is neither dynamic nor adaptable enough to adjust to a world of disruptive technological change. Witness how it has failed to compete in the market for mobile devices, which Siemens has now quit, or in information technology more generally, where SAP has lost ground in business software. More broadly, observe how it has failed to create new companies: all of the stalwarts of the German economy, large and middling, are old and entrenched. None of this necessarily means Germany will become the "sick man" of Europe again. Such epithets are usually exaggerated. But nor, on current policies, does Germany's future look that bright. The German eagle never soared very high – and just as the sun also set for Japan, so the German eagle will also land.

9

REFORMS THAT ADD UP

Why economies ought to be more adaptable, dynamic and decent

> *The interactions of millions of people, making decisions, en-*
> *gaging in strong reciprocal behaviour, acting out their cultural*
> *norms, cooperating, competing, and going about their daily*
> *lives, creates an emergent phenomenon that we call society...*
> *Within society are the constructs of states, markets, and com-*
> *munities, the three of which create the economic world that we*
> *live in. We may not be to control or predict the future direc-*
> *tion of society, but we can endeavour to ensure that these three*
> *elements work together to create wealth, social capital, and*
> *opportunity.*
> Eric Beinhocker, *The Origin of Wealth*, 2006[515]

515 Eric Beinhocker, *The Origin of Wealth: Evolution, Complexity and the Radical Remaking of Economics*, Harvard Business School Press: 2006

To get out of the mess they are in, Europe's economies need to tackle their balance-sheet problems decisively and fairly by restructuring banks, writing down debts and implementing an investment-led growth and adjustment strategy. But looking beyond the immediate crisis, they also require deeper reforms that generate lasting shared prosperity. Not an Osborne-style return to bubble and bust. Not Schäuble-style stability – stagnation masquerading as success. But rather reforms to make economies more adaptable, dynamic and decent and thus create better societies. Europe needs reforms that ADD UP.

Many institutions produce blueprints for economic reform that are ostensibly objective but are actually based on subjective judgments about what a good society should look like and particular assumptions about how economies work. They do this by design: organisations such as the OECD and the IMF are meant to be apolitical. Much of the work they do is excellent. But many people will disagree with their value judgments and others will question their economic models. While their technocratic blueprints do reflect political constraints, not least the views of their more powerful members, they tend to neglect the political economy of reform: how one effects the desired change. Again, this is by design. But it means they are less effective than they ought to be and even their sound recommendations are often not implemented.

I am going to take a different approach. First, I will put my cards on the table and sketch out my vision of a good society. You may disagree with parts or all of it; in any case, many of the reforms advocated in this book can be justified more broadly. Second, I will outline how I think economies work and how this differs from the models that policymakers tend to use. Again, you may disagree with some or all of it, but I will also try to point out why the reforms make sense even if I am wrong. Third, I will touch on the political economy of change:

how to convince people that change is needed, how to mobilise them and how to overcome (or at least neutralise) the lobbying and lies of entrenched vested interests – and if necessary how to buy them off.

Clearly, Europe's economies, societies and politics are very different. Desirable reforms differ country by country, as do the political constraints. I do not pretend to be an expert on all of them. Indeed, I don't think policymakers in general have the information needed to craft a detailed blueprint for reform of complex, advanced economies, still less effective levers to fine-tune them. They don't know enough about the particulars of each economy, how economies work in general, how people might react to a particular change and what the future might bring. Central planning failed in the Soviet Union, and the EU's ten-year plan, the Europe 2020 programme, is also misconceived.

Even so, all European economies would benefit from becoming more innovative, being better able to cope with change and offering greater opportunities to everyone in society. They also all face common challenges – overmighty yet fragile finance, climate change, ageing, the rise of China and other emerging economies, a loss of faith in traditional politics – and common obstacles to change: the influence of bad ideas, the grip of vested interests, the erosion of the power of national governments and other institutional weaknesses, the difficulty of mobilising people, and limited resources. So I am going to suggest broad principles of what ought to be done, outline some big reforms that are widely applicable and discuss in general terms how to achieve change.

A good society

My idea of a good society is one where everyone is free to be different while also being equal and able to belong. It is an open society: one where everyone is free to speak out, challenge authority and demand change; one that is open to newcomers and outsiders, to everyone in society and to the world; one that embraces new ideas, different ways of doing things, the future and all its possibilities for technological and social progress. It is a colour-blind society that transcends petty nationalisms and erases divisions of class, gender and sexuality – one where people treat others as they would wish to be treated themselves. It is one where concern for others does not stop at an arbitrary national border, any more than it should at an individual family or extended clan. Those who argue that it is "natural" for it to do so forget that nation states are not extended families. If people can be persuaded to conceive of an Us that stretches to strangers who happen to live in a large political territory, there is no reason why Us couldn't ultimately extend to all of humanity.

My idea of a good economy flows naturally from that. It is one that tries to make the best use of all our diverse talents, one where everyone has an equal opportunity to flourish and one where everyone enjoys a decent minimum standard of living, and so can participate fully in society. It is an open economy that does not discriminate against foreigners, newcomers or anyone else in society. It is an adaptable economy that takes change in its stride and adjusts to evolving tastes, technologies and circumstances rather than trying to cling to the past. It is a dynamic economy that always strives to do better: encouraging and embracing new and different ways of doing things and seeking to surpass the limits imposed by current technologies and institutions. And it is a decent economy: one where there is a rough correspondence between rewards and merit, where inequalities of wealth and power are not so great that they become entrenched and where suffering is minimised. A good economy generates sustained rises in living standards that are widely shared. It's an open economy that adds up.

There are many facets to economic progress. Many reports have been written, books penned and conferences held on the deficiencies of gross domestic product (GDP) as a yardstick of economic performance. It struggles even with the basics: distinguishing between increases in the quantity of spending on cars and improvements in their quality, let alone measuring the value-added of advertising or the contribution of financial services to the economy. Often, it measures inputs – teachers' salaries – rather than outputs: the value of the education that they provide. Worse, it counts some negatives as positives, flows but not stocks, and omits many important things altogether. When an earthquake demolishes a town, GDP rises: the destruction isn't counted, but the rebuilding effort is. A country that suffers a crime wave and ups its spending on security seems better off. The economic contribution of a factory that emits choking smoke is triply exaggerated: the harm to locals of breathing in filthy air isn't deducted, while increased healthcare spending and the cost of cleaning up the pollution add to GDP. Services for which people aren't paid aren't counted: if two neighbours look after their own children, this adds nothing to GDP; if each pays the other to look after their children, GDP rises. It records neither assets, nor liabilities (debts). Nor does it make allowance for the size of the population – although GDP per person does – or for how income is shared out.

Clearly, governments ought to try to measure economic performance better. They should try to measure national wealth – physical, human, natural and social capital – as well as incomes. They should care about how they are distributed, not just the total amount. They should try to gauge welfare too: the value of leisure, health, security and so on. The United Nations Development Programme's Human Development Indicators are one attempt to do this. Clearly, though, no measurement is perfect. It is impossible for any of us to pin a number on our wellbeing that captures all the various facets of what makes a good life, still less to aggregate those numbers reliably.

We need to be bold in our aspirations for what a good economy can achieve, realistic about what it can't and be careful not to confuse means and ends. We set our sights too low if we only try to hold on to what we have. We have a limited vision of progress if we think a safety net is a substitute for a springboard. We have a poverty of ambition if we don't dream of a boundlessly better future –tapping the limitless energy of the sun and the atom, understanding ever more of the wonders of our world, exploring space. A richer, fairer, more advanced economy would not only make us individually better off, it would help pay for better education and healthcare as well as funding non-commercial goals: art, enlightenment, pure scientific research. It can also provide greater freedom and security: freedom to pursue whatever we want to do, security to fall back on if we fail and to help us start again. But while economic progress is crucial, it isn't everything. Higher consumption cannot buy us love or self-respect. The purpose of life is the pursuit of happiness, whatever form it may take, not to be the richest corpse in the cemetery. Ethics matter as well as economics. At a philosophical level, I agree with people who say that being richer doesn't necessarily make us happier (although few people genuinely want to be poor). But that doesn't mean that happiness, an intensely subjective and personal thing, ought to be the object of economic policy. If you take it literally, it gives licence for an authoritarian government to brainwash children or put Prozac in the water. If you take it as a metaphor, it provides cover for a wide range of policies that policymakers might subjectively favour and that may or may not make people happy, but if sensible ought to be justifiable in other ways. An ingenious way of capturing the fact that higher incomes are desirable but are only a means to a much wider range of aims is Amartya Sen's conception of "Development as Freedom"[516] – the notion that

516   Amartya Sen, *Development as Freedom*, Oxford: 1999

economic development is about expanding people's "power to do things", the freedom and the capacity to achieve their dreams.

That implies an economic role for government even in a notionally perfect market economy: to set the rules of the game, to enforce rules that prevent discrimination and abuses of power, and to try to ensure that have people have equal chances, or at least more equal ones. Such a prospectus ought to muster broad political support. But while most pay lip service to it, few actually prioritise it. That is short-sighted as well as shameful. When European countries extended education to everyone in society, they didn't just open up new possibilities to children of all backgrounds, they also unleashed economic progress. By making full use of everyone's talents, economies can innovate faster, so that even today's poor have greater capabilities than yesterday's rich. Nathan Rothschild, Britain's richest man at the time, died in 1836 of an infected abscess that antibiotics now available cheaply to everyone could have cured. Of course, if one cares only about status, one might make a different calculation – but I bet that a feudal lord from medieval England would still prefer the comforts of a middle-class life in modern Britain. Equality of opportunity is certainly in *nearly* everyone's long-term enlightened self-interest. So the reasons for making it a lodestar of a good economy are both ethical and practical.

By the same token, combating vested interests that capture others' economic contributions, impede their opportunities and hinder technological and social progress promotes better economic performance as well as justice. It is also an inherently political task: breaking up concentrations of economic and political power – or at least ensuring that power is not abused. That, in turn, requires openness about how power is exercised and accountability for what is done – to governments, in the marketplace, to civil society, through the legal system and to voters – and countervailing powers. Like equality of opportunity, openness and accountability are concepts to which most politicians subscribe in principle, but which they rarely prioritise. After all, most politicians want to exercise power as unconstrained as possible.

Countervailing power can come from government regulation and antitrust enforcement, from market competition, through the media and social networks, through the law and through the ballot box. What happens, though, when governments are captured by vested interests – as all are, to varying extents? Market discipline is highly ineffective: it punishes profligacy rather than cronyism. Elections are crucial, but these only occasionally focus on abuses of economic and political power, so in the meanwhile vested interests multiply largely unconstrained. The media can certainly play a constructive role, albeit unevenly. The legal system can punish the most egregious abuse. Ultimately, it is about mobilising people through the power of ideas and of example and overcoming the lobbying and lies of entrenched vested interests. With luck, this book can play a small part in that.

Whether or not you share my vision of a good society and economy, the reforms recommended in this book can also be justified more broadly. After all, most politicians at least claim to want to improve the living standards of everyone in society.

It's not perfect, but it's progress

I don't think it is possible to create a perfect society – human beings are too imperfect for that and their needs and desires inevitably clash to some extent – and it is dangerous to try. But we can surely create a better one. Since European societies in 2014 are clearly better in nearly every respect than those of 1914, 1934, 1954, 1974 – and in many respects than those of 1994 – the possibility of further progress ought to be uncontroversial, however painful recent years have been. Yet it isn't:

many Europeans think Europe's best days are behind it, and that their children will live worse than they do.

A century ago, in 1914, Europe was marching towards four years of senseless massacre, mostly orchestrated by imperial elites who sent millions of ordinary people to their deaths. Ireland was part of the British Empire, while central and eastern Europe was carved up between the German, Austro-Hungarian and Russian ones. Democracies were rare and limited: women generally did not have the vote and neither did all men.[517] Societies were stratified along class lines. While a rudimentary welfare state existed in Germany and Britain, social protections were generally minimal.[518] Compulsory education for all was a novelty and the school leaving age in Britain was twelve. Lives were much shorter: life expectancy at birth was fifty-nine years in Denmark, fifty-two in Britain, forty-three in Germany and thirty-five in Albania.[519] People were much poorer: income per person in Britain, the richest country in Europe, was lower than Jamaica's today.[520] Electricity, cars and the telephone were novel luxuries: remember the first season of Downton Abbey. Since even the richest did not have access to technologies that we take for granted, such as antibiotics,

---

517   The Grand Duchy of Finland was the first European country to grant women full voting rights, in 1907, followed by Norway in 1913. Several countries allowed women to vote in municipal elections but not national ones. Women gained the right to vote in national elections in many countries just after the end of the First World War, but not until 1945 in France and only in 1971 in Switzerland.

518   Bismarck introduced the first elements of a welfare state in Germany in the late nineteenth century: old age pensions, accident insurance and medical care. The Liberal government in Britain introduced old-age pensions in 1908, free school meals in 1909 and national insurance for unemployment and health benefits in 1911.

519   www.gapminder.org

520   GDP per person was $6,934 in 2005 dollars adjusted for differences in purchasing power. www.gapminder.org

airplanes and television, their living standards were lower than today's poor in many respects.

By 1934, Europe was in the grips of the Great Depression, with millions unemployed and scarcely a social safety net (although the school leaving age in Britain had risen to fourteen). The working classes were flexing their muscles. Democracies were rare and under threat. Many of the new states that emerged from the crumbling of empires after the First World War had lapsed into authoritarianism. Fascists were in power not just in Hitler's Germany and Mussolini's Italy but also in Pilsudski's Poland, Dollfuss's Austria, Horthy's Hungary, Salazar's Portugal and elsewhere, while they had many sympathisers in Britain too. Spain was on the brink of civil war that the fascists would win. The forced collectivisation of farmers in the Soviet Union had caused mass famines, leading Stalin to embark on purges to tighten his grip on power. Life expectancy at birth had reached sixty-seven years in the Netherlands and sixty-one in Britain and Germany, but was still only forty-five in Portugal and forty in Albania. Income per person in Switzerland, the richest country in Europe, was lower than Turkey's or China's today; Britain was poorer than Thailand is today.[521]

In 1954, Europe was recovering from the horrors of war but was now divided by the Cold War. Those on the eastern side of the Iron Curtain were trapped in communist dictatorships, while those fortunate enough to be in western democracies lived in fear of a Soviet Union that had just developed nuclear weapons. Fascists still ruled Franco's Spain and Salazar's Portugal. Britain and France still controlled large global empires. The leaders of France, Italy, Belgium, Netherlands and Luxembourg were starting to bury the hatchet with West Germany, tying their economies together and building common institutions with the aim of making war between them unthinkable.

---

521   GDP per person in Switzerland was $9,038 in 2005 dollars adjusted for differences in purchasing power. In the UK it was $7,892. www.gapminder.org

Kickstarted by Marshall Plan aid from America and burgeoning trade, western Europe was booming. But class divisions were rife. The middle classes had knocked the upper classes off their pedestal. Bolstered by the fear of communism, the working classes had gained much more clout too: unions were in the ascendant, working conditions had improved and welfare provision was expanding. Britain had created its now-revered National Health Service. Governments played a much bigger role in the economy generally: industries had been nationalised, taxes and spending had risen and planning was all the rage. Determined to avoid a repeat of the Great Depression, governments' priority was maintaining full employment. While the school leaving age in Britain had risen to fifteen, university was still the preserve of a privileged few. Life expectancy at birth had reached seventy-three years in Norway and Iceland, seventy in Britain and sixty-eight in West Germany, but was still only fifty-six in Albania. Income per person in Switzerland, the richest country in Europe, was the same as Argentina's today; Britain was poorer than Romania and Venezuela are now.[522] Television was generally a single channel in black and white. Washing machines were a luxury. Many people still used outside toilets.

Few Europeans nowadays think 1914 or 1934 were better than today. But many social conservatives look back fondly on the Europe of 1954, albeit through rose-tinted spectacles. This was a glorious time before the horrors of the 1960s when women still knew their place – at home cleaning, cooking and caring for their children and their husband – discrimination was legal and homosexuality illegal, and society was almost uniformly white. Respect for church, army and tradition remained strong, while government censors ensured people didn't read, see or hear anything they shouldn't. Contraceptive pills didn't

---

522   GDP per person in Switzerland was $15,739 in 2005 dollars adjusted for differences in purchasing power. In the UK it was $10,723. www.gapminder.org

exist. Abortions took place in back streets.[523] Divorce was difficult in most countries and still illegal in some.[524]

In 1974, Europe was still sundered by the Cold War, albeit in a period of détente. The Carnation Revolution finally killed off fascism in Portugal, while Franco was on his last legs in Spain. Greece's military dictatorship collapsed too. Only a few outposts of Europe's global empires remained. The six countries that founded the European Economic Community (EEC) in 1958 had just been joined by Britain, Ireland and Denmark. The social revolution of the 1960s had also liberated people as never before. Italy had at last legalised divorce. Switzerland had finally allowed women to vote in federal elections. In Britain, women had won the right to equal pay with men; sexual and racial discrimination were about to be outlawed.[525] The school leaving age in Britain had risen to sixteen. But political and social progress contrasted with economic regress. A thirty-year boom had ended abruptly when soaring oil prices plunged economies into recession. Inflation soared to double digits. In the following years, unemployment rose to what seemed like an alarmingly high rate – 5 per cent in Britain and France – that would now be considered low. Recession pitted people against each other as they fought for the scraps of a shrinking pie. Richer northern European countries slammed their doors on newcomers from southern Europe, North Africa and their former colonies, and tried to force settled immigrants to leave. The post-war economic model was breaking down.

On the plus side, life expectancy at birth had crept up to seventy-five years in Sweden[526] and seventy-three in Britain, while even in

---

523   Iceland legalised abortion in limited cases in 1935, Sweden in 1938.

524   For example, Italy only legalised divorce in 1970 and Ireland in 1995.

525   The Equal Pay Act of 1970 gave women the right to equal pay. The Sexual Discrimination Act of 1975 and the Race Relations Act of 1976 outlawed discrimination.

526   As well as Norway, Iceland and Switzerland.

Albania it had reached sixty-nine. Thanks to massive improvements in healthcare, people in the poorest country in Europe could expect to live twice as long as sixty years earlier; the average Albanian could also expect to live seventeen years longer than the average Briton born in 1914. Income per person in Switzerland, still the richest country in Europe, was similar to that in South Korea today.[527] Britons were more than twice as rich as they were in 1934, but were still poorer than Hungarians are today. Cars and foreign holidays were no longer the preserve of the rich. While television was now in colour, nobody had a computer at home.

By 1994, Europe had made another huge leap forward, but also a step back. The Berlin Wall had fallen and the Cold War was over: both Germany and Europe were reunited. Communist dictatorships had given way to democracies; Estonia, Latvia and Lithuania were freed from the Soviet empire. Only Belarus remained frozen in old-style totalitarianism. Mercifully, the Soviet Union broke up peacefully; tragically, Yugoslavia descended into war and ethnic cleansing. What was now the European Union may have made war unthinkable among its members – which now included Greece (1981), Spain and Portugal (1986) and were soon to include Austria, Finland and Sweden (1995) – but it did not prevent war on its doorstep.

Economies had resumed their growth, albeit more slowly than before 1974. Inflation had been beaten back and the overriding priority was now keeping it down. High unemployment lingered, however. Governments were retreating in some respects: nationalisation had given way to privatisation, many industries were deregulated (not least finance) and economies were opened up to trade, investment and capital flows. But as a share of national income, taxes and spending had continued to creep up, as had public debt. The fall of

---

527   GDP per person in Switzerland was $26,353 in 2005 dollars adjusted for differences in purchasing power. In the UK it was $16,690. www.gapminder.org

communism, the decline of industry and in the case of Britain laws pushed through by Margaret Thatcher had weakened the power of the labour movement. The school leaving age in Britain was still only sixteen. Across Europe, university education had been massively expanded (albeit much less so in Britain). Denmark, Sweden and Norway had just introduced registered same-sex partnerships. Ireland was about to legalise divorce.

Life expectancy at birth had crept up by another four years over the past twenty, reaching seventy-nine in Sweden[528] and seventy-seven in Britain; Albania was up to seventy-two but Latvia could only manage sixty-five. Oil-rich Norway was now Europe's most prosperous country, but it was poorer than Ireland is today.[529] Britain was roughly as rich as Slovenia is today and poorer than South Korea now is. Two decades may not seem like such a long time, but back then mobile phones were a luxury, the internet a painfully slow novelty and flights within Europe prohibitively expensive at a time when Ryanair was tiny and Easyjet didn't even exist.

It should be self-evident that progress – creating a better society – is not only possible, it has actually been achieved, dramatically, in almost every dimension: economic, social and political. But while few would dispute that life in Europe now is better than in 1974, many might argue that things have not improved since 1994 or have even gone backward.

In former communist countries, life has clearly got better. Take Estonia. Despite the crisis, which hit it particularly hard, income per person in 2012 was two-and-a-half times what it was in 1994.[530]

---

528   As well as Iceland and Switzerland.

529   GDP per person in Norway was $35,547 in 2005 dollars adjusted for differences in purchasing power. In the UK it was $24,119. www.gapminder.org

530   GDP per person in Estonia was $7,734 in 1994 and $18,858 in 2012 in 2005 dollars adjusted for differences in purchasing power. www.gapminder.org

Estonians are now as well off as Spaniards were in 1994. Life expectancy at birth rose by seven years to seventy-four over the same period. Estonia has been particularly successful, but what about Romania, which is often depicted as a basket case? Average incomes in Romania rose by nearly 60 per cent between 1994 and 2012 – Romanians are now better off than Hungarians were in 1994 – while life expectancy increased by four years to seventy-four.[531] Politically, things have improved too. Eight ex-communist countries, including Estonia, joined the EU in 2004, followed by Bulgaria and Romania in 2007. The war in the former Yugoslavia is over; conflict over Kosovo was avoided; Croatia became the twenty-eighth member of the EU in 2013. Their citizens can now trade and travel freely throughout Europe. Most can work freely too; restrictions on Bulgarians and Romanians were lifted in January 2014, but still remain on Croatians. Unlike in the interwar period, all have remained democracies, although Hungary is taking a worrying turn towards authoritarianism. War is not unthinkable – remember Russia's invasion of Georgia in 2008 – but certainly much less likely. Don't get me wrong: I'm not saying things are perfect, far from it, simply that they have got better.

In western Europe, the picture is more mixed. On average, people are considerably better off than in 1994. GDP per person in Ireland nearly doubled between 1994 and 2012.[532] Income per person in Spain rose by more than 40 per cent between 1994 and 2012; Spaniards are as rich as the Germans were in 1994.[533] Living standards in Britain rose by 30 per cent over the same period; Britons are as rich as the Swiss were

---

531   GDP per person in Estonia was $6,976 in 1994 and $11,058 in 2012 in 2005 dollars adjusted for differences in purchasing power. www.gapminder.org

532   GDP per person in Ireland was $38,856 in 2005 dollars adjusted for differences in purchasing power in 2012, up from $18,869 in 1994. www.gapminder.org

533   GDP per person in Spain was $26,458 in 2005 dollars adjusted for differences in purchasing power in 2012, up from $18,783 in 1994. www.gapminder.org

back in 1994.[534] Even the Greeks were 27 per cent better off by 2012, although they have fallen back considerably since then. Italians have made the least progress: incomes are up by only 15 per cent.

But some Europeans have done much better than others. Between 1995 and 2010, households' disposable income rose much faster in Sweden (2.87 per cent a year), Britain (2.67 per cent) and France (2.17 per cent) than in laggards such as Germany (0.74 per cent) and Italy (0.37 per cent).[535] Before the crisis (1995–2008), incomes in Britain rose pretty equally for everyone except the bottom tenth (whose incomes still inched up by 0.51 per cent a year) and the top tenth (whose incomes soared by 3.98 per cent a year). In France, the pattern was very even, with only the top tenth pulling ahead. In Sweden, the poor did worst and each decile above them did progressively better. In Italy and Greece, the pattern was reversed: the poor did best. But in Germany, only the top 10 per cent did reasonably well. Most people's incomes stagnated, while the bottom 30 per cent got poorer.

Since the crisis, most people have fallen back and the poor have often suffered most. Median income – that of a household richer than half of the population and poorer than the other half – plunged by more than a fifth in Greece between 2010 and 2012.[536] The poorest tenth lost a third of their income – falling back to where they were in 2001.[537] The poorest tenth in Germany have not experienced a sudden fall in income,

---

534   GDP per person in Britain was $31,295 in 2005 dollars adjusted for differences in purchasing power in 2012, up from $24,119 in 1994. www.gapminder.org

535   Kaja Bonesmo Fredriksen, "Income Inequality in the European Union", OECD Economics Department Working Papers, No. 952, 2012. http://dx.doi.org/10.1787/5k9bdt47q5zt-en

536   Personal calculations from Eurostat, median equivalised net income, at purchasing power standard. Code: ilc_di03

537   Personal calculations from Eurostat, income of first decile, top cut-off point, at purchasing power standard Code: ilc_di01

but are scarcely richer than they were in 2001. Median income has fallen by 5 per cent in Britain, while the poorest tenth have stood still.

Technological progress has continued, however. Home computers, then laptops and now tablets have proliferated. An unimaginable wealth of information can now be googled anywhere for free. You can skype your friends across the world and have a video chat without it costing you a penny. A global conversation is beginning on Twitter. Mobile phones are ubiquitous, most of them smart. As a student in 1994, I used to copy mix tapes for my friends; now you can carry all your music in your pocket, or stream it from a massive jukebox in the cloud. Amazon has revolutionised shopping. Big boxy televisions have been junked for cheaper flat-screens with pin-sharp images. Thanks to imports from China and elsewhere, the cost of clothing, toys and much else has plummeted. Supermarkets provide a wider range of better food. Flying around Europe is no longer a luxury. High-speed rail has proliferated; even Britain has one short link. Cars are starting to drive themselves. 3D printing shops are opening on high streets. Fears that we would run short of fossil fuels have proved false: shale oil and gas (and coal) are plentiful. AIDS has become a chronic disease, not a quickly fatal one. Viagra has given many men a new lease of life. Starting with the Netherlands in 2001, ten European countries have allowed gays to marry; England and Wales are due to do so in 2014. Britain introduced a minimum wage in 1997. Finally, in 2013, the school leaving age in Britain rose to seventeen and it is due to rise again to eighteen soon. University education has expanded almost everywhere. Life expectancy in Switzerland has risen to eighty-three, up four years within the space of eighteen; even Albania is up to seventy-seven. So it's not all bad – and with the right reforms, it could get much better.

How economies work

Europe can build better economies and societies. Progress is possible. But how?

While many excellent economists have shed light on a wide variety of subjects, we still have only a sketchy grasp of how economies work – and what passes for economic "science" is often bunk. Fortunately, technological progress doesn't depend on our economic understanding of why it occurs – although it can be stunted by bad policies.

Political economy – as it was then called – emerged in the eighteenth century, when the Scottish philosopher Adam Smith pursued "an inquiry into the nature and causes of the wealth of nations".[538] His key insight – that competition between selfish profit-seeking producers tends to advance the common good – is profound and often true.[539] At the time, political economy was descriptive, analytical and firmly anchored in a political and social context. In the nineteenth century, it was rebadged as the science of economics, akin to a branch of mechanical engineering. In keeping with the science of the time, economies were thought of as gigantic, self-equilibrating machines.

Increasingly, economics ran away with itself. Instead of trying to describe the world as it is, with the economy as a form of human interaction, it imagined a mathematical ideal detached from its social,

---

538   Adam Smith, *An Inquiry into the Nature and Causes of the Wealth of Nations*, 1776

539   In *The Theory of Moral Sentiments* (1759), Smith also argued that people had regard for others: "How selfish soever man may be supposed, there are evidently some principles in his nature, which interest him in the fortunes of others, and render their happiness necessary to him, though he derives nothing from it, except the pleasure of seeing it. Of this kind is pity or compassion, the emotion we feel for the misery of others, when we either see it, or are made to conceive it in a very lively manner. That we often derive sorrow from the sorrows of others, is a matter of fact too obvious to require any instances to prove it; for this sentiment, like all the other original passions of human nature, is by no means confined to the virtuous or the humane, though they perhaps may feel it with the most exquisite sensibility. The greatest ruffian, the most hardened violator of the laws of society, is not altogether without it."

political and historical context. Assumptions that were not approximately right but completely wrong became doctrine: that people have known, stable, independent and well-ordered preferences; that based on those preferences, they "maximise" rather than operate by rules of thumb and make do; that they know how the economy works and have "rational expectations" about what the future holds, which conforms to a known probability distribution; and that as a result, markets (not least financial ones) are "efficient" and tend towards equilibrium. On the basis of these false assumptions, economists created a fantasy world – that's fine, lots of people love Harry Potter – and then proceeded to give advice as if the real world was like their fantasy. And people believed them. Which is bonkers.

Simplifying (false) assumptions allowed macroeconomists to model economies as if they consisted of an all-seeing, all-knowing single representative agent rather than as the complex interaction between many types of agent; to abstract from the financial system altogether; and to ignore the role of particular institutions. As a result, mainstream economics has very little to say about how new ideas come about and how they are deployed across the economy – which is a pity considering they are the two main drivers of growth in advanced economies. Because it has no coherent account of innovation, it often misses the point. Immigrants are seen as generic drones who fit into vacancies into the labour market, rather than diverse sparks of new ideas. Free trade purportedly delivers a tiny one-off gain instead of being a stimulus for competitive improvement. Entrepreneurs don't exist. Likewise, it has no coherent account of how the financial sector interacts with the economy. Standard models ignore it altogether; newer ones tack it on in an ad hoc way. Milton Friedman, a famous American economist, once countered that theories should be judged by their ability to predict events rather than by the realism of their assumptions. On that basis, orthodox economics is a flop. Physics is a wonderful science that told us how to send a man to the moon; economics pretending to be physics is a disaster that led to the crash.

The notion that economies are stable and predictable and tend towards a steady state – in effect, a linear forward projection of equilibrium over time – is nonsense. Ironically, this neo-classical theory is often advanced by free-marketeers who don't understand its implications. If this really was an accurate description of how an economy works, a central planner could do the job just as well as the market system.

I don't pretend to know how economies precisely work. I don't think anyone does. That's the point. Economies are in fact complex systems that are forever changing in often unpredictable and non-linear ways as a result of the interaction between different economic agents with a limited grasp of how the economy works and little idea of what the future holds. The best synthesis of thinking about economies as complex, adaptive systems is Eric Beinhocker's *The Origin of Wealth: Evolution, Complexity and the Radical Remaking of Economics*.[540]

Economies are inherently unstable, not (as conventional economics assumes) because of shocks from outside the system that knock them out of equilibrium, but because of the continual interaction between agents within the economy who are both jostling for advantage and cooperating, taking their cues from others and striking out on their own, and whose ever-changing expectations about an unknown future are often self-fulfilling. Left to its own devices, the system does not settle down, it continues changing and evolving. The case for markets, then, is not that they are right or "efficient" at any point in time, but rather that they help chart a course towards an unknown future, enlightening us about what works and what doesn't, what people want

---

540   Eric Beinhocker, *The Origin of Wealth: Evolution, Complexity and the Radical Remaking of Economics*, Harvard Business School Press: 2006

and what they don't. On that point Hayek was right and Friedman wrong.

In a complex, ever-changing economy, policymakers need to do more than stand back and let markets rip – but the belief that they know best is a delusion. Throw in insights from political economy, namely how policymakers get caught up with the crowd or captured by it, and the dangers of micromanagement become clear. The task for policymakers is particularly tricky because while the inherent instability of capitalism is a source of progress – the "gales of creative destruction" produced by innovators and entrepreneurs, as Joseph Schumpeter put it – it can also be extremely damaging: when the financial system runs away with itself and then crashes. Economies need to try to capture the benefits of entrepreneurs' efforts – or the animal spirits of investors, as Keynes put it – while limiting the financial sector's excesses. Governments need to encourage the dynamism of technological and business progress, while stepping in to rekindle its spirits in a slump. As Keynes pointed out: "If the animal spirits are dimmed and the spontaneous optimism falters, leaving us to depend on nothing but a mathematical expectation, enterprise will fade and die."[541] While Keynes and Schumpeter are often viewed as polar opposites, there is merit in synthesising their insights. Keynes is right that governments need to step in to support demand in a slump, while Schumpeter is correct that we need to enable economies to adjust so that the process of creative destruction can resume. "In the long term, it is absolutely necessary for insolvent banks, firms, and households to go bankrupt and emerge anew; keeping them alive indefinitely only prolongs the problem," economist Nouriel Roubini rightly observes.

What does that mean for economic policy? It should be bold and modest. Bold in trying to unleash and channel waves of innovation and enterprise. Modest in realising that policymakers' ability to shape

---

541   John Maynard Keynes, *The General Theory of Employment, Interest and Money*, 1936

the future is limited. Bold in intervening to remedy obvious dysfunctions: an economic slump, a bond market panic, stifling monopolies. Modest in realising that no system of rules or human oversight is going to make the economy stable or predictable. What we need, rather, are rules and institutions that encourage trial and error, can cope with a wide range of unexpected events and inevitable policy mistakes, enable economies to adjust, and provide greater equality and security.

What Europe needs is reforms to make its economies more adaptable, more dynamic and more decent – and thus lift up living standards. We need reforms that ADD UP. The next three chapters look at each of these in turn.

10

ADAPT!

How to cope with and adjust to change

We have involved ourselves in a colossal muddle, having blundered in the control of a delicate machine, the working of which we do not understand.

John Maynard Keynes, *The Great Slump of 1930*, 1930[542]

The curious task of economics is to demonstrate to men how little they really know about what they imagine they can design.

Friedrich von Hayek, *The Fatal Conceit*, 1988[543]

Change happens all the time. Some of it is reasonably predictable: higher demand for ice cream in summer. Some of it isn't: out of nowhere, Gangnam Style became a global hit. Big changes often

---

542 John Maynard Keynes, *The Great Slump of 1930*, 1930
543 Friedrich Hayek, *The Fatal Conceit: The Errors of Socialism*, Chicago: 1988

happen unexpectedly. The Berlin Wall falls. The Fukushima earth-quake knocks out a big chunk of the Japanese economy and with it crucial links in global supply chains. Hydraulic fracturing ("frack-ing") leads to a shale-gas boom that transforms America's energy landscape – and Europe's – within a few years. Apple was left for dead at the turn of the century, then vaulted to being the world's most valuable listed company. American house prices never fell – and then they did. The Western financial system collapses. When such unexpected changes happen, it is often hard to know whether they will last. Harry Potter did, Gangnam Style didn't. The rise of East Asia seemed inexorable; then out of the blue the 1997–98 crisis happened and it was widely written off; then it bounced back. The Arab Spring took everyone by surprise, then seemed like one-way traffic – until Egypt had its counterrevolution. Other changes are more predictably enduring, such as the ageing of European socie-ties. Still others are probable but shrouded in uncertainty, not least climate change.

If you believe that economic systems, like all forms of social in-teraction, are complex and always in flux, often in unpredictable and non-linear ways – or if you simply observe that changes and "shocks" are all too frequent – adaptability is a key feature of any successful economy. An adaptable system can cope with a variety of circum-stances – boom and bust, both high and low oil prices, the emergence of new technologies, the rapid development of other economies, a financial crash – and adjust where necessary. In contrast, a fragile system may collapse when confronted with change, while a rigid one will struggle to adjust. This chapter will first look at how to make the economy less fragile, notably in the face of financial upheaval. Then it will examine how to make economies more flexible. Lastly, it will suggest how to adjust to reasonably predictable changes, such as de-mographic trends, and hugely uncertain ones, such as climate change.

Change often comes out of the blue, so this chapter cannot, and does not aim to, cover every conceivable one.

Less fragile finance

Europe's biggest source of fragility is its over-reliance on debt. Banks and other financial players, companies and households all finance an excessive share of their investments with debt. For individual borrowers, this magnifies the upside but leaves them perilously exposed if asset prices fall. Relying on short-term debt also makes you vulnerable to refinancing problems, as banks that rely on overnight funding and small companies that depend on overdrafts know all too well. Short-term borrowing in foreign currencies is particularly precarious. Equity financing, on the other hand, is much safer. If you buy a house with a 25 per cent deposit (equity) and 75 per cent debt, both you and the bank can absorb a large fall in house prices with minimal risk. If the bank finances itself with 20 per cent equity and 80 per cent debt, it likewise has a big cushion against losses. If companies rely more on equity, they are more resilient to a recession or a rise in interest rates.

For the system as a whole, an over-reliance on debt amplifies rises in asset prices, making bubbles bigger and more frequent. On the downside, it exacerbates the costs of price falls and spreads their consequences more widely, causing bankruptcies and defaults, disrupting the flow of credit and deepening recessions. Contrast the bursting of America's dotcom bubble in 2000–1 with the US housing crash in 2006–7. The dotcom bust wiped $5.1 trillion off the value of companies on the Nasdaq stock exchange between March 2000 and November 2002, a collapse exacerbated by 9/11.[544] But while many dotcoms folded, the wider economic consequences were relatively limited. Internet companies were largely equity-financed and most investors had bought their shares with cash. (Had they also

---

544   http://articles.latimes.com/2006/jul/16/business/fi-overheat16

borrowed from banks, imagine how much higher internet share prices might have soared – and how much worse the bust would have been.) So when dotcoms crashed, investors suffered a loss of wealth, but were not left with a massive debt overhang. Banks were largely unscathed and so could continue lending to the rest of the economy. While growth slowed, the US did not even suffer two consecutive quarters of shrinking output.[545] In contrast, the housing bust wiped out less wealth directly – $4.7 trillion between 2006 and 2008 – than the dotcom crash even in dollar terms, and a much smaller percentage of total US wealth. Yet whereas the impact of the dotcom crash was dampened and contained, that of the housing bust was magnified and spread by the layer upon layer of interconnected debt built up against the "security" of US housing values.

Among the many reasons why both Europe and America are over-reliant on debt one of the biggest is the tax system. For businesses (including banks), interest payments are tax-deductible; the cost of equity is not. Perversely, governments subsidise debt finance, making the economy as a whole more fragile. One way to remove this tax bias towards debt would be to provide an equivalent "allowance for corporate equity", as advocated by the Mirrlees Review on taxation conducted for Britain's Institute for Fiscal Studies.[546] A more radical (and better) change would be to abolish tax deductions for interest payments and depreciation and instead allow companies to write off all their investments against tax when they are incurred.[547] In effect, this would involve taxing companies' net cash flows (their incomings less their outgoings) instead of their taxable income or profits. As

---

545   The unemployment rate rose by only two percentage points.

546   James Mirrlees and others, "Mirrlees Review: Reforming the tax system for the 21st century", Institute for Fiscal Studies, 2010. http://www.ifs.org.uk/mirrleesReview/design

547   http://www.ifs.org.uk/mirrleesreview/design/ch17.pdf

well as removing the tax bias towards debt, this would make corporate taxes much simpler and therefore less open to accounting manipulation. Taxing interest payments would also enable governments to lower corporate tax rates without losing revenues. So eliminating the tax bias towards debt would boost growth as well as making the economy less fragile.

Additional measures are needed to limit banks' particularly severe overreliance on debt. Very few companies finance assets with 97-per-cent debt and 3-per-cent equity as banks do. No sensible banker would lend to businesses with such precarious balance-sheets. Moreover, banks' excessive borrowing enables them to lend more to each other and to the rest of the economy, destabilising the economy as a whole. Worse, when banks become distressed, they stop lending, harming the economy. And when they go bust, the consequences can be devastating, which enables them to blackmail policymakers into bailing them out.

The new EU and global rules enacted since the crisis are wholly inadequate – perhaps unsurprisingly, since they were drafted by the same compromised insiders who gave the financial system a clean bill of health before the crash.[548] Instead of recognising that the old system was fundamentally flawed, they toughen it a little, complicate it further and leave huge loopholes untouched. Astonishingly, banks will still be able to finance £100 of assets with up to £97 of debt. Their holdings of government bonds, which are still deemed risk-free, can be wholly financed with debt. Banks will also still be able to use their dodgy and biased risk-weighting models to determine how much equity they need to use to fund specific assets. Since bank bosses' bonuses are typically based on their return on equity – without allowing for any extra risk they incur – they have a huge incentive to game the system and load up

---

548 The new Basel III capital-adequacy rules, which have been transposed into EU law through a package of regulations known as CRD IV.

on debt. While policymakers are aware of all these risks, they are relying on supervisors to keep tabs on excessive risk-taking not just within individual banks but also across the system as a whole.

Unfortunately, even wise and impartial supervisors don't know enough to get to grips with the immense complexity of the financial system – and bankers have every incentive to muddy the waters even further. It is also a delusion that they can remain detached from the system they oversee: they got caught up in the bubble before 2007 and panicked along with markets in the eurozone in 2010–12. Getting to grips with complexity requires simple solutions. As well as taking away the tax bias towards debt, banks should be forced to fund their assets with much more equity. Anat Admati and Martin Hellwig argue that banks should rely on at least 20-per-cent equity – which is actually low compared to most companies. Banks should also be compelled to hold more liquid assets to reduce the risk of cashflow problems.

Ideally, big financial institutions ought to be broken up into a diverse range of smaller, simpler and safer ones, many of them partnerships with unlimited liability (as they used to be). If you gamble with other people's money, you ought to have skin in the game. A financial system with a greater diversity of investors could cope better with disruptions: witness how cash-rich, long-term investors such as Warren Buffett, the American billionaire investor, and sovereign-wealth funds helped stabilise banks by buying into them in the crash. Healthy financial systems require investors with a wide range of investment horizons, a diversity of ability to bear risk, and a mix of bulls and bears. If investors are affected differently by a particular change – and react differently to it – the system as a whole will be better able to cope.

Curbing property speculation

While banks are the biggest source of fragility, households' predilection for debt-financed property speculation is another. Individual decisions are skewed by both the availability of credit and the tax system.

Say you get a £100,000 windfall from winning the lottery. You have a choice between investing it in shares or in property, both of which yield a return of, say, 10 per cent a year. If you buy property, the bank is willing to lend you 90 per cent of the value at 5 per cent a year, so your £100,000 deposit will stretch to a £1 million home – and if it yields a 10 per cent return a year, you have made £100,000 less the £45,000 cost of the debt, so £55,000. If you buy shares, though, the bank refuses to lend to you, so you still have only £100,000 to invest and your return is £10,000. Thus the availability of cheap credit for investment in bricks and mortar but not shares biases households' investment decisions towards an asset that is both illiquid – in a downturn it is hard to sell your property quickly except at a big loss, if at all – and unproductive: unlike investment in companies, investment in property doesn't boost future growth. This also encourages property buyers to load up on debt, although they do face a bigger downside than bank bosses: the prospect of losing their home and – in countries that (unlike America) do not have non-recourse mortgages – personal bankruptcy.

The tax system is even more skewed. When you own shares, both the income they yield (the dividends) and the capital gains you realise when you sell them are taxed. When you own property that you live in, the "income" you derive from it (the rent that you would otherwise have to pay) is generally not taxed, nor are the capital gains when you sell.[549] Moreover, mortgage interest payments are tax-deductible in many European countries.[550] While many countries do impose property

---

549   Some countries, such as Switzerland, Iceland, Luxembourg, Netherlands and Slovenia do tax the imputed rental stream of owner-occupied housing. http://ec.europa.eu/economy_finance/events/2011/2011-11-24-property_taxation/pdf/andrews_housing_taxation_for_stability_and_growth_en.pdf

550   http://ec.europa.eu/economy_finance/events/2011/2011-11-24-property_taxation/pdf/andrews_housing_taxation_for_stability_and_growth_en.pdf

taxes – for instance, council tax in Britain – these are typically payable by tenants as well as owner-occupiers, so they are not an additional cost of property investment. (They also tend to be based on outdated valuations: from 1991 in Britain, 1970 in France).There is thus a huge tax bias towards property speculation – sorry, home ownership – financed by fragile debt. This results in higher and more volatile house prices. These tax subsidies not only tend to benefit the rich most, they actually harm the poor because by bidding up house prices, they make home ownership unaffordable for many.[551] As discussed in Chapter 7, the UK government's Help to Buy subsidies are particularly pernicious. In short, the tax bias towards debt-fuelled property speculation is destabilising, regressive and anti-growth.

At the very least, then, tax deductions for mortgage interest payments should be phased out, as they have been in Britain, where the tax deductibility of interest payments on properties that investors "buy to let" (ie, buy to rent out) should also be abolished. Limits should be placed on how much people can borrow: say, 80 per cent of the value of a home. How, though, might one equalise the tax treatment of property more generally? The OECD suggests taxing capital gains on people's primary residence. But that would deter people from moving, not least to a better job – as indeed do taxes on buying a property such as stamp duty in Britain and much bigger taxes elsewhere, notably in Greece and Belgium. A more radical (and better) idea would be to replace both income tax and capital-gains tax with an expenditure tax, while also introducing a tax on land values.

The beauty of scrapping taxes on income and capital gains and replacing them with one on expenditure is that saving would be tax-free until the proceeds were spent – akin to how pension plans are taxed today. That would eliminate the tax bias towards certain types of

---

551   http://ec.europa.eu/economy_finance/events/2011/2011-11-24-property_taxation/pdf/andrews_housing_taxation_for_stability_and_growth_en.pdf

investment – property, restrictive tax-exempt savings schemes, pension plans – and against shares, bonds and savings accounts. All the various, complicated tax-exempt savings schemes could be scrapped. People would no longer be forced to sign up to a pension plan – and hence to paying exorbitant fees to pensions providers – in order to save tax-free. Eliminating the tax bias against saving would also provide more funds for investment in future growth.

Like taxing companies on their net cash flows, an expenditure tax is, in effect, a tax on people's cash flows: on their income less their investments. Each year people would declare their income, subtract the amount they have invested in shares, bonds, property, savings accounts, pension plans and so on, add their withdrawals from savings and capital receipts, and pay tax on the difference. Tax rates could be modulated to be as progressive as voters want.

Since people would only be taxed when they spent the proceeds of their investments, people would not face a huge tax bill when they sold their property (or shares). Conversely, those who borrowed against their property to spend would be taxed at that point. But while shifting to an expenditure-tax system would eliminate the tax bias towards investing in property rather than shares, it would not eliminate the tax advantages of property altogether, because the imputed income from living in a property that you own – the rent you would otherwise have to pay – would not be taxed in most countries. More fundamentally, the tax system ought to distinguish between gains from hard work and investment and unearned gains that derive from the efforts of others. As Chapter 12 will explain, a good way to encourage greater dynamism and decency would be to slash taxes on labour and replace them with a tax on land values.

Policy changes

Capitalism is inherently unstable. Often this is a good thing. Economic growth rarely proceeds in a straight line; rather it involves waves of creative destruction: entrepreneurial innovation that ditches the old for the new, as Chapter 11 will discuss. Trying to curb this inherent dynamism tends to lead to stagnation. So policymakers ought to unleash it, while helping people to adapt and providing them with the security they need to embrace change.

Unfortunately, the financial system has an inherent tendency to amplify this instability and indeed create its own through the "destructive creation" of bubbles that end in busts. While the financial system plays a vital role in funding innovation and enterprise, it often channels resources into both unproductive speculation and activities that allow it to appropriate wealth created by others. Reducing its reliance on debt would mitigate these problems. When the financial system crashes, however, governments need to cushion the blow. The best way to do so is through fiscal policy combined with measures to restructure banks and write down debts. Relying exclusively on monetary policy is likely to be increasingly ineffective and ultimately destabilising.

Economic policymaking goes in fads. In post-war Europe, where growth came mainly from rebuilding what had been destroyed and emulating what America did better, the importance of creative destruction was forgotten. So too was the financial cycle, because the financial sector was caged and overwhelmingly national. This deceptively stable environment tricked policymakers into thinking they could plan economic development while fine-tuning demand to maintain full employment. But the system broke down in the early 1970s as the post-war economic boom ran out of steam, efforts to boost employment resulted in ever higher inflation, the Bretton Woods system of currencies pegged to the US dollar collapsed and the oil shocks of 1973–74 resulted in the previously unthinkable combination of stagnation and inflation: stagflation. In this new stop-go world, controlling inflation became the top priority of economic policy and monetary policy the preferred tool for economic management, with central banks causing short, sharp recessions by raising interest rates whenever inflation looked like getting out of hand. Governments increasingly delegated this task to independent central banks. Policymakers gave freer rein to markets domestically – through deregulation and privatisation – and internationally, by opening up to foreign trade and investment. With the rise of East Asian economies, the opening up of China and then India, the collapse of communism and a broader trend of pro-market reforms, the world economy became more globalised. Better still, the benefits of a new wave of creative destruction through the collective power of computers (and people) communicating with each other began to be felt in the 1990s.

Governments also deregulated and opened up their financial systems in the 1980s. Despite warnings that the explosive growth of a poorly regulated and increasingly global financial system was dangerously destabilising – first the Nordic banking crises in the early 1990s, then the crisis that began in Asia in 1997 and threatened to drag down the global financial system in 1998 – central bankers' near-magical powers were believed to safeguard stability. When LTCM, an American hedge fund, collapsed in 1998, the US Federal Reserve brokered a rescue, cut interest rates and the global panic abated. But this reliance on – and faith in – central bankers' powers to stabilise the financial system created ever greater instability: first the dotcom bubble and bust, then the financial and property bubble and the current crisis. Lulled into a false sense of security by the supposedly superior powers of Alan Greenspan and other central bankers, everyone assumed the good times were here to stay and that central bankers could fix any problems that might emerge. But in the current slump, monetary policy has proved to be largely ineffective and increasingly destabilising. In effect, it is trying to create a new bubble to save us from the last.

The best long-term solution is to cut the financial system down to size again. In the mean time, policymakers need to adapt their toolkit. They need to focus more on the financial cycle than the business cycle. Instead of trying to prop up the existing system through hyperactive monetary policy and fiscal backstops for banks, causing stagnation in the short term and even greater instability longer term, they need to allow banks to fail safely and write down debts promptly. At the same time, they need to rely much more on fiscal policy to prop up demand and promote economic adjustment, not least in the eurozone, but also in Britain and elsewhere.

Versatile

To cope with change better, Europe's economies need to be less financially fragile, less prone to property speculation and rely more on debt write-downs and fiscal policy in crises. To adjust to change, they also need to be less rigid.

At the very least, economies need to cope with reasonably predictable variability. Shop assistants need to work longer hours in the run-up to Christmas. Accountants have to burn the midnight oil at the end of the quarter. Seaside resorts need to recruit extra staff during the summer. Farmers require temporary workers at harvest time. So it ought to be easy for companies to hire people on temporary contracts, with variable hours. People also need to be willing and able to move to where the jobs are: Brits to promote bars in Ibiza in the summer, Asians to pick berries in Sweden, people from all parts to work at the Olympics or the Glastonbury music festival.

It's not just labour that needs to be flexible, it's capital too. Electricity companies need enough capacity to cope with peak demand. Car rental companies require sufficient vehicles for the holidays. Cities need enough hotel rooms for the peak tourist season. In part, this requires sufficient investment. But technology also offers exciting new opportunities to make better use of our existing assets. Smart electricity meters in your home could turn the washing machine off and the heating down at peak times when prices are high and also allow you to sell surplus electricity to the grid from solar panels or a wind turbine on your roof. A global pioneer is Italy's Enel, the state-owned energy utility, which has deployed more than 30 million smart meters to its customers since 2001.[552]

The internet is also making it easier to connect people who want to rent out rooms, cars and all sorts of other things with those who want to borrow them – a new sharing economy that offers huge potential for growth. Airbnb, a company based in San Francisco, allows people to rent out accommodation for the night; by the end of 2013 ten million people had used its services, many of them in Europe.[553] It now has several European rivals: Wimdu and 9flats, both based in Berlin, and London-based onefinestay, which also offers upmarket services. Car-sharing services have mushroomed too. Some are, in effect, more flexible car-rental companies that allow you to hire a vehicle by the hour off the street. The world's biggest, America's Zipcar, snapped up European rivals such as Britain's Streetcar and Spain's Avancar, before itself being bought by Avis, a traditional car-rental company, in 2013.[554] Others allow people to hire out their own car. One is Paris-based Buzzcar, founded by the founder of Zipcar. Tamyca is a German equivalent. (Whipcar, a British one, closed in 2013.) Still others offer taxi-like services, notably Uber, that can call on additional drivers at peak times. In France, La Machine du Voisin even allows people to rent out the use of their washing machine.[555]

---

552 http://www.economist.com/node/13725843

553 http://www.indyposted.com/226135/airbnb-adds-250000-properties-6-million-guests-2013/

554 http://www.bbc.co.uk/news/business-20890174

555 http://www.lamachineduvoisin.fr/

Such peer-to-peer rental schemes make better use of an economy's assets, provide extra income for their owners and are often cheaper and more convenient for borrowers. Just find somewhere nearby with your smartphone, check out the reviews and pay online: simple.

Or at least it should be. Unfortunately, vested interests and bureaucratic regulation sometimes impede collaborative consumption. Taxes can be prohibitive. Amsterdam requires people to obtain a permit to rent out their place. Hotel groups lobby for their stringent health and safety regulations to be applied to private rentals: just think of the prohibitive cost and inconvenience of fitting a fire exit to your flat. In many cities, taxis operate legal cartels that are threatened by peer-to-peer cab services like Uber. Taxi drivers' lobbying persuaded the French government to insist on a fifteen-minute delay between a person booking a private cab online and being picked up – a move that has since been overruled (for now).[556] Insurance can also be a big problem. Policymakers looking to boost growth should update and where necessary scrap regulations that prevent economies from using their assets more flexibly.

Adaptable

As well as coping with unexpected change and predictable variability, an adaptable economy needs to be able to adjust to changes that seem more enduring: the rise of emerging economies, the spread of new digital technologies, a desire for more eco-friendly products. To do so, people, businesses, organisations and governments need the freedom, the capacity and the willingness to adapt. At least four types of barrier may impede them. Laws and regulations may restrict hiring and firing, prevent businesses from growing or shrinking, or forbid them from deploying a new technology. A lack of competition may also impede adjustment: dominant players may stifle the growth

---

556   http://www.ft.com/cms/s/0/fd8a20ca-3b3a-11e3-a7ec-00144feab7de.html

of nimbler upstarts or the deployment of technologies that undermine their core business. The absence of suitable labour, capital and supportive infrastructure is a third barrier: companies may not be able to find people with the right skills locally, attract the investment they need to grow or access the competitively priced high-speed internet (or efficient ports) that they need. Last but not least, there are cultural barriers to change, such as a reluctance to ditch old ways of doing things and embrace new ones or a prejudice against hiring foreign workers.

As well as requiring adjustments, the rise of China, the spread of the internet and climate change all open up huge new opportunities for growth. Take trade with emerging economies. Cheaper imports benefit consumers, allowing them to spend more on other things. Companies that source better-value parts and components overseas can in turn export more. Foreign competition spurs local companies to up their game. Fast-growing emerging economies are also Europe's export markets of the future, as I detailed in *Aftershock*. But barriers to adaptability may prevent economies from seizing these new opportunities, resulting in higher unemployment and stagnation.

Mature economies can only grow if workers and capital are deployed to more productive uses – which means they need to stop doing less productive things. They need both the freedom and the capacity to adapt. Reforms that remove regulatory restrictions are necessary but not sufficient. Thus while Britain has admirably flexible labour markets, its narrow skills base, increasing restrictions on immigration, lack of small-business finance and inadequate infrastructure prevent it from being as adaptable as it ought to be.

An economy with a diversity of firms, skills and perspectives is better able to cope with change. Britain's overreliance on finance and Germany's overdependence on manufacturing seem like strengths when demand is booming, but leave them very vulnerable to a downturn – unless they can quickly shift resources to other areas. That is especially true at a local level: towns that rely on a single employer or industry are much more fragile than a big city with a variety of industries. Often, though, the requisite skills won't be available locally: that's why the mobility of people, both within and between countries is so important. Likewise with capital: foreign investors often have funds and attributes that local ones lack. Last but not least, the willingness to adapt is also crucial. People must be prepared to move to where the jobs are. Managers must be ready to shed unproductive business lines and invest in new ones. Flailing owners must be willing to sell up. Society as a whole must be willing to embrace change and take risks.

Flexible labour markets often get a bad rap because they are associated with swapping good, secure jobs for inferior, insecure ones. Eurozone policymakers have made matters worse by single-mindedly and self-defeatingly pursuing wage cuts to boost "competitiveness". But the point of making labour markets more adaptable is not to destroy jobs and drive down wages, it is to create new jobs and enable productivity gains that boost wages. So governments should seek to protect people, not particular jobs or businesses. Just as it is misguided for the US to tie people's healthcare to their employment, it is wrongheaded that European trade unions often try to tie economic security to a particular job. In the Nordic countries, notably Denmark, flexible labour markets go hand-in-hand with lifelong learning, government help in finding a new job and generous unemployment benefits in the interim. This security gives people the confidence to be adaptable.

The good news for Europe is that because the cumulative damage of all the restrictions on economies adjusting is so large, there is huge potential for growth simply by adapting what works well elsewhere. While Europe is in part a global leader that can only grow by innovating, it is also partly a laggard that can grow by imitation, just like emerging economies. That is true in northern as well as southern Europe: witness Germany's hidebound service sector.

Looking to the future, Europe faces two huge, but very different adjustment challenges. One is adjusting to a reasonably predictable trend: ageing societies. Another is curbing highly uncertain and potentially catastrophic climate change.

Predictable adjustment: ageing

Unless Europe welcomes more migrant workers, the population of working age – those aged fifteen to sixty-four – will decline over the next fifteen years. Everyone who is going to reach the age of fifteen by then has already been born – and they are greatly outnumbered by the baby-boomers who are going to reach sixty-five (or die) over that period.[557] That is true even in the UK, which has a better demographic profile than most.[558] In the absence of migration, Eurostat projects that the EU's working-age population will fall by 0.5 per cent a year between 2015 and 2020 and by 0.7 per cent a year between 2020 and 2030.

Barring a pandemic or other disaster, the number of Europeans aged sixty-five and over is set to soar as the baby boomers retire and people generally live longer. In the absence of migration, Eurostat projects that their numbers will leap from 87 million in 2010 to 122.7 million in 2030.[559] By then, they would account for a quarter of the EU population, up from 17.4 per cent in 2010.[560]

---

557 On 1 January 2012 there were 78.6 million under 15s in the EU and 98.4 million people aged 50–64. All figures are from Eurostat, population on 1 January by five years age groups and sex. Code: demo_pjangroup

558 In Britain there were 11.1 million under 15s and 11.5 million people aged 50–64 on 1 January 2012

559 Eurostat, Europop2010 (Eurostat Population Projections 2010-based. Code: proj_10c2150zmp

560 A quarter of a diminished EU population of 491.8 million in 2030.

Since, in the absence of migration, the working-age population is going to shrink while (barring a disaster) the number of over-65s is set to soar, society will change dramatically in all sorts of ways, from attitudes to risk to voting patterns. Economic cleavages between young and old could become acute. In 2010, there were nearly four people of working age for every over-65; by 2030 there will be fewer than two and a half.[561] Since many Europeans retire before sixty-five and many people of working age aren't working – they are studying, looking after children, unemployed, ill, disabled or have taken early retirement – there are actually far fewer workers per pensioner. Already in 2010 Britain had only around two workers per pensioner.[562] So unless Britain gets more people working, there may be scarcely more workers than pensioners in 2030.[563] In some other European countries, the trends are even more dramatic. Germany had only 1.65 workers per pensioner in 2010, Italy 1.38. Without reform, there could be only one worker per pensioner in Germany in 2030 and less than one in Italy.

Projecting out to 2050 or even 2060, as both the UN and the EU have done, makes these demographic changes seem even starker. But that far out, all sorts of imponderables cloud the picture, not least how many babies Europeans choose to have and how far average lifespans extend. Worse, it makes the issue seem distant, when it is in fact pressing. The post-war baby boomers have started retiring en masse. On current policies they will almost all be pensioners by 2030. Unless

561   Personal calculations from Eurostat, Europop2010 (Eurostat Population Projections 2010-based). Code: proj_10c2150zmp. The ratio of 15–64s to 65 and overs is 3.86 in 2010 and 2.45 in 2030.

562   Britain had 28.9 million workers in 2010 (Eurostat, code: lfsi_emp_a) and 13.9 million pensioners (Eurostat, code: spr_pns_ben), a ratio of 2.08.

563   In 2010, Britain had 4.02 people of working age per person 65 and over. By 2030, without migration, this ratio is projected to fall to 2.64, ie, by a third. If the ratio of workers to pensioners (2.08 in 2010) declines by a third, this would be 1.37 in 2030.

governments change things soon, they will be closing the door after the stampede has bolted. Worse, the longer they delay, the harder reform is likely to become, because pensioners may form such a big and effective lobby that politicians dare not touch them. Witness how state pensions in Britain have risen in recent years, even as wages have plunged and other government spending has been slashed.

What, then, needs to be done? Governments ought to do lots of things to increase investment and productivity growth, as this book argues at length. That would boost economic growth and thus the potential for everyone to enjoy higher living standards. But if societies want to guarantee pensioners some proportion of average incomes, there would still be a distributional issue, namely that a big chunk of workers' income gains would need to be taxed away (or siphoned off as a higher profit share to a retired rentier class) to pay for old people's pensions. It is also debatable whether a greying population with a shrinking workforce would invest more: Masaaki Shirakawa, a former governor of the Bank of Japan, argues that one reason why Japan has stagnated is because an ageing society with a shrinking workforce tends to consume and invest less, relying entirely on exports for growth.[564] So three further changes are needed: getting more people into work, bringing in migrant workers and reforming state pension systems.

A wider workforce

Start with getting more people into work. Employment rates vary hugely across the EU. On average, just under two-thirds of people aged 15–64 were in work in 2012,[565] ranging from 75.1 per cent in the Netherlands and 70.1 per cent in Britain to only 51.3 per cent in

---

564   http://www.boj.or.jp/en/announcements/press/koen_2012/data/ko120530a1.pdf

565   The exact figure is 64.2 per cent.

Greece. Tackling the crisis would help a lot, but many people are not working for other reasons. Some are physically or mentally unable to. Others, often young people, are studying or in training; if their learning is valuable, it would be short-sighted to curtail it. Leaving those aside, there are many people who could be working but aren't.

While countries vary a lot, employment rates tend to be lower among young people, those with few qualifications, women and those aged fifty-five and over. To strip out the effect of the crisis, let's look at figures for 2007, when economies were buoyant. Back then, 93 per cent of university-educated European men aged 25–54 were working, with Britain a bit above average; only in Italy was the figure below 90 per cent.[566] In contrast, among those with lower secondary education or less – the equivalent of GCSEs in Britain – only 79.9 per cent were working (a bit less than that in the UK), with big disparities across countries.[567] The gender gap is huge too: women of all education levels are much less likely to be in work than men. Whereas 86.8 per cent of European men aged 25–54 worked in 2007, only 71.2 per cent of women did. Again, countries vary a lot: while three-quarters of British women of that age group work, the Nordic countries do much better, Italy and Greece much worse.[568] The young and the old are also disproportionately out of work. Even in 2007, one in seven youngsters aged 18–24 – and an even greater proportion of 25–29s – was not in employment, education or training, rising to one in five

566   Eurostat, employment rates by sex, age and highest level of education attained: employment rate for men aged 25 to 54 with tertiary education. Code: lfsa_ergaed

567   The employment rate among men aged 25–54 with lower secondary education or less as high as 89.1 per cent in Greece, 76.3 per cent in the UK but only 71.2 per cent in Germany and much less in parts of central and eastern Europe

568   In 2007, more than 80 per cent of women aged 25-64 worked in the Nordic countries (Denmark, Iceland, Finland, Norway, Sweden) plus Estonia, Lithuania and Slovenia. Only three in five Italian and Greek ones did.

in Italy.[569] The biggest shortfall and differences were among 55–64s. Across the EU, fewer than half of 55–64s were in work, ranging from seven in ten Swedes and 57.4 per cent of Britons to only one in three Belgians.[570] So, to get more people into work, policymakers need to combine reforms that make the labour market in general work better with specific measures to boost employment among young people, older ones, women and the less-qualified.

Once demand for labour picks up, there will still be three broad obstacles to getting people into work. In many European countries, the availability of jobs is artificially restricted even in good times by taxes that make it prohibitively expensive to hire people and employment regulations that make it difficult and costly to fire them. Jobseekers may also lack the skills and attributes that employers are looking for – and because hiring and firing is expensive, employers are deterred from taking a chance on them and training them. Last but not least, some are dissuaded from working by welfare rules that penalise work, while others do not want to work and welfare gives them the option of remaining idle. In order to succeed, reforms need to tackle all three aspects of the problem together.

Politicians agree that decent work is a good thing. It doesn't just provide people with an income, it gives them autonomy and dignity and, at best, a sense of achievement and fulfilment. It gives people a stake in society and the opportunity to get ahead. And it saves on social spending. So it is insane that all European governments tax work so heavily. Because of income tax and social-security contributions by employees and employers (known as national insurance in Britain), the cost to companies of hiring someone is much higher than their take-home pay. For every €100 that a single person with no children

---

569   Eurostat, young people not in employment and not in any education and training, NEET rates. Code: edat_lfse_20

570   Across the EU 44.6 per cent of 55–64s were in work in 2007.

earning average wages takes home in pay, it costs their employer twice that in France and Germany and more than twice that in Belgium.[571] In Britain, it costs employers nearly 50 per cent more than workers receive. In contrast, the tax wedge drives up labour costs by only a third in Ireland and a fifth in Switzerland. Worse, this tax on work is huge even for people on low wages. For a single person with no children earning two-thirds of average wages, it inflates the cost of labour by around a quarter in Ireland and Switzerland, 40 per cent in Britain, nearly 60 per cent in Spain, more than 80 per cent in Germany, 90 per cent in France and more than 100 per cent in Belgium.[572] Slashing taxes on work would create more jobs, especially for people with fewer qualifications, and boost take-home pay. Some of the lost tax revenues would be recovered from getting people off benefits and into work. The rest could be made up by cutting wasteful spending and raising taxes on harmful things, like carbon emissions, and introducing a tax on land values.

As well as slashing taxes on labour, governments ought to make it easier for companies to adjust their labour needs as conditions change. In an uncertain world where tastes, technologies and circumstances are forever changing, trying to protect specific jobs is incredibly costly. It deters companies from hiring in the first place – especially the young, the unemployed, newly arrived immigrants and anyone else whose performance is unproven. It tries to cling on to yesterday's jobs at the expense of tomorrow's. It can end up costing many more jobs if it ends up dragging down the company too. And it hinders economic growth by trapping economies in outmoded patterns of production, preventing them from seizing new opportunities. Many European

---

571   OECD, tax wedge, 2012 http://www.oecd.org/tax/tax-policy/taxingwages. htm

572   http://www.oecd.org/els/emp/oecdlabourmarketpolicies-labourtaxesunemploymentbenefits.htm

countries have dual labour markets where the privileged few enjoy jobs for life while others are on temporary contracts. As a result, companies may be forced to shed a bright and hard-working temporary worker rather than an underperforming permanent one in a redundant job. That is not just inefficient, it is unfair.

The OECD compiles indicators that gauge the rigidity of employment rules. While Britain's labour market is admirably flexible, with Ireland and Estonia close behind, many other European countries are much more rigid. It is hardest to shed a permanent worker in Italy, France, Netherlands, Belgium and Germany.[573] Temporary work is very flexible in the Netherlands, but much less so in southern Europe, with France worst of all.[574]

There is nothing progressive about protecting permanent workers at the expense of temporary ones, with those trapped in unemployment harmed most of all. Often, the security is illusory: it protects jobs in declining industries and failing companies for a while until finally they collapse and workers are left stranded. In an unpredictable, ever-changing world, the greatest security is for people to have plentiful opportunities to find new jobs, versatile skills and a capacity to learn new ones, and a willingness to adapt and if necessary move to where the jobs are. Lowering labour taxes, loosening employment regulations and removing barriers to competition and enterprise would create more job openings as successful companies grow and new ones emerge. Everyone should be encouraged to acquire a wide range of skills that they update throughout their career, for instance, through subsidised evening classes and training days, online courses and mentoring programmes. While academic qualifications are important, so are practical skills such as computer programming and personal ones such as being pleasant with colleagues and customers.

573 http://www.oecd.org/els/emp/oecdindicatorsofemploymentprotection.htm
574 *Idem*

The unemployed should get more intense coaching. Free training courses that get people into work tend to pay for themselves in extra tax receipts and saved social spending; governments could also offer training loans repayable through the tax system.

Enabling more women to work involves many things, such as better childcare facilities and more flexible working arrangements. Countries ought to learn from more successful ones, notably in Scandinavia. Last but not least, governments need to get rid of tax incentives for early retirement and encourage businesses to keep on older workers. Within companies, senior workers should be able to carry on working for fewer hours at lower wages; pension arrangements tied to final salary should be reformed. The Netherlands has boosted working among older men more than any other EU country over the past twenty years by banning age discrimination, cutting financial incentives to retire early, scrapping early retirement options and setting limits on the receipt of unemployment and disability benefits.[575] It is often hard for governments to know what works and what doesn't. Sometimes they can learn from others, though what works well in one country might not translate well to another. They should also trial policies and then test their effectiveness better, as Chapter 11 explains.

European governments also need to raise the official retirement age, with exceptions for people in particularly physically demanding work. This should start as soon as possible, so that baby boomers also participate. For example, the official retirement age could rise by three months each year until it reaches the age of seventy. So in Britain, where the retirement age is sixty-five in 2014, this would reach seventy by 2029.

In the absence of migration, the working-age population is set to shrink. Without reform, ever fewer workers will have to sustain

---

575   http://www.ft.com/cms/s/0/b12953b8-14a7-11e3-b3db-00144feabdc0.html

ever more pensioners. Radical reforms to get more people into work could partly offset these demographic trends, especially in southern European countries where employment rates are low. In northern European countries where employment rates are generally higher, the biggest boost would come from raising people's actual retirement age (see footnotes for detailed calculations).[576]

Foreign youth

While boosting employment and encouraging people to retire later would make a big difference, migration would also help smooth the adjustment in several ways. However much countries reform, an influx of foreign workers would make it easier to sustain the massed ranks of pensioners. With public debt often high and the cost of paying for the pensions, healthcare and social spending of retiring baby-boomers huge, admitting migrants would spread that cost over

---

576   In 2010, there were 335.8 million people aged 15–64 in the EU and 215.5 million people in work. Without migration, the population aged 15–64 is set to shrink to 300 million by 2030. So without radical reforms, the workforce is set to shrink. But in the very optimistic case that by then everyone aged 15–19 was in education or training as were half of those aged 20–24, the employment rate among 25–64 year olds was 80 per cent and that among 65–69 year olds was 60 per cent, the workforce would actually rise to 231.5 million. If nobody could claim a pension before 65, while 40 per cent of 65–69 year olds did and all those 70 and over did, the number of pensioners would be 102.9 million. So 2.3 workers would be supporting each pensioner. Since northern European countries generally have much higher employment rates, they have less potential to offset the impact of ageing by getting more people into work, although increasing the effective retirement age would still make a big difference. For example, in 2010, 28.9 million people were employed in Britain and 4.5 million in Sweden. If by 2030 they managed to raise employment as described in the paragraph above, employment in Britain would edge up to 29.5 million and they would be supporting 12.4 million pensioners, that is, 2.4 pensioners per workers. In Sweden, employment would still fall to 4.3 million and they would have to support 2.1 million pensioners, or just over two pensioners per worker.

a wider number of taxpayers. Migrants can also play a vital role in caring for the elderly: the population aged eighty and over is set to soar from 23.3 million to 36.4 million, with the biggest increase among those aged eighty-five and over.[577] Migrants' youth is a particular bonus. Healthy economies need a workforce with a wide range of skills and ages: older, more experienced types, as well as young, dynamic workers who are physically and mentally at their peak, keen to work hard to get ahead and can help generate new ideas about how to do things better. With the share of Europe's population aged 20–39 set to slump from 27.3 per cent in 2010 to 21.6 in 2030, young migrants are a perfect fit.[578]

Let me be clear, I am not arguing that migration is a solution to ageing. Nor do I think countries should have specific migration targets. But countries should be much more open towards migration. Ideally, governments should let people come and go freely, as they do across the twenty-eight members of the EU. By 2030, central and eastern Europeans are likely to be much richer, and therefore less tempted by higher wages in western Europe, while the number of young people in those countries is set to plunge – by 40 per cent in the case of Polish twentysomethings. So Europe also needs to open up to the rest of the world.

The Swedish model

The third element of adjusting in a sustainable and flexible to way to changing demography is creating pension systems that are affordable for contributors and adequate for beneficiaries. From an individual perspective, the more you save during your working life, and

---

577   That is, from 4.6 per cent of the population to 7.4 per cent.

578   Without migration, the population aged 15–64 is set to fall by 35.8 million between 2010 and 2030. Of that fall, 30.3 million is among workers aged between 20 and 39, while the population aged 55 and over will increase.

the better those savings are invested, the higher your retirement income will be – and the longer you stay in work, the more you can save and the less time your savings will need to last in retirement. All European governments also provide state pensions. These are generally financed on a "pay-as-you-go" basis – today's workers pay for today's pensioners – with defined benefits: either a flat-rate pension for everyone or one that is linked to earnings. Pay-as-you-go worked a treat when there were lots of workers and few pensioners. But it is a disaster in the making as the baby boomers retire and smaller younger generations are expected to pay for them. Unless governments change their pension systems, the tax burden on workers will become unbearable – and if those pensions are paid for by social-security contributions, their rising cost will price people out of work, adding to the burden on existing workers. Moreover, unless governments act soon, the swelling ranks of pensioners and soon-to-be pensioners will be able to block reforms: in the absence of migration, Eurostat projects that the population aged over fifty-five will soar from three-eighths of the population of voting age in 2010 to just under half in 2030. Over-fifties will by then have a comfortable voting majority.[579]

One way to make reforms future-proof is to adjust pensions automatically in line with the national wage bill that pays for them, how long people stay in work and how long they are expected to live once they retire. That is what Sweden has done since the 1990s. It fixes how much people pay in (rather than how much they take out), so public spending on pensions remains affordable as the population ages. Swedes contribute 16 per cent of their earnings to a pot that pays for today's pensions and is also added to notional personal pension accounts, which look like those in a private pension plan (but without the gouging fees). The notional capital in these accounts increases in

---

579 Personal calculations from Eurostat, Europop2010 (Eurostat Population Projections 2010-based). Code: proj_10c2150zmp

line with the total wage bill in Sweden on which the pension contributions are levied. At retirement, the notional capital is converted into an annuity, an annual payment based on average life expectancy, like in a private pension plan, albeit with the payments actually funded by the contributions of people then working.

Sweden's "notional defined contribution" system has huge advantages. While the 16-per-cent pension contribution is a tax, there is a clear link between how much you put in and how much you get out, so it feels more like compulsory savings. If workers think of it as deferred pay, it will not have the same disincentive effects as the tax wedges discussed earlier. The second big advantage is that provided the workforce remains stable, the capital in the account rises in line with average wages. That gives voters a big incentive to support reforms that boost employment and to allow in migrants who will help pay their pensions. A third bonus is that the system adjusts automatically to an ageing population: lower pension contributions translate into lower payouts and longer life expectancy leads to lower annuity payments. Fourth, the system gives people an incentive to stay working if they want a higher pension. Unlike in most pension systems, which give workers an incentive to retire sooner rather than later, those who carry on working accumulate both a bigger notional account and, because they retire later, a higher annuity payment on that account. Fifth, as *The Economist* notes, the system "avoids costly procrastination and piecemeal interventions by politicians".[580] No system is insulated from the pressure of lobby groups, but because Sweden's system is transparent and its costs and benefits to everyone are clear, it is less susceptible to capture than opaque systems where, for instance, pensioner lobbies can sucker people with sob stories about

---

580   See *The Economist*, "The autopilot solution", 2 February 2013. http://www.economist.com/news/finance-and-economics/21571116-how-notional-savings-accounts-could-put-state-pensions-sustainable

poor pensioners to justify measures that actually benefit rich ones. There is much to recommend the Swedish model.

Unpredictable adjustment: climate change

While it is impossible to know how many and which migrants will be willing and able to come work in Europe over the next fifteen years, many of the parameters of how Europe's population is set to age are reasonably predictable. But in other areas, economies need to adjust in conditions of radical uncertainty. Climate change is a good example.

Environmentalists tend to argue that Europe needs to act now to reduce greenhouse-gas emissions as if there were great certainty about how best to proceed.[581] By and large, they backed the EU's emissions-trading scheme, which was meant to curb emissions in a predictable and cost-effective way by putting a market price on them. They support specific targets for reducing the emissions produced in Europe and further ones for how those reductions should be achieved, notably by increasing the share of renewable energy and improving energy efficiency. Many categorically reject certain types of emissions-reducing alternatives, notably nuclear power and shale gas. In essence, they tend to have a rigid, command-and-control mentality, which presumes that they know best what needs to happen and how.

Sceptics, who have multiplied during the crisis, point out that every aspect of the issue is shrouded in uncertainty and that current policies are both costly and ineffective. Scientists have only a limited understanding of how today's climate works and even less grasp of how it might change in future. The sensitivity of the global climate to

---

581   See, for instance, Friends of the Earth Europe, "2030 Climate and Energy Policy: The Time is Now", May 2013 http://www.foeeurope.org/sites/default/files/publications/2030_briefing_may2013.pdf and Greenpeace EU, "The Next Step in Europe's Climate Action: Setting Targets for 2030", June 2013 http://www.green-peace.org/eu-unit/Global/eu-unit/reports-briefings/2013/ecofys_PolicyPaper.pdf

rising levels of carbon dioxide in the atmosphere is highly uncertain and the local impacts are even more unpredictable. For example, contrary to climatologists' predictions, global temperatures have scarcely risen over the past decade, yet paradoxically sea ice in the Arctic is melting much faster than they expected.[582] The most recent report by the Intergovernmental Panel on Climate Change (IPCC) highlights that the many of the predictions in previous reports are actually much less certain than they claimed.[583] This is red meat for sceptics, some of whom don't believe that man-made climate change is actually happening. Sceptics can also point to the many follies of EU climate policy, such as massive subsidies for biofuels, or the fact that Germany subsidises both clean energy and filthy coal.

While both sides are partly right – environmentalists are right to worry about climate change, sceptics that current climate policies are often misconceived – both their arguments are flawed. The case for curbing climate change is not that its consequences are certain. Nor is the uncertainty about its impact an argument for inaction. Rather, the case for action is that the consequences of climate change are highly uncertain and could be catastrophic. Since the only liveable planet we know of is Earth, it makes sense to take out insurance against disaster. But as with any insurance policy, you want it to provide effective cover at as low a cost as possible. Since we don't know how best to proceed, rigid bureaucratic prescriptions are not the solution. Ineffective policies are not just a waste of money, they are politically corrosive. Unfortunately, both environmentalists and well-meaning EU officials are often the worst enemies of sensible climate policy.

---

582   http://www.economist.com/news/leaders/21574490-climate-change-may-be-happening-more-slowly-scientists-thought-world-still-needs

583   http://www.ipcc.ch/?utm_source=Newsletter&utm_campaign=525d05a1c0-June_Mailout7_5_2013&utm_medium=email&utm_term=0_b63698abdf-525d05a1c0-61519721

With so much uncertainty, what is the best way to proceed? To insure ourselves against a potential climate catastrophe, the level of carbon dioxide and other greenhouse gases in the atmosphere needs to be capped. This will only happen if all major economies curb their emissions. While Europe is responsible for a big chunk of the increase in carbon dioxide in the atmosphere since the Industrial Revolution, it accounts for a diminishing share of new emissions – less than a seventh. Emission reductions in Europe over the past two decades have scarcely offset a much bigger rise in the rest of the world, not least China and other fast-growing emerging economies. Since it doesn't make a blind bit of difference to the planet what Europe's share of global emissions is, European policy can only be effective if it encourages others to curb their emissions too. In other words, it must either stimulate the development and spread of low-carbon technologies and energy sources that are cheaper than existing ones or spur other countries to adopt policies that make emitting carbon more expensive. Nothing else will make much difference.

In practice, though, EU policies have had scarcely any impact on the rest of the world – indeed, they have arguably increased global emissions. The EU led the big push towards a global deal on limiting carbon emissions, but its efforts in Copenhagen in 2009 and the jamborees since then have so far achieved little. It has also set a target of reducing carbon emissions in Europe by 20 per cent from 1990 levels by 2020, with further cuts mooted by 2030. But while emissions generated by production in Europe have fallen, those generated by Europeans' consumption have soared. For example, "carbon production" in Britain fell by 15 per cent between 1990 and 2005, while "carbon consumption" rose by 19 per cent, according to Dieter Helm of Oxford University, author of *The Carbon Crunch: How We're Getting Climate Change Wrong – And How to Fix It*.[584] Shifting production of

---

584   Dieter Helm, *The Carbon Crunch: How We're Getting Climate Change Wrong – And How to Fix It*, Yale: 2012

carbon-intensive goods abroad does no good to the planet whatsoever – in fact, it makes things worse if they are produced in a more polluting manner elsewhere. Worse still, carbon production in the energy sector is now rising again because of the failure of the EU's flagship emissions-trading scheme and the shale-gas bonanza in the United States. The explosive growth of shale gas in the US has caused gas prices there to plunge, leading power companies and other industrial users to replace coal with cheaper gas. As a result, US carbon emissions have fallen, because shale gas generates only half the carbon emissions of coal. Meanwhile, the surplus coal is being shipped to Europe, where gas remains expensive and the cost of burning coal has fallen as the price of carbon emissions on ETS has plunged (because too many emissions permits have been doled out). So while America is shifting to cheaper, lower-carbon gas, Europe is burning more filthy coal.[585] Ironically, then, despite all the EU's costly policies, America is becoming greener and Europe less so.

As well as seeking to cut carbon emissions produced in Europe by 20 per cent, the EU aims to meet 20 per cent of Europe's energy needs from renewable sources.[586] In principle, creating a guaranteed market for renewable energy could stimulate innovation and generate economies of scale, together creating new and cheaper alternatives to fossil fuels. But in practice, it has often led to exorbitant and often misdirected subsidies for substandard technologies. Cloudy Germany is now covered with pricey solar panels. Offshore wind farms in Britain generate eye-wateringly expensive electricity intermittently. In a return to pre-industrial ways, Europe is now burning vast amounts of wood. Specific subsidies and targets for biofuels that by some reckonings generate even higher emissions than fossil fuels displace crop production, pushing up food prices. Meanwhile, Angela Merkel has

585   International Energy Authority, Medium-term coal market report, 2012

586   10 per cent in the transport sector.

committed Germany to phasing out one economical form of zero-carbon energy: nuclear power. France and Bulgaria have imposed a moratorium on developing shale gas, which is much cleaner than coal and a backstop to intermittent wind and solar power. Some greens lobby against capturing and storing the emissions generated by burning coal, a technology that is in any case not yet economical. In short, Europe is neither a global leader in developing low-carbon technologies that could be deployed elsewhere, nor a role model for the rest of the world in crafting low-emissions policies.

Tax carbon consumption

How could Europe do better? It is worth persevering with efforts to agree a global deal to limit carbon emissions; the chances of success are slim but the costs of trying are low. More importantly, the EU should provide incentives for research into low-carbon technologies. As well as traditional research funding, why not offer prizes for developing promising new technologies? If that research bears fruit, it would more than pay for itself from the profits of deploying those new technologies worldwide. The next step is to jettison the ineffective, corporate boondoggle that is the ETS and replace it with a tax on carbon consumption. A carbon tax that rose steadily over time would provide some predictability for businesses, enable them to better plan long-term investments and encourage them to try to develop new low-carbon technologies. It would also give clean-tech companies a good idea of the price target they need to achieve to be competitive, allowing them to raise funds and have a go at developing promising technologies. Importantly, governments wouldn't be trying to second-guess the best technologies or pick winners among the many clean-tech companies. A carbon tax would be flexible: it could be raised or lowered at will, depending on how conditions evolve. It would be transparent and impartial, imposing the same price on all firms, with no opaque special favours for politically connected companies. And it would provide revenues that would enable governments to cut other taxes, rather than providing corporate handouts to polluters as ETS emissions permits do.

A tax on carbon consumption would be better than both the ETS and a tax on carbon production because it would actually reduce Europeans' carbon emissions, rather than shifting them overseas (or achieving very little). While taxing carbon production would have a similar impact if the whole world was doing it, taxing carbon consumption is much more effective if only Europe and a few others are going ahead first. Better still, it doesn't put European companies, or production in Europe more generally, at a disadvantage. Carbon-intensive products consumed by Europeans would be taxed whether they were made in Europe, America, China or elsewhere. As a result, carbon-intensive European companies would have less incentive to lobby politicians against putting a price on carbon and politicians would no longer have an incentive to impose protectionist "border-adjustment taxes" on carbon-intensive imports. Instead, the carbon consumption tax could be levied much like value-added tax is, on local as well as foreign production. Better still, with the EU single market still the world's biggest, EU standards often have a global impact, because firms that invest in tailoring their products for the European market then sell them elsewhere too. So a carbon-consumption tax would encourage firms everywhere to make their products in a low-carbon way, to gain a cost advantage in EU markets. Once that investment is made, it tends to be cheaper to deploy it elsewhere too.

Dynamic adaptability
This chapter has set out how to make our economies better able to cope with and adjust to change. Reducing our reliance on debt would make the financial system and the economy as a whole less fragile.

Ending the tax bias towards debt in general and property speculation in particular would make a big difference. When financial crashes do occur, governments should tackle excessive debts head on and support the economy fiscally rather than exclusively by monetary means. Both labour and capital need to be more versatile to cope with reasonably predictable variability, and the new sharing economy offers huge potential for growth. As workforces shrink and societies age in pretty predictable ways, economies need to adjust by getting more people into work, admitting more newcomers and reforming pension systems. Last but not least, to cope with radically uncertain climate change, Europe needs better incentives for research and a tax on carbon consumption.

Adaptability is a key feature of a successful advanced economy; dynamism another. Adaptability involves coping with and making the most of changing circumstances; dynamism is about trying to change those conditions by crafting new opportunities. To put it differently, if the economy was a stable system that had settled down in equilibrium, there would be no forces requiring it to adapt. But a dynamic economy would continually propel itself forward, as innovators and entrepreneurs, policymakers and citizens try to improve things. Thus while an economy needs to be adaptable in order to be dynamic, it isn't sufficient.

11

DYNAMIC

How to create new ideas and businesses

There's a temptation in our networked age to think that ideas can be developed by e-mail and iChat. That's crazy. Creativity comes from spontaneous meetings, from random discussions. You run into someone, you ask what they're doing, you say 'Wow', and soon you're cooking up all sorts of ideas.

Steve Jobs, co-founder of Apple[587]

Capitalism... is by nature a form or method of economic change and not only never is but never can be stationary... The fundamental impulse that sets and keeps the capitalist engine in motion comes from the new consumers' goods, the new methods of production or transportation, the new markets, the new forms of industrial organisation that capitalist enterprise creates...

---

587   Quoted in http://www.thetimes.co.uk/tto/opinion/columnists/danielfinkel-stein/article3865753.ece

The opening up of new markets, foreign or domestic, and the organisational development from the craft shop and factory to such concerns as U.S. Steel illustrate the same process of industrial mutation... that incessantly revolutionises the economic structure from within, incessantly destroying the old one, incessantly creating a new one. This process of Creative Destruction is the essential fact about capitalism. It is what capitalism consists in and what every capitalist concern has got to live in.

Joseph Schumpeter, *Capitalism, Socialism and Democracy*, 1942[588]

To get a glimpse of Europe's future, you need to get down and party. Hackers, coders, gamers, developers, designers, DJs, technologists, entrepreneurs – they come together from all over Europe each year at Campus Party for a week of inspiring talks, eye-opening demos, informal networking and creative sparking. Even in a digital age, meeting face to face counts. In September 2013 they congregated in London for the first time, at the magnificent O2 Arena in Greenwich. The buzz was incredible. Against a backdrop of pessimism and high unemployment, young Europeans are determined to build a brighter digital future. Their modest agenda: to revolutionise the economy and society, everything from education, entertainment and e-commerce to design, drones and big data.

Where do new ideas come from – and how do they generate economic growth? These are perhaps the most important questions in economics, yet orthodox theory has very little to say about them. Statistically, most growth in advanced economies is accounted for by "total factor productivity growth" – generating more output for a given input of capital and labour – but that is just a black box. In

---

588 Joseph Schumpeter, *Capitalism, Socialism and Democracy*, Routledge: 1942 pp. 82–83.

effect, new technologies are assumed to fall like manna from heaven. A slightly more sophisticated analysis emphasises the importance of investment in both skills and research and development (R&D). That view is reflected in European policymaking. In the EU's ten-year plan for delivering "smart, sustainable and inclusive growth", the Europe 2020 programme, the two targets for delivering smart growth are raising the proportion of Europeans who graduate from university to 40 per cent and boosting investment in R&D to 3 per cent of GDP.[589] But while investment in skills and research can be important, they are merely inputs to innovation. What really matters are the process and outcomes: how new ideas come about and how they shake up the economy to make people better off.

A fundamental fallacy of orthodox economics is viewing economies as computable machines that tend towards a steady state. A theoretical framework that suggests economies naturally settle down is going to find it hard to explain disruptive innovation and enterprise as anything more than a contrived device. But in fact, economies are dynamic organisms that are forever evolving in unpredictable ways as the millions of human beings within them interact. As people spark off each other, they generate lots of new ideas. Enterprising individuals, businesses and organisations try some of them out. Some succeed, most don't. When markets work well, they ruthlessly weed out bad ideas and propagate successful ones across the economy as innovative, enterprising companies grow and their competitors imitate them. Old ways of doing things are discarded and better new ones replace them. (Sometimes, though, the financial system propagates bad ideas like a virus, as previous chapters explained.) Thus economic growth is an ongoing voyage of discovery into an unknowable future, fuelled by

---

589   The education targets are reducing the rates of early school leaving below 10 per cent and at least 40 per cent of 30-34–year-olds completing third-level education. http://ec.europa.eu/europe2020/europe-2020-in-a-nutshell/targets/index_en.htm

ingenuity and energy, trialled by enterprising businesses and stimulated by competition within a framework of supportive institutions. In effect, it is a bit like evolution, which proceeds by mutation, selection and replication. While I do not agree with much of what Joseph Schumpeter wrote, his insight in 1942 that capitalism is an evolutionary process of continuous innovation and creative destruction seems fundamentally correct.

Developing economies can grow simply by imitating what works well in more advanced ones – as can the less developed parts of every advanced economy. Advanced ones can also inch forward by making incremental improvements to existing ways of doing things. But to grow fast, dynamic economies need to generate lots of genuinely new – and often disruptive – ideas. While these sometimes arrive from individual geniuses coming up with incredible insights in isolation, they mostly emerge from creative collisions between people, as the Steve Jobs quote at the top of the chapter suggests. For those interactions to be fruitful, people need to bring something extra to the party. The saying "two heads are better than one" is true only if the two heads think differently. So to generate lots of new ideas, you need to bring lots of people with different talents and viewpoints together. That's why diverse cities and people from different disciplines working together are so important. Before discussing how new ideas emerge, let's quickly review where Europe stands on the standard measures of innovation.

Not so novel

Measuring innovation is fraught with difficulties. Start with inputs such as education and R&D. In terms of schooling, Finland ranks highest in Europe in science and maths; Britain is strong in science but not maths; while both the US and southern Europe lag.[590] Nearly

---

590   http://www.oecd.org/site/innovationstrategy/45187823.pdf

all Finns graduate from secondary school and the Irish do nearly as well; together with the Danes, those two also have the highest university graduation rates. Here too the US is a laggard, and Germany is among the worst, far behind Spain and Italy.[591] But in terms of doctorates, Sweden tops the list and Germany also scores highly, while the US is middle-ranking.[592] As far as R&D spending goes, the EU's was estimated at 23.4 per cent of the global total in 2013, down from 24.8 per cent in 2010, according to Battelle, a US technology research group.[593] China's was up to 14.7 per cent and the US down to a projected 28 per cent. The EU spent 2 per cent of its GDP on R&D in 2010, much less than the US's 2.79 per cent in 2008.[594] Finland spent most (3.87 per cent), followed by Sweden (3.42 per cent); Britain spent 1.77 per cent and Italy a mere 1.26 per cent. Clearly, skills and R&D are important, but they don't guarantee results. Students may be good at passing tests but lack questioning minds that think creatively; often, R&D yields no benefits. Conversely, despite generally poor education results, the US is very innovative, while many firms innovate without doing any R&D.[595]

Gauging how much innovation takes place is just as tricky. This can take many different forms: new or better products, a novel or better service or experience, a superior production process, a more efficient supply chain. Frugal innovation involves making a much cheaper, basic version of an existing product, as Tata did with its £1,000 Nano car. Business models can be innovative, such as giving away a product

591   http://www.oecd.org/site/innovationstrategy/45187845.pdf

592   http://www.oecd.org/site/innovationstrategy/45187873.pdf

593   http://www.ft.com/cms/s/0/c74be3b8-adc3-11e2-a2c7-00144feabdc0.html

594   http://epp.eurostat.ec.europa.eu/statistics_explained/index.php?title= File:Gross_domestic_expenditure_on_R%26D,_2000-2010_%28%25_share_of_ GDP%29.png

595   http://www.oecd.org/site/innovationstrategy/45183382.pdf

for free and earning money from associated ones. So can business formats. In retailing, huge hypermarkets vastly increased productivity and satisfied consumers' desire for a good-value, one-stop shop. More recently, traditional retailers have responded to competition from online ones such as Amazon through hybrid distribution models, where customers order online and collect in store. The most famous institutional innovations date back centuries: limited-liability companies enabled businesses to tap a much wider pool of capital and thus expand more rapidly; stockmarkets allowed shares to be traded easily and cheaply. Social enterprises, self-financing (and therefore scalable) business ventures that serve a social purpose, are a more recent one.

The standard measure of innovation – patents – captures only a fraction of this. For what it's worth, Europe's share of global patent applications was 6.7 per cent in 2011, down from 7.6 per cent in 2008, with China's proportion climbing to almost a quarter, from 15.1 per cent in 2008. Moreover, counting patents doesn't distinguish between big leaps forward and insignificant ones. "Triadic patents" that have been registered in Europe, the US and Japan may be more important than most. The US notched up 53.5 per million inhabitants in 2005–7, ahead of the EU's 30.3. But individual European countries are far ahead: Switzerland managed 119.7 per million and Sweden 87.8. Britain had a paltry 27.9 and Italy only 13.2.[596] Yet many truly great breakthroughs aren't patented at all: think of Crick and Watson's discovery of the molecular structure of DNA, the basis of much of biotechnology, or Tim Berners-Lee's invention of the World Wide Web and hence the internet.

Perhaps the best long-term yardstick of an advanced economy's dynamism – its ability to generate new ideas and deploy them across the economy – is labour productivity growth. Even so, it is subject to all the same measurement problems as GDP (see Chapter 9). In the

---

596 http://www.oecd.org/site/innovationstrategy/45184357.pdf

short term, moreover, it is distorted by changes in employment: as less productive workers start working, they drag down the economy-wide average (and conversely, firing the least productive people can boost average productivity). With those provisos, the productivity figures presented in Chapter 1 are deeply worrying. Productivity growth in Europe has slackened over the past fifteen years, especially since the crisis. Europe urgently needs to innovate more, starting in creative cities.

Creative cities

The stimulus for innovation may be a questioning mind, a pressing demand for solutions to problems, or the pressure of competition. Fostering creative thinking among students is therefore much more fruitful than rote learning. Often, innovation comes from entrepreneurs' desire to steal a march on their rivals. So their energies need to be unleashed. Remarkably, around 15 per cent of technical change in Europe can be attributed directly to competition from Chinese imports. Firms have responded to the threat of Chinese imports by increasing their productivity through adopting better information technology, higher spending on R&D and increased patenting.[597] So opening up the economy and boosting competition more generally are vital for innovation and growth in Europe.

Wherever the demand for innovation comes from, it tends to be supplied in cities. Jane Jacobs, a great American urbanist, pointed this out in the 1960s.[598] More recent research by Ed Glaeser of Harvard University documents this. In his masterful *Triumph of the City: How*

---

597   Nick Bloom, Mirko Draca and John Van Reenen, "Trade Induced Technical Change: The Impact of Chinese Imports on Innovation and Productivity", CEPR Discussion Paper No. 1000, 2011 http://www.voxeu.org/article/who-s-afraid-big-bad-dragon-how-chinese-trade-boosts-european-innovation

598   Jane Jacobs, *The Death and Life of Great American Cities*, Random House: 1961

Our Greatest Invention Makes Us Richer, Smarter, Greener, Healthier and Happier, he explains how most innovation takes place in diverse, densely populated cities, where people are forever interacting with each other and experiencing new things.[599] "We are a social species and we learn by being around clever people," he observes.[600] "Cities have long sped this flow of ideas. Eighteenth-century Birmingham saw textile innovators borrow each other's insights – and gave us the industrial revolution... Physical proximity allows the free flow of goods, services and ideas – and this powers the collaboration that creates everything from Ford's Model T to Facebook, and economic growth too." Even most advances in agricultural technology have been developed in cities.

Denser cities are more inventive. Patent rates (patents per person) tend to rise by 20–30 per cent for each doubling of the number of employed people per square kilometre, according to Gerald Carlino of the Federal Reserve Bank of Philadelphia. This outsize contribution will surely grow as economies become more knowledge-based.[601] Cities not only generate many more new ideas. They rapidly disseminate them too. When one firm comes up with a new technique, product or design, nearby ones tend to quickly imitate or improve on it. As Alfred Marshall, a British economist, observed in 1890, "When an industry has thus chosen a locality for itself, it is likely to stay there long: so great are the advantages which people following the same skilled trade get from near neighbourhood to one another. The mysteries of

599   Edward Glaeser, *Triumph of the City: How Our Greatest Invention Makes Us Richer, Smarter, Greener, Healthier and Happier*, Macmillan: 2011

600   http://www.ft.com/cms/s/0/d6074404-48f5-11e0-af8c-00144feab49a.html

601   http://www.economist.com/news/business/21581695-city-leaders-are-increasingly-adopting-business-methods-and-promoting-business-mayors-and-mammon

the trade become no mysteries; but are as it were in the air, and children learn many of them unconsciously."[602]

While the internet makes it easier to collaborate from afar, interacting face to face remains crucial. Despite the huge costs of being in Silicon Valley, technologists still congregate there. Isolating yourself makes you less influential: one study finds that when a prominent researcher moves to another city, their patents are less likely to be cited by peers in their previous city.[603] Moreover, innovation today often requires an ever-larger crowd of experts, preferably working nearby. Benjamin Jones of Northwestern University finds that it takes ever more people to produce new research, a trend he attributes to the increasing "burden of knowledge" associated with rising technological complexity and an expanding knowledge base.[604]

One reason why Europe is not as innovative as America – in particular, why it has nowhere that rivals Silicon Valley – is that its digital innovators are spread across many locations, where there is not a dense enough network to produce as many new ideas. Ed Glaeser and Matthew Resseger of Harvard University find that in highly skilled areas, city size explains 45 per cent of the variation in worker productivity.[605] It's not just that smart workers choose to live in bigger cities. The cities themselves seem to promote learning: newcomers tend to enjoy faster wage growth over time. The McKinsey Global Institute

602   Alfred Marshall, *Principles of Economics*, 1890

603   Pierre Azoulay, Joshua Graff Zivin and Bhaven Sampat, "The diffusion of scientific knowledge across time and space: Evidence from professional transitions for the superstars of medicine", NBER Working Paper #16683, January 2011

604   Benjamin Jones, "The burden of knowledge and the 'death of the renaissance man': Is innovation getting harder?", *Review of Economic Studies*, 2009. Quoted in http://www.economist.com/node/21564536.

605   Edward Glaeser and Matthew Resseger, "The complementarity between cities and skills", National Bureau of Economic Research Working Paper #15103, June 2009

reckons that around three-quarters of the productivity gap between the US and Europe is due to Europe's relatively small cities.[606]

At the very least, then, Europe should stop subsidising people to stay in rural areas. The Common Agricultural Policy, a monstrous protectionist racket, is a brake on economic growth. Governments should also lift barriers that prevent cities from growing in size and density. Paris is like a museum preserved in aspic; not all of it is beautiful and needs to be kept intact. London is constrained by the often mucky green belt that surrounds it. Planning restrictions and zoning laws ought to be relaxed: by limiting the supply of property and driving up its cost, they price out creative people. This "regulatory tax" amounts to over 300 per cent in the office markets of Frankfurt, Paris and Milan, according to a 2008 study by Paul Cheshire and Christian Hilber of the London School of Economics.[607] One reason why Berlin is the most creative city in Germany is that rents are cheap. Likewise, London's Tech City sprung up in Hoxton because rents were affordable.

No silo

A single-industry town is much less creative than a metropolis where lots of different people jostle together. Breakthrough ideas generally occur when people from different disciplines interact and bring concepts from one field into a new, unfamiliar territory, as Frans Johansson documents in *The Medici Effect: Breakthrough Insights at the Intersection of Ideas, Concepts, and Cultures*.[608] He asked Alan Leshner, the

---

606   James Manyika, Jaana Remes, Richard Dobbs, Javier Orellana and Fabian Schaer, "Urban America: US cities in the global economy", McKinsey Global Institute, April 2012

607   Paul Cheshire and Christian Hilber, "Office space supply restrictions in Britain: The political economy of market revenge", *Economic Journal*, 2008

608   Frans Johansson, *The Medici Effect: Breakthrough Insights at the Intersection of Ideas, Concepts, and Cultures*, Harvard Business School: 2004

chief executive of the American Association for the Advancement of Science (AAAS), the world's largest science organisation, what the future holds for scientific discoveries within disciplines. "Disciplinary science has died," Leshner replied. "It's gone. Most major advancements involve multiple disciplines. It is rarer and rarer to see single-author papers. And often the multiple authors are from different disciplines." For precisely that reason, the Santa Fe Institute in New Mexico devotes itself to the "creation of a new kind of scientific research community pursuing emerging syntheses in science." For example, biologists work with economists and stockmarket analysts to generate new ideas about how markets behave. "The models we use to explain the evolution of financial strategies are mathematically similar to the equations biologists use to understand populations of predator-prey systems, competing systems, and symbiotic systems," says Robert Hagstrom of Legg Mason Focus Capital. The European Institute at the London School of Economics, where I had the honour of being a visiting fellow from 2007 to 2010, follows a similar multidisciplinary approach.

In *Imagine: How Creativity Works*, Jonah Lehrer documents the importance of different perspectives in generating creative solutions.[609] 3M, an old but not staid American conglomerate, encourages its employees to take risks. It spends a lot on research – and also expects workers to spend around 15 per cent of their time pursuing speculative ideas. Most of these efforts fail, but some, such as masking tape, an early 3M product, generate profit for the company. A much newer firm, Google, has gone further. It encourages its employees to spend 20 per cent of their time experimenting with their own ideas. Among many things, this generated Gmail, the world's most popular online email service. As *The Economist* notes, "The reason why this approach works... is because many breakthroughs come when people venture

---

609   Jonah Lehrer, *Imagine: How Creativity Works*, Houghton Mifflin Harcourt: 2012

beyond their area of expertise. Often it takes an outsider to ask the kind of dumb questions that may yield an unconventional solution."[610]

Another way in which tech employees are encouraged to pursue their own experiments is at hackathons, programming marathons followed by brief presentations and often prizes too.[611] Corporate hackathons are now commonplace, including at Twitter, Facebook, Google, Yahoo, LinkedIn and eBay. Through LinkedIn's InCubator, creators of top experiments can get up to three months to develop their ideas, along with coaching from founder Reid Hoffman.

Creativity is partly innate, but it can also be nurtured by an education system and work environment that encourage people to question established ways and think for themselves. Young people tend to be the most innovative thinkers in nearly any field, from physics to music, Lehrer notes. The ignorance of youth "comes with creative advantages", as the young are less jaded by custom and experience. But anyone can stay creative as long as they work "to maintain the perspective of the outsider". This can be done by considering new problems at work (3M regularly rotates its engineers from division to division), travelling to new countries or simply spending more time staring "at things we don't fully understand". Thus another reason why cities are such potent drivers of productivity is that they expose people to unexpected experiences and force the exchange of ideas. Among the policies Lehrer calls for to boost our "collective creativity" is increased immigration.

The diversity dividend

Along with density and different disciplines, the third key ingredient of innovation is diversity. Since I first wrote about this in *Immigrants:*

---

610   http://www.economist.com/node/21550235

611   http://www.wired.co.uk/news/archive/2013-08/22/20-percent-time-here-to-stay

Your Country Needs Them in 2006, there has been a huge amount of research backing up my case that both immigrants individually and the interaction between diverse people more generally generate new ideas. As Scott Page, a professor of complex systems, political science and economics at the University of Michigan, Ann Arbor and also a faculty member at the Santa Fe Institute, explains in *The Difference: How the Power of Diversity Creates Better Groups, Firms, Schools, and Societies,* groups that display a range of perspectives outperform groups of like-minded experts.[612] His research shows that "organisations, firms and universities that solve problems should seek out people with diverse experiences, training and identities that translate into diverse perspectives and heuristics." Adding women to an all-male corporate board, a minister educated in a Northern state school to a cabinet full of privately educated Southerners and people with diverse cultural backgrounds to a team of locals boosts productivity as well as equal opportunities. New ideas tend to come from the creative exchange between people of different viewpoints, backgrounds, cultures, educations and experiences. It's what makes a global city like London so creative, despite the fact that so many talented people are diverted into finance. It's why Berlin is more innovative than Frankfurt.

Donald Campbell, one of the leading psychologists in creativity research in the sixties, concluded that "persons who have been uprooted from traditional cultures, or who have been thoroughly exposed to two or more cultures, seem to have the advantage in the range of hypotheses they are apt to consider, and through this means, in the frequency of creative innovation."[613] Simply by being aware that

---

612   Scott Page, *The Difference: How the Power of Diversity Creates Better Groups, Firms, Schools, and Societies,* Princeton: 2007

613   Donald Campbell, "Blind Variation and Selective Retention in Creative Thought as in Other Knowledge Processes", *Psychological Review* 67, no. 6 (1960): 380–400.

there are several ways of approaching a problem, someone from a multicultural background is more likely to view any situation from multiple perspectives. "The mere fact that an individual is different from most people around him promotes more open and divergent, perhaps even rebellious, thinking in that person. Such a person is more prone to question traditions, rules, and boundaries – and to search for answers where others may not think to."[614] People who are fluent in several languages also tend to be more creative. "Languages codify concepts differently, and the ability to draw upon these varied perspectives during a creative process generates a wider range of associations," Johansson notes.

Diversity can also act as a magnet for the innovative, entrepreneurial talents of what Richard Florida calls the "creative class". "A great city has two hallmarks: tolerance for strangers and intolerance for mediocrity. These are precisely the qualities that appeal to members of the creative class – and they also happen to be qualities conducive to innovation, risk-taking, and the formation of new businesses."[615]

The boost to innovation from diversity in general and immigration in particular is potentially huge. They are associated with increased patenting as well as higher productivity. While the benefits are typically biggest in America, they are significant in Europe too – and they could be even greater with a change of policies and cultural mindset.

An exhaustive study by Richard B. Freeman and Wei Huang of over 1.5 million scientific papers written in the US between 1985 and 2008 found that those co-authored by people of different ethnic backgrounds tended to be published in higher-impact journals and cited more often, leading them to conclude that "diversity in inputs into

614   Dean Simonton, *Origins of Genius*, Oxford: 1999

615   Richard Florida, *The Rise Of The Creative Class: And How It's Transforming Work, Leisure, Community And Everyday Life*, Basic Books: 2002

papers leads to greater contributions to science."[616] Migrant scientists tend to outperform domestic ones, according to a study of 14,299 scientists across sixteen countries and four fields of science.[617]

More than three in four patents generated at the top ten patent-producing US universities had at least one foreign-born inventor in 2011, according to a study by the Partnership for a New America.[618] For example, Chinese-born Wenyuan Shi, a professor at the University of California, Los Angeles, developed an ingredient in a lollipop that works as a dental treatment for children and has since started a business to commercialise it. More than half of all patents were awarded to students, postdoctoral fellows and staff researchers, a group more likely to face immigration problems, rather than to professors.[619] Foreign-born inventors are especially important in cutting-edge fields such as semiconductors (where they help generate 87 per cent of patents), information technology (84 per cent), pulse and digital communications (83 per cent), pharmaceuticals (79 per cent) and optics (77 per cent). Contrary to the popular perception that only Asian immigrants are innovators, the patents awarded to these top universities boasted inventors from eighty-eight different countries.

Studies show that skilled migrants to the United States boost patent activity – and that foreign graduate students give their universities

---

616   Richard B. Freeman and Wei Huang, "Collaborating with People Like Me: Ethnic co-authorship within the US", NBER working paper #19905, February 2014 http://www.nber.org/papers/w19905

617   Chiara Franzonia, Giuseppe Scellatob and Paula Stephand, "The mover's advantage: The superior performance of migrant scientists", *Economics Letters*, Volume 122, Issue 1, January 2014, Pages 89–93 http://www.sciencedirect.com/science/article/pii/S0165176513004874

618   http://www.renewoureconomy.org/research/patent-pending-how-immigrants-are-reinventing-the-american-economy-2/ 76 per cent of patents, to be precise.

619   54 per cent of all patents, to be exact.

an especially big lift.[620] They make a greater contribution to scientific publications and citations than their US-born counterparts. A 10 per cent fall in the share of doctoral students who are foreign leads to a 5–6 per cent decline in science and engineering output by US universities.[621] The critical factor is the diversity of national origin among researchers and the complementarities that this creates.[622] Another study finds that increasing the share of migrant graduates in the US population by one percentage point lifts the patent rate by at least 6 per cent – and perhaps as much as 18 per cent due to positive spillovers to fellow US-born researchers, the attaining of a critical mass in specialised fields and contributions in complementary fields such as management and entrepreneurship.[623]

Globally, around 30 per cent of Nobel laureates were living outside their country of birth at the time of their award. They include Professor Venkatraman Ramakrishnan, who received the 2009 Nobel Prize in chemistry for his studies of ribosomes, the parts of living cells that translate genetic information into proteins. He was born in India, studied in the US and works in Britain at the Laboratory of Molecular Biology at Cambridge University. Like many Nobel

---

620   A 10 per cent increase in international graduate students would raise patent applications by 3.3 per cent, university patent grants by 6.0 per cent and non-university patent grants by 4.0 per cent. G. Chellaraj, KE Maskus & A Mattoo, "The contribution of skilled immigration and international graduate students to U.S. innovation"', *Review of International Economics* 16(3), 444-462, 2008

621   Keith Maskus, Ahmed Mobarak, Eric Stuen, "Skilled Immigration and Innovation: Evidence from Enrollment Fluctuations in U.S. Doctoral Programs", CEPR Discussion Paper 7709, February 2010 http://ideas.repec.org/p/cpr/ceprdp/7709.html

622   *Idem*

623   J Hunt, and M. Gauthier-Loiselle, "How much does immigration boost innovation?", *American Economic Journal*, 2010

laureates, Professor Ramakrishnan has been a prolific inventor and applied for numerous patents.[624]

Using a global patents database, Carsten Fink, Ernest Miguelez and Julio Raffo of the World Intellectual Property Organisation (WIPO) find that in the US, by far the most popular destination for migrant inventors, migrants account for 18 per cent of all inventors.[625] While more inventors emigrate from Britain, Germany and France than move there, the first two do receive quite a few immigrant ones. Andre Geim, a Russian-born physicist at the University of Manchester, won a Nobel in 2010 for developing graphene, a revolutionary super-material that has all sorts of potential applications. He is not alone: 12 per cent of all inventors in Britain are immigrants. In some smaller European countries – notably Belgium (19 per cent), Ireland (20 per cent) and Switzerland (38 per cent) – immigrants account for an even bigger share of inventors than they do in America. Unfortunately, foreigners account for only 3–6 per cent of inventors in Germany, France, Italy and Spain. Worse, Geim warns that new UK restrictions on non-EU migrants, including minimum salary requirements of at least £31,000 and tighter student visa rules, are blocking the brightest sparks from working at British universities. Had the restrictions been in place at the time, he says, they would have prevented him and his team from identifying graphene.[626]

In Europe, diversity is beneficial at an economy-wide level, in specific sectors and within individual firms. Francesc Ortega from the City University of New York and Giovanni Peri of the University of California at Davis find that an increased share of skilled migrants

---

624   Based on information available at http://www.nobelprize.org/.

625   Carsten Fink, Ernest Miguelez, Julio Raffo, "The global race for inventors", Vox.eu, 17 July 2013 http://www.voxeu.org/article/global-race-inventors

626   http://www.independent.co.uk/news/uk/politics/nobel-winner-slates-britains-stupid-immigration-reforms-8433324.html

boosted economy-wide productivity across advanced OECD economies between 1980 and 2005.[627] Critics often cite a paper by Alberto
Alesina of Harvard, who found that ethno-linguistic diversity had a
negative impact on economic growth.[628] But as I argued in *Immigrants*,
that is comparing apples and pears.[629] Longstanding divisions within
countries – polarised relations between whites and the descendants of
African American slaves in the US, the ethnic and linguistic antago-
nism between Flemish people and Walloons in Belgium – may very
well be harmful; that does not mean the impact of diverse newcomers
is. Indeed, new research by Alesina himself confirms this. His more
recent study finds that "diversity of skilled immigration has a positive
impact on the income and productivity levels of the richer countries in
our sample."[630] Alessandra Venturini of the University of Torino and
others find that migrants in Britain, France and Germany boost innovation in particular sectors too.[631] For example, highly skilled migrants
in Britain boost patent applications. In Germany, they are a particular
boon in the high-tech sector. Such sectoral studies underestimate the
broader impact of immigrants on innovation, as they omit the spillovers across sectors and disciplines that are so vital. In the Netherlands,

627   Francesc Ortega and Giovanni Peri, "The effects of Brain Gain on Growth,
Investment, and Employment: Evidence from the OECD countries, 1980–2005",
in Boeri T., Brucker H, Docquier F., Rapoport H. (eds) *Brain Drain and Brain Gain*,
Oxford: 2012

628   Alberto Alesina, A Devleeschauwer, S Kurlat and R Wacziarg,
"Fractionalization", *Journal of Economic Growth*, 8(2): 155-194, 2003

629   I pointed this out in *Immigrants* in my rebuttal of David Goodhart's anti-diversity
arguments.

630   Alberto Alesina, J Harnoss and H Rapoport, "Birthplace diversity and economic prosperity", NBER Working Paper #18699, January 2013

631   Alessandra Venturini, F. Montobbio and C. Fassio, "Are migrants spurring
innovation?", MPC Research Report 2012/1 http://www.migrationpolicycentre.eu/
docs/MPC%202012%20EN%2011.pdf

having a more diverse immigrant workforce boosts companies' product innovation – and the greater the number of unique birthplaces among staff, the more process innovation there is.[632]

In Germany, regions with a more culturally diverse workforce innovate more.[633] A study of twelve countries across Europe found that an increase in the foreign-born share of the population, in migrants' skill level and in the region's diversity were all associated with increased patenting activity.[634] A further study of twenty European countries between 1995 and 2008 finds that "cultural diversity plays a role not only through the direct channel of increasing skilled labour, but also by an indirect effect on skilled labour productivity. Foreigners positively affect natives' productivity, as new ideas are likely to arise through the interaction of diverse cultures and diverse approaches in problem solving. Not only do high-skill immigrants display high rates of patenting, but they also allow natives to produce greater innovation."[635]

In a study of 7,600 firms in London, perhaps Europe's most diverse big city, Max Nathan of the London School of Economics and

632   Ceren Ozgen, Peter Nijkamp and Jacques Poot, "Measuring Cultural Diversity and its Impact on Innovation: Longitudinal Evidence from Dutch Firms", IZA Discussion Paper No. 7129, January 2013

633   A Niebuhr, "Migration and innovation: does cultural diversity matter for regional R&D activity?", Hamburg Institute of International Economics (HWWI) Research Paper 3-1, 2006

634   Ceren Ozgen, Peter Nijkamp and Jacques Poot, "Immigration and innovation in European regions", 2010 draft paper, Migrant Diversity and Regional Disparity in Europe (MIDIREDIE) project, Migration in Europe – Social, Economic, Cultural and Policy Dynamics, Department of Spatial Economics, VU University, Amsterdam.

635   Valentina Bosetti, Cristina Cattaneo and Elena Verdolini, "Migration, Cultural Diversity and Innovation: A European Perspective", Fondazione Eni Enrico Mattei, Working Papers 2012.69 http://www.aiel.it/bacheca/Capua/papers/Cattaneo.pdf

Neil Lee of the University of Lancaster found significant evidence of a diversity dividend in all types of firms.[636] Companies whose management is diverse are more likely to introduce new product innovations than are those with homogeneous "top teams". Diversity is particularly important for reaching international markets and serving London's cosmopolitan population. Migrant status is also positive linked to entrepreneurship.

Diverse societies not only tend to create more new ideas, they are also generally more receptive to them. Exposure to different cultures tends to broaden people's horizons and make them more accustomed to difference. Psychological research shows that this is especially true of people from a mixed cultural background and those who speak two or more languages. This mental flexibility helps both managers and employees to think "outside the box", to be more open to change and to adapt more readily to it, not least because diverse workforces have a wider variety of skills at their disposal.

While Silicon Valley has attracted the best and brightest from around America and the world, many European countries tightly restrict migration. By curbing immigration for nativist reasons, Britain's blinkered government may end up killing the golden goose that makes a global city like London so great. To boost innovation, the EU should make it easier for people to move within Europe – for instance, by making pensions portable and more professional qualifications mutually recognised. European governments should also open up to outsiders. Sweden is a model in that respect: firms there are allowed to hire workers of all skill levels from anywhere in the world on two-year renewable visas. Stockholm may be too small to become a European Silicon Valley and unfortunately barriers within

---

636 Max Nathan and Neil Lee, "Cultural Diversity, Innovation, and Entrepreneurship: Firm-level Evidence from London", *Economic Geography*, 89: 367–394, 2013 http://onlinelibrary.wiley.com/doi/10.1111/ecge.12016/abstract

the country often hold back newcomers. Even so, Sweden has the best immigration policy in Europe.

Migrants don't just bring with them skills and knowledge. They interact with the rest of society within a particular institutional, organisational, regulatory, cultural and policy context. Those who arrive as students are more attuned to existing national institutions and thus presumably more likely to boost innovation, according to David Hart of George Mason University.[637] They make the biggest contribution when their technological and cultural insights blend with those of natives, rather than if they live separate lives or are expected to assimilate.

As I argued in *Aftershock*, the benefits of diversity are not automatic.[638] Diverse people need to interact productively. They need to be able to communicate. They need to have open minds. They need to mix at school, at work, in the street and socially. Their insights and difference need to be valued. Governments needs to help everyone fulfil their potential – invest in education and training; remove the barriers to employment and enterprise, especially for minorities and immigrants; vigorously enforce anti-discrimination laws; and encourage social mobility more generally – as the next chapter elaborates. Last but not least, government, businesses and organisations all need to be geared towards promoting innovation and enterprise, and to invest in new ideas.

What role for government?

New ideas come from creative interactions between diverse people. That's why density, different disciplines and diversity are so vital for

---

637   David Hart, "Understanding immigration in a national systems of innovation framework", *Science and Public Policy*, vol.34, no.1, pp.45–53, 2007

638   Philippe Legrain, *Aftershock: Reshaping the World Economy After the Crisis*, Little Brown: 2010

a dynamic economy. European governments need to foster them – a 3D approach to promoting innovation. And they can also play an important role in other ways.

Funding investment in education, research and infrastructure can make a big difference. All EU governments rightly provide children with free public schooling. Most also fund free university education, albeit of varying quality. That is less justifiable: while a better-educated workforce may be more innovative, most of the benefits of higher education tend to go to graduates, while the typical taxpayer paying for it has not been to university. Student loans repaid through the tax system once incomes reach a certain level, as advocated by Nick Barr of the London School of Economics, are generally preferable.[639] Scholarships for promising post-graduates ought to be generous.

Government also ought to fund scientific research in areas where the commercial applications are not immediately obvious. Both the internet and the Global Positioning System (GPS) used for satellite navigation are based on technologies developed for military purposes by the US government's Defense Advanced Research Projects Agency (DARPA). Its funding for biomedical research through the National Institutes of Health plays a vital role in developing new medicines.[640] And its Small Business Innovation Research programme gave tech giants such as Amgen and Qualcomm some of their earliest funding.

Governments can help to set market-creating standards that allow industries to develop and companies to flourish. For example,

---

639 See, for instance, Nicholas Barr, "Paying for higher education: What policies, in what order?", February 2010 http://econ.lse.ac.uk/staff/nb/Barr_HEReview100215.pdf

640 Of the twenty-one most important drugs introduced between 1965 and 1992, fifteen were developed using knowledge and techniques from federally funded research. Of these, NIH research led to the development of seven drugs used to treat patients with cancer, AIDS, hypertension, depression, herpes, and anaemia. http://www.faseb.org/portals/0/pdfs/opa/2008/nih_research_benefits.pdf

by agreeing on a common GSM digital standard in the late 1980s, EU governments gave the mobile-telecoms industry a big boost, enabling network providers and equipment manufacturers to compete on a European basis. Governments can also create a supportive legal framework and promote competitive markets. Patent protection, however, is a double-edged sword. While it may stimulate innovation, it limits its diffusion – and may also stunt further innovation. Jonah Lehrer argues that stemming the flood of vague patents and copyright claims would enable more cultural borrowing and adaptation. Intellectual-property laws in Europe, though not as restrictive as in US, are unduly weighted towards the interests of patent holders. One study finds that the loss of patent protection boosts subsequent citations to the focal patent by 50 per cent on average – and thus that patents block cumulative innovation.[641] Governments ought to look at reducing the length of software patents – or abolishing them altogether. Prizes are often a better of encouraging innovation, as Alex Tabarrok argues in *Launching The Innovation Renaissance: A New Path to Bring Smart Ideas to Market Fast.*[642]

Governments can play a vital role in mobilising resources and energies towards a well-defined goal. As Chapter 10 argued, public funding for research into ways of tackling climate change, together with a carbon-consumption tax, could be decisive. Often, though, priorities aren't clear and governments that think they know best make big mistakes. In *The Entrepreneurial State: Debunking Public vs Private Sector Myths*, Mariana Mazzucato of Sussex University argues that "Nations that have achieved innovation-led growth have not only created the conditions for innovation – funding education, training and infrastructure – or fixed market failures by funding basic research. They

---

641   http://www.voxeu.org/article/do-patent-rights-impede-follow-innovation

642   Alex Tabarrok, *Launching The Innovation Renaissance: A New Path to Bring Smart Ideas to Market Fast*, TED Books: 2011

have also actively provided direct support to innovators. This is true even in red-in-tooth-and-claw capitalist America. The IT revolution did not happen with the federal government on the sidelines. The US backed the microchip, as it did the internet and, more recently, nanotechnology and biotechnology. Each was funded through public agencies such as the National Science Foundation and National Institutes of Health. This spending worked because it was 'mission oriented': the state picked an idea and supported it, from putting a man on the moon to tackling climate change. And when government can pursue missions with big enough budgets, it is easier to hire bright minds and to think big – as Darpa did with the internet. It is just as cool to work at Arpa-E, a research agency run by the US Department of Energy, as at Google. It is no surprise that the DoE was recently run by a Nobel Prize-winning physicist."[643] While she is right to point out the importance of public research spending, she overstates her case by omitting the many examples of misdirected government efforts. The many billions that the EU has spent on research have so far yielded few benefits. Regrettably, recipients of EU research funding tend to be established players who know how to work the system and systematically call for more research once a project is completed. Let's hope against hope that the more than €70 billion that the EU is planning to invest in research and innovation between 2014 and 2020 is better spent.

Governments are generally on treacherous ground when they try to pick winners. Fans of EU industrial policy point to the success of Airbus, the pan-European rival to Boeing, which now bests its US rival in global competition. Yet given Boeing's previous quasi-monopoly and the particular characteristics of the airplane business – huge entry costs and massive economies of scale – Airbus subsidies could be seen as a pro-competition policy, albeit a huge costly one

643   http://www.ft.com/cms/s/0/738da524-08f2-11e3-8b32-00144feabdc0.html

for taxpayers. Moreover, unlike in computing, the contours of the industry are pretty well-defined, so there is less scope for making big mistakes.

The fundamental reason why industrial policy that favours specific industries, technologies or firms is generally flawed is that policymakers lack the information to make judgements about the best way forward. In the 1990s, a fortune was wasted on the HDTV project for a European standard for satellite television broadcasting, which was made redundant by technological advances in the US.[644] Even industry experts are often wrong. If in 2006 you had asked Nokia, then the world's leading mobile-phone company, about the future of its industry, their vision would have been a poor guide, since they were upstaged by the launch of Apple's iPhone in the summer of 2007 and then by Google's Android – so much so that Nokia sold its shrivelled mobile-phone division to Microsoft in 2013. Likewise, energy "experts" told policymakers that fossil-fuels were scarce and would continue rising in price, so that renewables would soon be cost-competitive even without subsidies. But they were blindsided by the explosive growth of shale gas (and oil) in America. This could deliver vast quantities of cheap fossil fuels all over the world, substituting for coal in electricity production and oil in transport.

Worse, policymakers are often captured by powerful lobby groups: they listen to industry insiders with a vested interest rather than the small voice of the upstart, the challenger or the company that has yet to be born. Industrial policy often subsidises sunset industries, rather than rising ones. Even when it is more future-oriented, its priorities tend to be distorted by fashion and favour. Antonio

---

644 For an excellent discussion of industrial policy in Europe see Geoffrey Owen, "Industrial Policy in Europe Since the Second World War: What Has Been Learnt?", ECIPE Occasional Paper No. 1/2012 http://www.ecipe.org/media/publication_pdfs/OCC12012-revised.pdf

Tajani, the buffoon appointed by Silvio Berlusconi to the European Commission, wants to craft a European industrial policy which – surprise, surprise – favours his chums in Italian industry. His six priorities are: new manufacturing technologies in areas such as robotics and 3D printing; basic "enabling technology" such as optical electronics and new materials linked to novel products; biotech-based production techniques; low-carbon and other low-pollution manufacturing techniques; "clean" vehicles, such as cars using new forms of hybrid engines; and equipment needed for new "smart grids" to facilitate more efficient energy use. Tajani wants the EU's manufacturing output to rise from 15.5 per cent of GDP in 2011 to 20 per cent in 2020.[645] That is an absurd target, given that manufacturing is shrinking as a share of the economy even in China. Even if his priorities turn out to be correct – a big if – any support he provides is unlikely to be well-directed. But one area where governments could make a big contribution to innovation is in the public sector itself.

Public-sector innovation

Government spending accounts for just under half of the EU economy. Nearly half of that takes the form of redistribution in cash and kind. But a big chunk goes on the funding, and often the provision, of public services, notably health (7.3 per cent of GDP) and education (5.3 per cent of GDP). As societies get older and richer, their demands for healthcare and other public services are set to grow. But with budgets tight, governments will struggle to meet those demands. The good news is that new technologies and institutional innovations can enable governments to deliver (or fund) better public services, tailored to people's individual needs – at lower cost. Precisely because

---

645   http://www.ft.com/intl/cms/s/0/c74be3b8-adc3-11e2-a2c7-00144feabdc0.html

government services tend to be so resistant to change, the potential for improvement is huge.

Estonia has made huge savings – and delivered a better service for taxpayers – by being a pioneer in e-government. The country's passion for all things digital starts at the top. President Toomas Ilves learned to program computers at 13.[646] The government's cabinet meetings have been conducted electronically since 2000. Citizens have been able to vote on the internet since 2005; nearly a quarter of votes were cast that way in the 2011 elections. Tax returns have been completed electronically since 2000. School reports and other information have been online since 2002, the land registry (for which there is no paper backup) since 2005, e-health records since 2008 and prescriptions since 2010. You can even register your newborn child electronically. All of which allows Estonia to employ only 1.9 per cent of its population as public-sector administrators (in contrast to France's 3.8 per cent). Ilves hopes that Europe will follow Estonia's technology lead.

E-stonia, as Ilves dubs his country, is particularly innovative in education. Estonian schools have long taught computer programming at secondary level; they now plan to teach kids as young as seven. "I think teaching them to program has lots of benefits," says 24-year-old Hannes Raimets, a child of the first e-generation, who is supervising a class of ten-year-olds designing their own computer games in a newly-built school in Lagedi, outside the capital, Tallinn. "It helps the children develop their creativity and logical thinking. Also, it's fun, building your own game. I think it's their favourite subject at school."[647]

The youngest generation of E-stonians encounter electronic communication as soon as they enter school through the eKool (e-school)

---

646   http://online.wsj.com/article/SB100014241278873234776045786537927127 4 3194.html

647   http://www.bbc.co.uk/news/business-22317297

system. Exam marks, homework assignments and class attendance are all available to parents at the click of a mouse. "For most kids in Estonia, eKool is their first connection to ICT [information and communications technology]," says its chief executive, Sander Kasak. "They will be at school for ten to twelve years, so they'll be learning about technological improvements all the time. So you could say eKool is not only a technological partner, but also an educational partner." For Mairi Tonsiver, whose eleven-year-old son Uku is a student at Lagedi School, eKool is a life-saver. He had just spent three school days at home sick, but by checking online, his mother found out what he had missed. "It was much more difficult and much more time-consuming when we didn't have eKool," she says. "And your kids can't now make the excuse that they didn't write down what homework they have to do, because now you can just go to the computer and check it."[648]

As Estonia's example shows, education in Europe is ripe for a shake-up. For the most part, it's trapped not in the twentieth century, but in the nineteenth. If you sent a surgeon from the 1890s into a modern hospital, they would be incapable of doing much more than sweep the floor. But if you sent a maths teacher from the same era into a typical European school, they could go straight into a classroom and start teaching. Despite the huge technological changes over that period, education has largely stood still. Consider the possibilities for better teaching of maths, a vital subject that many children find very difficult with conventional teaching methods. Kids intuitively seem to know how to use tablets; even toddlers can work out how an iPad (or a Nexus 7) works. Smart apps could enable children to learn interactively, at their own speed, with the technology learning from their strengths and weaknesses and tailoring the teaching, coursework and quizzes to their different needs. The power of social networks could

648 *Idem*

be harnessed to stimulate students: badges for completing tasks, chat forums to learn from each other, and so on. Instead of being stuck at a blackboard with pupils passively copying what they write, teachers would be freed to inspire, coach and supervise children's active learning. Fewer of them would be needed – and they ought to be better paid and accorded a higher status in society, so as to attract higher-calibre people. (This example is meant to illustrate the possibilities, not prescribe how change ought to happen; I do not claim to be an educational expert.) More to the point, individual schools ought to be allowed to innovate – within limits and subject to appropriate monitoring – since there is no single right way of teaching and we can only find out what works well by trying out different things.

The possibilities are even greater in higher education. Already, students around the world can benefit from rather primitive "moocs" – massive open online courses – which so far mostly consist of watching videos of top professors giving a lecture. That is a huge step forward, but it is surely only scratching the surface of what a genuinely interactive, personalised online learning experience could be like. With potentially millions of people learning from the best teachers and clever new technologies, the prohibitive cost of higher education could be slashed. That would be a huge bonus for students in countries such as Britain, where young people have to pay for their university education. It would democratise access to higher education, since it would open up many more possibilities for low-cost, part-time degrees. It would save taxpayers money while enhancing young people's prospects. It is an obvious way of providing lifelong learning. Since better education is key to a more prosperous and fairer society, the broader benefits would be huge.

Plenty could also be done to revolutionise healthcare. Change is essential, since an ageing population will otherwise place an unbearable burden on public finances. In some respects, healthcare systems are highly innovative: think of all the expensive new drugs, procedures and equipment that are developed each year. Combine all that pricey new technology with rising labour costs, insatiable individual demand and a rapidly ageing society and no wonder health spending is soaring. Insofar as all this spending enables people to be healthier and happier, that is a good thing. As we get richer and live longer, it is perfectly reasonable that we wish to spend a bigger share of our incomes on improving our quality of life, rather than piling up ever more goods. But if there are ways of making us healthier and happier that cost less, we should embrace them. Again, technology can help. Much of the work done by general doctors – general practitioners in Britain – could be done by more junior staff (or patients themselves) equipped with the latest interactive, online databases of medical conditions. Self-diagnostic gadgets could replace a battery of expensive laboratory tests and provide reams of data that would allow better, more personalised care. Taking a leaf from low-cost "frugal innovation" in emerging economies, routine operations could be mechanised – a technique that has slashed costs in India while improving patient outcomes. Barriers to international trade in healthcare services should also be lowered. People increasingly travel to Brazil, Thailand and South Africa for low-cost cosmetic surgery, so why not reimburse them for having other operations done abroad that would otherwise be provided or paid for by public healthcare systems in Europe? Institutional innovation could also help. Locally managed hospitals should be able to experiment with better ways of delivering services more efficiently. Again, these examples are indicative, not prescriptive. Expertise and experimentation are needed to find out what works best. As in the case of education, it would be best if healthcare professionals went along with the necessary changes. But insofar as they are unwilling, their vested interests must not be allowed to hijack change. Healthcare should be driven by patients' preferences, not doctors' desires.

Testing what works

When companies operating in competitive markets innovate, their new products, technologies and business processes are subject to a market test: are they profitable or not? But in the case of public policies, that isn't so. While voters can throw out the whole government, their views on individual policies are generally not decisive. Often, administrations tend to proceed on the basis of political prejudice (or lobbying) rather than informed decision-making. Policymaking that purports to be evidence-based often degenerates into policy-based evidence making. Instead of prejudging how best to proceed or second-guessing what works and what doesn't, governments ought to conduct randomised controlled trials – testing public policies as pharmaceutical companies do a new drug – and replicate policies that consistently outperform. That method was pioneered by Esther Duflo, a brilliant French economist, together with Abhijit Banerjee, an Indian one, in their work on how best to alleviate poverty. Not content with being a professor at the Massachusetts Institute of Technology (MIT), advising President Obama and winning prestigious prizes, Duflo set up the Abdul Latif Jameel Poverty Action Lab with Banerjee and others to put their ideas to the test. What they have learnt from their work in trying to reduce poverty has wider applications – not least in Europe, where governments push out all sorts of new policies without rigorously testing whether they will work. At a time when public services need to cater to people's growing needs for personalised care against a backdrop of tight public finances, it is more important than ever that we find out what works and what doesn't. Governments could also help by making government data public: witness how many useful apps have been created in London using data from Transport for London. Innovation in all areas of the public sector is vital. So too is lifting the barriers to private enterprise, where Europe is generally far behind America.

Where is Europe's Google?

If you look at the titans of the US economy, it's striking how many of them are young. As of May 2013, when the latest Forbes 2000 list of leading global companies was compiled, America's most valuable listed company was Apple, founded in 1976.[649] In third place was Google (1998), with Microsoft (1975) in eighth. In total, twenty of America's top 100 listed companies have been founded (as opposed to spun off or formed by a merger) since 1975. Many are in computing – Oracle (1977), Cisco (1984), Qualcomm (1985), EMC (1979), VMware (1998) – or internet-related: Amazon (1994), eBay (1995), Facebook (2004), Priceline.com (1997). Three are in biotech: Amgen (1980), Gilead (1987) and Biogen Idec (1978). A couple of older ones are bricks-and-mortar retail: Home Depot (1978) and Costco (1976). The final three are Starbucks (coffee retail, 1985), Blackrock (finance, 1998) and Kinder Morgan (energy, 1997). In contrast, while a few of Europe's top 100 companies were incorporated since 1975, these are all spin-offs or mergers of older firms. Not a single one of Europe's 100 most valuable businesses has been founded since 1975.[650]

European capitalism is much less dynamic than America's. Fewer Europeans than Americans want to be entrepreneurs. Fewer actually start a company. European start-ups tend to grow more slowly. Hardly any new companies become world-beating giants. Stodgy old ones rarely die. Europe's biggest post-war entrepreneurial successes predate 1975. Ingvar Kamprad established Sweden's IKEA, the world's largest furniture retailer, in 1943. Amancio Ortega, the founder of Spain's Inditex, the world's largest fashion company which owns Zara, started off in 1963. Britain's Richard Branson launched his Virgin Group, which began in music and now embraces everything from planes, trains and space tourism to finance and health clubs, in 1970. Even the

---

649   http://www.forbes.com/global2000/list/

650   Personal research from Forbes 2000 list and wikipedia.

leading post-1975 successes are not quite global giants. Red Bull, an Austrian company co-founded in 1984 by Dietrich Mateschitz which makes the world's most popular energy drink, may be among them, but it is privately held so it is hard to know how much it is worth.[651]

The gap is glaring in the digital world. Europe lacks an equivalent to Silicon Valley; Tech City in London and Silicon Allee in Berlin are tiny in comparison. The global giants that dominate the industry – such as Google, Amazon and Facebook – are all American. The closest European equivalent is SAP, the world's biggest business software company. Founded by five former IBM engineers, it is Germany's most valuable company – but it dates back to 1972. ARM Holdings, a British-based company founded in 1990 that designs the chips used in most smartphones, is also a world-beater, but is not yet among Europe's most valuable 100 companies. Many promising European start-ups get bought up by bigger American firms. Skype, the world's leading online call service, was co-founded in 2003 by a Swede and a Dane working with Estonian programmers. They sold it to eBay, then bought it back and sold it for even more to Microsoft. Lastminute.com, a British travel site co-founded by Martha Lane-Fox and Brent Hoberman in 1998, was bought by America's Sabre in 2005 and merged into Travelocity. Sparrow, an email client co-founded in Paris by French entrepreneurs and Vietnamese-born Dinh Việt Hoà, was a huge hit before being bought by Google. Others successes remain independent, but frustratingly small. Vente Privée, a French pioneer of online flash sales, had sales of €1.3 billion (£1.1 billion) in 2012 – which is excellent but tiny compared to Amazon.com's $61 billion (£38 billion).[652] Angry Birds has been downloaded more than a billion times, propelling its Finnish developer, Rovio, to revenues

---

651   http://www.forbes.com/profile/dietrich-mateschitz/

652   Converted at average 2012 exchange rate of £ = €1.2337 = $1.5851

of €152 million (£123 million), but in the global electronic-games industry it is dwarfed by America's Electronic Arts (revenues: $4.1 billion, or £2.6 billion), not to mention market-leader Nintendo.[653] While France's Dailymotion is the world's second largest video-sharing website, it is miles behind YouTube. There are lots of other wonderful digital start-ups in Europe. Spotify, a Swedish music-streaming service, is superb. From its base in Southwark, south London, Swiftkey saves people countless keystrokes with its intelligent predictive smartphone keyboards. Shazam, the most down-loaded app developed in Britain, has been used to tag more than five billion songs. I doff my cap to them. But it is still troubling that none can match America's global giants.

Silicon Valley sparks off a diverse mix of dynamic people from around the world. More than half of start-ups founded there between 1995 and 2005 had a migrant as a chief executive or lead technologist.[654] While a tightening of visa rules and the rise of China and India have reduced immigrants' contribution somewhat, they still co-founded 43.9 per cent of Silicon Valley start-ups between 2006 and 2012.[655] Companies co-founded by migrants – many of whom arrived as children, not through some pseudo-scientific government selection process – include stand-out successes such as Google, Yahoo, eBay, PayPal, YouTube, Hotmail, Sun Microsystems, Intel and WhatsApp. Steve Jobs, the co-founder of Apple, had a mixed heritage too: his biological father was Syrian-born, his biological mother Swiss American and his adoptive one Armenian American. Across the US economy, migrants make an outsized contribution: a quarter of start-ups are

---

653   Converted at average 2012 exchange rate of £ = €1.2337 = $1.5851

654   National Venture Capital Association, "American Made: The Impact of Immigrant Entrepreneurs and Professionals on US Competitiveness", 2006

655   http://www.kauffman.org/newsroom/immigrant-entrepreneurship-has-stalled-for-the-first-time-in-decades-kauffman-foundation-study-shows.aspx

co-founded by them.[656] They co-founded a quarter of start-ups in manufacturing, defence and aerospace; more than a fifth in bioscience; and a fifth in clean tech.[657]

Many US-based entrepreneurs are European. There are about 50,000 Germans in Silicon Valley and an estimated 500 start-ups in the San Francisco Bay area with French founders. Pierre Omidyar, the co-founder of eBay, was born in Paris to Iranian immigrant parents who moved to the US when he was six. Eric Benhamou left Paris aged twenty and went on to co-found a computer network technology company that was bought by 3Com, of which he later became chief executive.[658] Bernard Liautaud co-founded Business Objects, an enterprise software company, in Paris before opening up shop in Silicon Valley and then being bought out by SAP in 2007. Jan Koum, the co-founder of WhatsApp, which Facebook bought for $19 billion in February 2014, was born in Kiev and moved from Ukraine to California aged sixteen. British entrepreneurs account for 6.3 per cent of immigrant-co-founded start-ups in the US, German ones 3.9 per cent and Dutch ones 2 per cent.[659]

Silicon Valley owes its success to many factors as well as its diversity. It started with initial demand and public funding for research into science and technology from the US Defence Department. It was fostered by entrepreneurial universities, notably Stanford, that train superb, go-getting graduates, help generate valuable new ideas and encourage the development of businesses to commercialise those ideas.

---

656   http://www.kauffman.org/infographic-americas-new-immigrant-entrepreneurs-then-and-now.aspx

657   http://www.kauffman.org//uploadedFiles/Then_and_now_americas_new_immigrant_entrepreneurs.pdf

658   http://en.wikipedia.org/wiki/Eric_Benhamou

659   http://www.kauffman.org//uploadedFiles/Then_and_now_americas_new_immigrant_entrepreneurs.pdf

It inhales a risk-taking culture where enterprise is celebrated. A dense network of mentors and potentially useful contacts provide help. It is easy to start a business, hire and fire people and bounce back from bankruptcy. Angel investors, venture capital and other forms of early-stage finance are readily available. Last but not least, it benefits from a huge and generally competitive domestic market with many people open to new ideas and products.

Running through that list, Europe falls short in every respect. Public spending on research and innovation is plentiful but often poorly spent. Europe lacks entrepreneurial universities with close links to businesses. It fails to make the most of its diversity (with the notable exception of a city like London) and is generally not an attractive destination for would-be immigrant entrepreneurs. It tends to have a risk-averse and often anti-business culture, with few entrepreneurial role models. It has much sparser networks of mentors and business contacts. The legal and regulatory framework varies: while it is relatively easy to start a business, hire and fire people and bounce back quickly from bankruptcy in some countries, it is much harder in others. It has a much smaller market for venture capital, while banks are often reluctant to provide finance to new and small businesses. It lacks a proper single market in services, not least digital ones. Many domestic markets are dominated by big players that deter (and stamp on) competition, cosseted by a host of regulations that impede new entrants.

Silicon Valley is the cauldron of many American start-ups. But the US is also much more enterprising generally. Witness how shale gas has revolutionised America's energy landscape within a few years. Cheap energy, in turn, could spark a new manufacturing revolution in the US, together with 3D printing. Genetic modification is breeding better, hardier, cheaper, tastier and more nutritious food. America is also pouring many more resources into the biotech revolution.

Stopped-up Europe

Four types of barrier hold European enterprise back: education systems that fail to encourage entrepreneurship; a cultural aversion to risk-taking, diversity and many new technologies; flawed regulations that restrict competition, stymie start-ups and hamper smaller businesses; and a shortage of finance. All four are related. For example, punitive bankruptcy laws exacerbate Europeans' fear of failure. Cartelised markets, burdensome regulations and a lack of risk capital encourage many go-getting Europeans to emigrate. Pessimism about the future can prove self-fulfilling.

The problems start young: European education systems generally don't encourage entrepreneurship. While 59 per cent of Americans think their schooling has helped them develop a sense of initiative and entrepreneurial attitude, only 50 per cent of Europeans and 35 per cent of Britons agree.[660] A majority of Americans believe their education has given them the skills and know-how to run a business, compared with 41 per cent of Europeans and a mere 27 per cent of Britons.[661] Only 17 per cent of Britons say their schooling has made them interested in becoming an entrepreneur.[662]

Once they start working, most Europeans prefer the security of being an employee to the excitement, freedom and potential rewards of being an entrepreneur. The first step towards setting up a company is often to become self-employed, yet whereas a majority of Americans would prefer to work for themselves, only 37 per cent of Europeans, a third of Britons and a paltry 22 per cent of Swedes

---

660   Eurobarometer, "Entrepreneurship in the EU and beyond", Flash Eurobarometer 354, July/August 2012, Q11.1 http://ec.europa.eu/public_opinion/flash/fl_354_en.pdf

661   54 per cent of Americans say their education has given them the skills and know-how to run a business. *Ibid* Q11.4

662   *Ibid.* Q11.3

would.[663] Policymakers are unenthusiastic too. "Freelancing is the wave of the future, yet the EU still calls it 'atypical work'," observes Ann Mettler of the Lisbon Council, a reform-minded think-tank in Brussels (at which I used to be a senior fellow).

Few Europeans go on to start a business. According to the Global Entrepreneurship Monitor's annual survey in 2013, some 13 per cent of Americans (and Estonians) were starting or had started a new business, but only 8 per cent of Europeans (and 7 per cent of Britons).[664] Fewer Europeans (31 per cent) perceive opportunities for entrepreneurship than Americans (43 per cent) and fewer think they have the necessary capabilities (42 per cent to 56 per cent). Many Swedes (66 per cent) see opportunities; far fewer have confidence in their abilities (37 per cent). Fear of failure is crippling in Greece and Italy.[665] Starting a business inevitably involves the risk of failure. Yet one in two Europeans – and a whopping two in three Portuguese – think that one should not start a business if there is a risk it might fail; only 28 per cent of Americans agree.[666] Britons (38 per cent) are the least risk-averse Europeans. Over their lifetimes, more Americans have started a business or are taking steps to do so (38 per cent) than Europeans (23 per cent).[667] Only 24 per cent of Britons have and a mere 15 per cent of French people. Men are much more likely to be

---

663 51 per cent of Americans would prefer to work for themselves. *Ibid.* Q1

664 Global Entrepreneurship Monitor, "2013 Global Report", Figure 2.3, early-stage entrepreneurial activity (TEA) rate http://www.gemconsortium.org/docs/download/3106

665 61 per cent in Greece, 58 per cent in Italy.

666 Eurobarometer, "Entrepreneurship in the EU and beyond", Flash Eurobarometer 354, July/August 2012 Q21.4

667 *Ibid* Q13

entrepreneurs than women: twice as likely in Britain. Surprisingly, the gap is even greater in generally female-friendly Scandinavia.[668]

European entrepreneurs are often held back by regulation. Starting a business ought to be quick, cheap and simple. It is easiest in Ireland, which ranks tenth globally, according to the World Bank's Doing Business rankings, followed by Britain, which is nineteenth worldwide.[669] But Germany ranks 106th out of 185 in the world (below Russia), Poland is 124th, Austria 134th, Spain 136th, Greece 146th (below Zimbabwe) and Malta 150th. A whopping 85 per cent of Italians and Greeks say that complex administrative procedures make it difficult to start one's own business.[670] Taxes can be punishing too. In 2012 a group of French tech entrepreneurs calling themselves "les Pigeons" (suckers) mounted a social-media campaign against the government's plan to tax their capital gains as ordinary income, doubling their tax rate to 60 per cent.[671] Punitive bankruptcy laws – and social stigma – are also a big deterrent. If your firm goes under in France, says Dan Serfaty, the French founder of Viadeo, a fast-growing business-networking website, you don't get a second chance.[672] In Germany it tends to take six years to be discharged from bankruptcy; in France nine. Bankrupts in Germany can face a lifetime ban on senior executive positions at big companies.[673]

Labour laws are another obstacle. If you are thinking of taking the plunge and hiring your first employee – a huge responsibility and

---

668   http://www.oecd.org/std/business-stats/Entrepreneurship-at-a-Glance-2013-Gender.pdf

669   http://www.doingbusiness.org/rankings

670   Eurobarometer, "Entrepreneurship in the EU and beyond", Flash Eurobarometer 354, July/August 2012, Q21.2

671   http://www.economist.com/node/21564609

672   http://www.economist.com/node/21559618

673   http://www.economist.com/node/21559618

potentially a massive burden – not being able to let them go easily if they don't work out (or business flags) is a huge deterrent. Yet French start-ups typically have to pay six months of severance pay even for very recent hires. After Mobuzz, a Spanish online-video firm founded in 2005, went bankrupt when the financial crisis hit, Spanish social security still pursued its founder Anil de Mello for five more years to extract repayment of severance money it had paid to the firm's employees on his behalf. Unsurprisingly, he started his next company, which seeks to lower roaming tariffs for mobile-phone users, in Switzerland, where labour laws are less punitive.[674] Immigration rules also make it hard for start-ups to hire the foreign talent that they need. Risk-aversion is an impediment too. Many Europeans prefer the perceived security of working for a bigger company. Start-ups often struggle to hire professional managers to help their firms grow because European executives are extremely risk-averse.

Entrepreneurs are often viewed with suspicion. While nearly all Americans and Europeans agree that entrepreneurs are job creators,[675] 57 per cent of Europeans – a whopping 91 per cent of Poles and a still hefty 46 per cent of Britons – think entrepreneurs take advantage of other people's work, compared with only 31 per cent of Americans.[676] Whereas half of Europeans (and Britons) think entrepreneurs only think about their own pockets, only 30 per cent of Americans do.[677] In both cases, the only Europeans who view enterprise more positively than Americans do are the Danes.

Once a business is up and running, successful ones need the scope to grow. While more than half of businesses tend to fail

---

674   http://www.economist.com/node/21559618

675   Eurobarometer, "Entrepreneurship in the EU and beyond", Flash Eurobarometer 354, July/August 2012, Q12.3

676   *Ibid*, Q12.4

677   *Ibid* Q12.2

within five years and the remaining ones tend to remain small, the fast-growing ones make a critical contribution to the economy.[678] Between 2007 and 2010, over 60 per cent of new jobs in the UK were created either by start-ups or by the 1 per cent of firms that grew fastest, according to Nesta, Britain's foundation for innovation. Yet many European companies stay inefficiently small. While a lack of credit or a reluctance to relinquish control to external shareholders may be part of the reason, taxes and regulations that kick in when businesses reach a certain size often stunt their growth. France is notorious for having many firms with exactly forty-nine employees.[679] In manufacturing, where economies of scale tend to matter, 97.6 per cent of Italian firms have fewer than fifty employees. In contrast, 10 per cent of German manufacturers have fifty employees or more, as do 14.2 per cent of (mostly foreign-owned) Irish-based ones. Britain is in between.[680] Limiting firms' growth is damaging to the economy as a whole because workers in companies with 250 or more employees tend to be much more productive than those in micro-firms with less than ten workers: more than three times more in Italy and nearly two times more in Britain.[681] But in services, where even more firms are tiny, micro-firms are often

---

678 http://www.oecd-ilibrary.org/sites/entrepreneur_aag-2013-en/03/04/index. html

679 Once a company has at least fifty employees inside France, management must create three worker councils, introduce profit sharing, and submit restructuring plans to the councils if the company decides to fire workers for economicreasons.http://www.businessweek.com/articles/2012-05-03/why-france-has-so-many-49-employee-companies

680 http://www.oecd-ilibrary.org/sites/entrepreneur_aag-2013-en/02/01/index. html

681 Two-and-a-halftimesmoreinGermanyandSweden. http://www.oecd-ilibrary. org/sites/entrepreneur_aag-2013-en/02/04/index.html

the most productive.[682] So technological change may make these burdensome regulations less binding for many digital firms.

Barriers to competition can also be crippling. It is hard to build up a business when established companies (and governments) tend to not like dealing with tiny ones. Established firms (both big and small) are often protected by a thicket of regulatory measures. Pharmacies, taxi drivers, notaries – all are cosseted in many countries. Forget building your local pharmacy into a big chain of chemists (along the lines of Britain's Boots) in Italy or – horrors – selling basic medicines in supermarkets; it's illegal. Before its relaunch, Deezer, a French music streaming service, was charged with copyright infringement by a French government agency and shut down in 2007.

Funding drought

European entrepreneurs are also deprived of finance. Conservative banks are often reluctant to lend. Angel investors – rich people who put money into start-ups in their early stages – are much rarer than in America. Venture capital is much scarcer. Because European venture-capital firms lost money after the dotcom bubble burst in 2000–1, institutional investors such as pension funds view it as a poor investment. The crisis has made matters worse: venture-capital investment has halved since 2007. Foreigners don't help much: American funds tend to invest only in the largest start-ups.

As previous chapters explained, European banks have been particularly reluctant to lend to smaller businesses, let alone risky start-ups, since the crisis. Many entrepreneurs are forced to resort to more expensive funding, such as the overdraft on their personal bank account or borrowing on their credit card. In any case, for entrepreneurs with a promising business plan or fledgling businesses that need

---

682   Micro-firms are the most productive in Britain, France, Sweden and Germany, although not in Spain or Italy.

capital to grow, equity is generally a more flexible form of finance than a bank loan.

Yet whereas American angel investors poured $22 billion (£13.9 billion) into US start-ups in 2012, European ones put in less than a third of that: €5.1 billion (£4.1 billion).[683] Even that figure is a heroic guesstimate: recorded investment is a mere €0.5 billion and the rest is the industry body's estimate of the "invisible" market.[684] Whereas European business angels funded 2,913 companies that created 17,881 jobs, American ones financed 67,030 ventures that created 274,800 jobs.[685] The US has ten times more business angels (268,000) than Europe does (26,000). American businesses have just received a further boost: private companies seeking capital are now legally permitted to advertise to all-comers through the websites of companies such as AngelList, WeFunder and RockThePost.[686] That promises a wider pool of capital for entrepreneurs – and hence better valuations for their shares.

Venture-capital firms are vital for larger investments. Yet the US invests three times more in venture capital, as a share of GDP, than the leading European countries – Sweden and Ireland – nearly five times more than Britain, eight times more than Germany and thirty-seven times more than Italy.[687] While venture capital is much more bountiful in America even at the seed capital and start-up stage, the gap is widest at the later development stage, where it is four times Sweden's and nine

683   Converted at average 2012 exchange rate of £ = €1.2337 = $1.5851

684   http://www.eban.org/e5-1-billion-market-shows-european-angels-on-the-rise/#. UkRitYYya-Y

685   http://www.unh.edu/news/releases/2013/apr/lw25cvr.cfm

686   http://www.ft.com/cms/s/0/ea20e300-2601-11e3-8ef6-00144feab7de.html

687   Venture capital is equivalent to 0.17 per cent of GDP in the US. That is three times the share in Sweden and Ireland (0.054 per cent), nearly five times more than in Britain (0.038 per cent), eight times more than in Germany (0.021 per cent) and thirty-seven times more than in Italy (0.005). http://www.oecd-ilibrary.org/sites/entrepreneur_aag-2013-en/06/03/index.html

times Britain's. America's huge capital market helps. Yet it is not essential: the world leader is Israel, where venture capitalists invest twice as much as in America as a share of GDP.[688]

In absolute terms, the gap between America and Europe is stark. Venture-capital investment in the US totalled $26.7 billion (£16.9 billion) in 2012, compared with only $4.1 billion (£2.6 billion) in the twenty-two European countries for which the OECD has figures.[689] America provides nearly nine times more venture capital in both life sciences and computer and consumer electronics, more than six times more in communications and nearly six times more in the industrial and energy sectors.[690] In Europe, Britain invests most: $929 million (£586 million). Tiny Israel (population: 8 million) invested more in venture capital ($867 million) than the $706 million invested in Germany (population: 82 million).

Start-up Europe?

Education, culture, regulation and finance – all four hold Europe back. It urgently needs to reform. One positive sign is that young Europeans are much more enthusiastic about being self-employed or starting a business than older ones. With so many young people unemployed, they have nothing to lose from starting out on their own. In Britain, the number of self-employed has soared since late 2009.[691]

---

688 Venture capital is 0.36 per cent of GDP in Israel.

689 The twenty-two countries are the EU-15 plus Norway and Switzerland, plus Estonia, Slovenia, Czech Republic, Poland and Hungary. Converted at average 2012 exchange rate of £ = €1.2337 = $1.5851

690 The US spends $10.3 billion on venture capital in life sciences to the EU's $1.2 billion. In computer and consumer electronics, the split is $6.9 billion to $0.8 billion. In communications it is $4.5 billion to $0.7 billion. In the industrial and energy sectors it is $2.8 billion to $0.5 billion.

691 http://www.oecd-ilibrary.org/sites/entrepreneur_aag-2013-en/01/03/index.html

Entrepreneurship ought to be lionised, as it is in America and Denmark. Sporting stars can be fine role models; start-up stars ought to be too. Grassroots campaigns like StartUp Britain, modelled on StartUp America, can help. They can raise awareness, spread enthusiasm, provide mentoring, create connections and help to solve problems. Launched by David Cameron in March 2011, StartUp Britain was wholly funded and run by the private sector. Over a three-year campaign, it engaged lots of people and helped boost start-up rates considerably.[692]

Education can make a big difference too. Gi Fernando, a Sri-Lankan born British entrepreneur and angel investor, set up Freeformers to teach digital skills: for every business person they train, they also train an unemployed youngster for free.[693] Britain's Gazelle Colleges are transforming their curriculum to encourage an entrepreneurial mindset in their students.[694] Working in partnership with Babson College in the US, they aim to create "entrepreneurial colleges" whose ethos, culture and values are geared towards enterprise. Start-up lounges help students develop new businesses. Entrepreneurs work on the curriculums. Students join a company rather than a course. Thus instead of sitting in a classroom studying graphic design, they set up a business that competes for local trade. They learn by doing. So far, Gazelle Colleges have scaled the idea to twenty further-education colleges in the UK, with plans to grow to more than forty in coming years. While nowhere in Europe compares to Stanford, traditional European universities are becoming more enterprising too. Silicon Fen clusters around Cambridge University. Paris is basing its start-up plans around scientific centres such as the Institut de la Vision and

---

692   http://www.startupbritain.co/news/2014-02-26/startup-britain-embarks-on-new-chapter

693   See http://www.freeformers.com/

694   http://www.gazellecolleges.com/

Institut Langevin and engineers from its high-powered *Grandes Ecoles* such as Polytechnique. More boldly, Xavier Niel, the billionaire founder of Free, an upstart mobile-phone and internet provider, has set up a programming school called 42 – the answer to the meaning of life, according to the Hitchhiker's Guide to the Galaxy – that breaks with the often-rigid methods and philosophy of the government-run education system wherever it can. Niel believes it will produce graduates who are more innovative, entrepreneurial and diverse as a result.[695]

Policymakers need to encourage Europeans to become entrepreneurs. Providing every young person with a capital lump sum, as Chapter 12 suggests, could make a huge difference. Making it easier to start a business can have an immediate impact. Start-up rates doubled in France in 2009, in the midst of the crisis, after legislation supporting *auto-entrepreneurs* (sole traders) was introduced.[696] Bankruptcy law should also be shaken up so that businesspeople who fail aren't scarred for life but rather can learn from their mistakes and start again. Britain discharges bankrupts from their debts after twelve months; in America it is usually even quicker. Europe should learn from Denmark, which has the most supportive bankruptcy laws of all.

Making hiring people more flexible is another priority. With so many Europeans unemployed, there is a huge pool of talent waiting to be used. Martin Varsavsky, an Argentinian entrepreneur who has founded a string of telecoms start-ups in Spain, says that since the crisis it is easier for his current venture, Fon, a global Wi-Fi community, to recruit. With bigger firms firing people, well-qualified people are more willing to join a new one. In a presentation to Spanish entrepreneurs called "Why you should not move your company to Silicon

695   http://www.nytimes.com/2013/11/16/world/europe/in-france-new-tech-academy-defies-conventional-wisdom.html

696   http://www.oecd-ilibrary.org/sites/entrepreneur_aag-2013-en/01/01/index.html

Valley", Varsavsky pointed out that salaries for software engineers are 70 per cent lower in Europe than in California. With luck, some of the European entrepreneurs who have struck it rich in the US can also be lured back to sprinkle some of their Silicon Valley ways in Europe.

Europe should also do more to try to attract dynamic foreigners, not least with start-up visas for would-be entrepreneurs. Better still, they should open up their borders more generally. They should also make the most of the talents of the diverse people already in Europe. Like in the US, immigrants in Britain are nearly twice as likely to start a new business as UK-born ones.[697] Contrary to the belief that only some immigrant cultures are entrepreneurial, data from GEM surveys show that all their categories of immigrant are more entrepreneurial than white UK-born people.[698] Other European countries need to unleash the potential of diversity too. In particular, more women need to be encouraged to become entrepreneurs.

One of the most dynamic women in Europe is aged seventy-two. Neelie Kroes, the EU's digital commissioner, has the energy of a woman half her age. She is determined to drive forward her digital agenda for growth. Among many other things, she set up the Start Up Leaders group, an independent group of European tech entrepreneurs and business-builders, to stimulate fresh thinking. Their initial thoughts have been enriched with ideas from the Founders Forum

---

697 Migrants to the UK had a total entrepreneurial activity rate of 16 per cent, compared to 9 per cent among UK-born people. Global Entrepreneurship Monitor UK Report 2012, cited in "Migrant Entrepreneurs: Building Our Businesses, Creating Our Jobs", Centre for Entrepreneurs, March 2014

698 Jonathan Levie and Mark Hart, "Global Entrepreneurship Monitor: United Kingdom 2008 Monitoring Report", 2009. Whereas 5.4 per cent of white UK-born people have started, or are trying to start, a new business, the figure is 6.8 per cent among Asian immigrants, 7.8 per cent among white immigrants, 8.5 per cent among black immigrants and 9.8 per cent among mixed immigrants. Interestingly, though, the highest enterprise rates are found among UK-born blacks (11.3 per cent).

in London, a community of leading global entrepreneurs, chief executives and key investors in media and technology. Their 22-point manifesto for entrepreneurship and innovation is chock-full of bright ideas.[699]

Europe also needs much tougher and more stringently enforced competition policies – Kroes's earlier EU job. Think back to how Orange, then owned by Hutchison Whampoa, shook up the UK mobile-phone market in the 1990s, forcing the other players to up their game. Compare that to Belgium's now, where prices are high, service is poor and 4G mobile broadband is delayed. An upstart like France's Free could do a world of good. To give competition policies teeth, fines should be swingeing. But since these end up being paid by shareholders (or customers), criminal penalties for the bosses of offending companies are the best deterrent. At EU level, completing the single market in services (not least digital ones) ought to be a priority, as Chapter 5 emphasised. Opening up more to foreign trade and investment would also do wonders to boost competition for everyone.

"Accelerators" can also help start-ups grow. Seedcamp, a London-based pan-European accelerator launched in May 2007 by thirty European investors, provides start-ups with seed money, mentoring, office space and support over a year-long programme. Wayra, one set up by Telefónica, a Spanish telecoms company that owns O2 in the UK, has fourteen academies in twelve countries in Europe and Latin America that provide funding of up to €40,000 plus office space and mentoring.

Europe needs to champion angel investors such as Niklas Zennström, the Swedish co-founder of Skype, who has raised $165 million for his second London-based venture-capital firm, Atomico Ventures II. "When it took us more than a year to get financing

---

699   http://startupmanifesto.eu/files/manifesto.pdf

for Skype, we knew what line of business we eventually had to get into," he observes.[700] Marc Simoncini, the French founder of Meetic, Europe's biggest dating website, has earmarked €100 million of his fortune for this.[701] Brent Hoberman, the co-founder of last-minute.com, is a partner in PROfounders, an early-stage investment firm. Germany's Samwer brothers, Oliver, Marc and Alexander, who made fortunes in the first dotcom boom have also become angel investors.

In venture capital, Europe ought to take a leaf out of Israel's book as well as America's. If private investors won't chip in enough, governments can lead the way. The EU's European Investment Fund, which invests in venture-capital funds rather than directly in start-ups, managed €7 billion of funds by the end of 2012.[702] Some governments provide generous tax breaks for venture capital. The European Commission is also trying to create a genuine single market for it. That said, investors who put money into very young firms tend to prefer operating in their own language and culture, so start-ups generally rely on backers from their own country.

Venture capitalists and entrepreneurs also need a way of re-alising their investments, whether by floating on the stockmarket or selling to a larger company. Streamlining the process for small companies to list on the stock exchange is vital. In March 2013 the London Stock Exchange introduced a new "high-growth" seg-ment of its main market – in addition to its existing Alternative Investment Market (AIM) for small firms – relaxing the listing requirements for fast-growing, mainly high-tech businesses. In May NYSE Euronext, which groups the stock exchanges of Paris, Brussels, Amsterdam and Lisbon, launched EnterNext, a marketing

---

700   http://www.economist.com/node/21559618

701   http://www.economist.com/node/17680631

702   http://www.eif.org/news_centre/publications/eif_-annual_report_2012.pdf

initiative to raise the profile of the mid-cap and small-cap segments of the main market, along with Alternext, the traditional market for smaller firms.[703] But "it takes a long time to build a successful growth market," says Alastair Walmsley, head of primary markets at LSE Group.

Crowdfunding – raising small contributions from a short pitch to investors online – is another promising possibility. Around 200 crowdfunding platforms in Europe together raised nearly €500 million in 2012, twice as much as in 2011. "Instead of saying I like this idea, brand or product, you are committing money to it," says Aernoud Dekker, the founder of Sellanapp, the first crowdfunding platform specialising in smartphone apps. Crowdfunding can also unlock finance from business angels and venture capitalists. "It can prove that the concept is attractive to other people," says Oliver Gajda, co-founder of the European Crowdfunding Network. "Plus it can de-risk the whole investment by bringing other investors on board."[704]

A bigger way to unlock finance for start-ups would be to shift corporate taxes to a net cashflow basis, as Chapter 10 advocates. That would allow investors to write off their investments against tax immediately and remove the bias towards unproductive property speculation.

Precisely because Europe's economies are so hidebound, there are huge opportunities for progress. Unleashing Europeans' entrepreneurial spirit could make a huge difference quickly. Existing companies, governments and society as a whole need to be more willing to embrace risk.

---

703   http://www.economist.com/news/finance-and-economics/21588384-stock-exchanges-are-courting-small-firms-never-capital-remedy

704   http://www.europecrowdfunding.org/2013/01/the-european-crowdfunding-network-on-euronews/

Think big

We live in an age of diminished expectations. Europeans in particular tend to be afraid to venture out and try new things, let alone reach for the stars. We need more people like Elon Musk, a South-African-born entrepreneur. After making billions in the US from PayPal, the on-line payments system, he didn't rest on his laurels. He founded Tesla, which makes fantastic (and profitable) electric cars. He set up SpaceX, a space travel company. Now he wants to build a Hyperloop – basically a solar-powered maglev train in a vacuum tube that would whisk passengers along at 760 miles (1,220 kilometres) an hour, three times faster than a high-speed train, and cost ten times less to build.[705]

Gloomsters argue that technological progress is grinding to a halt. The low-hanging fruit have all been picked, argues Tyler Cowen in *The Great Stagnation*.[706] Nothing can ever compare to the great leap forward ushered in by electricity and other advances during the second wave of the Industrial Revolution between 1870 and 1900, such as cars, running water, petroleum and chemicals, claims Robert Gordon of Northwestern University.[707] "Many of the original and spin-off inventions of IR #2 could happen only once – urbanisation, transportation speed, the freedom of females from the drudgery of carrying tons of water per year, and the role of central heating and air conditioning in achieving a year-round constant temperature." Yet he is wrong to dismiss the importance of exponentially increasing computing power, communications (through both the wired and the mobile internet) and data gathering ("big data") – and many previous advances since 1900. The improvements in life expectancy over the past hundred years are breathtaking. That information about almost anything – not

---

705 http://www.bbc.co.uk/news/technology-23681266

706 Tyler Cowen, *The Great Stagnation*, Dutton: 2011

707 Robert J Gordon, "Is US Economic Growth Over? Faltering innovation confronts the six headwinds", NBER working paper #18315, August 2012

to mention all the entertainment we desire – is now at our fingertips everywhere is amazing. That in future we could harness the power of the sun and the atom to generate almost limitless cheap energy – and therefore as much desalinated water as we need – could be transformational.

We are surely only at the beginning of what the digital revolution can achieve. By enabling energy to be used far from where it was generated, electricity eventually rewired the entire economy and sparked many new industries – but it took decades for all these gains to be realised. Likewise, by enabling people to make calculations and connections far beyond their unaided capacity, the digital revolution is likely to transform our economies and our lives, creating new possibilities that we can scarcely imagine. For example, internet-connected gadgets that continually monitor and analyse our vital signs, together with genetic profiling and personalised medicine, could transform healthcare.[708]

The notion that we have picked all the low-hanging fruit is flawed. Previous generations probably thought so too. But until recently we were tapping the brainpower of only a tiny fraction of humanity. Just think how much faster and further humanity could progress if Africa emulated China's success, if women were liberated in the Arab world, if people were set free to live and work wherever they want, if Silicon Valley's entrepreneurial magic cast its spell on Europe, and if every young person got a fair start in life.

Knowledge is cumulative: by standing on the shoulders of giants we can reach ever-higher branches. Each invention also creates new demands, argues Jan Mokyr, an optimistic counterpoint to Robert Gordon at Northwestern University.[709] Antibiotics have given us a

708 http://www.economist.com/news/briefing/21569381-idea-innovation-and-new-technology-have-stopped-driving-growth-getting-increasing

709 http://www.voxeu.org/article/technological-progress-thing-past

new lease of life, but as bacteria become resistant, we need to develop new ones. Using nitrates as fertilisers helped us feed billions but their overuse pollutes the water; perhaps the solution will be genetic engineering to enable plants to fix more of their own nitrates or bacteria that convert nitrates into nitrogen at more efficient rates. Fossil fuels have made possible all the comforts of modern life; now we need clean energy to limit climate change.

Above all, we don't know what we don't know and have no idea what the future holds. Only a decade ago, even technologists thought self-driving cars were scarcely on the horizon, yet Google has successfully developed them. Future advances in computing, biotech, nanotechnology or something else entirely are likely to surprise us.[710] We have surely only scratched the surface of what is possible. Astronomy, nanochemistry and genetic engineering are advancing in leaps and bounds. New materials and digital manufacturing techniques such as 3D printing are leading to what some are dubbing a New Industrial Revolution.

Paradoxically, while some are gloomy that technological progress has stalled, others fret it is proceeding so fast that is eliminating the need for workers. This is an old fear. Undeniably, adjusting to change can be wrenching and take time – hence the need for all the supporting policies advocated in this book. But ultimately, getting computers and robots to do ever more tasks that humans currently do ought to be liberating. As they do, people will specialise in the things that they do best (or enjoy most). A few examples among many: teaching meditation, yoga or

---

710   Tools such as DNA sequencing machines and cell analysis through flow cytometry are revolutionising molecular microbiology. Our ability to crunch vast amounts of data – petabytes (a million gigabytes) or zettabytes (a million petabytes) – could be transformative. Artificial intelligence programmes are interpreting medical data from scans and sifting through reams of legal documents faster and better than the most diligent radiographer or paralegal http://www.cityam.com/article/let-optimists-run-economy-and-innovation-will-charge-growth#sthash.oenNqTPm.dpuf

martial arts; preparing and serving meals; sales; managing people; caring for the young and the old; motivating students; writing books and music; entertaining people; and many other things. Technology will also create new jobs: not just in technology companies themselves but also in complementary lines of work: for example, marketing jobs for businesses on social networks. Ultimately, if robots could do everything, humans could lead a life of leisure; the key issue would then be distributional: ensuring ownership of robots was widely shared.

Think positive

Pessimism is self-fulfilling. If we don't believe we can do better, don't take risks and don't make big, bold investments, Europe *does* risk stagnation. Business investment in Europe was low even before the crisis and is now plumbing historic depths. Governments too have slashed capital spending. Demographic trends and hostility to diversity are damaging. But decline is not inevitable. If we shake up and open up our economies, the future can be much brighter.

By lowering our sights, we are forsaking our future. Even though the future is fundamentally unknowable, we can still try to shape it. Uncertainty is not a reason for inaction. Research by Tali Sharot, an economist at University College London, shows that optimists are worse than pessimists at guessing what the future will hold, but that they tend to be more successful anyhow, partly because they have the guts to try but also because their can-do attitude carries others along. "Imagination can be just as important as reasoned analysis," points out Stian Westlake, executive director of policy and research at Nesta, the UK's foundation for innovation. "After all, it was science-fiction writers who first envisaged robots, satellites and cyberspace."[711]

We need to open our minds. We need to harness our collective creativity. We need to experiment. We need to encourage people,

711   http://www.ft.com/cms/s/0/31f366de-03f8-11e3-8aab-00144feab7de.html

businesses and governments to take risks. As Westlake rightly argues: "If we're to reap the harvest of these new technologies, the government needs to create a world where optimists can flourish. This means liberalising planning and immigration so that entrepreneurs brave enough to expand aren't stopped by government. It means creating a culture where angels and VCs [venture capitalists] can back growth firms in the expectation that, if they succeed, they'll be able to float on public markets. And it means prioritising Plan I: ingenuity, innovation and inspiration."[712]

Europeans need to overcome their cultural resistance to change. GM crops have been tried and tested around the world, yet they continue to be rejected in Europe: only two have been licensed by the European Commission. Shale gas is cleaner, safer and cheaper than coal yet some governments have banned it, while Britain's is meeting fierce resistance in trying to develop it. While many Europeans obsess about the costs and risks of new technologies, what about the costs and risks of forsaking them? Our world of plenty – and the political progress that this makes possible – depends on science, technology and risk-taking. As Ryan Avent of *The Economist* rightly remarks, "a lack of big discoveries doesn't strike me as the binding constraint on growth. Conceivably it is the pace of entrepreneurial adaption that matters. I'm most inclined to think that it's the pace of *societal evolution* that is most binding: growth proceeds at the fastest pace that legal and social institutions can tolerate."[713]

Europe's most important challenge is to nurture a risk-taking, can-do, optimistic mindset. People who don't accept limits and try to push boundaries, forcing everyone else to try to up their game. The determination to lift the obstacles that are holding us back. The

---

712   http://www.cityam.com/article/let-optimists-run-economy-and-innovation-will-charge-growth?

713   http://www.economist.com/blogs/freeexchange/2012/06/innovation

optimism that leads us to open our economies, our societies and our minds to all the many possibilities for progress.

Europe desperately needs more creative destruction. We need to oust tired old ways and replace them with fresh new ones. While some may object that they prefer Europe's more caring capitalism to America's more cutthroat variety, that is a false choice. For a start, Europe's capitalism is often cosily corporatist and cartelised rather than genuinely caring. It tends to prioritise wage-squeezing competitiveness over dynamic competition that offers opportunities to outsiders, benefits consumers and generates growth and jobs. And while change can be unsettling, it is surely preferable to stagnation. After all, without growth, Europe's generous social policies are unaffordable. A dynamic economy is perfectly consistent with a decent society that promotes equality of opportunity and protects people throughout life. A society open to everyone widens the talent pool. A welfare state that catches people when they fall and helps them back on their feet can encourage people to take greater risks. Dynamism and decency are complements, not alternatives. So Europe can emulate the best of America's more dynamic capitalism without adopting its model wholesale. The next chapter explains how to make our economies and societies more decent.

12

DECENT

A fairer society with opportunities for all

Men did not make the earth. It is the value of the improvements only, and not the earth itself, that is individual property. Every proprietor owes to the community a ground rent for the land which he holds.

Thomas Paine, *Agrarian Justice*, 1797[714]

Land monopoly is... by far the greatest of monopolies – it is a per-petual monopoly, and it is the mother of all other forms of monopoly. Unearned increments in land are not the only form of unearned or undeserved profit, but they are the principal form of unearned incre-ment, and they are derived from processes which are not merely not beneficial, but positively detrimental to the general public.

Winston Churchill, 1909[715]

---

714   Thomas Paine, *Agrarian Justice*, 1797

715   http://www.progress.org/banneker/chur.html

I see nothing objectionable in fixing a limit to what anyone may acquire by mere favour of others, without any exercise of his faculties, and in requiring that if he desires any further accession of fortune, he shall work for it.

John Stuart Mill, *Principles of Political Economy*, 1848[716]

Inheritance taxes could, of course, be made an instrument toward greater social mobility and greater dispersion of property and, consequently, may have to be regarded as important tools of a truly liberal policy.

Friedrich von Hayek,
Individualism and Economic Order, 1948[717]

Hurrah: the world has become a much less unequal place over the past thirty years. Living standards in many poorer countries – not least China and India – have risen much faster than those in the West. Over the past decade, much of Africa has started to catch up too. Across Europe, the gap between rich and poor has also narrowed. In southern Europe until the crisis and even now in central and eastern Europe, the EU has been an engine for economic progress – a "convergence machine", as the World Bank's *Golden Growth* report puts it.[718] But at the same time, the gap between rich and poor *within* many countries has widened. Some attribute this to globalisation, which has expanded opportunities for some while eliminating others' jobs. Others point to new technologies, notably computing, that make some

716 John Stuart Mill, *Principles of Political Economy*, 1848, quoted in Richard Reeves, *John Stuart Mill: Victorian Firebrand*, Atlantic: 2007

717 Friedrich Hayek, *Individualism and Economic Order*, University of Chicago: 1948. http://library.mises.org/books/Friedrich%20A%20Hayek/Individualism%20and%20Economic%20Order.pdf

718 http://www.worldbank.org/en/region/eca/publication/golden-growth

people much more productive, while replacing others' jobs. Politically, trade is much more controversial than technology, but economically they are analogous. In both cases, society as a whole is better off because it is able to produce more with less. Stifling such growth would be a mistake; it would be much better to help people to adapt, while also redistributing some of its proceeds. Ideally, a tax system should be progressive – the rich should contribute a bigger share of their incomes than the poor – but not punitive. But a much bigger issue is that some get outsized rewards that they don't deserve.

Europe is often a desperately unfair place. Financiers have looted the wealth created by businesses and prudently put away by savers, wrecked the economy and pillaged public coffers. Even failed company bosses get huge golden goodbyes. Landowners get richer through others' investment and hard work while taxing successful businesses and people through higher rents. Some businesses – both big and small – enjoy monopolistic profits at the expense of their customers and challenger companies. Privileged employees on permanent contracts and inflated salaries price young people out of work. The undeserving rich (who may, of course, be perfectly decent people) inherit wealth passed on from previous generations. Talented young people and outsiders are denied opportunity or locked out of the country altogether. This unfairness is not just unethical; it eventually stunts economic dynamism.

As well as becoming more adaptable and dynamic, Europe's economies ought to be more decent. A decent society is one where equal opportunities are a priority, there is a closer connection between people's contribution to society and their rewards, inequalities of wealth and power are not so great that they become entrenched and everyone enjoys a decent minimum standard of living. In principle, many politicians would agree. In practice, they often don't want (or dare) to tackle privileged vested interests. Even well-meaning ones tend to tackle symptoms rather than causes – and may make things worse.

A decent society is desirable in itself. But it is also a means of boosting economic growth more generally. If bright children from disadvantaged backgrounds are denied opportunities to better themselves, this unfairness is also a waste of talent: ideas not developed, businesses not started, jobs not created, taxes not paid. If wealth, status and power are inherited rather than earned, they may contribute nothing to the greater good and the incentives of those who inherit may be dulled. If people reap huge rewards by appropriating value created by others, that unfairness distorts incentives and makes society as a whole worse off. If some scrape by in penury while others live in luxury, such indecency fragments society, preventing the interchange of ideas from which innovation springs.

A dynamic economy will inevitably create huge disparities of wealth. Those who seize business opportunities and develop new technologies that create value for the rest of society ought to be rewarded for it. Few would begrudge James Dyson, a British inventor whose eponymous bagless vacuum cleaners have cleaned up, his fortune. Xavier Niel, the founder of Free, has done France a huge service by freeing up internet provision there. Anyone who has shopped at Ikea can thank Sweden's Ingvar Kamprad.

But alongside Europe's deserving billionaires are many undeserving ones. Britain's richest man, Gerald Cavendish Grosvenor (also known as the Duke of Westminster), contributes nothing to society; in fact, he leeches off it. He owes his wealth to the accident of birth, having inherited three hundred acres of land that are now Mayfair and Belgravia, London's priciest real estate. This land was not created by him or by any of his ancestors. Nor did it soar in value from his or their efforts. It is now worth some £5 billion because of the hard work and investment of millions of Londoners and successive governments who together have made London a global powerhouse. Did Grosvenor pay for or build the roads, the Tube, water pipes, sewerage, electricity, phone lines? No. Did he build the businesses that operate around there? No. Without them, his land has little value. The more wealth that others create on and near his land, the wealthier he gets and the more he can extract from their enterprise in higher rents. It is a monstrous racket that penalises the people, companies and taxpayers who actually create wealth.

The explosive growth of the financial sector in the decades before the crisis has also enabled a gilded few to appropriate wealth created by businesses and households in the rest of the economy. In Britain, the profits of the financial sector soared from 1.5 per cent of the total between 1948 and 1978 to 15 per cent in 2008, often at the expense of the rest of society.[719] In 1989 the bosses of Britain's four biggest banks already earned a whopping fifty times average incomes; by 2007, just before the crash, their pay had soared to £4.3 million, 230 times average household income.[720] Fred Goodwin, the man whose hubris blew up Royal Bank of Scotland, arguably deserves to be in jail, not on a munificent taxpayer-funded pension.

The property and financial bubbles, which are being rekindled by the global spillovers from America's QE and government subsidies for property speculation in Britain, are a big reason why the distribution of income – not to mention wealth – has become much more unequal. No European country is as extremely unequal as the US. The top 1 per cent of Americans took home nearly a fifth of national income in 2012, while the top 0.1 per cent alone amassed 8.82 per cent of total incomes – and the richest 0.01 per cent an astonishing 4.08 per cent![721] The 0.01 per cent include Larry Page and Sergey

---

719   http://www.bankofengland.co.uk/publications/Documents/speeches/2010/speech442.pdf

720   http://www.lrb.co.uk/v34/n04/andrew-haldane/the-doom-loop

721   Facundo Alvaredo, Tony Atkinson, Thomas Piketty and Emmanuel Saez, "The World Top Incomes Database" http://topincomes.parisschoolofeconomics.eu/#Database:

Brin, the co-founders of Google, whose achievements are admirable. But the superrich also include Dick Fuld, the man who sank Lehman Brothers, and other scoundrels who have kept their ill-gotten gains. In Britain, the top 1 per cent received 13.88 per cent of national income in 2009 (up from 9.8 per cent in 1990), their biggest share since the 1930s. The top 0.1 per cent got 5.11 per cent. Even in more equal Sweden, the richest few are pulling further ahead. The top 1 per cent earned 7.02 per cent of national income, nearly twice the 3.97 per cent they received in 1981, while the top 0.1 per cent obtained 2.19 per cent, nearly three times the 0.77 per cent they obtained in 1986. The top 0.01 per cent took home 0.75 per cent, nearly five times the 0.17 per cent they got in 1980. Looking at the Gini coefficient, a measure of a society's overall income inequality, Britain and Italy are the most unequal societies in western Europe, while Denmark is the most equal, with Sweden just behind.[722] The distribution of wealth is generally much more unequal. And as Thomas Piketty of the Paris School of Economics has pointed out, as growth slows and with it the creation of new wealth, old (inherited) fortunes weigh more heavily than before.[723]

A decent society should want to encourage effort and enterprise – by everyone, not just those who end up billionaires – without rewarding undeserved or unearned income. Battles between right and left about how high tax rates should be generally fail to make this distinction: those who want to cut taxes point to people like James Dyson, those who want to raise them point to Fred Goodwin. But while no economic system can perfectly distinguish between deserved income and wealth and the undeserved variety, societies could still do much better.

---

722   *Ibid.* Table 4

723   Thomas Piketty, *Capital in the Twenty-First Century*, Harvard: 2014

The starting point is to tackle problems at their source, since undeserved income is generally a symptom of an underlying problem that also has wider costs. Ending the tax privileges of debt, as Chapter 10 suggested, would curb the size and profitability of the financial system, and thus the outsized rewards to financiers. Abolishing the tax advantages of property speculation and private pensions would likewise reduce undeserved rewards in those sectors. Reforms to corporate governance would reduce bosses' bloated pay, as David Sainsbury suggests in *Progressive Capitalism*.[724] Injecting competition into monopolistic markets and taking away the privileges of labour-market insiders likewise. But that would still leave two big problems: undeserved earnings from land and inherited wealth.

Tax land, not labour

It is perverse that all European governments tax labour so heavily and not land. As a result, some strive less – and since hiring is more expensive, fewer jobs are created. The poorest and least productive (including the young) are most likely to be priced out of a job. Cutting taxes on work would create more jobs, especially for those people. This could be accompanied by a (smaller) rise in the minimum wage to ensure that existing low-paid workers benefit too. The holy grail of higher employment and higher wages for the low-paid could thus be achieved – a key plank of a decent society. If people on lower incomes were exempt from taxes on work altogether, this would make society much fairer. At a time of high unemployment, it ought to be a no-brainer.

The shortfall in tax revenues would be filled by taxing land values. This wouldn't reduce the supply of land, which is fixed and immovable: Mayfair can't be spirited away to a tax haven. Nor would it push

724   David Sainsbury, *Progressive Capitalism: How To Achieve Economic Growth, Liberty and Social Justice*, Biteback: 2013

up rents, which depend on what tenants are prepared to pay rather than landlords' expenses.[725] Thus, unlike most taxes, it wouldn't crimp economic activity, as Adam Smith explained in *The Wealth of Nations*. On the contrary, a land tax would encourage development. Since it would be payable irrespective of how land is used, it would stimulate the regeneration of derelict and unused sites. Infrastructure investment that raises surrounding land values, such as new Tube (metro) lines or a high-speed rail network, would pay for itself and thus escape short-sighted budget cuts. Unlike with property taxes, people who do up their homes would not be penalised. Taxing land values could also curb property bubbles – and the inevitable busts – without discouraging mobility (unlike Britain's stamp duty and other taxes on property transactions) or business investment (unlike interest-rate rises). In Britain, a 0.5 per cent a year tax on land values would raise roughly £25 billion a year. Since the government raises a bit over £100 billion from national-insurance contributions, this could be used to slash those by a quarter, ideally by raising the lower limit on contributions

---

725 "Ground-rents are a still more proper subject of taxation than the rent of houses. A tax upon ground-rents would not raise the rents of houses. It would fall altogether upon the owner of the ground-rent, who acts always as a monopolist, and exacts the greatest rent which can be got for the use of his ground. More or less can be got for it according as the competitors happen to be richer or poorer, or can afford to gratify their fancy for a particular spot of ground at a greater or smaller expense. In every country the greatest number of rich competitors is in the capital, and it is there accordingly that the highest ground-rents are always to be found. As the wealth of those competitors would in no respect be increased by a tax upon ground-rents, they would not probably be disposed to pay more for the use of the ground. Whether the tax was to be advanced by the inhabitant, or by the owner of the ground, would be of little importance. The more the inhabitant was obliged to pay for the tax, the less he would incline to pay for the ground; so that the final payment of the tax would fall altogether upon the owner of the ground-rent." Adam Smith, *The Wealth of Nations*, Book V, Chapter 2, Article I: Taxes upon the Rent of Houses

dramatically. Over time, the aim would be to shift the tax burden off hard-working families and on to idle landlords.

Above all, a land tax would be fair. In many European countries, land ownership is concentrated in the hands of a few: in Britain land is parcelled out more unequally than in Brazil.[726] The country's biggest private landowner, the Duke of Buccleuch, owns 277,000 acres, not because of his talent or industry, but because his ancestors seized vast swaths of Scotland. Crucially, land values have soared over the past twenty years through no effort of the likes of the Duke of Westminster. Surely it would be better to tax that windfall gain, rather than the employees and entrepreneurs who generate it?

Take Tech City. Internet start-ups sprang up around London's Old Street roundabout in part because of the low rents in what was a down-at-heel area. By creating valuable businesses there, they have made it a desirable place to work. For local landowners, this has been a boon. One internet entrepreneur told me that Derwent, a big office owner, raised the rent more than five-fold overnight after David Cameron drew attention to Tech City, and thus to the value local start-ups were creating. Derwent, in effect, expropriated much of the value that those young entrepreneurs created. That is not just unfair, since it has been rewarded for doing nothing: neither creating the land nor taking a risk. It is also inefficient, since it acts like a private tax on enterprise. Surely it would be better to tax that socially created value and use the proceeds to slash the taxes on effort and enterprise? Since most of us earn most of our lifetime income from work rather than from rent, taxing land instead of labour would make most people better off. Neither tenants nor leaseholders would pay a penny; only freeholders and landlords would; the owner of a large estate could pay a higher rate than someone who owns a small suburban semi.

---

726   0.3 per cent of the population owns 69 per cent of the land in Britain. Kevin Cahill, *Who Owns the World: The Hidden Facts Behind Landownership*, Mainstream: 2006

Farmers and big landowners would doubtless kick up a mighty fuss. But since the typical family of four shells out £850 (€1,000) a year to farmers in higher taxes and food prices because of the EU's Common Agricultural Policy, which also inflates land prices, it's only fair to claw some of that back. While landowners would point to the impact on a poor granny in a big house – a bogus argument that Churchill called the "poor widow bogey" – she wouldn't be forced out of her home; her tax bill could be deferred. Another old objection – that land is hard to value – is outdated in an era of big data in which land is routinely valued each year as property changes hands.[727]

Globally, Hong Kong has prospered by taxing land values, which has allowed it to keep taxes on enterprise low. In Europe, Austria charges a 1 per cent tax on land values and Denmark a tax of between 1.6 and 3.4 per cent. Estonia levies between 0.1 per cent and 2.5 per cent a year to fund local councils. It works well. Others should emulate them.[728]

Tax spending from capital bequests

Shifting the tax burden off labour and on to land would tackle one source of unearned wealth. Another is large inheritances. These are objectionable for two reasons. Like landowners, heirs have not worked for their windfall – and large inheritances entrench privilege and impede equality of opportunity. Often the two inequities are combined, when huge parcels of real estate are passed down from generation to generation.

---

727   Land in Denmark is valued using a "hedonic" pricing model based on the compulsory registration of all land transactions. This model uses information about the characteristics of land (location, transport links and so on) that is sold to estimate the value of other land.

728   http://aysps.gsu.edu/isp/files/ISP_CONFERENCES_PROPERTY_TAX_06_TIITS_PAPER.pdf

Large inheritances aren't just bad for society as a whole; they may be harmful for the individual concerned. As Andrew Carnegie, a Scottish-American steel magnate, wisely remarked, "The parent who leaves his son enormous wealth generally deadens the talents and energies of the son, and tempts him to lead a less useful and less worthy life than he otherwise would." His 1889 article proclaiming "The Gospel of Wealth" called on the rich to use their wealth to improve society, and stimulated wave after wave of philanthropy. More recently, Bill Gates has pledged to give most of his fortune from Microsoft to the Gates Foundation, now the world's largest private philanthropic foundation. This aims to improve health-care and reduce extreme poverty around the world and expand educational opportunities and access to information technology in America. Warren Buffett, a billionaire investor, has selflessly decid-ed to throw in his billions to a foundation that doesn't even carry his name. George Soros, another financier turned philanthropist, has pledged billions to advance human rights and open societies, notably in central and eastern Europe. After the Berlin Wall fell, he personally gave more aid to eastern Europe than the British govern-ment did. British examples include the Wellcome Trust, which funds medical and scientific research, the Barrow Cadbury Trust, which helps the vulnerable and marginalised, and the Joseph Rowntree Foundation, which funds work on poverty. Other European ones include the Robert Bosch Stiftung in Germany and the Knut and Alice Wallenberg Foundation in Sweden. Even so, there is gener-ally much less of a tradition of philanthropy in Europe. Charitable giving is often only a tiny fraction of people's wealth. A European Carnegie ought to pen his or her own Gospel of Wealth to motivate others.

There is also a role for public policy. Unfortunately, inheritance tax is wildly unpopular and often quite easy to evade, notably by giv-ing wealth away before death or putting it in trust. Revenues from inheritance tax in Britain are a mere £3 billion a year.[729] Some countries, including Sweden, have abolished it altogether over the past decade.[730] Even so, most OECD countries levy a tax on estates, gifts or inheritances, typically on the recipient rather than on the donor (as in the UK). Many also tax gifts given prior to death as a tax-avoidance measure. Some, such as Ireland, try to tax all gifts and inheritances received over a lifetime.

A better way of tackling the issue is to incorporate it into the expenditure-tax system advocated in Chapter 10. Someone who received a capital bequest would include it in their taxable income; as with normal income, they would only pay tax on it when they spent it. Those who gave capital would have an incentive to declare it, because they could deduct it from their taxable income – thereby limiting tax avoidance. In effect, unearned income would be taxed in the same way as the earned variety. Such a system might be less unpopular than inheritance tax because it would not force families to sell their home or business when someone dies. Those who inherited wealth would only pay tax when they sold a house or shares and spent the proceeds. Additional revenues from taxing capital bequests when they are spent could help fund measures to boost equality of opportunity.

Equal chances

That human beings are born unequal is an inescapable fact of life. Intelligence, dexterity, drive, charm, confidence, looks and many other factors that help people get ahead are given to some more than others. Some have loving and supportive parents; others don't. While David Beckham's success required both effort and discipline, he was also extremely fortunate to be born with innate footballing

---

729 http://www.ifs.org.uk/bns/bn09.pdf

730 http://www.ippr.org/images/media/files/publication/2013/03/wealth-taxes-context_Mar2013_10503.pdf

skills that happen to be extremely valued in modern Britain (but would have been of no value two hundred years ago) – and handsome to boot.

No public policy could have given me Beckham's skills. Even so, it is self-evidently possible to create societies where life chances are more equal. Capitalist economies offer greater opportunities than feudal ones did. Modern societies in which everyone receives a free education offer better prospects than those where many received little or none. If one thinks of life as a race to achieve whatever your goals may be (admittedly, an imperfect analogy) a society that strives to improve equality of opportunity is one where there is a more equal starting point, the race is fair – one's chances of success depend solely on relevant qualities such as aptitude and effort – and those who fall at one hurdle have a chance to pick themselves up again.

One gauge of equality of opportunity is social mobility: the extent to which people's prospects are determined by their parents' economic status. An OECD study finds that people's earnings and educational achievements are strongly determined by their parents' incomes in Britain and France, but much less so in Nordic countries.[731] That social mobility is low in both France, where welfare provision is lavish, and Britain, where it is more meagre, highlights that the key to equality of opportunity is not necessarily higher welfare spending, but rather improving education and other factors that enhance young people's life chances. Studies show that poorer children fall behind even before they start school, so good nurseries and pre-school classes for all should be a priority. The OECD study suggests that this makes a significant difference. So too does financial support targeted at helping poor families invest in their children's education. Increasing the social mix within schools tends to boost disadvantaged students

---

731   OECD, *Economic Policy Reforms: Going for Growth*, 2010, Chapter 5. http://www.oecd.org/tax/public-finance/chapter%205%20gfg%202010.pdf

without any apparent negative effects on other children. However, streaming children by ability at an early age impedes social mobility.

Governments ought to prioritise education spending, especially on children from poorer backgrounds. Manifestly, money makes a difference: witness the dominance that Eton, a school for the rich, has over British public life. Equally clearly, private, non-profit schools have no problem delivering a good education. So one way of ensuring there are Etons for everyone would be to provide parents with generous education vouchers, with top-ups for kids from underprivileged backgrounds. That way schools would be motivated to attract them and then have the resources to provide them with better education. Paying higher salaries to attract better teachers would help; as would valuing teaching more highly as a profession; perhaps one would lead to the other. Let a wide range of new schools open. Combine that with choice over which school to attend, with successful schools allowed to expand and failing ones either taken over or closed down, and access to excellent education could be democratised. To the extent that existing institutions, teachers and education professionals are willing to embrace change, they should be helped and encouraged to. But if they aren't, new schools should be established and more open-minded teachers recruited. Children's needs should be paramount, not teachers'.

Providing each young person with one or two lump sums of capital – one when they reach eighteen and another, say, when they reach thirty – could also make a huge difference. The lump sum – say £10,000 (€12,000) – would not be enough to live on for a long time, so it would not deter people from working much. But it would provide everyone with capital and thus a buffer against bad times and a springboard for starting one's own business (or pursuing one's studies). It would also give everyone a stake in society: because they would have something to lose. The lump sum could be conditional on, for instance, school attendance or avoiding a criminal record, and thus provide a strong incentive for young people to improve themselves and avoid trouble. Overall, the aim would be to ensure that everyone had a fairer chance in life and fewer ended up wards of the state. In Britain, roughly 1.7 million people will turn eighteen or thirty in 2015. If each received £10,000, this would cost £17 billion a year.

Ensuring the race is fair involves enforcing anti-discrimination laws more vigorously. But it would also be a consequence of the reforms to make economies more adaptable and dynamic. Businesses in competitive markets have a greater incentive to hire the best person for the job than cartelised clubs where profits flow from connections rather than creativity. If it is easier to start a business or make a name for yourself by writing a blog, appearing on YouTube or organising a social movement online, those who are neglected by traditional companies have alternative routes to get ahead. Last but not least, countries need a welfare system that protects people when they lose their job while helping them to find a new one, as Denmark does. As Chapter 10 explained, that should involve help retraining and finding a job, which is much easier and cheaper now there are online job exchanges.

The past four chapters have outlined how to make Europe's economies and societies more adaptable, dynamic and decent through reforms that ADD UP. How, though, does one drive change? The next chapter looks at how to make the EU more democratic. The concluding chapter looks at how to resist the twin dangers of extremism and stagnation and instead embrace a European Spring: economic and political renewal.

13

DEMOCRACY IN EUROPE

Why the EU is still a good thing, but needs to change

> *If democracy has been one of the strong commitments with which Europe emerged from the 1940s, an understanding of the necessity of social security and avoidance of intense social deprivation has surely been another. Even if savage cuts in the foundations of the European systems of social justice had been financially inescapable (I don't believe they were, but even if they had been), there is a need to persuade people that this is indeed the case, rather than trying to carry out such cuts by fiat. The disdain for the public could hardly have been more transparent in many of the chosen ways of European policymaking.*
>
> Amartya Sen, professor of economics and philosophy
> at Harvard University, 2012[732]

---

732   http://www.bis.org/publ/bppdf/bispap69.pdf

It may not seem like it now, but the European Union is an amazing achievement. A continent devastated by two World Wars, disgraced by Nazi genocide, disfigured by fascist dictatorships and divided by communist ones has largely reunited in peace and democracy. Its original objective – to make war among its members unthinkable – has been achieved. It also helped entrench democracy and the rule of law and spread prosperity southwards (to post-fascist Greece, Spain and Portugal) then eastwards (to former communist countries). That relatively smooth transition is now taken for granted, but it wasn't certain at the time. While it took American intervention to end the wars in the former Yugoslavia two decades ago, peace has been secured by the lure of EU membership: Croatia joined in 2013, while Serbia and Bosnia are candidates. Without the prospect of joining the EU, many countries might have gone off track: witness Ukraine. The EU's positive influence on candidate countries stands in contrast to the catastrophic consequences that America's "war on drugs" and lax gun laws have on its neighbourhood. Spreading peace, prosperity and democracy eastwards and southwards through closer ties to (and eventual membership for) neighbouring countries ought to be at the heart of the EU's mission in decades to come.

Trade in Europe is also freer than ever. While former European Commission President Jacques Delors once said it was impossible to fall in love with Europe's single market, Europeans disagree: they rate the free movement of people, goods and services within the EU as its most positive achievement.[733] Europeans are much better off as a result – a family of four is €2,000 a year richer, by one reckoning.[734] There is a wider choice of better-value products in shops. The cost

---

733   European Parliament Eurobarometer (EB79.5), June 2013, QD5T

734   One European Commission study in 2007 found that the single market had boosted EU GDP by 2.2 per cent (€233 billion) and created 2.75 million jobs between 1992 and 2006.

of flights within the Europe has plunged: it is thanks to the EU that Ryanair can fly freely anywhere in Europe. Using your mobile phone in another EU country is less exorbitant. Your taxes stretch further because big government contracts have been opened up to competitive tendering, generating better value for money. For some countries, the EU's single market has been transformational: thanks in large part to foreign investment attracted by its access to the EU market (and its low taxes), Ireland's Celtic tiger economy leapt from poverty to prosperity within two decades.

Freedoms that were unimaginable thirty years ago – that five hundred million people could move freely across the EU, from Lisbon to Lithuania and Leipzig to Liverpool – now seem normal. Asked what the EU means to them personally, Europeans' top answer is the freedom to travel, study and work anywhere in the Union.[735] The EU's Charter of Fundamental Rights enshrines Europeans' basic freedoms. The EU's official motto, "United in diversity", is admirable. At its best, it is a vehicle for overcoming narrow nationalisms and embracing open, diverse societies.

Connected by economic exchange and personal contact, Europe has also evolved a novel form of political collaboration, a hybrid between intense and intricate intergovernmental cooperation and pan-European institutions, notably the European Commission, the European Parliament and the European Court of Justice. No other region in the world comes close to this. Acting together through the EU, Europeans also have more global influence than apart. Their clout is greater in trade and investment talks. Even big American companies call off mergers if EU watchdogs object that they would harm competition in Europe. If the EU could muster a collective energy policy, even the hoodlums in the Kremlin would have to take note.

---

735   European Parliament Eurobarometer (EB79.5), June 2013, QA14. In Greece, however, more people associate the EU with unemployment.

It is precisely because the EU is such an amazing achievement that the bad turn it has taken in recent years is so tragic. While public dissatisfaction with the EU is nothing new – the French came within a whisker of rejecting the Maastricht Treaty in a referendum in 1992 and, together with the Dutch, put paid to the constitutional treaty in 2005, while the Danes and the Irish have also rejected EU treaties (and then accepted amended ones) – support for the EU has collapsed since the crisis. Only 50 per cent of Europeans now think the EU is a good thing.[736] A mere 26 per cent believe it is going in the right direction.[737] Three in five no longer trust it.[738] Only 44 per cent are satisfied with the way democracy works in the EU.[739] Only 39 per cent think their voice counts in the EU.[740]

Scepticism about the EU was once confined to Britain and the margins of other European countries; now it has gone mainstream. Support for anti-EU parties has soared. Many French Socialists are disenchanted with the EU. Many British Conservatives want the UK to leave the EU altogether. The Liberal-Labour coalition that runs the Netherlands wants more powers back from Brussels. The European Parliament elections in May 2014 could produce a swathe of anti-EU MPs.

Policymakers in Brussels tend to think the EU is simply misunderstood. But while it is true that Europeans are not always aware of

---

736   *Ibid*, Q22

737   Eurobarometer 80, Autumn 2013, QA9.2 "At the present time, would you say that, in general, things are going in the right direction or in the wrong direction, in the European Union?"

738   *Ibid*, QA10.8 "I would like to ask you a question about how much trust you have in certain institutions. For each of the following institutions, please tell me if you tend to trust it or tend not to trust it: The European Union"

739   European Parliament Eurobarometer (EB79.5), June 2013, Q30b

740   *Ibid*, Q24.1

its benefits and that national governments have a tendency to blame difficult decisions on Brussels, the EU has also taken a wrong turn in recent years. As this book has detailed, EU and eurozone institutions helped create the crisis in the eurozone – and their response to it has been deeply flawed. There has also been a dangerously inflexible and deeply undemocratic centralisation of fiscal powers in Brussels. Worse, the EU's political institutions have been captured by Angela Merkel's government to serve its selfish ends as a creditor. No wonder Spaniards, who were once exuberantly pro-European, are now increasingly resentful. Only 24 per cent think the EU is going in the right direction, the same proportion as in Britain.[741] More than two-thirds of Spaniards and Britons no longer trust the EU.[742] Most Europeans don't think the EU is creating the conditions for more jobs.[743] Two-thirds think the EU is responsible for austerity.[744]

The economic crisis has exacerbated a political one that predates it. Designed as an elite project that advanced integration through agricultural subsidies and industrial development, the EU now meddles in everything from defence and foreign policy to food safety, education and culture, not to mention economic policy. Some object that the EU should not be handling such matters at all. Others oppose specific decisions. Still others have problems with the process through which it reaches decisions. For a variety of reasons, support for the EU was already much lower at the height of the boom in 2007 than fifteen years earlier.

---

741   Eurobarometer 80, Autumn 2013, QA9.2

742   *Ibid*, QA10.8

743   *Ibid*, QA13.1 "Please tell me to what extent you agree or disagree with each of the following statements. The EU is creating the conditions for more jobs in Europe"

744   *Ibid*, QA13.2 "Please tell me to what extent you agree or disagree with each of the following statements. The EU is responsible for austerity in Europe"

In countries where there was previously a strong political, cultural or ideological attachment to the EU, this goodwill has been eroded. Many Germans no longer feel a need to immerse themselves in Europe to atone for their Nazi past. Many French people resent that what was once perceived as a vehicle for projecting power in an American-dominated West has seemingly become a Trojan Horse for imposing globalisation on them. Many Italians who saw Europe as a means of escaping from their dysfunctional politics now see EU governance as deeply flawed too. Many Greeks, Spaniards and Portuguese who were ecstatic about rejoining the European club after the pain and isolation of fascist dictatorships have lost their rose-tinted spectacles. Many Irish people who saw Europe as a way of escaping from Britain's shadow and modernising their society now resent Germany instead. When that goodwill is gone, what remains is a British-style transactional view of the EU: do its benefits outweigh its costs? At the moment, many think not. To change that, the EU needs to convince Europeans that the future benefits of the EU outweigh its current perceived costs, while rekindling goodwill towards it. An economic recovery and lower unemployment would doubtless help. But the problem is more deep-seated than that. The basic issue is that the EU is not democratic enough. Before going into why and what ought to be done about it, let me explain why it would be a terrible mistake for Britain to leave even an unreformed EU.

Britain in Europe

Most Britons have never been particularly enthusiastic about European integration. In 1946 Winston Churchill proposed a United States of Europe – of which Britain would be a "friend" and "sponsor" but not a member.[745] When six European countries began to tie their destinies together in the 1950s, Britain stood aside. Very soon, though, British

---

745   http://assembly.coe.int/Main.asp?link=/AboutUs/zurich_e.htm

policymakers regretted their decision. While considering Britain different from the Continent (an "island nation") and superior (undefeated in the Second World War, unoccupied since 1066, master of a massive Empire), they were also insecure (Britain was in economic and political decline) and afraid of isolation. Edward Heath's Conservative government finally took Britain into what was then the European Economic Community (EEC) in 1973. Soon after, the new Labour government asked voters whether they wanted to stay in. In a referendum in 1975, two-thirds of Britons voted Yes. Among the most vigorous Yes campaigners was the Conservative leader, Margaret Thatcher. Contrary to the belief that she and British voters generally were misled into joining what they thought was only a Common Market, she saw the case for membership as primarily political: "Almost every major nation has been obliged by the pressures of the post-war world to pool significant areas of sovereignty so as to create more effective political units."[746] The tables turned in the late 1980s, however. The opposition Labour Party, which had favoured withdrawal in the 1983 elections, was won over by European Commission President Jacques Delors, a French socialist. Meanwhile, despite the momentous decision in 1986 to create a European single market by the end of 1992, a big advance for free trade that she strongly supported, Thatcher soured on Europe. Her ejection as prime minister in 1990 after a dispute over Europe's exchange-rate mechanism, from which Britain itself was ejected on Black Wednesday in September 1992, started a civil war in the Conservative Party during John Major's premiership that ended in victory for EU-phobes.[747] After 1997, Britain played a

---

746   http://www.euromove.org.uk/index.php?id=6505 In 1978 Thatcher also favoured closer European cooperation in defence.

747   Ironically, Thatcher's dispute with her Chancellor, Nigel Lawson, was over whether to take the pound into Europe's exchange-rate mechanism (ERM). Lawson, who now thinks Britain should leave the EU, was determined to take the pound into

more constructive role in Europe under Tony Blair, but decided not to join the euro. Ironically, Gordon Brown, who had been strongly in favour of the euro before becoming Chancellor in 1997, subsequently changed his position, in part because of knee-jerk opposition to Blair, but also because he did not want to cede power to Europe. I played a small part in the debate at the time as chief economist and then director of policy at Britain in Europe, the cross-party pro-European campaign, from late 2002 to early 2005.

Back then, our polling showed that while British people were not enthusiastic about the EU, they strongly supported the status-quo option and were afraid of isolation. While it is still not a pressing issue for most Britons – hence David Cameron's earlier appeal to his more extreme backbenchers to stop "banging on" about Europe – public opinion has become more negative, for several reasons. Unlike in the eurozone, Britain's lurch into austerity cannot be blamed on Brussels; nor are falling wages the result of demands from Olli Rehn, the EU's economic enforcer. But as boom has turned to bust, Britons have generally turned inwards. They increasingly blame foreigners of all kinds – immigrants, other Europeans, the Chinese – for their troubles. Since the EU is now associated with both the eurozone crisis and east European immigration, it is doubly damned. Being insulated, if not isolated, from the rest of Europe now seems more appealing. The contrast between Europe's sluggishness and the rapid growth in China and other emerging economies also makes it seem more plausible that Britain could prosper as a global trader (although so far it exports less to China as a share of its economy than Greece does). Worse, if the crisis in the eurozone leads to

---

the ERM. Thatcher, who had criticised the Labour government for not joining the ERM in 1978, was set against the idea. After Lawson resigned in 1989, his successor, John Major, bounced her into joining the ERM in October 1990, only to replace her as prime minister a month later after she was forced out of office. The pound was subsequently ejected from the ERM on Black Wednesday in September 1992.

closer integration within it, Britain risks being marginalised even within the EU. So why not be free?

Economic benefits

Deluded by nostalgia for the Empire, hardline EU-phobes fantasise about a Britain, freed of EU shackles, that bestrides the globe. But whether Little Englanders like it or not, geography still matters – and Britain's places it in Europe. Even in a globalising economy, most trade remains regional – and in Britain's case more than half of it is with the rest of the EU. Surely it ought to trade on the best terms possible?

It is because Britain is part of an EU single market of 500 million consumers that Toyota and other Japanese carmakers, India's Tata (which has turned around Jaguar Land Rover) and Germany's BMW, which has revived the Mini, have invested in the UK. They have revitalised the manufacture of cars – four in five of which are exported. While Eurosceptics tend to portray global trade as an alternative to the EU, that is a false choice. If Germany successfully exports to both China and France, so too could Britain. Far from being an impediment to international trade, being part of the EU single market is a platform for British businesses to engage with the world.

While Britain has lots going for it, it would be worse off trying to go it alone. American presidents would call less. Chinese companies would invest less. European partners would be sad to see Britain go but would get on with life without it. While EU-phobes seem to think that Britain would be in the driving seat in any future negotiations with the EU, the EU matters much more to Britain – exports to the EU amount to 14 per cent of the UK economy – than Britain does to the rest of the EU: their exports to Britain are a mere 2.5 per cent of their collective GDP.

Paradoxically, the biggest reason why Britain would lose out from leaving the EU is that European countries are going to matter much less in coming decades as the centre of gravity of the world economy tilts east and south. In global terms, Britain matters less and less. On its own, it would have to play by others' rules or else be isolated and ignored. But within the EU, Britain is big enough to matter – if only it would play a constructive role – and through the EU, it can have influence on the global stage.

In 1970, when Britain was last an independent trader, it was a heavyweight in world trade: its 8 per cent share of total exports and imports was greater than China's 7 per cent share in 2008.[748] But Britain's share of world trade has now fallen to 3.5 per cent and is likely to continue declining as the weight of non-Western economies grows. By global standards, Britain is becoming a small economy.

So long as Europe lives under a *Pax Americana* and global trade is reasonably free, small economies are perfectly viable both inside the EU (Sweden) and outside it (Switzerland), but those outside the EU have much less autonomy than British Eurosceptics tend to imagine. In order to buy everything they want from the rest of the world, they need to export – and that means accepting the terms set by their major export partners. In Britain's case, exports of goods and services account for around a third of the economy.

More than half of Britain's goods exports go to the EU and a further eighth to the US.[749] While the EU and the US impose relatively low import taxes on most foreign goods, they stipulate all sorts of standards on everything from acceptable specifications to product safety and environmental requirements. Because the EU and the US are such heavyweights in world trade, their standards apply much more widely. EU members have a say in setting EU standards – and hence those that often apply elsewhere too; countries outside the EU just have to comply. For Britain, which is a heavyweight within

---

748   Personal calculations from WTO statistics

749   World Trade Organisation, Trade Profiles 2012

the EU, but would be a small player in global markets outside it, the loss of influence over its own destiny from leaving the EU would be considerable.

Goods make up two-thirds of Britain's exports; services account for the other third. Unfortunately, global trade in services is much more restricted. For example, foreigners are not allowed to buy American airlines and only US ones are allowed to fly on domestic routes there. Despite its supposedly special relationship with the US, the UK is as discriminated against in the airline business and many other protected service sectors as other foreigners are. Contrast that with the EU's open-skies policy: a British airline such as Easyjet, which did not even exist before the old airline cartels were dismantled, can now fly anywhere in the EU, slashing the price of airfares, opening up new routes and democratising air travel. Hardly anyone went on stag weekends in Barcelona, city breaks in Prague or regular trips to their holiday home in Tuscany before European airspace was opened up.

Britain's financial sector is intimately linked with Europe. The UK's trade surplus with the EU in financial services was £16.6 billion in 2012, more than a third of the country's total financial sector surplus, according to The City UK, an industry lobby group.[750] London dominates several European financial markets: it has 74 per cent of trade in over-the-counter interest-rate derivatives, 85 per cent of hedge-fund assets and 51 per cent of marine-insurance premiums. Whether or not financial players left London if Britain exited the EU, Britain would have no say in shaping EU financial regulation with which they would have to abide in order to trade with the EU.

Given the importance of services exports to the British economy – not just banking, but also insurance, accounting, consultancy, commercial law, advertising, education, healthcare, creative industries

---

750   http://www.ft.com/cms/s/0/f0acf3dc-2604-11e3-8ef6-00144feab7de.html

such as film, music, design, fashion and publishing, and much else – Britain has a huge stake in trying to drive forward further liberalisation within the EU and in shaping the terms on which it happens. Outside the EU, Britain might be able to negotiate access to the EU market for British Airways and Easyjet, but it would have no say in the pace, nature or scope of future market-opening measures.

Since efforts to free up global trade at the World Trade Organisation have all but stalled, the alternative is to open up foreign markets through bilateral (or plurilateral) trade agreements. As Chapter 5 mentioned, the EU is negotiating a Transatlantic Trade and Investment Partnership (TTIP) with the US that aims to reduce remaining tariffs (import taxes), which are particularly high in agriculture, as well as tackling standards, regulations and certification processes that impede trade and investment. Reaching a deal won't be easy. But with the combined clout of the EU, the UK would get a better deal out of the US than it could alone. When negotiating trade deals with smaller countries, the US tends to impose its terms; the smaller country has to take it or leave it, as negotiators from those countries can testify. For example, the US typically insists on extremely strong intellectual-property protections for American firms or a watering down of data-privacy rules. On its own, Britain would have to accept those terms in order to get better access to US markets. Negotiating as an equal with the US, the EU cannot be bullied as easily.

Outside the EU, the UK wouldn't just have less leverage with the EU or the US. It would also have to renegotiate existing trade agreements that the EU has signed and pursue separately those that the EU is currently conducting.[751] The EU has a customs union with Turkey and three dots on the European map (Andorra, Monaco and San Marino). It also has free-trade deals with western European countries that are not in the EU (the Faroe Islands, Iceland, Liechtenstein,

---

751   http://trade.ec.europa.eu/doclib/docs/2012/november/tradoc_150129.pdf

Norway, Switzerland) as well as with eastern European ones (Albania, Bosnia and Herzegovina, Macedonia, Montenegro, Serbia). Deals with Georgia and Moldova are done but not yet implemented; one with Ukraine could be signed soon. It also has free-trade agreements with its Mediterranean neighbours (Algeria, Egypt, Israel, Jordan, Lebanon, Morocco, Palestinian Authority, Syria and Tunisia) and is negotiating a deeper deal with Morocco. In Latin America, it has free-trade deals with Mexico, Chile, Colombia and Peru plus three Central American countries (Honduras, Nicaragua and Panama). Agreements with a further three (Costa Rica, El Salvador and Guatemala) are done but not yet implemented. Negotiations with Mercosur, a trade-grouping that includes Brazil and Argentina, are stalled, but separate talks with Brazil are in the offing. The EU has a free-trade deal with South Africa and has concluded or is negotiating "economic partnership agreements" with a bevy of African, Caribbean and Pacific (ACP) countries. In Asia, it has recently inked deals with South Korea and Singapore and is negotiating with Japan, Malaysia, Vietnam, Thailand and India. It has also recently concluded a trade deal with Canada. That is a lot of trade deals to renegotiate, many doubtless on worse terms.

The disruption to investment would be smaller, because until now EU members have negotiated investment treaties bilaterally. But the EU recently acquired the power to negotiate such deals on behalf of EU members. Investment is a key part of the negotiations with the US and talks on an investment-protection treaty with China are also in motion. Again, on its own, Britain would be at a disadvantage.

Outside the EU, Britain would be able to restrict immigration from the EU – and the EU could reciprocate. That would be a problem for Nigel Lawson, a former finance minister who favours Britain leaving the EU while himself living in France – although perhaps he thinks that he deserves special treatment. It would also be a problem for the 2.2 million more humble Britons who live, study, work and retire in the rest of the EU.[752] Brits working in Germany, with homes in France and Italy, retired in Spain and doing business in booming Poland. Contrary to popular perception, Brits living in Europe are comparable in number to the 2.34 million EU citizens living in the UK. As an economy that relies so much on services, Britain is particularly vulnerable to restrictions on mobility in both directions. To work on German building sites, British brickies need to have the right to live and work there. To build up a client base in a country, a British consultancy will typically need to open an office there. Conversely, British schools and universities can't provide an education to foreign students who cannot obtain a UK visa. Nor can British boutiques sell big-ticket luxuries to foreigners unless they are allowed into the country. So if Britain leaves the EU, a sensible government would continue to allow free movement to and from the EU, disappointing those who want Britain to raise the drawbridge. If the government wasn't sensible, the damage to the British economy would be considerable – not to mention the restrictions on the freedom and lifestyle of Brits who take for granted the right to move freely around the EU.

On the plus side, Britain would save its net contribution to the EU budget. Or perhaps not: Norway has to pay to access the EU single market. In any case, it is not a huge sum of money. While the figure varies year by year, in 2011, the most recent year for which there is a complete breakdown, Britain's net contribution was €7.25 billion (£5.85 billion).[753] That was only 0.87 per cent of public spending that year. It is equivalent to £92.70 a year per person, or twenty-five pence a day. It is hardly an exorbitant price to pay for access to the world's biggest market and all the other benefits of EU membership.

---

752   http://www.ft.com/cms/s/0/5cd640f6-9025-11e3-a776-00144feab7de.html

753   http://ec.europa.eu/budget/library/biblio/publications/2011/fin_report/fin_report_11_en.pdf

Most of that net contribution goes to pay for the Common Agricultural Policy. It would be fantastic if Britons (and Europeans in general) no longer subsidised agribusinesses and landowners and could enjoy better-value food by abolishing import taxes on farm produce. (I explain at length why the CAP fails to deliver its purported benefits to the environment, rural development, food safety, animal welfare and so on in a pamphlet for the Lisbon Council.)[754] But even if Britain left the EU, it might still subsidise agriculture. Before joining the EEC, Britain had its own farming tariffs and subsidies. Nowadays European countries outside the EU – notably Norway and Switzerland – lavish even more loot on their cosseted farmers than the EU does. If Britain left the EU, the agri-lobby would doubtless feed us sob stories about the suffering of small farmers and scare stories about the perils of foreign food. They would talk of the need for "transitional payments" to cushion the impact on jobs and rural communities. They would portray industrial agri-businesses as environmental stewards and inefficient smallholders as kindly guardians of animal welfare and local food. With big rural landowners and the National Farmers Union on the Conservative side and eco-romantic urbanites on the Labour side, it is quite plausible that they would succeed. In any case, British produce would face high EU tariffs – and the threat of punitive sanctions – on farm exports that are deemed too cheap. Even Norway, a country that accepts all EU single-market rules without any say in setting them and contributes to the EU budget without receiving payments in return, has been a victim of such "anti-dumping" duties, on its farmed salmon.

---

754   Philippe Legrain, "Beyond CAP: Why the EU Budget Needs Reform", Lisbon Council, September 2010 http://www.lisboncouncil.net/publication/publication/61-beyondcappublication.html

Undeniably, there are many things wrong with the EU. Some of its policy priorities are misguided. The CAP is a grotesque, protectionist racket. The Common Fisheries Policy has emptied the seas of life. Other priorities are sound – helping poorer regions catch up, boosting innovation, tackling climate change – but often poorly executed. Still other aims – a single market in both energy and services – are laudable but incomplete. Unfortunately, the EU has got diverted into trying to micromanage national reforms through a ten-year plan. But with a constructive attitude, Britain could build coalitions for change within the EU. Outside it, Britain would just be a bystander, affected by what happens in Europe, but not shaping it. But the biggest change that needs to happen not just for Britons but for all Europeans is that the EU needs to become more democratic.

Democratic deficit

For all its flaws, the EU is much more democratic than other international organisations. Every transfer of powers to the EU level has been freely agreed by all elected national governments in changes to the EU treaties that have been ratified by national parliaments and in some countries put to a referendum too (as will happen in Britain from now on). Both the president of the European Commission, the EU's quasi-executive body and civil service, and the Commission as a whole have been appointed by a supersized "qualified majority" of EU leaders and approved by the European Parliament. While the Commission has the sole right to propose legislation, such as the rules granting it the right to override national budgets, this must then be approved by both EU governments (the European Council) – typically by qualified majority, sometimes by unanimity – as well as by the directly elected European Parliament. In the case of the new fiscal powers granted to the European Commission, however, a qualified majority of EU governments is required to block its decision. EU laws can also be challenged and reviewed by both the European Court of Justice in Luxembourg and national courts.

But while the EU is democratic, it is not democratic enough. It is much more than a typical international organisation: it is a "union" of member states with supranational institutions that increasingly takes intensely political decisions that require much more open debate, proper scrutiny and democratic choice. That is especially but not exclusively true within the eurozone. These are decisions about fundamental issues, such as how much governments can tax and spend and how economies should be run, on which national governments can be outvoted and their behaviour constrained, decisions that create winners and losers – and over which there are important differences of opinion about how best to proceed. So Europeans need to have a bigger say over what direction the EU takes – and the right to change course. That requires a genuine democratic contest over who should exercise power and what political direction to take.

Yet neither the European Parliament elections nor the selection of the European Commission president provide this. The Parliament now has greatly enhanced powers to shape EU legislation. Unlike most national parliaments, it is not controlled by a government that can whip a majority of MPs into line. Nor can it be dissolved by the Commission or the Council. Thus it has the potential to become as independently powerful as the US Congress. Yet because many voters are unaware of its new powers and the electoral stakes seem small – since it does not appoint a government – European elections tend to be low-key, second-order affairs. Europe is scarcely debated. Few bother to vote. Only 43 per cent of Europeans and 35 per cent of Britons did in 2009.[755] Those who do often see it as an opportunity

---

755   Eurostat, voter turnout in national and EU parliamentary elections. Code: tsdgo310

to give their national government a kicking and let off steam. The European elections on 22–25 May 2014 are unlikely to be any different – and such is popular anger that they will probably see particularly big swings towards cranks and extremists. But if people knew that the European elections could produce a genuine change of course, they would be more engaged – and opposition to austerity and other EU policies need not morph into support for extremists and anti-EU sentiment.

The president of the European Commission is also potentially a very powerful role. Since the Commission has the sole right to initiate EU legislation, its president could set Europe's political agenda, as Jacques Delors did. He or she also has a say over which commissioner each government sends to Brussels and decides their portfolios. Yet the Commission president is selected through a backroom deal rather than an open contest. As Simon Hix of the London School of Economics points out in his brilliant book, *What's Wrong With the European Union & How to Fix It*, "the election of the Commission president is closer to the election of a pope – who emerges from a secret conclave of cardinals – than to an open and competitive battle between politicians with rival policy agendas for their term in office."[756] Who are the actual candidates (as opposed to the declared ones) to replace José Manuel Barroso when his term ends at the end of October 2014?[757] What might their policy priorities be? Are they up to the job? Nobody really knows.

Because there is not an open democratic debate about what political direction Europe should take, the Commission does not have a proper mandate for anything it tries to do. That makes it easier for vested interests to block what it proposes, resulting in gridlock. Worse,

---

756 Simon Hix, *What's Wrong With the European Union & How to Fix It*, Polity: 2008
757 As of 10 March 2014, the declared candidates were Jean-Claude Juncker, Martin Schulz, Guy Verhofstadt, Alexis Tsipras, José Bové and Franziska Keller.

when it does get something done, people feel like it has been imposed on them and those who object or suffer as a result often do not accept the decisions as legitimate. If Europeans feel that they have no say in shaping what the EU does and are told that in any case there is no alternative to current policies, it is not surprising that they increasingly reject the EU and turn to charlatans and populists who peddle false solutions and want to pull the house down.

When Olli Rehn, the EU commissioner for economic and monetary affairs, told the Belgian government to cut more than €1.2 billion from its budget over a weekend, a Belgian minister asked: "Who knows who Olli Rehn is? Nobody. Yet he tells us how we should conduct our economic policy."[758] Quite. As a British citizen who disagrees with George Osborne's policies, I recognise that he argued (albeit not entirely candidly) for austerity at the 2010 election; that the coalition government of which he is a leading member enjoys the support of a majority of MPs chosen by voters at that election; that he is accountable to the UK parliament, the media and others; and crucially that he can be booted out at the next election and his policies changed. British (or French or German) democracy is far from perfect, as the next chapter will explain, but it is still much healthier than EU democracy. European citizens did not elect Rehn, cannot hold him accountable for his mistakes and cannot force him to change his misguided policies, still less get rid of him. Each time a new national government is elected, Rehn pops up immediately on television telling it to pursue the same policies that voters have just rejected. His successor will be appointed by the next unelected European Commission president, not the people. Voters' ability to elect the politicians who make vital decisions about taxation and spending, hold them to account subsequently and periodically throw them out is of the essence of democracy.

---

758   http://theeuropeancitizen.blogspot.be/2012/01/brussels-v-brussels-belgium-and-eu.html

Without representation, taxation is confiscation – the stuff of revolutions. Likewise, who the hell is Olli Rehn to (wrongly) insist on cuts in Spanish wages – or tell the French government to cut spending?

Centralised fiscal decision-making is the most egregious example of the lack of democratic choice and accountability in the EU. As Chapter 6 argued, it would be better to replace it with a common eurozone budget, or failing that to decentralise budget decisions again. But so long as we are stuck with the current system, it needs to be more democratic. The same is true for all the other political decisions the EU makes – on energy, climate change, labour-market reforms and many other things.

Eurosceptics argue that because the EU is not democratic enough, powers should be handed back to member states – or their country should leave the EU altogether. Federalists counter that the EU needs to become a federal state – in effect, a decentralised state, like Switzerland writ-large. Realists point out that dismantling the EU would be undesirable while federalism is not feasible for now. The good news is that neither is needed for democratic reforms to make the EU work better.

Openness, accountability, choice

The EU needs three big reforms to make it more open, accountable and democratic. While EU decision-making is already more open than in many member states – EU documents and the various stages of the legislative process can be tracked online (although the Byzantine europa.eu website ought to be easier to navigate) – Council decisions are opaque. Since the Council – representatives of EU governments – operates in part as a legislative arm of the EU, its law-making functions ought to be much more transparent. Which other democratic legislature debates and takes decisions in secret, without a public record of who said what and how people voted?

All Council legislative documents ought to be made public, all its law-making debates take place openly and all decisions reached by public vote. Voters have a right to know what their government representatives said in a meeting, whether it squares with their public position, how they voted and how legislative compromises were reached. Greater openness would also reduce governments' ability to blame the EU for decisions that they took themselves. It is particularly important that meetings of ECOFIN (EU finance ministers) and the Eurogroup (eurozone ones) take place in public, notably when discussing the Commission's fiscal plans.

To increase accountability, a new committee made up of two representatives of each of the finance or budget committees of national parliaments ought to be created. While members of the European Parliament could also be involved, on its own it has neither the legitimacy nor the expertise to grill Olli Rehn (or his successor) on his decisions about, for instance, the Belgian budget. This new budget committee would connect the Brussels debate about fiscal issues to that in member states (and vice versa). For instance, Belgian parliamentarians could question Rehn and he would have a better grasp of their concerns. It would also enhance understanding and coordination across member states. Thus members of the German parliament could build a rapport with their counterparts in Greece's and each might understand the other's views better. It would also hold the European Commission, ECOFIN and the Eurogroup to account. To be effective and legitimate, this new committee would need to sit regularly, have broad powers to compel relevant decision-makers to explain and justify their actions and be able to hold them to account for their decisions and mistakes.

Above all, the EU needs an open, democratic contest for power with genuine political choice. There ought to be a meaningful political debate about the future direction of Europe tied to the European elections every five years. How? Each political grouping in the European Parliament (and potential new ones) could hold open primaries with online (or televised) debates to choose their candidate for president of the European Commission. Each candidate could then seek the endorsement of national politicians and other stakeholders and participate in a series of online or televised debates where they present their platform for the next five years. Should the EU be more conservative, social democratic, liberal, green or libertarian? Should it be more integrated or less – and if so in which areas? Should it be more open or less? Wider or deeper – or a bit of both? What specific policies should it prioritise? The new European Parliament could then act as an electoral college for the new Commission president. It should also hold confirmation hearings for each individual commissioner and have the right to reject any individual, as the US Senate can do with many senior US officials.

Another way to make the European elections more significant would be for the Parliament to behave more like a proper legislature. Instead of splitting top jobs (two-and-a-half years for the centre-right, two-and-a-half for the centre-left), one grouping should battle to get it for the full five-year term. Like in most national parliaments, bigger parties should get more committee chairs. To make the Parliament itself more representative and legitimate, party lists should be opened up so that a wider range of candidates can contest elections. It should also make a point of passing stringent new laws to prevent parliamentarians abusing their expenses, punishing any corruption severely and thus burnishing its reputation for probity.

A proper political contest and an open debate about policies would help create a genuinely European politics for the first time. It could generate a battle of ideas and help stimulate new ones. It could encourage joined-up thinking and explicit political trade-offs. It would allow coalitions that span institutions and national borders to form. It would attract media interest and work against the capture of institutions by insider lobbies. It would engage Europeans more both in the European elections and in the EU political process over the next five years, giving them both a say and a stake in what was decided. It would give a mandate for what the next Commission and Parliament tried to achieve. Crucially, it would also give the Commission president the democratic legitimacy to speak for Europe, acting as a counterweight to German hegemony and the power of vested interests. EU decisions would also have much greater legitimacy if they were seen to happen through an open and fair process whose outcomes could be contested and changed at the next election, if not before. Last but not least, it could help form new political identities. Contrary to the view that European politics is not possible because there is no European "demos", proper politics could help produce one. "Rather than assuming that a common democratic identity is a prerequisite for democracy, a democratic identity usually does not emerge until there is genuine democratic politics," Hix points out. In any case, nothing proposed here involves a transfer of new powers to the EU level.

The beauty of these proposals to make the Council more open, fiscal decision-making in particular more accountable, and the Commission and the Parliament more explicitly political is that they do not require a painful and laborious change to the EU treaties. The Parliament could simply decide to have an open contest to select the Commission president. The Council could acquiesce, while also deciding to become more open.[759] Likewise, a committee of national parliamentarians could be set up initially on a consultative basis, although a

---

759 Article 17 of the Lisbon treaty now gives the Parliament the right to elect the Commission president. It states: "Taking into account the elections of the European Parliament and after having held the appropriate consultations, the European Council acting by a qualified majority shall propose to the European Parliament a candidate for the president of the Commission. This candidate shall be elected by the European Parliament by a majority of its members."

treaty change would be needed to formalise its powers. Once the new way of working had bedded in, governments might eventually wish to formalise it through a change in the treaties.

Some change is in the offing. The various party groups in the Parliament have nominated candidates for Commission president – but unfortunately not through open primaries with genuine policy debate. The Greens went about it best: they held an online ballot to choose their candidate, who did not even have to be a party member. However, it is unclear how much weight EU leaders will give to the candidates selected by the Parliament. If the Socialists end up the biggest grouping in the next Parliament, as polls suggest they might be, their candidate, Martin Schulz, would doubtless press his case vigorously. But he is unlikely to be acceptable to his Christian Democrat compatriot, Chancellor Merkel, who is likely to want to impose a candidate of her choice. A constitutional moment could be in the offing.

Some will argue that the EU isn't ready for a democratic leap forward. But that is not what voters think. Indeed, 70 per cent of Europeans support an even more ambitious reform: directly electing the president of the European Commission in the near future; there is a big majority in favour in every EU member state, including Britain (62 per cent).[760] That is a good idea longer term, but it could not happen immediately because it would require treaty change. Why do Europeans favour directly electing the president of the European Commission? The top two answers are that "EU decisions would seem more legitimate to Europeans" and "It would reinforce democracy within the EU", the latter being the key selling point for Britons.[761]

---

760   European Parliament Eurobarometer (EB79.5), June 2013, Q32 "Would you be in favour or opposed to the President of the European Commission being elected directly by the European citizens in a near future?"

761   *Ibid*, Q33

Critics will object that politicising the EU would fundamentally change its nature. The Commission would no longer be officially apolitical. Council decisions would be more openly contested and overtly political. But the Commission already is a political body. Even though commissioners are meant to "be completely independent in the performance of their duties", they tend to represent national positions and those of their political party. Council decisions are clearly political too. The policy direction taken during the crisis – austerity and structural reforms focused on competitiveness – was a political choice. Far from transforming an impartial system into a political one, the reforms I am suggesting would recognise its political nature, make it more democratic and thereby make it both more effective and more legitimate.

At the same time, the president of the Commission would still require broad support across all EU institutions to get things done, not least from his or her own commissioners, who would still be nominated by national governments. (Eventually they too could stand for election.) All the existing checks and balances in the EU would also remain. Powers exercised at the EU level would still be circumscribed by treaty. National governments would still have a veto in many areas, while a supermajority would be needed in others. The approval of the European Parliament would still be needed for legislative decisions. There would still be recourse to judicial review.

Many will argue that since opening up the system is not in elites' interest, they won't do it. That may be true. But some members of that elite may support change because they think they could gain from it, while the crisis and popular pressure could force even recalcitrant players to change. France's President Hollande might see it as a way of countervailing German power and setting out a distinct social democratic agenda. Britain's David Cameron might make it one of his objectives. Smaller countries could see it as an opportunity to make their voices heard. Within the Parliament, even the centre-right European

People's Party (EPP) might be persuaded that change is essential if the new Parliament throws up a big constituency of extremists, populists and Eurosceptics.

From the Commission's point of view, delegating technical powers – for instance, spinning off its antitrust powers to a European Competition Authority – and refocusing it as a more political actor would greatly enhance its diminished stature. Ultimately, though, Europe needs a big political campaign for European democracy that puts citizens first, involves all sorts of stakeholders, organises petitions through means such as Avaaz as well as official ones through the European Citizens' Initiative, and mobilises a grassroots movement for change.

Anyone who genuinely wants Europe to succeed ought to realise that change is essential. If the EU is misunderstood, it is partly because there is never a proper political debate about where it should be going. If the EU is underappreciated even when it delivers benefits to citizens, it is because it is not seen to have a democratic mandate. If mainstream political parties and EU institutions refuse to have this debate about Europe's future in the open, it will not disappear. It will simply happen elsewhere. That will strengthen the voices of those who propose extremist and often noxious solutions, while frustrating those who want a reasonable voice in the EU debate but have nowhere to turn. The biggest beneficiaries of the status quo are the likes of Marine Le Pen, Geert Wilders and Nigel Farage.

Ultimately, just as elites in the nineteenth century and the twentieth century agreed to open up politics and broaden the democratic franchise under popular pressure, so all Europeans who want the EU to succeed must demand to shape its future. If Europeans are told that there is no alternative to current policies or the existing system, many will reject it altogether. Demanding political reform is not anti-European. On the contrary: it is precisely because I believe in European cooperation that I want it to work well. If elites fail to respond to popular pressure for a more open, accountable and democratic Europe with genuine competition and choice over political decisions, the extremists will gain support and the EU will weaken. It would be a tragedy if, like the Habsburgs, Europe's rulers failed to change with the times, only for the EU to collapse. But it is not just EU politics that needs to change, so too do national democracies, as the concluding chapter explains.

14

THE POLITICS OF CHANGE

Why we need a European Spring

If Europe is to escape from its depression and save the euro and the EU, it needs politicians who can speak a language both of hope and of liberalism, selling reform as a source of opportunity and renovation, one that retains social justice even while reinventing it.

Bill Emmott, 2013[762]

Due to recent budget cuts, the light at the end of the tunnel has been switched off. That poster captures the way many Europeans feel. Long before the crisis, many were pessimistic. Now, many more are in a funk; some have sunk into despair or resignation. People assume that computers and the Chinese will take their jobs. Most Europeans expect the next generation to have a worse life in nearly every respect: less time with their families, less comfortable housing, less job security, less

---

762   http://www.ft.com/cms/s/0/998c7346-60cb-11e3-b7f1-00144feabdc0.html

job satisfaction and less secure pensions. To paraphrase Hobbes, they think their children's lives will be "solitary, poor, nasty, brutish" (and long). A mere 16 per cent of Spaniards, 11 per cent of French and 7 per cent of Italians think young Europeans will have more opportunities than their parents' generation to earn a high salary; Britons (24 per cent) and Germans (26 per cent) are scarcely more optimistic.[763] This negativity is so deeply ingrained that people scarcely notice it any more. Witness how Europeans tend to focus on the perceived risks of new technologies rather than their potential rewards. One in two thinks one should not start a business if there is a risk of failure – as there inevitably is. Investment is at a record low. Hope of a better future – a belief that progress is possible – is fading.

It doesn't have to be that way. Yet most politicians and technocrats are overcautious, ineffective and uninspiring: they try to muddle through, when what Europe needs are bold reforms. Worse, public officials are often in the pockets of powerful vested interests: not least the financial sector, but also landowners, farmers, cosseted companies (big and sometimes small), unions – and increasingly pensioners' lobbies too. No wonder people increasingly believe that economies are run for the benefit of privileged insiders rather than society as a whole. Many have lost faith in politicians, in political parties, in parliaments – and some in democracy itself. Only 14 per cent of Europeans tend to trust political parties in their country.[764] Only one in four trust their national parliament and a similar proportion their government; a mere 9 per cent of Spaniards do.[765]

---

763 http://www.debatingeurope.eu/2013/05/17/new-poll-dramatic-rise-in-pessimism-in-the-eu/#.Uk_yuYbrzlY 92 per cent of Italians, 77 per cent of Spaniards, 72 per cent of the French, 56 per cent of Germans and 53 per cent of Britons think they will have fewer opportunities.

764 Eurobarometer 80, Autumn 2013, QA10.5

765 *Ibid,* QA10.6 and QA10.7

Democracy is in distress. Only one in two Europeans is satisfied with how it works in their country – and vanishingly few in southern Europe.[766] Over the centuries, people have died for the right to vote. A century ago, British women chained themselves to railings in order to secure it. Now, fewer and fewer people bother to cast a ballot. Across the EU, the average turnout in national elections plunged to 69.4 per cent in 2012.[767] Even in a crisis, with so much at stake, fewer than two in three Britons voted in 2010, a paltry 58 per cent in Portugal in 2011 and a mere 62.5 per cent in Greece (where voting is supposedly mandatory) in 2012. This economic and political crisis should trouble everyone – even those among Europe's elites and insiders who are only in it for themselves. They cannot take their gilded status for granted. Europe's economic slump has been longer and deeper than the Great Depression. Greece is suffering more than Germany did in the 1930s. The prospect of perpetual sluggishness as sclerotic economies slumber into senescence is soul-destroying. At some point, societies will snap.

Some are already trying to break them. The crisis is a golden opportunity for charlatans and extremists: from the bigots of Britain's UKIP to the neo-Nazis of Greece's Golden Dawn. While it is understandable that people are looking for alternatives to discredited established parties, it is regrettable that they are increasingly turning to reactionary and often racist parties that peddle a return to a romanticised past when the world seemed less threatening: when Europe was less open, less diverse and everyone knew their place.

---

766   European Parliament Eurobarometer (EB79.5), June 2013, Q30a. Fewer than two in three Britons, 55 per cent of French, a mere 35 per cent of Italians, 27 per cent of Spaniards, 19 per cent of Greeks and 14 per cent of Portuguese are satisfied with how democracy works in their country.

767   Eurostat, Voter turnout in national and EU parliamentary elections. Code: tsdgo310. Average turnout in national elections was 78.5 per cent in 1990.

The politics of hate, fear and grievance are sweeping through Europe. In the European Parliament elections, nasty extremists of various kinds are likely to do extremely well. These parties have many differences – some hate gays, others purport to defend them – but for the most part they are economically interventionist, socially conservative and culturally xenophobic. In other words, they are illiberal.

Worse, they are polluting politics more generally. Some established parties have long been nativist. Spain's ruling Partido Popular is issued from Franco's fascism. Silvio Berlusconi, the convicted criminal who leads Forza Italia, lambastes diversity. Others are heading in that direction. Hungary's government is increasingly nationalist and authoritarian. Listen to the abuse heaped on immigrants, who did not cause today's crisis, by supposedly respectable politicians and pundits in Britain, France or the Netherlands these days. Substitute "black people", "women" or "poor people" for immigrants in their sentences and the vile nature of their sentiments becomes clear. The dehumanisation of people is how the march towards fascism began.

Reactionaries' scapegoating of foreigners is vile but effective. The solutions they propose are false: stop the world, stamp on difference, turn the clock back. But their success is symptomatic of a genuine sickness. Europe's sluggish economies are strangled by vested interests that stifle opportunity and steal the value created by others. EU institutions have become instruments for creditors to impose their will on debtors. Democracy is lacking at an EU level and ailing at a national one. Our open societies – post-war Europe's most wonderful achievement – are at risk.

Europe desperately needs to change. It needs hope, a politics of genuine optimism, a prospectus for a better future. It needs a European Spring: economic and political renewal.

Economic spring

The starting point is to tackle the balance-sheet problems that are weighing down many economies. In Britain, the combination of austerity, easy money and a cheap currency without meaningful reform generated three years of stagnation – and now the authorities are cranking up yet another cycle of debt-fuelled consumption, housing bubble and bust. Far from a "march of the makers", it is a flight of the speculators. In the eurozone, where the policy-induced panic has been halted for now, front-loaded, slash-and-burn, collective austerity has been a dismal failure too. Southern Europe is being pushed into a deflationary debt trap – and ultimately default. What Europe needs instead is to restructure the banking system: inject fresh capital into viable banks so they start lending again and kill off zombie ones. Unpayable debts need to be written down. Governments need to support spending in ways that push the economy towards healthier patterns of growth, not least by boosting investment (both public and private), while embracing innovation and lifting the barriers to enterprise.

Germany must play its part. Often set up as a success that others should emulate, its much-vaunted current-account surpluses are actually a symptom of a sick economy, not a strong one. Stagnant salaries swell corporate surpluses, while subdued spending, stifled service sectors and stunted start-ups suppress investment, so savings are instead squandered overseas. It is in Germans' own interests to enjoy the fruits of their labour in higher wages, invest more, not least in their dilapidated infrastructure and decaying education system, and reform their economy so that so many would-be entrepreneurs aren't forced to emigrate to start a business. It is also in their enlightened self-interest to give the rest of the eurozone a hope of escaping their debtors' prison. Do Germans want to be surrounded by a wasteland of resentful vassal states – or a prosperous and contented community of equals?

The bigger challenge is to revitalise Europe's senescent economies. Sluggish productivity growth, low investment and rapidly ageing societies are a recipe for stagnation. Curing the crisis and then opening up the labour market to those excluded from it is an economic imperative as well as a moral one. Unless European societies get more people into work – not least the young, the old, women and the less-skilled – the ageing of the population will place an intolerable burden on social systems and polarise politics. So cutting taxes on labour, making it easy to hire and fire, and helping people to retrain and find a new job should be priorities. As Denmark's example shows, a flexible labour market can also be a secure one. Opening up to migrants can also make a big difference. They tend to be young. They can help care – and pay – for the old. And their efforts tend to complement those of locals. As Europeans live longer, they also need to work longer and retire later. Other European countries can learn from what the Dutch have done to encourage senior work. They also need to fix their pension systems, as Sweden has, in a way that is affordable for contributors and decent for beneficiaries, while giving everyone an incentive to work longer and embrace reform.

More generally, European economies need to become more adaptable: better able to cope with change and make the most of it. The good news is that large parts of Europe's economies are so inefficient that they can grow fast simply by imitating what works well elsewhere. Set businesses free, stimulate the necessary investment, encourage people to embrace change and many countries could grow by leaps and bounds. Imagine how much richer – and happier – Spaniards would be if their employment rate was as high as that of the Swiss. Consider how Italy's prospects would improve if its manufacturers could match Germany's. Think how much more vibrant Germany would be if its retail sector was as competitive as Britain's. Dream of a Britain with roads and railways as good as those in Spain. Completing the EU's single market, inking a free-trade agreement with America, signing an investment deal with China and reinvigorating the WTO could restore the convergence machine that the EU once was (and still is for the ex-communist east). Europeans should also embrace new technologies that work well elsewhere, such as genetically modified crops that require less water, insecticides and pesticides, as well as shale gas, which is cleaner than coal and a stepping stone to, and a back-up for, intermittent renewable energies.

As well as imitating what others do well, Europeans need to innovate more. Start with schools that give everyone a fair start in life, stimulate open minds, spur creative thinking and, like Estonia's, embrace our new digital world. Create prizes and competitive tenders for research funding. Relax patent laws. Encourage the cross-fertilisation of ideas across disciplines in dense, diverse cities. Capitalise on Europe's biggest resource: the diversity of its people, both within countries and across them. Open up to go-getting newcomers from around the world. Stimulate a healthy mix of competition and cooperation. Create enterprising universities and colleges. Champion risk-takers, business angels and successful entrepreneurs. Unleash Europeans' entrepreneurial spirits. Make it easy to start a business (like in Ireland and Britain), grow one, and close one (like in Denmark). Look on failure as a lesson learned not a lifelong stigma. Jumpstart finance for risky ventures through both private capital (like America) and public (like Israel). Provide every young person with a capital lump-sum and thus the potential to build their own business.

Europe also needs to insulate itself from the excesses of a fragile and often dysfunctional financial system. Finance will always be unstable, but it need not be so big, so powerful, so destructive and so subsidised. Eliminating the tax advantages of debt and property speculation would cut it down to size and make it less fragile. Forcing banks to fund themselves with much more equity would reduce the risk of failure and government bail-out – and hence their implicit taxpayer subsidy. Folding banks when they fail – or bailing in their private creditors – would end their grotesque looting of public coffers.

Nobody likes paying taxes. But reshaping the tax system could create a cleaner, more decent and more dynamic economy. Scrap the EU's ineffective emissions-trading scheme and its costly command-and-control approach to tackling climate change and introduce a transparent and flexible tax on carbon consumption and ample incentives for research. Replace income tax with a progressive expenditure tax that would boost savings and productive investment and tax unearned income. Shift the tax burden off labour and on to land to encourage hard work and enterprise, boost wages and create jobs, and claw back the undeserved rewards that landowners accumulate from others' efforts and investment.

Reforms to make economies more adaptable, dynamic and decent literally ADD UP. An adaptable economy that can cope with change and adjust to it better is also likely to be more dynamic. A dynamic economy that breaks down barriers to competition and enterprise will also be a more decent one, where even outsiders have a chance and there is a closer correspondence between rewards and merit. A decent society that gives everyone a more equal chance in life and thus makes better use of all our talents will also be more dynamic.

Political spring
European Spring has put forward an agenda for change. An agenda for dealing with the balance-sheet crisis decisively and fairly and for creating lasting shared prosperity through reforms to make our economies and societies more adaptable, dynamic and decent – reforms that

ADD UP. It has sought to dispel bad ideas such as the austerity delusion, the "competitiveness" myth, the bubble mentality and the notion that economies are inherently stable and predictable. It has suggested reforms that would break the power that vested interests have over our economies and our politics. It proposes changes to institutions to make them work better, not least a more open, accountable and democratic European Union with genuine political choice and a fiscally federal (or flexible) eurozone that restores national governments' budgetary freedom. It's an agenda of standing up for those locked out of the system, not in the noxious, hateful way that populist extremists do, but rather by opening up opportunities for everyone to get ahead. An equal chance to get a good education and a decent job. The capital to give every young person a start in life. The opportunity to start your own business and build it up. Shifting tax off hard work and enterprise and on to unearned rewards from land ownership and inheritance. The ability to save for your retirement tax-free without your returns being gobbled up in fees. A future-proofed state pension system. The security that enables you to sleep easily at night – and take risks. Open capitalism, not crony capitalism. The freedom to be who you want to be, live the life you want to lead and still have a place in society.

How, though, can one overcome entrenched vested interests? Sometimes war – or revolution – wipes out the old power structure. Change can also come about peacefully. Reform can be precipitated by external forces or domestic ones. The lure and then the process of joining the EU have a huge impact on candidate countries. The EU's trustbusters can crack open cartels and inject competition into monopolistic markets. With luck, the EU's trade and investment negotiations with the US will help lever open Europe's sheltered service sectors. Domestically, reform can come from above – decisive political leadership – or below: by mobilising the forces who desire change to overcome the resistance of those who oppose it. It can happen in a big bang or incrementally. A crisis can provide an opportunity for radical reform. The internet can be a fantastic instrument for mobilising it. And the fuel can be the power of ideas, as well as enlightened self-interest.

To make it happen, and to defang the nasty xenophobes and extremists, politics needs to change too. Our political systems are no longer fit for purpose. The world has changed. The era of mass-membership parties based on class belongs to a bygone industrial age, yet the old parties endure. Our economies are dominated by services, not industry. Class divisions have blurred. Tribal party allegiances are fading. Many people, especially younger ones, feel no connection to traditional parties. In all established democracies, party membership has plunged.[768]

Above all, people no longer trust the competence, motives and honesty of politicians in general. Their perceived competence has been shredded by their failure to prevent or tackle the crisis. Their imputed motives have been blackened by the sense that they serve their own interests and those of lobby groups rather than those of society as a whole. In many cases, their honesty is questioned too. Understandably so, given the slush-fund scandal in Spain, the court cases that have implicated successive French presidents, the MPs' expenses scandal in

---

768 Membership of political parties has plunged by at least a quarter and sometimes up to two-thirds since 1980. While it varies hugely across countries – more than 17 per cent in Austria, nearly 6 per cent in Italy and Belgium, 4 per cent in Sweden, just over 2 per cent in Germany, just less in France, a mere 1 per cent in Britain – it is falling everywhere. On average, the absolute number of members has almost halved since 1980.

http://onlinelibrary.wiley.com/doi/10.1111/j.1475-6765.2011.01995.x/abstract and http://blogs.lse.ac.uk/europpblog/2013/05/06/decline-in-party-membership-europe-ingrid-van-biezen/

Britain, the corrupt client state in Italy and Greece and the nepotism and fraud in EU spending.

Open democracy

The country in Europe where democracy is healthiest is Sweden. It is the only sizeable European country where a significant majority (57 per cent) trusts the government (and 70 per cent trust the parliament).[769] (Trust in political parties is also highest, albeit still only 34 per cent.)[770] All in all, a whopping 87 per cent of Swedes are satisfied with how their democracy works (just behind the Danes) and five in six Swedes voted in their last general election (ditto).[771]

Since Swedes are so content with their democracy, perhaps the rest of Europe should take a leaf out of their book. All parties that poll more than 4 per cent of the vote in elections get seats in parliament in proportion to their votes cast. As a result, a wide spectrum of views is represented –left-wing (the Left Party), centre-left (Social Democratic Party), green (Green Party), social liberal (Centre Party), liberal (Liberal People's Party), liberal conservative (Moderate Party), social conservative (Christian Democrats) and far-right (Sweden Democrats) – and political debate isn't narrowly focused on swing voters. Power is decentralised, with much of it exercised at a regional and local level. Government is conducted openly.

Across Europe, democracy ought to more open. Political parties ought to be more open to new and different views and more open in how candidates are recruited. One way to achieve both aims is to have open primaries to select candidates, so that they aren't all machine politicians. Parties should also be forced to be honest about their funding,

---

769   Eurobarometer 80, Autumn 2013, QA10.6 and QA10.7

770   *Ibid*, QA10.5

771   European Parliament Eurobarometer (EB79.5), June 2013, Q30a. 87.7 per cent of Danes voted in 2011, 84.6 per cent of Swedes did in 2010

with large donations banned. Lobbying needs to be more transparent too. Lobbyists should be registered. All politicians should have to declare all their interests and all their meetings. Former public officials should be banned from working for the companies that they regulated.

Europe should also experiment with new forms of democracy. Direct democracy – referendums, ballot initiatives and recall votes – has its place. While California's ballot initiatives have often resulted in conflicting and incoherent policies, they have also led to innovative ones, such as legalising marijuana and gay marriage. Switzerland seems to thrive on direct democracy, though the 2014 vote to cap immigration from the EU is regrettable. But since referendums are costly, time-consuming and ill-suited for making the compromises and trade-offs between competing claims on which politics depends, they should be used sparingly. Worse, they give little place for deliberation and can result in the tyranny of the majority rather than a proper respect of minority rights.

A healthy democracy should aim to do three things. It should ensure wide participation in decision-making by the people affected. It should involve deliberation: a rational discussion where all major points of view are aired and evidence considered. And it should be based on equality: an equal chance for everyone to have their views taken into account. At a local level – think of a town-hall meeting – it may be possible to achieve all three aims. But at a national or European level, it traditionally hasn't been. "Consulting elites offers deliberation but without political equality," observes James Fishkin of Stanford University, "whereas consulting the people offers political equality but without deliberation." He argues that "we need to experiment with different modes of democratic consultation and use social science to ensure that processes are balanced and representative."

Like the best academics, Fishkin doesn't just theorise, he tests his ideas in practice. On the eve of the European elections in 2009, he brought together a representative sample of citizens from all twenty-seven EU member states to deliberate in twenty-one languages about the issues in the upcoming elections. It would never work, sceptics asserted. Europeans don't share a common politics. They speak so many different languages. Yet the experiment was a huge success. This "deliberative polling" enhances understanding of the issues and encourages people to weigh the trade-offs that public policy involves.[772] Similarly, AmericaSpeaks aims to "engage citizens in the public decisions that impact their lives" through methods such as 21st Century Town Hall Meetings.

An elaboration of this approach is to set up citizens' assemblies made up of a representative sample of the population that come together to deliberate on important issues. Canada is a pioneer. In 2004, the British Columbia Citizens' Assembly on Electoral Reform convened a policy jury to look at alternatives to the first-past-the-post electoral system.[773] In 2007, a similar grouping considered alternative electoral systems in Ontario. Three of that province's Local Health Integration Networks have also referred their budget priorities to a policy jury for advice and refinement. At the very least, both European countries and the EU should explore greater use of deliberative democracy on a consultative basis. If it works well, citizens' assemblies, chosen by lot, might ultimately replace the upper house of parliament. Sound far-fetched? Actually, it was a key feature of democracy in ancient Athens – and it is how the modern jury system works too.

A coalition for change

Disenchantment with traditional political parties and democratic institutions is often interpreted as apathy. But that is incorrect. Political activism has changed, not disappeared. A better educated, better informed and more demanding citizenry is actually more engaged than

---

772   http://cdd.stanford.edu/polls/docs/summary/

773   http://en.wikipedia.org/wiki/Deliberative_democracy

ever. Single-issue groups, notably non-governmental organisations (NGOs), have proliferated and gained support. In Britain, for example, Friends of the Earth has 75,000 volunteer campaigners – many more than the ruling Conservative Party.[774] Amnesty International and Oxfam mount campaigns on issues that narrow-minded nationalists claim people don't care about, such as human-rights abuses around the world and global poverty. Transparency International monitors and publicises government and corporate corruption worldwide.

The internet has also unleashed new forms of politics. People can create their own campaign group on Facebook. Twitter storms mobilise public opinion and real-world protests. Change.org, a social enterprise funded by advertising in the form of "sponsored petitions", enables anyone to start their own online petition. People can also lobby for change through online campaigns such as those organised by Avaaz – which in February 2014 had 3.3 million members in France, 1.8 million in both Germany and Italy, and more than a million in both Britain and Spain.[775]Avaaz, which is wholly funded by small donations, organises online petitions and then uses them as a basis to campaign for changes that people want. In Britain, 38 Degrees mobilises nearly a million campaigners. We need to harness these new forms of political action to mobilise a coalition for change: a European Spring.

With luck, some mainstream politicians will seize on the need for economic and political reform. Like the economy, politics is going through a huge upheaval that offers opportunities for political entrepreneurs of all persuasions. Among conservatives, witness how Boris Johnson, the mayor of London, has crafted an optimistic, pro-investment, pro-immigration alternative to the narrow-minded negativity in Downing Street. See how a new centrist party, the Unión

---

774 http://www.foe.co.uk/resource/faqs/fund_how_many.html

775 http://www.avaaz.org/en/community.php accessed on 28 February 2014

de Progreso y Democracia, is thriving from disenchantment with traditional parties in Spain. Admire the reform drive of Denmark's centre-left coalition government. Observe how Matteo Renzi, who became prime minister in February 2014 aged thirty-nine, is trying to shake up post-Berlusconi Italy. Doff your cap to the unabashedly pro-openness message of Sweden's Centre Party and Greens. Let others embrace change too.

Dare to dream of a more decent and dynamic Europe. A Europe set free from dead-end ideologies, liberated from the clasps of vested interests, supported by strong and broad-based institutions. A Europe truly "united in diversity" – where everyone can be different, equal and belong. And then demand change. Debts can be defaulted on. Banks can be broken up. Entrepreneurs can be emancipated. Every child in Europe can get a better start in life.

The suffering is terrible, the injustice shocking. But the prevailing pessimism is corrosive. Europe has bounced back from far worse than this. Stagnation and decline are not inevitable. With bold reforms and a broad movement for change, a better future is possible. We desperately need a European Spring.

ABOUT THE AUTHOR

Philippe Legrain is an independent thinker and communicator who also has practical experience of policymaking at the highest level. He is the author of three critically acclaimed books – *Open World: The Truth about Globalisation* (2002); *Immigrants: Your Country Needs Them* (2007), which was shortlisted for the *Financial Times* Business Book of the Year; and *Aftershock: Reshaping the World Economy After the Crisis* (2010). After seeing him debate on television and reading *Aftershock*, the president of the European Commission, José Manuel Barroso, asked Philippe to advise him. From February 2011 to February 2014, he was independent economic adviser to President Barroso and head of the team that provides the president with strategic policy advice.

Philippe's earlier career spanned academia (at LSE's European Institute), journalism (at *The Economist*; as contributing editor to *Prospect*; as editor of *World Link*, the magazine of the World Economic Forum; and independently), policy advice (as special adviser to the director-general of the World Trade Organisation), political campaigning (at Britain in Europe, the pro-European campaign) and independent commentating, consultancy and advocacy. He has a first-class degree in economics and a master's in politics of the world economy, both from the London School of Economics. He has written for a wide variety of international publications, including the *Financial Times*, the

Wall Street Journal, the *Guardian* and *The Times,* as well as those affiliated to Project Syndicate, and is a frequent commentator on BBC, Sky and international TV and radio. In 1999, he was highly commended as Young Financial Journalist of the Year in the Wincott awards. He has author pages on Facebook and Google+ and tweets as @plegrain. His personal website is www.philippelegrain.com

Philippe is now setting up OPEN: the Open Political Economy Network, a new kind of think-tank that will function as an international platform for ideas, advocacy and debate on international political economy and openness issues in particular, at www.opennetwork.net

Printed in Great Britain
by Amazon.co.uk, Ltd.,
Marston Gate.